W9-AQL-714

SOUTH AFRICA

WHITE RULE BLACK REVOLT

Ernest Harsch

COLUMBIA UNIVERSITY
THE
LIBRARIES
WITHDRAWN
THE CITY OF NEW YORK

SOUTH AFRICA

SOUTH AFRICA

WHITE RULE BLACK REVOLT

Ernest Harsch

MONAD PRESS / NEW YORK

Library of Congress Catalog Card Number 80-82042
ISBN cloth 0-913460-78-8; ISBN paper 0-913460-77-x

Manufactured in the United States of America
First edition, 1980

Published by Monad Press for the Anchor Foundation

Distributed by:
Pathfinder Press
410 West Street
New York, NY 10014

Contents

Capitalism and National Oppression

The Struggle for Freedom 1488-1980

Charts and Tables

Maps

I

Capitalism and National Oppression

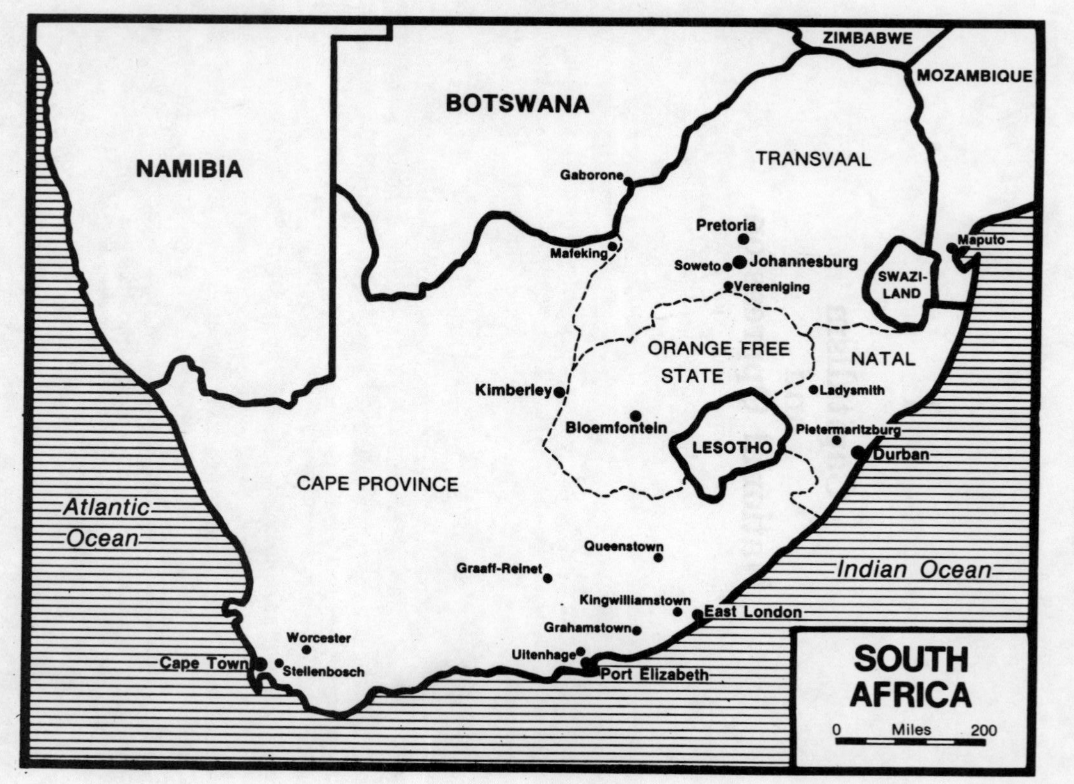
SOUTH AFRICA
0 Miles 200
ZIMBABWE
MOZAMBIQUE
BOTSWANA
NAMIBIA
TRANSVAAL
Gaborone
Pretoria
Maputo
Mafeking
Soweto
Johannesburg
Vereeniging
SWAZI-LAND
ORANGE FREE STATE
NATAL
Kimberley
Ladysmith
Bloemfontein
Pietermaritzburg
LESOTHO
Durban
CAPE PROVINCE
Atlantic Ocean
Queenstown
Graaff-Reinet
Indian Ocean
Kingwilliamstown
East London
Grahamstown
Worcester
Uitenhage
Cape Town
Stellenbosch
Port Elizabeth

1

Soweto, South Africa

In the mornings, Soweto is shrouded by a greyish-brown smoke. It emanates from numerous coal and wood stoves and clings to the unpaved streets and small brick houses.

Even before it gets light, thousands of figures emerge and move through the haze. In overalls, well-worn suits, and work dresses, they wend their way along the wide lanes of reddish dirt, from all corners of Soweto, and converge on the train stations. Crowds gather on the concrete platforms. They disappear within seconds as the trains pull up. Packed shoulder to shoulder in old and rundown railway cars, they are whisked off to their jobs a few miles to the northeast, in Johannesburg.

Picking up and discharging workers, the fast-moving trains roar back and forth continuously from 4:00 a.m. until just after midnight. They are the lifelines that connect the twin cities: Soweto, with its segregated, all-Black population, and Johannesburg, the economic hub of "white" South Africa.

From Johannesburg's modern apartment complexes, office buildings, skyscrapers, plush homes, and luxury hotels, it would be difficult to imagine that just a few miles away lies Soweto, the largest single urban ghetto anywhere on the African continent. In fact, few of Johannesburg's whites have ever visited Soweto, though Johannesburg's prosperity depends on that township's existence.

Viewed through the telescopes atop the Carleton tower in downtown Johannesburg, Soweto is barely visible. Unlike Johannesburg, with its numerous tall buildings, Soweto is flat, sprawling over thirty-three square miles of generally level terrain. Just a handful of structures are more than one story high.

Soweto is a teeming urban concentration, the home of nearly a million and a half Blacks, with a social, cultural, and political life as rich and vibrant as that of any large city in Africa. But alongside its bustle of activity exists an overwhelming physical bleakness: monotonous rows of almost identical red or grey brick houses stretching for mile after mile, unpaved dirt roads scarred by mammoth potholes, an absence of sidewalks, litter in the streets and open fields, wrecks of old cars, a lack of any malls or downtown areas.

Like all Black townships in South Africa, Soweto has few of the social amenities usually associated with urban life. It has only three movie theaters, one hotel, three banks, three post offices, one hospital, and few stores that sell anything more than groceries or the commonest household items. There are no supermarkets or shopping centers, and only one produce market. Most sports fields are bare stretches of dusty land. Telephones are rare, and street lighting is nonexistent in large parts of the township.

The white authorities have repeatedly promised to "modernize" Soweto, but with little result. "The health services are terrible," according to Dr. Nthato Motlana, chairman of the Soweto Committee of Ten, a broad-based community group. "I haven't seen roads being tarred in the last ten years and there's barely any street lighting. And as for housing, thousands have no hope of ever having their own homes."[1]

Those who are lucky enough to get houses have little to boast about. The houses themselves are tiny, unadorned cubicles, most with only four rooms. Sowetans call them "matchboxes." They are grossly overcrowded with an average of six or seven persons living in each.

Despite Soweto's expanding population, the regime has refused to construct enough housing. In fact, the number of new houses built each year steadily declined from the mid-1960s. As a result, some twenty-five thousand Soweto families—well over one hundred thousand persons—were on the official waiting list for new houses as of 1978; many others did not even bother to apply, since they were in Soweto illegally or were ineligible to obtain houses (a category that includes widows, deserted or divorced wives, and unmarried mothers). But they had to live somewhere. So they simply squeezed in with friends or relatives.

A mere 15 percent of Soweto's houses have bathrooms; almost all toilets are enclosed outside pits. Two-thirds lack hot running water. Most are without electricity, despite the towering presence

1. *Sunday Times* (Johannesburg), November 19, 1978.

within Soweto of the Orlando power station, which provides electricity for Johannesburg. Most homes are lighted by candles and kerosine lamps. Some areas of Soweto have only one bed for every three occupants. Three-fourths of the houses lack ceilings; since most have uninsulated roofs of corrugated iron sheeting, they can become quite hot in the summer and chilly in winter.

The inhabitants of Soweto have almost no security of residence and cannot own the land they live on; it is owned by the government, to which they must pay up to a quarter of their incomes in rent. The cost of ownership of the houses themselves is prohibitive to all but a privileged few; among them are a handful of large and impressive houses with well-manicured flowerbeds and exteriors that speak of affluence, the homes of Soweto's "millionaires"—those few who are favored by the authorities for their collaboration with the apartheid system.

For the vast bulk of Soweto's population, however, poverty is the norm. It can be seen in the unpainted walls and old furniture in countless houses, in the worn and faded clothes of children and adults alike, in the skinny limbs and short stature of many young Sowetans. In 1976, fully 80 percent of all Soweto households lived below the Effective Minimum Level, a common poverty indicator.[2] That level is supposed to be enough to keep a family of six in a state of subsistence. But in practice, even those families who earn that much have trouble making ends meet.

Hunger is constant. A 1975 study found that protein malnutrition was a "major clinical problem" among Blacks in the Johannesburg area. In the Diepkloof section of Soweto, some 45 percent of all children aged ten-to-twelve years suffered from it.[3]

Disease is also prevalent. Tuberculosis is among the most common. In addition, a survey of twelve thousand Soweto schoolchildren conducted by Dr. Margaret McLaren of the University of the Witwatersrand found the highest known incidence of rheumatic heart disease in the world, nearly eighteen times greater than anywhere else.[4]

Given the overcrowding and poverty—combined with the frustrations generated by white supremacist society—it is not surprising that Soweto has one of the highest crime rates in the

2. John Kane-Berman, *Soweto,* p. 54.

3. Ibid.

4. Joyce Sikakane, *A Window on Soweto,* p. 48.

world. Apartheid, a system of institutionalized violence against Blacks, produces violent reactions.

The problem of crime has been intensified by widespread alcoholism, for which the white authorities are directly responsible. The West Rand Administration Board, which ran Soweto until 1979, had a monopoly on all legal sales of alcoholic beverages in Soweto, selling 160 million barrels of beer a year, at nine cents a liter. Seen as symbols of the regime's attempts to keep Blacks submissive, many beer halls and liquor stores in Soweto were put to the torch during the 1976 rebellions.

Soweto, too, mirrors the continual repression that Blacks face everywhere in South Africa. The bristling police stations stand in the township surrounded by barbed-wire fences, like outposts in an occupied territory. The police do not hesitate to use their weapons; each year dozens of Blacks are shot to death during "routine" police activities. At times of political ferment, the cars of the security police converge on houses at any time of the day or night to round up suspected political "agitators" for the terrifying ride to John Vorster Square, the main police headquarters in Johannesburg. The newspapers in Soweto carry virtually daily reports of political arrests and trials, and every now and then of yet another death of a political prisoner while in police custody.

The plight of Soweto's residents is a common one in South Africa. Wherever one goes, the contrasts between the wealth and power of the white settler minority and the poverty and oppression of the Black majority are stark and sharply drawn. Those contrasts are part of the very fabric of South Africa's social, economic, and political system, a system that has been evolving for more than three hundred years, ever since the first European settlers began to subjugate the indigenous peoples and take away their land.

The widespread poverty of South Africa's Blacks springs from a society based on class exploitation and white supremacy—commonly called apartheid. It springs from an entrenched and all-pervasive policy of keeping Blacks down, to serve only as cheap, rightless laborers.

Blacks in South Africa are totally excluded from any political representation. The regime in Pretoria formally represents only the 4.3 million whites; the more than 22 million Blacks—composed of 18.6 million Africans, 746,000 Asians (mostly Indians), and 2.4 million Coloureds, who are of mixed ancestry[5]—are

5. Estimates released by South African Department of Statistics, June 30, 1976.

barred from voting. They have no say over the laws adopted by the all-white parliament, and have no legal recourse to change or oppose the regime's oppressive policies.

To keep Blacks under control, the white authorities have imposed racial segregation throughout the country, in most spheres of life. By law, Blacks must live in separate townships like Soweto. They must go to separate and inferior schools. Where they can travel, whom they can marry, what jobs they can hold, how long they can stay in a particular area, all are restricted and rigidly controlled.

The myriad laws, ordinances, and regulations that govern the lives of Blacks from the cradle to the grave are not the result of racist attitudes or sentiments that are somehow inherent to whites. They exist for the simple reason that they are *profitable.* They materially benefit the white employers, factory owners, and landlords, who use the system of racial oppression to keep down Black wages and living standards and thus substantially increase profits. White racism is but the surface reflection of that material reality.

Black labor is the bedrock upon which South Africa's economy rests. Despite the regime's depiction of South Africa as a "white man's country," Black workers are everywhere: hanging on scaffoldings at Johannesburg construction sites, digging drainage ditches in Cape Town, hauling cargo on Durban's docks, harvesting Natal's sugar cane, drilling and breaking up rock in the Witwatersrand gold mines, assembling auto engines in Port Elizabeth.

Blacks, in fact, are allowed to do little except work. The white expropriation of most of the land has left Blacks propertyless, with no recourse but to sell their labor power, the only thing of value that they have left. The development of Black businesses has been stifled by legal restriction and a white economic monopoly. The overwhelming majority of Blacks thus belong to the working class. The basic function of townships like Soweto is to serve as dormitories for the Black workers who keep the economy running; they are economic appendages of the "white" cities. The whole system of apartheid—the pass laws, "influx control," industrial legislation, the African reserves (Bantustans)—has one central goal: to keep the reins on South Africa's large and powerful Black working class.

The exploitation of this underpaid work force is the source of the country's extensive wealth, the bulk of it concentrated in the hands of a tiny class of white capitalists who live and prosper off the labor of others. Their affluence is especially garish in contrast to the depressed living conditions of Blacks: the plush, exclusive, all-white suburbs; the yachts, private planes, and pleasure resorts; the bank accounts running into figures of seven digits or more; the investment portfolios containing holdings in dozens of companies.

To these people, the "masters" of South Africa, the survival of white supremacy is vital to their own class position. By depressing Black wages to the barest minimum, profit rates have been boosted to among the highest in the world.

While the national oppression of Blacks has favored a rapid accumulation of capital in South Africa, the development and growth of the country's capitalist economy has in turn led to a strengthening of white supremacy. The two elements—national oppression and capitalism—are inseparably intertwined and mutually reinforcing.

Throughout the development of this social system, Blacks have not remained passive victims. They have fought back every step of the way. From the early wars against colonial conquest; through the emergence of the first Black political organizations at the turn of the century; to the innumerable strikes, marches, demonstrations, and uprisings since then, Blacks have striven to regain their national independence and wipe the country clean of white supremacy and class exploitation. As it has grown in numbers and social power, the Black working class has played an increasingly central role in these political battles.

The series of large-scale urban rebellions that began in Soweto on June 16, 1976, and subsequently spread to every corner of the country, was part of this long struggle. The uprisings, general strikes, and protest marches marked an elemental clash between the white rulers' efforts to preserve their profitable system of white supremacy and the Black population's fight to attain class and national emancipation. Azania—as many young Blacks hope to rename a liberated South Africa—is the goal.

The struggle for freedom in South Africa has already lasted a long time and claimed countless martyrs. How much more sacrifice will it take? "As much as the struggle demands," a young Soweto student told me. "The regime tried to keep us down with fear. But in 1976 we conquered fear. We showed them we were ready to shed our blood." With just a hint of emotion, he added, "We will not stop until we have won."

2

Foundations of a Colonial-Settler State

The roots of colonial rule and white supremacy in South Africa run deep. They stretch back more than three hundred years. From the very beginning, when the first Dutch settlers started to arrive in the seventeenth and eighteenth centuries, the history of white colonization was one of conquest, plunder, and dispossession of the indigenous Black peoples and societies.

The official white version of South Africa's history, however, tries to hide the violent and oppressive origins of white rule. As this version goes, most of what is now South Africa was uninhabited before the arrival of the white settlers, who were supposedly the first claimants to the land. Shortly thereafter, so the "historians" claim, Africans originating from further north migrated into the region, settling for the most part in those areas now demarcated as the Bantustans. The sole aim of this myth is to provide a historical justification for white dominance and white ownership of most of the land, including the most fertile and mineral-rich parts.

But the area that is now South Africa was far from barren or uninhabited when the first whites set foot there. Fossils of tools and human bone fragments found in South Africa have been dated back hundreds of thousands of years. In fact, a large proportion of all archaeological discoveries in Africa have been found within South Africa's present borders.

According to the available archaeological evidence, the San and Khoikhoi peoples, who lived in the west, originated in South Africa about eleven thousand years ago. There were signs of copper mining in what is now the northern Transvaal as early as the eighth century; the African inhabitants of the area mined and smelted iron, copper, and tin over hundreds of years. Both the

Sotho and Tswana peoples built stone towns, some of which were quite large. Toward the south and east, in what are now the Eastern Cape and Natal, lived the Xhosas and the predecessors of the Zulus. In the 1550s, a century before the arrival of the first Dutch colonists, shipwrecked Portuguese sailors found these areas densely populated.

Though their societies were not free of strife, these early African peoples were at least able to enjoy their self-determination. They had some say over the social relationships and norms that governed their daily lives. They did have chiefs, tribal elders, and others of political and social authority, but to the San hunters, the Khoikhoi pastoralists, and the Tswana, Sotho, and Xhosa herders and agriculturalists, the existence of social classes or of class exploitation was outside their realm of experience. Almost everyone in a tribe lived at the same general level of subsistence as everyone else. According to one South African socialist historian:

> The equalitarianism of this tribalism, embracing first everyone and later only the men, was due to backwardness of productive techniques. There had to be equality because one person's labour could not then support both himself and a non-producer. Exploitation was thus impossible, for all were engaged in the struggle with nature, all had to work or die.
>
> In the absence of exploitation, private property was of no material advantage. In the absence of an incentive—to live or gain from the exploitation of another's labour—the very notion of private property could not arise. Technical backwardness hence excluded not only exploitation but also private property. And so the land, the rivers, forests, minerals, the fruits of the earth and, in the early stages of "tribalism," . . . even the animals belonged to the people in common. Equality in ownership sprang out of backwardness, yet ensured the very physical existence of the primitive societies. For since the means of production belonged not to individuals but to all, none died of want in the midst of plenty.[1]

This early egalitarianism did not long survive after the Dutch and British settlers landed on South African soil. It was shattered by the advance of European civilization. For Africans, starvation in the midst of plenty was to become the established way of life.

South Africa first aroused significant interest among the

1. Mnguni [pseudonym], *Three Hundred Years,* 1:7.

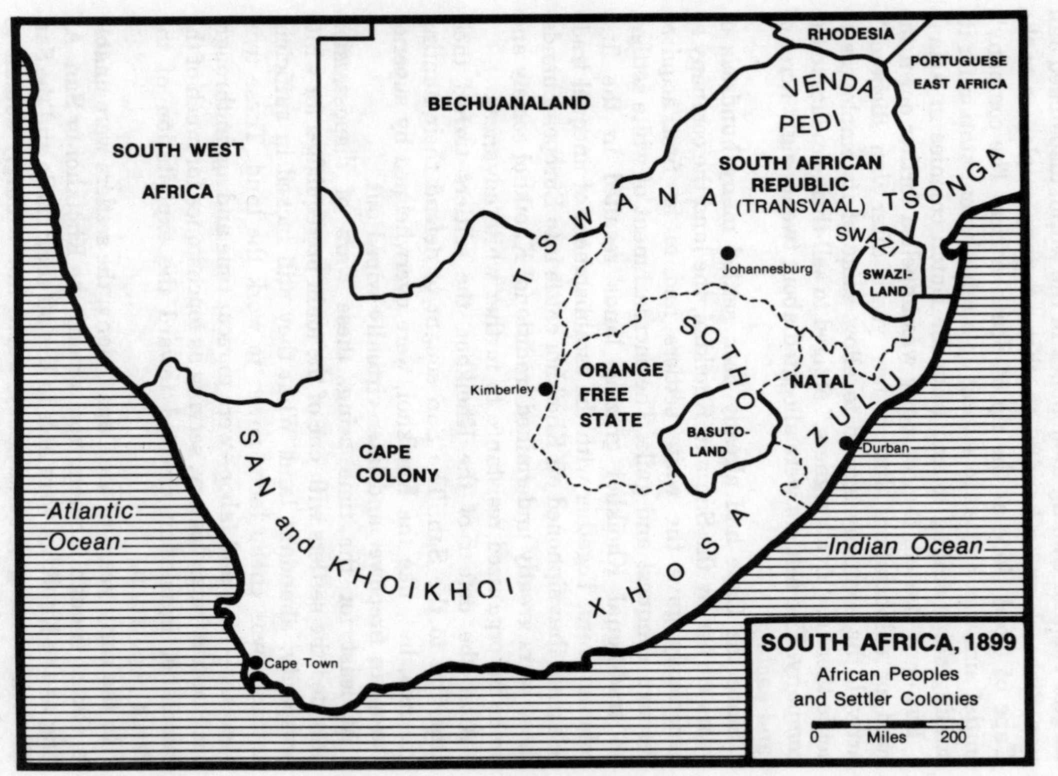
SOUTH AFRICA, 1899
African Peoples
and Settler Colonies
0 Miles 200
RHODESIA
PORTUGUESE
EAST AFRICA
BECHUANALAND
SOUTH WEST
AFRICA
VENDA
PEDI
SOUTH AFRICAN
REPUBLIC
(TRANSVAAL)
TSONGA
SWAZI
SWAZI-
LAND
TSWANA
Johannesburg
SOTHO
ORANGE
FREE
STATE
Kimberley
NATAL
ZULU
BASUTO-
LAND
Durban
CAPE
COLONY
SAN and KHOIKHOI
XHOSA
Atlantic
Ocean
Indian Ocean
Cape Town

emerging European colonial powers in the last half of the seventeenth century.

In 1652, the Dutch East India Company, then one of the largest colonial trading monopolies in the world, dispatched Jan van Riebeeck and a handful of other company employees to the Cape of Good Hope at the tip of South Africa. The company's initial aim was limited to setting up a refreshment station for its trading ships sailing to and from the Dutch colonies in Asia.

But once started, the company was impelled further down the road of colonization. Just a few years after van Riebeeck's arrival, the company agreed to allow some of its employees to settle there as "free burghers," obliged to sell their produce to the company. The settlers were allocated about twenty-eight acres of land each.

Since the Cape had already been settled many hundreds of years earlier by the San and Khoikhoi, the land the company so generously gave the white settlers had to be first acquired through conquest and guile. The encroachment of white settlers on traditional Khoikhoi grazing lands resulted in the first colonial wars. Together with the establishment of unequal trade relations that siphoned off Khoikhoi cattle into European hands, these wars greatly undermined traditional Khoikhoi society and broke its organized resistance to further white advances.

After the defeat of the Khoikhoi, the settlers turned their attention to the San. The San sought to defend their hunting grounds, but, like the Khoikhoi, were overwhelmed by superior European firepower and later virtually wiped out.

At least for the time being, these wars of dispossession provided the settlers with one of the main prerequisites for white prosperity: abundant land. What they still lacked in sufficient amounts was cheap labor power to work the land. These twin concerns—land and labor—were to recur time and again throughout South African history, serving as touchstones for much of the colonialist legislation directed toward the exploitation of the Black population.

In the early years of the Cape Colony, the settlers were unable to attract enough laborers from among the Khoikhoi or San. As long as the Khoikhoi were able to live off their cattle and the San off their hunting grounds, they would not willingly submit to employment by the conquerors. Van Riebeeck complained that "the natives here are not to be induced to work."[2] It was to take

2. Ibid., 1:27.

decades before Khoikhoi society had disintegrated to such an extent that they were compelled by economic necessity to seek jobs with whites.

To supply the settlers' immediate labor demands, the Dutch East India Company agreed in 1657-58, after repeated requests by van Riebeeck, to allow the importation of slaves into the Cape. By the end of the following century, about twenty-five thousand slaves (most of them African, but also many from Asia) had been pressed into servitude in the Cape Colony.

As the number of slaves increased, the social restrictions and laws against them were stiffened. In 1760, one of the first versions of South Africa's infamous pass laws was adopted to restrict their freedom of movement. It was similar to the more extensive and elaborate pass laws of later years, which are now among the white regime's principal instruments of control over the Black population as a whole. According to the 1760 law, every slave traveling "from the town to the country or from the country to town" was required to carry a pass signed by the slave owner authorizing the journey.[3]

As in all slave societies, the punishments meted out in South Africa were barbaric. Severe beatings by slave owners were administered routinely and the use of torture against slaves was legally sanctioned. Even minor offenses were punished with whippings, binding in chains, branding, or cutting off of ears. Upon recapture, slaves who had tried to escape were usually mutilated. More serious "crimes"—such as raising a hand against a slave owner—brought mandatory death sentences, carried out by strangulation, breaking on a wheel, decapitation, quartering and chopping off of limbs, and burning.[4]

Throughout the eighteenth century, slavery was the predominant form of labor. Slaves from India, Ceylon, and other Asian countries performed almost all of the jobs in the mechanical trades in Cape Town. Outside of the city itself most of the slaves were put to work on white-owned farms. Thanks to slave labor, wheat and wine production increased substantially.

Although the number of "free" wage laborers did not rise appreciably until the following century, when slavery was formally abolished, some Khoikhoi did begin to seek work with

3. Monica Wilson and Leonard Thompson, eds., *The Oxford History of South Africa,* 1:196.

4. Albie Sachs, *Justice in South Africa,* p. 26.

white employers in the eighteenth century. By 1800, many of the fifteen thousand Khoikhoi living in the Cape Colony were employed as servants or laborers.

The large-scale importation of slaves was a momentous development in South African history. While the institution of slavery itself did not survive beyond the early part of the nineteenth century, it left a strong imprint on future social relations through the entrenchment of the master-servant relationship. The importation of slaves—and later the emergence of a class of landless Black laborers from within South Africa—tended to close the door to the settlement of large numbers of poor and unskilled whites. Those whites who did settle in South Africa in that period rapidly became part of a privileged layer. According to a report in 1743, ". . . the majority of the farmers in this Colony are not farmers in the real sense of the word, but owners of plantations, and . . . many of them consider it a shame to work with their hands."[5]

The white settler population nevertheless continued to grow at a steady, though modest, rate. And so did the land area occupied by them. White-owned farms of six thousand acres or more became common. The sons of plantation owners soon came to expect large farms of their own as a virtual birthright. This system of white land tenancy led to a rapid expansion of the colony's frontiers.

The dispersion of the Boers (the Dutch word for farmers) inevitably brought them into contact with yet more African peoples and led to a new wave of colonial wars. In 1779 the first of a long series of wars against the Xhosa began. But Xhosa society was more developed and organized than that of the Khoikhoi and San, making them much more formidable opponents. The armed conflict along the eastern border of the Cape Colony was thus to drag on for another century.

The last two decades of the eighteenth century marked the twilight of Dutch colonial rule in South Africa. In the 1780s, the Dutch East India Company began to founder under an avalanche of debts. Despite efforts to generate more revenues and cut back on costs in the Cape and other colonies, the company went bankrupt in 1794. The following year the Cape was occupied for the first time by British troops.

By that time, industrial Britain was already a mighty imperialist power, with a vast colonial empire of its own. The biggest

5. Eric A. Walker, *A History of Southern Africa*, p. 85.

prize in it was India, and the Cape assumed a strategic and commercial importance in relation to the naval and trade routes to India. As long as Britain's Dutch allies were in firm control of the Cape, those routes were considered relatively secure. But after the French revolution and the subsequent French defeat of the Dutch royalist forces, the British colonialists feared that their French rivals would press onward to occupy the Cape and thus jeopardize British dominance in India itself. The British occupation of the Cape in 1795 was designed to forestall such a possibility.

The British takeover brought the colony into a period of economic growth. The white settlers were granted freedom of internal trade and the right to export their surplus produce. New towns sprang up and roads and bridges were built. Like the Dutch before them, British settlers began to arrive in South Africa. By 1820 the British recognized that the Cape was potentially the most important commercial port in the southern hemisphere and that it was a valuable market for British manufactured goods. From the position of economic isolation imposed by the former Dutch monopoly, the Cape Colony was now drawn into the main channels of world capitalist trade.

There was no fundamental difference between the policies of the British and the Dutch toward the indigenous African population. The British settlers enjoyed the same privileged status that the Boers had already carved out before them. Blacks were kept in a totally subservient position. In fact, the economic and military strength of the British colonialists enabled them to bolster and extend white supremacy in southern Africa far beyond what the Dutch had ever dreamed of achieving.

Only a few years after the British takeover, the new administration made its intentions clear by continuing the wars begun by the Dutch against the Xhosas. Farms of four thousand acres each—on land taken from the Xhosa—were parcelled out to the settlers. "Though official reports told of deeds of soldiery daring," historian C. W. de Kiewiet wrote, "the real warfare was directed against the cattle and food supply of the Kaffirs [Xhosas]. Their fields were burned, their corn destroyed, and their cattle driven off. . . . Nothing was more calculated to bring them to their senses and, when the war was over, to leave them impoverished."[6]

Over time, this policy not only had the desired effect of weak-

6. C. W. de Kiewiet, *A History of South Africa,* p. 51.

ening Xhosa society, but also of inducing some Xhosas to seek employment with white farm owners. As early as the 1820s, there was a steady trickle of Xhosas into the colony, prompting the adoption of an ordinance giving passes to any Xhosa willing to work for whites.

As long as the Xhosas were able to defend themselves militarily, the policy was to push them back physically before the Cape's expanding borders. Once they had been defeated and impoverished, however, they were allowed into the colony, but only (at least in theory) on the basis of their labor as a conquered people. This was a pattern that was to unfold, slowly at first, throughout the subsequent wars on the eastern frontiers of the Cape.

By the early 1800s, those social forces in Britain favoring the abolition of slavery had gained the ascendancy. Among them were the new captains of industry, who viewed slavery as an inefficient and costly form of labor. Rather than buying slaves outright—and then having to provide at least a minimum of food and lodging whether the slaves were usefully employed at the moment or not—these entrepreneurs preferred to purchase only the actual labor time of so-called free workers.

The slave trade was formally abolished in the British Empire in 1807. The more than thirty-five thousand slaves in South Africa were officially "freed" in 1834, although they still had to be "apprenticed" to their old masters for four more years.

This signified the definitive transition of the Cape Colony from a slave-labor society into one in which the laws of the capitalist market were beginning to dominate. For Blacks, however, the change meant little real improvement in their material position; for many years wage levels rose only slightly above the former cost of slave subsistence.

Even before the abolition of slavery, "free" contract labor had become increasingly important in the Cape, much of it provided by the remnants of the Khoikhoi people, who had been almost completely landless since the end of the eighteenth century. The growing urbanization of the Khoikhoi threw them into close social contact with ex-slaves, other African peoples, and whites. Through years of intermarriage, the Khoikhoi gradually lost their specific ethnic identity and became absorbed into the racial category now known as Coloureds, which also includes descendants (usually mixed) of the San and other Africans, of Asian slaves, and of whites.

Since the abolition of slavery did not mean that the Cape had ceased to be a colonial society, Black workers—both Coloured and

African—were still unable to experience much freedom, either on the labor market or in social life in general. They were fettered by various laws, pass regulations, and labor ordinances, such as the Masters and Servants Act of 1841, which made it a criminal offense for a worker to break a labor contract.

In the Eastern Cape, the wars against the Xhosa continued to disrupt African life, creating the prerequisite for an even larger supply of propertyless African laborers for the white farm owners by robbing the Xhosas of enormous herds of cattle and hundreds of square miles of land. Following a severe famine in 1857, about thirty thousand Xhosas were forced to seek work on the white-owned farms in the eastern districts of the Cape.[7]

Various laws were enacted to control this African labor force. The Masters and Servants Act was repeatedly strengthened. The Kaffir Employment Act regulated the terms of employment of "Natives of Kafirland and other Native Foreigners," requiring them to sign labor contracts and carry passes.[8]

The Xhosas, Coloureds, ex-slaves, and other Black peoples had no legal way of abolishing or altering the laws that governed them. Theoretically, some of them could gain the vote, but the property, income, and education qualifications were pegged so high that few of them actually did, leaving the government of the Cape a whites-only institution.

In the decade from 1836 to 1846, a number of social and economic factors affecting the Boer settlers in the Cape combined to prompt a mass migration beyond the colony's borders. Known as the Great Trek, the emigration of ten thousand settlers—one-sixth of the Cape's white population—rapidly extended the limits of white colonization and greatly affected the future history of southern Africa.

7. The famine was a product of the Xhosas' own desperation. Just before it, Xhosa prophets arose who preached that if Africans killed their cattle and destroyed their seeds a great wind would sweep the whites into the sea and Xhosa prosperity would be restored. Under the conditions of the time, many Xhosas were ready to snatch at anything that appeared to offer a possibility of salvation. They followed the prophets' instructions by slaughtering more than a hundred thousand head of cattle. Instead of the expected end to white domination, famine swept the land. Thousands of Xhosas died and thousands more were left impoverished.

8. Sheila T. van der Horst, *Native Labour in South Africa*, pp. 32, 34-35.

The trekkers cited a number of reasons for their original departure from the Cape. Some expressed dissatisfaction over the abolition of slavery and vowed to "preserve proper relations between master and servant" in the new regions that they conquered. Others complained about the "proud and defiant attitude" of the Xhosas.[9] Perhaps one of the most important compulsions was the relative "shortage" of land and labor the growing Boer population faced within the confines of the colony. As they moved northward and eastward, the trekkers satisfied their economic wants by seizing yet more land and cattle and by forcing Africans to work for them.

Some of the first groups of trekkers skirted the remaining Xhosa regions and occupied land on the fringes of the Zulus' traditional territory in what is now southern Natal. After the Boers inflicted a major defeat on the Zulus, thousands of them streamed into the area, and in 1840 the trekkers proclaimed an independent white republic of Natalia. The Zulus within the republic were distributed among the settlers as laborers, with about five families working on each white-owned farm. Zulus captured in battle were "apprenticed." Passes were issued to Africans. Those Africans not needed to work for the Boers were subject to residential segregation.[10]

British merchants in Cape Town feared that the Boers' Port Natal (Durban) would develop into a rival port to that of the Cape, so in 1843 the British annexed Natal as another direct colony and took over its administration.

The British continued many of the labor policies against the local African population developed by the Boers. Between 1845 and 1875 Theophilus Shepstone evolved a policy of territorial segregation in Natal that was to provide the model for the present apartheid regime's Bantustan program. As in the Cape, Africans in Natal theoretically had the franchise, but because of high property and other qualifications they were effectively denied the vote.

The British annexation prompted the Boers to trek once again, this time further into the interior. They set out to conquer the areas that are now the provinces of the Orange Free State and the Transvaal. The British colonialists tried to impose their direct political authority over these territories for a few years after 1848,

9. W. A. de Klerk, *The Puritans in Africa,* p. 23; Freda Troup, *South Africa,* p. 110.

10. Van der Horst, *Native Labour,* p. 42.

but largely for financial reasons were compelled to pull back from any new expansionist undertakings. By 1854 they had agreed to withdraw south of the Orange River. This allowed the Boers to set up two independent white settler states, the Orange Free State and the South African Republic (Transvaal).

Before temporarily relinquishing their claims to the region north of the Orange River, however, the British helped the Boers establish themselves in the Orange Free State by waging two wars against the original inhabitants, the Sotho people. The Boers also conducted a few military campaigns of their own after the British departure. This combined British and Boer assault was eventually to leave most of the Sothos' land, especially the rich wheat fields west of the Caledon River, under white ownership, while the Sothos themselves retained only the territory that is now the formally independent country of Lesotho (then known as Basutoland), a mountainous, desolate region with only 13 percent of its land surface suitable for cultivation.

Farther to the north, beyond the Vaal River, the Boers carved out another white supremacist "republic," defeating the Ndebele, Sotho, Tswana, and other peoples in the region.

Both of the Boer republics were explicitly based on the principles of white supremacy. Neither had even a pretense of a franchise for Africans as the Cape and Natal did. The constitution of the Transvaal frankly stated, "The people want no equality of Blacks with white inhabitants, either in Church or State."[11]

The African inhabitants were reduced to farm laborers or "squatters" on their former lands. They were required either to pay rent or to work for 90 to 180 days a year for their "right" to continue living on those lands. The land wars and the disruption of the African communal economy compelled many Africans to seek work with the white plantation owners.

Where these economic pressures did not yet bring forth enough laborers to satisfy the Boers, measures were adopted to force Africans onto the labor market. In the Orange Free State, Boer commando units burned Sotho crops in the hopes that they would be driven by hunger to seek work with white employers. In the Transvaal, military expeditions were sent out to capture African children, who were forced to work for the Boer landowners. Labor taxes were imposed, instituting a system of virtual forced labor.

11. N. J. Rhoodie and H. J. Venter, *Die apartheidsgedagte* [The apartheid idea], p. 91.

To control the African population, both white regimes introduced pass laws. The Transvaal regime developed an early form of "influx control," decreeing that Africans would not be allowed to live "too close to the vicinity of any town."[12]

Over the years, the Boers in the two republics, as well as those who had stayed behind in the Cape, gradually acquired a new cultural and national identity. The Dutch that they spoke became modified, picking up a number of African and Malay words, expressions, and grammatical constructions from their Black servants, until it was transformed into a new language, which they called Afrikaans. They began to refer to themselves as Afrikaners.

The period of white geographical expansion in the early and mid-nineteenth century was also accompanied by a degree of initial capitalist economic growth in southern Africa. Wool was exported and maize production on the white-owned farms in the Eastern Cape spread rapidly. The exploitation of the Namaqualand copper mines in the 1850s elevated copper into a major export item, at least for a time. The first private bank in the Cape was established in 1836. A quarter of a century later there were twenty-nine. Between 1820 and 1860 the volume of shipping that passed through the port of Cape Town increased eightfold.

The merchant class gained in strength and wielded considerable political influence. But although capitalist trade was extensive, capitalist *productive* relations had thus far gained dominance for the most part only in the regions around the two main ports, Cape Town and Durban, Within a few decades, however, the discovery and exploitation of diamonds and gold was to totally transform the economy. Capitalism was to become rapidly entrenched in South Africa's heartland, built on the foundations of white supremacy that had already been laid by the early settlers.

12. G. D. Scholtz, *Die ontwikkeling van die politieke denke van die Afrikaner* [The development of the political thought of the Afrikaner], 2:603.

3

The Consolidation of White Supremacy

Diamonds and gold. Nothing else changed the settler colonies of southern Africa so radically and suddenly. By whetting the acquisitive appetites of hundreds of financiers, entrepreneurs, and adventurers in Europe and South Africa, they catapulted the previously little-known British and Boer states into the international limelight. They quickly spurred the growth of large-scale mining industries, drawing capital and labor toward the mine fields at a rate unprecedented on the African continent.

In a pattern that was to repeat itself time and again in later years, this rapid development and expansion of the capitalist mode of production was to bring with it an entrenchment, extension, and systemization of white racist rule. Where the one flourished, so did the other.

In 1870, extensive diamond fields were discovered at the site where the city of Kimberley now stands. One passing hindrance to the British colonialists in exploiting them was the fact that the diamond fields were on land that was occupied by the Griquas, a Coloured people. After first posing as protectors of the Griquas, the British annexed the area and threw the diamond fields open to white miners. When the Griquas finally rose in rebellion, they were brutally put down.

Barely a few years after the first diamonds were unearthed, about 15,000 whites, 10,000 Coloureds, and 20,000 Africans had poured onto the diamond diggings. The town of Kimberley mushroomed. The first sizable Black industrial work force was created; between 1871 and 1895, some 100,000 Africans worked at the mines, supporting another 400,000 with their wages.

With the aid of low Black wages, the dividends generated by the diamond mines were exceptionally high, reaching about £2 million to £3 million a year by 1910 on an issued capital of only about £10 million.[1]

Out of the early jumble of hundreds of individual mining claims, one person, Cecil John Rhodes, managed to secure control over all of the Kimberley mines by 1889, under the name of De Beers Consolidated Mines. Rhodes's monopoly over the South African diamond mines enabled him to build De Beers into an international giant. "All but a tiny proportion of diamond production was controlled by De Beers," biographer Anthony Hocking wrote, "and all but a fraction of sales were handled by a single sales organisation. De Beers and the [Diamond] Syndicate were so interlinked that they seemed inseparable. It was the most impregnable monopoly in the world."[2]

As important as the diamond mines were in launching the industrial revolution in South Africa, they were soon dwarfed by the emergence of another mining industry—this time based on the extraction of gold.

White settlers first found gold in South Africa in the 1850s, but the major discoveries—the extensive gold veins along the Witwatersrand in the southern Transvaal—were made only in 1886. These veins were later revealed to be only part of a series of gold reefs that stretch in an arc for at least three hundred miles from Evander in the Transvaal to Welkom in the Orange Free State. For the white conquistadors, it was at last the discovery of a new El Dorado: South Africa's reefs hold by far the largest known gold deposits in the world.

The Boer government of the Transvaal proclaimed the Witwatersrand (or Rand for short) a public goldfield in 1886. Although the economy of the Boer republic was based on farming, the regime nevertheless opened the way for the further penetration of capitalist productive relations into the African interior.

Unlike the early diamond diggings, there was no room for individual claim holders or small mining companies on the Rand. The difficulties and costs of underground mining and of extracting gold from the ore-bearing rock required massive concentrations of capital and labor. The gold mining companies thus had to be heavily capitalized from the start. Much of the money for these operations came from the mining barons who had already made a killing in diamonds, as well as from foreign investors,

1. Mnguni, *Three Hundred Years,* 3:132.
2. Anthony Hocking, *Oppenheimer and Son,* p. 15.

predominantly British. Of the £200 million invested in the gold mines until 1932, roughly £120 million came from abroad.[3]

By the turn of the century most of the gold industry was controlled by six mining finance houses, including Cecil Rhodes's Consolidated Goldfields of South Africa. These monopolies were in turn closely associated with each other through the Chamber of Mines, which sought to protect the interests of the gold industry as a whole.

In his study of the gold industry, Frederick A. Johnstone called it "the first really large-scale capitalist industry in South Africa."[4] In fact, the Chamber of Mines was the greatest single employer of labor in any one area of the world at the time.

The rapid development of the gold and diamond mines spurred capitalist economic growth throughout South Africa. By 1910 Johannesburg, which was bare pasture land before the opening of the gold fields, had surged ahead of both Cape Town and Kimberley to become the largest city in South Africa. Thousands of miles of railway were built. The gold mines directly influenced the growth of coal mining in the Transvaal and Natal, spurred the development of banking, and induced the beginnings of a manufacturing industry. The domestic market for agricultural produce was greatly widened, further enriching the white plantation owners. Trade expanded greatly.

Most importantly, this economic growth forged—and was dependent on the creation of—a numerous and powerful Black working class. Like magnets, the mines and other industries drew toward them hundreds of thousands of Black workers from throughout southern Africa.

Rather than breaking down the political and social restrictions on the Black population and creating a class of "free" Black workers, the white financiers and mining magnates who presided over this capitalist economic growth adapted the existing system of national oppression to their own ends, wedding white supremacy to class domination. To maintain high profit levels, the mineowners sought to keep labor costs at the barest minimum. They employed racial oppression to help create a large class of propertyless Blacks who had no option but to sell their labor power and to carry out unskilled work in the mines at ultralow wages.

3. Ralph Horwitz, *The Political Economy of South Africa*, p. 214.
4. Frederick A. Johnstone, *Class, Race and Gold*, p. 2.

One encumbrance the mineowners had to overcome, however, was the competition between the various mining companies in the recruitment of Black labor. Many Africans still had some access to land in the reserves (those areas that had not been directly seized for white land ownership) and thus were not compelled by economic necessity to seek full-time wage employment. This created a relative shortage of available mine labor. In order to attract workers, the companies were forced, to an extent, to outbid each other by offering slightly higher wages and better working conditions. According to a contemporary observer, "The dream of the mine manager is to cut down the cost of native labour by getting a larger and more regular supply. . . ."[5]

Acting in the interests of the gold industry as a whole, the Chamber of Mines adopted two measures to prevent the labor shortage from raising wage costs and reducing profit levels. One was the hiring of African workers from beyond South Africa's borders and the other was the coordination of recruitment policies and the elimination of competition. Several bodies, including the Witwatersrand Native Labour Association and the Native Recruiting Corporation, were established to lessen competition, cut recruitment costs, and fix wages and working conditions more or less uniformly throughout the gold mining industry.

From its earliest days, a cornerstone of labor policy on the mines was the migratory labor system. To get a mining job, a Black worker had to sign a labor contract specifying a minimum amount of work required, ranging from about nine months for Africans recruited within South Africa up to fifteen months for those hired elsewhere. When the contract was over, the worker had to return home before being allowed to reapply for another stint in the mines. This prevented many Black workers from becoming permanently urbanized.

The entrenchment of this migratory labor system was absolutely central to the chamber's policy of driving down Black wages. The modest agricultural output in the African reserves (or in other African countries), to which the migrant workers remained tied, made it possible for the mineowners to pay them below what it would cost to maintain both the worker and his family in an urban setting. The Chamber of Mines itself admitted this several decades later, declaring:

5. James Bryce, *Impressions of South Africa,* p. 303.

> It is clearly to be the advantage of the mines that native labourers should be encouraged to return to their homes after the completion of the ordinary period of service. The maintenance of the system under which the mines are able to obtain unskilled labour *at a rate less than ordinarily paid in industry* depends upon this, for otherwise the subsidiary means of subsistence would disappear and the labourer would tend to become a permanent resident upon the Witwatersrand, with increased requirements. . . .[6]

The mining barons thus sought to harness the subsistence agricultural relations in the reserves to the needs of capitalist industry.

While working in the mines, Blacks were kept under tight rein. Breaking a labor contract was a criminal offense under the Masters and Servants Act, punishable by imprisonment. Strikes and other acts of "insubordination" were also illegal. One key mechanism of social control was the confinement of Black workers in prison-like compounds, called hostels. The compound housing system was first developed at the diamond mines, initially to prevent Africans from quitting their jobs or walking off with the fruits of their labor—the diamonds. When not actually working in the mines, they were obliged to stay in the compound areas during the whole period of the labor contract. This system was later extended to the rest of the mining industry.

Another important instrument of labor control was the pass. In 1895 the Transvaal government adopted a pass law drafted by the Chamber of Mines in order, according to a mine official, "to have a hold on the native."[7] Within twenty-four hours of entering a labor district, an African seeking work had to obtain a special pass, which was good for only six days. If no employment was found in that time, he was subject to fines, imprisonment, and expulsion from the area. This short period weakened the bargaining position of the worker, forcing him to accept whatever job was offered. By controlling movement, the pass system also kept out "unwanted" Africans from the cities and restricted the workers' ability to quit or change jobs.

As a result of these combined measures, the Chamber of Mines

6. Harold Wolpe, "Capitalism and Cheap Labour-Power in South Africa," p. 434. Emphasis added.

7. Sheila T. van der Horst, *Native Labour in South Africa,* p. 133-34.

was successful in reducing annual African mine wages from the equivalent of R78 in 1889 to R58 in 1897.[8]

It was primarily the low wage costs achieved by the Chamber of Mines that made possible the profitable development of the gold mines. As the chamber itself acknowledged, "It was not so much the richness of these fields that attracted the necessary capital, as it was their apparent continuity and the fact that they could be worked efficiently by cheap native labour."[9]

The tightening control over African workers was accompanied by increasing restrictions on the political rights of Africans in general. In 1865 the British-dominated settler state in Natal disenfranchised virtually all Africans. Cecil Rhodes, the diamond and gold baron who was also prime minister of the Cape Colony, adopted measures that struck some thirty thousand Africans off the voting rolls in the Cape as well.

The accelerating capitalist economic growth in South Africa, particularly the opening of the diamond and gold fields, created a tremendous appetite for cheap Black labor. But throughout this period the white capitalists were unable to fully satisfy their needs. The main obstacle they faced was the continued possession of or access to land by broad sections of the African population in the areas that were still nominally independent, and even in the conquered territories themselves.

To try to break those African ties to the land, the rise of mining was accompanied by the last stages of the white conquest and the wars of colonial dispossession. It ended by the turn of the century with the defeat and subjugation of the last independent African societies in South Africa.

Africans living beyond South Africa also fell victim to this colonial expansion. Lured on by rumors of more fabulous mineral wealth north of the Transvaal, Cecil Rhodes used the fortune he had made to establish the British South Africa Company in 1889 for the purpose of extending white domination even further into the interior of the continent. Through a combination of guile and military force, he subjugated the Ndebele and Shona peoples and carved out a personal empire, which was named after himself—Rhodesia.

The conquest of the African territories—and in many cases

8. As used throughout this book, one rand is equivalent to US$1.15.

9. Johnstone, *Class, Race and Gold*, p. 47.

their actual incorporation into the British colonies and the Boer states—was insufficient by itself to create a class of propertyless wage earners. To be sure, a portion of the African population became proletarianized from a fairly early date, but many others continued to eke out an existence from the land, either as "squatters" or labor tenants on the white-owned farms or as more or less self-sufficient producers in the areas later demarcated as African reserves.

In fact, the growth of capitalist market relations provided an opening for the emergence of a small layer of African peasants, and even commercial farmers, who began to produce for the market in competition with white farm owners. The first sizable African peasantry, composed mostly of Mfengu, arose in the Ciskei area of the Eastern Cape around 1835, and later in the Transkei and northeastern Cape. This process accelerated after the rise of mining, which gave a further boost to agricultural production.

The growing economic weight of the African peasants worried the settlers and the colonial authorities. In Natal, the Native Affairs Commission of 1852-53 complained that African peasants were "rapidly becoming rich and independent" and that they "preferred the most independent state, and hence has arisen the uniformly insufficient supply of labour."[10] In the white republics of the Orange Free State and the Transvaal the Boer settlers were too weak to push Africans off the land and Africans began to use their saved earnings to buy back the land that had originally been taken from them.

In response, the white plantation- and mineowners launched a political and economic war against the African peasants and subsistence farmers, attacking their position as sellers of agricultural produce and driving them off the land to serve as wage workers.

The first major campaign in this war began as early as the 1840s in Natal, where Theophilus Shepstone established the first Native Reserves, the forerunners of today's Bantustans, which serve as vast labor reservoirs. With the aim of impoverishing the Africans in the reserves and driving them onto the labor market to earn cash wages, an annual tax was imposed on every hut. The reserves themselves were fragmented and scattered with, according to Pierre van den Berghe, "the dual purpose of making farm labour more easily accessible to White farmers, and of averting

10. Colin Bundy, "The Emergence and Decline of a South African Peasantry," p. 376.

the threat of large concentrations of Africans."[11] Just before the British war against the Zulu state in 1879, Shepstone expressed the hope that the defeated Zulus would be "changed to labourers working for wages."[12]

For the whites, this assault on African land ownership acquired a new urgency with the opening of the diamond and gold mines. As prime minister and minister of Native affairs of the Cape Colony, Cecil Rhodes once again led the charge. In 1894 he pushed through the Glen Grey Act, which he called his "Native Bill for South Africa." It imposed individual tenure on African land in the Glen Grey district that had previously been worked on a communal basis. The purpose was to limit the number of Africans with access to land and drive the rest out of the reserve to work. An annual hut tax was levied to push this process along. "Every black man cannot have three acres and a cow," Rhodes said. "We have to face the question and it must be brought home to them that in the future nine-tenths of them will have to spend their lives in daily labour, in physical work, in manual labour."[13] The provisions of the Glen Grey Act were later extended to other parts of the country.

Combined with the further displacement of Africans from the land were other measures designed to drive them into the hands of white employers. Through law, social compulsion, and economic inducement, new wants were fostered among Africans, such as the use of European clothes and manufactured goods, which could only be obtained through purchase. To get money to buy, Africans first had to work. The imposition of hut taxes and other monetary levies, though a cruder form of compulsion, had the same effect. Speaking in 1899 at an annual meeting of Consolidated Goldfields, one company official stated, "If we could only call upon one-half of the natives to give up three months of the year to work, that would be enough. We should try some cogent form of inducement, or practically compel the native through taxation or in some other way. . . ."[14]

The efforts to draw Africans onto the labor market took effect

11. Pierre van den Berghe, *South Africa,* p. 31.

12. Monica Wilson and Leonard Thompson, *Oxford History of South Africa,* 2:266.

13. Mnguni, *Three Hundred Years,* 3:136.

14. J. A. Hobson, *Imperialism,* p. 269.

only gradually—and could not be systematized for several more decades. The white employers were thus forced to look elsewhere, at least for the time being, for enough workers to fulfill their labor needs.

In Natal, the plantation owners along the coast brought in contract workers from India, the first of whom arrived in 1860. The Indian workers, mostly from the lower castes, were indentured to their white employers for a period of five years, after which they were allowed either to return home to India or to stay on in Natal. Most decided to stay. They were employed primarily in the burgeoning sugar plantations. Some got jobs as domestic servants. From 1876 to 1900, the number of Indians in Natal increased from ten thousand to sixty-five thousand, outnumbering the whites themselves. They soon constituted 90 percent of the labor force on the sugar plantations.

Not all of the Indians who came to South Africa were workers. Shortly after the first indentured laborers arrived, a significant number of Indian merchants immigrated to Natal to engage in trade. Fearing competition from this merchant class, as well as the potential political influence of the large Indian population, the authorities in Natal explicitly excluded Indians from voting in 1893 and four years later barred the entry of virtually all nonindentured Indians. Indian competition in trade was checked, and when Indian merchants began to move into the Transvaal in the 1880s they were shackled with further restraints.

The mineowners sent recruiters into other African countries as well. Between 1890 and 1899 the number of Africans employed in the gold mines alone increased from 14,000 to 97,000, about half of them coming from Portuguese East Africa (Mozambique). After the turn of the century the proportion reached about two-thirds. Migrant workers for the mines and other sectors were recruited from almost all the other countries of southern Africa, and even from as far away as Zanzibar.

The extension of white supremacy, the continued wars against the various African peoples, the rapid capitalist growth based on diamonds and gold, and the consequent demands for large numbers of African workers, all highlighted a key anomaly facing the white colonialists: This vast territory was still being ruled by four separate white settler states—the British colonies of the Cape and Natal and the Boer republics of the Orange Free State and Transvaal—whose policies were often uncoordinated and at times divergent. Many whites, mostly among the English-speaking population, saw this disunity as the chief obstacle to the effective entrenchment and protection of white supremacy, as well as to the unfettered growth of the newly emergent system of capitalist production.

Raising the well-worn alarm of a "Black peril," an English-language newspaper in the Orange Free State stridently declared in May 1851, "We see a war of races—the declared aim and intention of the black man being to drive the white man into the sea. . . . and what we ask in the name of reason are we to present as a counterpose? We answer in one word UNION."[15]

Such attitudes were prevalent in official circles as well. In 1858, Sir George Grey, the governor of the Cape Colony, stressed the advantages of white confederation or union, primarily in military terms. After describing the situation of almost constant warfare at the time, including the possibility of a "general rising" of Africans, he stated:

> The smallness and weakness of the [white] states, the knowledge that they are isolated bodies . . . has encouraged the natives to resist and dare them, whilst the nature of the existing treaties and the utter abandonment of the natives by Great Britain, to whom they had hitherto looked up, has led the natives to combine for their mutual protection, and thus to acquire a sense of strength and boldness such as they have not hitherto shown. . . . [The white states'] revenues will be so small that they cannot efficiently provide for their protection. Hence a new incentive is given to the surrounding natives to attack them.[16]

Broader British imperial interests were also involved, particularly at a time of sharpening competition among the European colonial powers over how to carve up the African continent. With the development of the gold mines, the Transvaal became the most important region of southern Africa, yet it was still outside direct British control. The British colonialists were concerned that the further strengthening of the Boer states, in alliance with a rival European power, could eventually challenge British dominance in southern Africa. In particular, there appeared to be the threat of a Boer alliance with imperial Germany, which had begun to conquer parts of South West Africa in the 1880s.

Rhodes, moreover, harbored extravagant ambitions of extend-

15. G. D. Scholtz, *Die ontwikkeling van die politieke denke van die Afrikaner,* 2:504.

16. Eric A. Walker, *A History of Southern Africa,* p. 271.

obvious. When British troops marched into Johannesburg in mid-1900, African mine workers, apparently expecting improvements in their position, burned their passes and greeted the British. But the British "were swift to disillusion the demonstrators," historian Donald Denoon wrote, "handed out severe punishments for breaking the (Republican) law, and set the labourers to work on road and railway building at arbitrarily low wages."[21] Encouraged by these measures, the mineowners slashed African wages by almost half, from more than fifty shillings a month to thirty shillings.

Negotiations for union among the four states were spurred after the end of the Anglo-Boer War partly by the emergence of new signs of Black unrest. A number of African, Coloured, and Indian political organizations were forged and a major Zulu rebellion shook Natal in 1906, reaffirming the dire need, from the viewpoint of the white supremacists, for an effective and uniform policy toward the Black majority.

The South Africa Act, passed by the British Parliament in 1909, provided for the formation of an independent Union of South Africa the following year. The four white settler states were incorporated as provinces. The provisions of the act entrenched the existing racist franchise laws, which barred all Blacks from voting in the Transvaal and Orange Free State, excluded almost all Africans and Indians from the voting rolls in Natal, and severely restricted the Black franchise in the Cape through high income, property, and literacy qualifications. The act specifically stated that all members of parliament had to be "of European descent."[22]

The establishment of the Union capped the consolidation of white minority rule and signaled the forging of a long-standing political alliance among the various ruling strata: mining and agricultural, English and Afrikaans speaking.

Union also marked an important shift in the relations between the South African settler state and Britain. For the white South African ruling class, it brought political independence from the former imperial power (although strong political ties were still retained with Britain until 1961, when South Africa became a republic and withdrew from the British Commonwealth).

For the Black majority, however, the establishment of Union

21. Donald Denoon, *Southern Africa Since 1800,* p. 104.

22. Mnguni, *Three Hundred Years,* 3:139.

signified no qualitative change in their position as a subjugated people. They still remained enslaved by a colonial-settler state, with no voice in the government and with their few surviving political rights destined for elimination. They still remained alienated from their land. Their country continued to be plundered of its natural and human wealth by white capitalists, who employed force and coercion to extract colonial-type superprofits. They still faced national oppression in all spheres of life.

In effect, the new South African state simply took over from Britain the role of direct colonial power over the subject Black population. Though it was now independent, having its own economic and political interests to defend, it nevertheless continued to function as an imperialist outpost on the southern tip of the African continent, a position it holds to the present day.

4

Land, Labor, and Segregation

> **Thus the coloured man is indispensable to the white man, and is brought into constant relations with him. He is deemed a necessary part of the economic machinery of the country, whether for mining or for manufacture, for tillage or for ranching.**
>
> **—James Bryce,**
> ***Impressions of South Africa***

With considerable fanfare, the Union of South Africa was officially proclaimed on May 31, 1910. The white rulers rejoiced and congratulated themselves over their triumph. But for the overwhelming majority of their subjects, who found themselves relegated to second-class citizenship, it was an especially grievous day. They watched with bitterness and foreboding as the white "masters" crowned the consolidation of white supremacy.

Once the vexing question of political union had been taken care of, the rulers could turn their attention to the more crucial economic and social problems that still hindered the effective exploitation of South Africa's natural wealth and plentiful labor power. To clear the way for further capitalist expansion, the twin problems of land and labor had to be firmly tackled.

In spite of numerous restrictive measures, many Africans throughout the country still clung tenaciously to whatever land they could. So long as Africans had access to their own means of production—land—the white mineowners, capitalist farmers, and urban employers faced continued obstacles in securing enough African workers.

The seriousness of this predicament became increasingly evident to the white employers. The Transvaal Labour Commission of 1903, which generally reflected the interests of the gold mining companies, observed that in the Transvaal "the natives are living practically under the same economic conditions as they were before Europeans came into the country. No considerable change can be reasonably anticipated in their industrial habits until a great modification of these conditions has been brought about." Its recommendations to increase the labor supply included "compulsion, either direct or indirect," the "imposition of higher taxes," and the "introduction of legislation modifying the Native Land Tenure."[1]

Similarly, the South African Native Affairs Commission of 1903-05 stated that if the process of Africans purchasing back their former land continued, "it is inevitable that at no very distant date the amount of land in Native occupation will be undesirably extended." This situation had already severely restricted the capitalists' labor supply. Estimating that the total number of African workers then required in the four South African colonies was 752,000, the commission pointed out that only a little more than 350,000 Africans were expected to seek work at any one time. The commission also foresaw the expansion of African land ownership as a threat to white supremacy itself, stating, "It will be far more difficult to preserve the absolutely necessary political and social distinctions, if the growth of a mixed rural population of landowners is not discouraged. . . ."[2]

It was only after Union that a coordinated offensive against African landowners was possible. The key weapon in it was the Natives' Land Act of 1913, known among Africans as the "law of dispossession."

The main forces behind the passage of the act were the mineowners and other capitalists. As the president of the Chamber of Mines declared in 1912, "What is wanted is surely a policy that would establish once and for all that outside special reserves, the ownership of land must be in the hands of the white race, and that the surplus of young men, instead of squatting on

1. D. Hobart Houghton and Jenifer Dagut, *Source Material on the South African Economy*, 2:87-89.

2. Ralph Horwitz, *Political Economy of South Africa*, pp. 39-40.

the land in idleness and spreading out over unlimited areas, must earn their living by working for a wage. . . ."[3]

The Natives' Land Act included two chief avenues of attack. One restricted the African right to purchase land in "white" South Africa and the other aimed to eliminate African "squatters."

Under the guise of "protecting" African-occupied lands in the reserves from white encroachment, the act formalized the territorial division of South Africa into "Native Areas," comprising at that time only 7.3 percent of the entire land surface, and the rest of the country, which was designated "white." Africans were prohibited from owning any land outside the reserves. Even within the reserves, the sizes of land allocations were carefully limited, so as to force African males onto the labor market to supplement their families' meager harvests.

The effects of the act were acute. The restrictions on African land occupation soon led to extreme overcrowding in the reserves, resulting in overutilization of the land and serious soil erosion. This process had already begun before the turn of the century in some areas, but spread throughout the African reserves during the 1920s and 1930s. Malnutrition became the rule, and outright starvation was not uncommon. African districts that had previously exported grain could now no longer grow enough food even to remain self-supporting.

In order to buy food—which was grown for the most part on white-owned farms—Africans were forced to go out and work for cash wages. Hunger was a basic impetus behind the rise in the number of available African workers.

By 1930, a majority of the men in the reserves were spending at least part of each year in employment in "white" South Africa. With the destruction of the African means of subsistence, the reserves had become little more than labor reservoirs.

The other major aspect of the land act was the suppression of African "squatting," a category that covered a variety of forms of land use on white-owned farms, in which African families grew crops and grazed cattle on part of the farms in return for occasional labor services, a share of the crops, or cash rents. To the mineowners and large-scale capitalist farmers, this was an inefficient use of African labor power. So the land act aimed to transform the squatters into wage laborers, pure and simple.

3. Frederick A. Johnstone, *Class, Race and Gold*, p. 27.

Those who refused to work for only a cash wage were subject to eviction.

The land act struck a fatal blow at an important sector of the African peasantry. Its impact was first felt in mid-1913 when thousands of Africans were expelled from their homes and sent wandering hopelessly in the rural areas in search of some new place to settle. Since it was winter, many lost their cattle to the cold, and some perished themselves. Sol Plaatje, an early leader of the African National Congress, toured some of the areas where squatters were being evicted and described their plight in his pioneering work *Native Life in South Africa.* "Look at these exiles swarming towards the Basuto border," he wrote, "some of them with their belongings on their heads, driving their emaciated flocks attenuated by starvation and the cold. The faces of some of the children, too, are livid from the cold. It looks as if these people were so many fugitives escaping from a war, with the enemy pressing hard at their heels."[4]

Some of the refugees migrated beyond South Africa's borders, to Basutoland or Bechuanaland. Some squeezed into the already overcrowded reserves. Many moved to the towns to look for jobs with a white *baas* (master). By the 1930s, squatting and labor tenancy had disappeared in the areas of commercial farming.

This deliberate impoverishment of the rural African population set off a large-scale migration to the towns and mining centers. Between 1921 and 1936 the number of Africans in urban areas nearly doubled. They even moved into towns and cities in the Western Cape, which until then had been populated predominantly by whites and Coloureds. Four-fifths of all wage workers were Black by the 1920s. Deprived of any means of livelihood in the countryside, African workers naturally sought to settle in the towns permanently and with their families.

The white employers were overjoyed at the availability of a large supply of cheap Black labor. But they were also worried about the potential political consequences of the rapid influx of Blacks into the "white" cities, a problem that has plagued the ruling class to the present day. The 1921 Native Affairs Commission bemoaned the appearance of "professional agitators" and warned that "the masterless native in urban areas is a source of danger. . . ."[5]

4. Sol T. Plaatje, *Native Life in South Africa*, pp. 105-6.

5. Monica Wilson and Leonard Thompson, *Oxford History of South Africa*, 2:187.

To safeguard against this threat, the Transvaal Local Government Commission that same year recommended that "the native should only be allowed to enter the urban areas, which are essentially the white man's creation, when he is willing to enter and to minister to the needs of the white man and should depart therefrom when he ceases so to minister."[6] Thus the apartheid regime's view that Africans are only laboring machines to be deprived of all political rights in "white" South Africa was officially adopted well before the National Party came to power in 1948. It is a basic policy from which many other restrictive measures flow.

The main piece of legislation in the 1920s designed to deal with this problem was the Natives' Urban Areas Act of 1923. It provided for the establishment of segregated African locations in the towns, barred Africans from owning land in urban areas, and imposed a uniform pass system for all African men throughout South Africa, except in the Cape. The act sought to control African movement into the towns and provided for the expulsion of "surplus" Africans not actually employed in the area.

African workers faced tighter restrictions on the job as well. It became virtually illegal for African workers to strike, and in the mines Africans were prohibited from jobs that were "reserved" for whites, a measure known as the color bar. The Industrial Conciliation Act of 1924 extended to the manufacturing sector the kind of labor relations that were already prevalent in the mines. It legally defined an "employee" as a worker who did not carry a pass, thus excluding from the category the vast majority of African males, who consequently had no right to negotiate with or strike against their employers. Instead, industrial councils composed of white bosses and white trade-union bureaucrats decided what African wages should be.

The effects of such measures were severe. Between 1916 and 1921 alone, the real wages of Blacks dropped by 13 percent.

The conditions of farm laborers tended to be even worse than those of workers in the cities. Their wages were much less, and they were fettered by additional laws that outlawed strikes on farms, tied farm workers to three-year labor contracts, and sanctioned whipping of those under eighteen years of age.

Other laws, of a more politically repressive nature, gave the governor-general virtual martial law powers to govern all African areas by proclamation; imposed stringent measures to banish

6. Francis Wilson, *Migrant Labour in South Africa*, p. 160.

individuals, control meetings, and outlaw the promotion of "hostility between the races"; and allowed police to arrest speakers and participants at public meetings.

However, despite the severity of these laws, the authorities were frequently incapable of enforcing them in practice, as shown by the many Black demonstrations, protest rallies, and strikes that erupted in this period. Although they were denied most political and trade union rights, Black workers responded to the assault on their living standards by flocking to the Industrial and Commercial Workers Union, the most powerful Black working-class organization in South African history, which flourished during the early and mid-1920s.

The political awakening of urban Blacks and the regime's incapacity to enforce fully the laws it had adopted against them prompted the authorities to look more closely at the overall apparatus of white supremacy. With the goal of further refining and systematizing it, Prime Minister J. B. M. Hertzog pushed through a series of far-reaching segregationist bills in 1936.

The Representation of Natives Act removed the ten thousand African voters in the Cape from the common voter registration rolls, putting them instead on a separate roll, from which they were allowed to elect only three representatives to the House of Assembly and three to the Cape Provincial Council. African chiefs in other parts of the country were allowed to choose an additional four senators. All the African "representatives," the act stipulated, had to be white.

As a cover for this attack on African rights, a Natives' Representative Council, with solely advisory powers, was established. It was composed of twelve elected and four nominated Africans, as well as five white officials, with the secretary of Native affairs as its chairman. This body served more than just a cosmetic purpose however. The white authorities realized that it was necessary to provide a safe outlet for African political energies and to make preparations for the later introduction of more indirect methods of rule. By winning the collaboration of a section of the African leadership through their participation in the council, Pretoria was successful for a time in sidetracking a wing of the Black liberation movement.

Finally, the Native Trust and Land Act extended the segregationist provisions of the 1913 Natives' Land Act to the Cape and accelerated the suppression of African squatting in that province as well. It also "released" additional land for the African reserves, eventually bringing the total amount of land legally allocated to Africans to 13.7 percent of the country. Since most of this "released" land was already occupied by Africans, the act did nothing to ease the severe overcrowding in the reserves.

The combined effect of these three acts was to strengthen the basic structure of white supremacy. The intensification of racial oppression that accompanied them was soon translated into higher profit rates and greater capital accumulation.

Side by side with the creation of a numerous Black working class, South Africa's capitalist economic expansion also proletarianized a section of the white population.

Drawn by promising job opportunities in the burgeoning mining industry, some white workers migrated to South Africa from Europe, particularly Britain. Many others had been farmers (mostly Afrikaners) who were driven off the land by the penetration of capitalism into agriculture, which favored the accumulation of land ownership by the big commercial interests and ruined many of the small-scale farm owners and *bywoners* (white squatters). The "scorched earth" policy of the British army during the Anglo-Boer War had uprooted many more. Tens of thousands of displaced farmers flocked to the cities and mining centers, many of them, at least initially, forced to take unskilled jobs. By the early 1920s some three-quarters of all white mine workers were Afrikaners, an indication of the extent of this rural-to-urban migration.

Despite all the myths about white "unity" and the supposed common interests of the entire white *volk*, white workers, like Black workers, were exploited by the capitalist class. As in any other capitalist country, the surplus value they produced was appropriated by the employers.

Owning no capital themselves, these white workers did not benefit from the exploitation of Black labor, although their relatively higher wages did make them a privileged layer of the working class.

The differences between white and Black wages were due to several factors. Far and away the most important was the national oppression of Blacks, which enabled the ruling class to exploit Black workers much more severely than whites, to drive down their wages and standard of living much further.

Another key element in the wage gap was the different degree of proletarianization of Black and white workers in that period. Most Black workers, especially in the mines, were migrant laborers with continued—though limited—ties to the land, which in effect subsidized their cash incomes. This enabled the bosses to pay wages sufficient to maintain only the individual Black worker. White workers, on the other hand, were more completely cut off from the land, living in the cities *with* their families, on a permanent basis. To ensure the maintenance of the white working class, the employers therefore had to pay out wages high enough to sustain both the white workers and their families, which meant covering costs like rent, schooling, health care, additional food, etc.

Finally, white workers, because of their stronger trade union organization, were able to wage a series of militant strikes in the early decades of the twentieth century, winning greater pay concessions from the employers than Blacks were able to.

In a study of the position of white workers in this period, Robert Davies concluded that it was not "that white unskilled wage rates were 'abnormally high.' On the contrary it would seem from contemporary evidence that they were extremely 'modest.' Rather it was that the wage rates applicable to African workers had been driven down . . . to levels which were 'abnormally low.'"[7]

The white ruling class saw the utility of such wage differentials for deepening the divisions within the working class as a whole, to hinder and block any moves white workers might make to ally with Blacks in a joint struggle against their common class enemy.

The capitalists' fears of a possible alliance between Black and white workers had a very real basis. With the rapid influx of whites into the cities, many of them got unskilled jobs in industrial enterprises, working side by side with Black workers, at wages only slightly higher than those of Blacks. Trade union militancy among these white workers was high. In the 1920s, there were an estimated 200,000 to 300,000 "poor whites," most of them Afrikaans speaking, throughout South Africa. A growing number of unskilled and unemployed whites ended up in multiracial urban slums, where they established closer social ties with Blacks.

One Afrikaner writer warned at the time that if nothing were done to bring these whites up to "civilized standards," they might seek an alliance with Black workers: "If the more privileged

7. Robert Davies, "The Political Economy of White Labour in South Africa," in T. Adler (ed.), *Perspectives on South Africa*, p. 148.

European grudges and refuses the poor his patronage and society, the latter will associate with non-Europeans. . . ."[8]

To head off such a potential threat to white supremacy and capitalist rule, the government, acting in the interests of the employing class as a whole, consciously sought to widen the social cleavage between white and Black workers. The Pact government[9] that came to power in 1924 instituted a "civilized labor" policy, in which "poor whites" were given secure and segregated jobs, largely in the public sector, such as the railways and post offices. To reinforce racial employment patterns, Black workers were barred, by law or practice, from holding skilled or semiskilled jobs.

The regime was greatly aided in this by the racist views and narrow craft outlook of most white skilled workers. When the mining companies sought to cut their costs by replacing some semiskilled white workers with lower-paid Africans, the white workers turned their anger not only against the mining barons, but also against the Black workers. They carried out a number of reactionary strikes to "keep Blacks in their place," culminating in a major uprising of white miners in the Witwatersrand in 1922. The Pact government, subordinating the immediate interests of the mining companies to those of the entire capitalist class, sought to prevent further white miner outbreaks by greatly strengthening the job color bar in the mines and extending it to the rest of industry.

The Industrial Conciliation Act of 1924, while excluding Africans from having any legal trade union rights, simultaneously emasculated the white trade unions by tying them to the regime's complex and proemployer straitjacket of industrial councils, wage boards, and compulsory arbitration. This blunted the militancy of the white unions and helped entrench the emerging layers of professional union bureaucrats who favored conciliation over struggle. By 1930, the number of white workers who went out on strike had fallen to only a fourth of the number in 1924.

A major political campaign was likewise launched to convince white workers that their interests lay not in allying with Black

8. Wilson and Thompson, *Oxford History*, 2:184.

9. A coalition government established in 1924 between the predominantly English-speaking and social-democratic South African Labour Party and the National Party, which represented the political interests of the aspiring Afrikaner capitalists.

workers, but in supporting national oppression. At the very time when class stratification was sharpening among Afrikaners, the emerging Afrikaner capitalists began whipping up Afrikaner nationalist sentiments in order to retain the allegiance of white workers to the *volk*. The Afrikaner nationalists also embarked on a drive to take over leadership of those unions that were predominantly Afrikaans speaking, so as to isolate the more radical trade unionists and win the unions to firm support of white supremacy.

Outright repression was also unleashed against white trade unionists who showed any inclination to help Black workers organize independent unions or struggle for higher wages and better working conditions. Scores of them were jailed and driven out of the union movement.

Based on the superexploitation of the Black working class, South African industry grew significantly in the period between the two world wars. Mining still occupied the paramount position in the economy, but manufacturing and capitalist farming were becoming increasingly important as well.

This capitalist industrialization had two long-lasting effects. It spurred the white authorities to tighten their stranglehold on Blacks, who were being drawn to the cities in ever greater numbers. And it gradually led to shifts in the relative weight and political influence of the various sectors of the capitalist class, especially between the so-called national bourgeoisie, part of which originated from rural-based Afrikaans interests, and foreign capital, which retained a strong, though diminishing, influence in mining and commerce.

The First World War had given a boost to South Africa's large-scale capitalist farmers, most of whom were Afrikaners, by disrupting foreign competition and increasing the demand, both within South Africa and abroad, for South African agricultural produce. Slowly at first, but later in greater numbers, these Afrikaner plantation owners began to reinvest their profits in commerce and industry.

The early Afrikaner capitalists—and those Afrikaners who sought to follow their example and enter business themselves—breathed new life into the traditional Afrikaner resentments against London and even against English-speaking white South Africans, who were still considered too closely tied to the former colonial power. They employed Afrikaner nationalism as a weapon against their more powerful competitors and as a tool for their own economic advancement. They issued emotional appeals for the upliftment of the *volk* to help mobilize capital and launch new, Afrikaner-owned businesses.

Their political instrument was the National Party, originally led by Hertzog, but later by D. F. Malan, who reforged the party after Hertzog joined with Smuts to form the United Party in 1934. The National Party leaders (contrary to the popular myth later spread by bourgeois critics of apartheid) were not backward farmers encumbered by "outmoded" racial concepts, but urbanized professionals and businessmen who clearly recognized the central importance of national oppression to maintaining capitalist superprofits.

The efforts of these aspiring capitalists began to bear fruit by the 1930s. The Broederbond, a secret Afrikaans society that formulated much of the policy of the Afrikaner nationalist movement from behind the scenes, had a direct hand in founding the first Afrikaans banking house, Volkskas, in 1934. Particularly important in focusing the Afrikaner business drive was a national economic conference organized by leading Afrikaner nationalists in 1939. At it, M. S. Louw, the managing director of the Afrikaans insurance company Sanlam, declared, "If we want to achieve success, we must make use of the technique of capitalism as it is employed in the most important industry of our country, the gold mining industry. We must establish a financial company like the so-called 'finance houses' in Johannesburg."[10] Shortly after the conference, the first Afrikaans investment company, Federale Volksbeleggings, was set up. It was later to grow into one of South Africa's largest companies.

By 1942, the Afrikaner capitalists were strong enough to found the Afrikaanse Handelsinstituut (Afrikaans Commercial Institute) as a counterpart to the English Chambers of Commerce and Industry.

During the same period, the largely English-speaking mineowners also continued to forge ahead, opening new mines, expanding their interests, and piling up profits. Between 1918 and 1939, the working profits of the gold mines increased by more than four times.

A new mining finance house, the first since the gold boom at the end of the preceding century, was set up in 1917. Drawing on capital from Rhodes's old De Beers diamond monopoly, as well as from the J. P. Morgan interests in the United States, Ernest Oppenheimer established the Anglo American Corporation. De-

10. Brian Bunting, *The Rise of the South African Reich*, p. 377.

spite its name and its links with foreign capital, the corporation was based in South Africa and was "a South African company," in the words of Harry Oppenheimer, Ernest's son and successor.[11] Although a late starter in relation to the other mining houses, it was destined to become the largest South African monopoly.

Reflecting the growing muscle of the South African capitalist class, the gold mining industry in general was coming under increasing South African control. In a study of foreign investment in South Africa, Barbara Rogers noted that the industry's "ownership was outside South Africa, but its management was largely in the hands of the newly rich South Africans or European immigrants who saw their personal future in a 'white South Africa.' Ownership, then, meant passively receiving dividends from a system controlled by local segregationist interests."[12] In 1920 the South African Reserve Bank was set up, taking over from foreign mineowners the right to sell gold. As a result of this increasing control, much of the accumulated capital from the mines was retained within South Africa for reinvestment, rather than being siphoned off abroad.

Ownership of the mines, too, was falling more and more into South African hands. As early as the 1920s, much of the capital put into the opening of a series of new mines on the eastern Rand was raised from within the country. By the following decade, South African ownership of gold shares had risen to 40 percent.

Mining was nevertheless still under the strong influence of foreign imperialist investors, particularly British. As a result, the mining houses showed little interest in—and even put up some resistance to—South Africa's industrialization. The profits of the members of the Chamber of Mines were largely plowed back into mining itself.

Because of the continued weakness of the local capitalist interests favoring industrialization, especially the Afrikaner nationalists and their allies, they were compelled to utilize their political strength and the apparatus of the state to further their economic aims, overcome British resistance—and more rigidly control the Black work force. It was no accident that the Nationalists, who favored greater capitalist industrialization, were also the most vociferous champions of extending and

11. Anthony Hocking, *Oppenheimer and Son*, p. 386.

12. Barbara Rogers, *White Wealth and Black Poverty*, p. 94.

systematizing the institutions of white supremacy.

Hertzog's Pact government, set up in 1924, was the first to begin reflecting the interests of the sector of the South African bourgeoisie that sought to push forward the country's industrialization. It adopted protectionist measures against foreign competition and subsidized capitalist agriculture through higher taxes on the gold mines. Following the failure of private capital to establish a South African steel industry, the regime stepped in and set up the Iron and Steel Industrial Corporation (Iscor) in 1928 as a public corporation with the government holding the controlling interest. It did so in opposition to the mining magnates. Steel was the first heavy manufacturing industry in South Africa and gave a strong impetus to other related industries, such as coal mining and engineering.

With the help of state protection and financing, manufacturing was well on its way by the 1930s. Between 1910 and 1940, South Africa's rate of industrialization was more than three times faster than that of the United States and more than seven times faster than Britain's.

The outbreak of World War II was a further blessing for the South African industrialists. It eliminated many foreign competitors and assured a home market for manufactured goods. During the war years, manufacturing output more than doubled.

Once manufacturing had become definitively established and the mining industry itself had come more under the control of South Africans and less under that of foreign investors, the last resistance to industrialization melted away. This was reflected in the measures adopted by Smuts's wartime cabinet. Smuts had long been identified with the Chamber of Mines, yet in 1940 he created the Industrial Development Corporation, one of the most important state-controlled companies in South Africa. It was specifically set up to help diversify the economy, with the purpose of filling any major gaps left by private capital.

The big expansion of capitalist industry during World War II inevitably brought with it another sharp rise in Black urbanization and proletarianization. Because many whites were serving in the military, Blacks were increasingly hired for semiskilled jobs that had previously been reserved for whites only. The relative scarcity of semiskilled labor strengthened the bargaining position of Black workers, leading to significant wage hikes for Blacks in manufacturing. The great demand for Black labor compelled the government to relax its pass laws. Africans streamed into the cities. While only 96,000 Africans (excluding those working in the mines) lived in the Johannesburg area in 1927, there were 400,000 there by the end of the war.[13] Enormous slums sprang up overnight. When the existing locations became too overcrowded, Africans squatted on vacant land and built unauthorized shantytowns. Administrative control over urban Blacks began to break down.

The Board of Trade and Industries spoke with alarm of the industrial and political implications of this rapid urbanization. "Racial and class differences" between Blacks and whites, it stated in 1945, "will make a homogenous Native proletariat. . . . The detribalisation of large numbers of Natives congregated in amorphous masses in large industrial centres is a matter which no government can view with equanimity. Unless handled with great foresight and skill these masses of detribalized Natives can very easily develop into a menace rather than a constructive factor in industry. . . ."[14]

The board's concern was not misplaced, as shown by a major series of strikes by Black workers. In defiance of wartime laws banning African work stoppages, scores of strikes broke out. Most significantly, about seventy thousand African mine workers walked off their jobs in 1946, the largest strike ever held in the mines.

Once again, South Africa's capitalist system required reinforcement of racial control over Blacks. Pass laws were tightened, resulting in the arrests of thousands of Africans who had come to the cities in search of jobs. Smuts strengthened and extended the regime's segregationist policies: The Native Urban Areas Consolidation Act of 1945 systematized even further the earlier laws stipulating where Africans could or could not live in the cities. The "Pegging Act" of 1943 and the "Ghetto Act" of 1946 restricted Indians from acquiring any new property in "white" areas and confined them to Indian slums.

Explaining these racist measures, Smuts asserted in parliament in 1945 that "all [white] South Africans are agreed . . .

13. Leonard Thompson and Jeffrey Butler, eds., *Change in Contemporary South Africa*, p. 139.

14. Martin Legassick, "South Africa: Capital Accumulation and Violence," p. 275.

except those who are quite mad . . . that it is a fixed policy to maintain white supremacy in South Africa."[15]

But waiting in the wings were the Nationalists—who promised to do an even more thorough job of safeguarding white capitalist dominance.

15. Freda Troup, *South Africa*, p. 278.

5

The Straitjacket of Apartheid

The word *apartheid*—an Afrikaans expression that literally means separation or segregation—was first coined in 1929. It did not come into popular usage until the 1948 elections, when the National Party of D. F. Malan adopted it as a campaign slogan. Since then, the term has come to connote the Nationalist regime's entire system of racist rule, ranging from segregated washrooms, playgrounds, and hospitals to the absence of nearly all Black political rights and the wide gap between Black and white incomes.

The adoption of apartheid as official policy with the victory of the National Party in 1948 represented an important watershed in the evolution of South African society. This shift was a direct result of the rapid industrialization of the 1930s and 1940s, which had drawn tens of thousands of Blacks to the urban centers, swelling the Black slum areas and fueling militant struggles around the country. As a proapartheid study in 1960 admitted, "Without the notable urbanization of the native, we would certainly not have had anything like apartheid today."[1]

The expansion of South Africa's capitalist economy thus required adjustments in the overall system of white control. To keep the lid on this increasingly urbanized Black population, the Nationalists institutionalized, extended, and systematized all aspects of white supremacy and Black oppression to a far greater degree than any previous regime. Segregation in particular was elevated into a central pillar of capitalist rule. While 49 explicitly racial laws had been placed on the books in the four decades

1. N. J. Rhoodie and H. J. Venter, *Die apartheidsgedagte* [The apartheid idea], p. 245.

before the National Party took office, the number trebled to 151 in the period between 1948 and 1971.

Segregation, of course, was no recent innovation. It was rooted in the very substance of South African society, in the enormous gulf between the rulers and the ruled. In this more general sense, apartheid was a policy as old as white supremacy itself. As N. J. Rhoodie, an Afrikaner academic, noted, "South Africa's apartheid policy is based on a racial ideology with an historical evolution of more than three hundred years."[2]

The ideological groundwork for the National Party's specific contribution to this established policy of segregation was laid in early 1941, when several Afrikaans organizations and churches prepared a draft constitution and program based on what they called "Christian-National principles." For the Black majority, these principles meant greater segregation and the entrenchment of the migratory labor system: "Every coloured group of races, Coloured, natives, Asiatics, Indians, etc. will be segregated, not only as regards the place of dwelling or the neighbourhoods dwelt in by them, but also with regard to the spheres of work. The members of such groups can, however, be allowed to enter White territories under proper lawful control for the increase of working power. . . ."[3]

The concept of using the African reserves for overtly political purposes was also explored more systematically during this period. In 1947, for instance, Geoffrey Cronjé, a Nationalist historian and sociologist, raised the idea of extending limited political "rights" to Africans in the Bantustans. Trying to present his proposal in a "positive" light, as a concession to Blacks that would allow them a degree of "equality" with whites, he wrote that "the destiny of every nonwhite community in this country is to become equal with the white community, not within the same homeland, socioeconomic system, and political context, but each community in its own homeland and with its own socioeconomic system and political structure."[4]

Although many apartheid theorists and ideologists claimed to see near-total geographical segregation as an "ideal," the actual

2. N. J. Rhoodie, *Apartheid en partnership* [Apartheid and partnership], p. 43.

3. Brian Bunting, *Rise of the South African Reich*, p. 108.

4. Geoffrey Cronjé, *Regverdige rasse-apartheid* [Righteous racial apartheid], p. 155.

measures enacted by the Nationalist regime have been aimed at a very different target: maintaining control of the Black population *within* a white-dominated society. The ideology of apartheid simply seeks to provide a theoretical justification for the denial of Black political rights in "white" South Africa.

Pretoria's policies and practice are designed to safeguard and advance the overall interests of the white capitalist class. With the expansion of manufacturing and other industries in the urban areas, the white authorities found it necessary to extend the repressive labor policies of the mines and the plantations to the economy as a whole. Apartheid is primarily a mechanism of social and political control aimed at shoring up white supremacy and ensuring that the Black labor force remains an underpaid one.

In accordance with the apartheid regime's goal of stripping Blacks of all political rights, it soon abolished even the fiction of Black political representation in the white Union government. One of Prime Minister Malan's first acts after the 1948 electoral victory was to withdraw the offer of a circumscribed franchise made by Smuts to the Indian population of Natal. The powerless Natives' Representative Council was dissolved in 1951, and eight years later parliament did away with the seats held by the white "African representatives."

While the Nationalists had made a few overtures to the Coloured population before coming to power, they soon launched a major assault against the Coloureds' traditional voting rights in the Cape, removing them from the common registration roll in the province in 1956 and giving them four elected white "representatives" in the House of Assembly. Twelve years later the regime abolished even this token Coloured franchise and barred the election of any new white "Coloured representatives." After their terms expired in 1971, the central government was officially representative of whites only.

The biggest problem the apartheid regime faced in its drive to strengthen white supremacy was securing control of the cities. The dangers to continued white rule that urban Blacks presented were obvious, but the white mineowners and industrialists could not do without them. They were dependent on cheap Black labor. So Pretoria sought to keep the economic advantages of maintaining a large Black working class, while at the same time eliminating the political disadvantages. To that end, the Nationalists have conducted a perpetual war against the ability of urban Blacks to organize politically—through systematized segregation, the tightening of the pass laws, the extension of the migratory labor system, the removal of "superfluous" or "undesirable" Africans, and outright repression.

Another motivation for the extension of segregation was the ruling class's fear of the effects that greater Black urbanization could have on *white* workers. One government supporter summed up this concern in 1954 when he wrote, ". . . how can we expect that the [white] child who grows up in the backstreets of the big city, whose parents have nonwhites for neighbors, and who plays with nonwhites in his youth will maintain the traditional concepts . . . on the relations between the races?"[5]

To reinforce and broaden urban segregation, the apartheid regime enacted the Group Areas Act in 1950. Prime Minister Malan described it as "the kernel of the apartheid policy . . . the most crucial for determining the future of race relations."[6] The act maintained that residential areas for whites, Africans, Indians, and Coloureds had to be segregated. Through its enforcement untold suffering and misery has been inflicted on entire Black communities, which have been uprooted from their traditional neighborhoods, often in the central cities, and trucked out to new segregated townships on the outskirts.

Since most Africans had already been forcibly segregated by earlier regulations, the main blow of this particular act fell on Coloureds and Indians, many of whom still lived in mixed residential neighborhoods, especially in the Western Cape and in Natal. By 1979, about 550,000 persons had been evicted from their homes under the Group Areas Act, and another 132,000 were slated for similar treatment.[7]

The evictions under this act, the exacting restrictions on African residency rights, the government's refusal to build enough housing in the official Black townships, and the overcrowding and poverty in the Bantustans have left many Blacks with little alternative but to set up makeshift shantytowns. These illegal squatters' settlements have sprung up around a number of major cities, especially Cape Town, which had about sixty camps as of 1978. The shantytowns are ramshackle collections of

5. G. D. Scholtz, *Het die Afrikaanse volk 'n toekoms?* [Do the Afrikaner people have a future?], pp. 116-17.

6. Ralph Horwitz, *The Political Economy of South Africa*, p. 273.

7. *Financial Mail* (Johannesburg), March 16, 1979.

pondoks (shacks) made out of corrugated iron sheeting, wood, plastic, cardboard, tarpaulin, or any other material that offers a measure of shelter. The settlements usually have no electricity, running water, or other services. Yet to several hundred thousand Africans, Coloureds, and Indians they are the only homes they know.[8]

To the apartheid authorities, however, these unauthorized—and unregulated—settlements are unwelcome obstacles to "separate development." Under the Prevention of Illegal Squatting Act of 1951, settlement after settlement has been bulldozed, and the inhabitants shipped off to the Bantustans or simply evicted with little prospect of finding legal homes. But since the roots of squatting lie in the system of apartheid and white supremacy itself, settlements have continued to proliferate despite frequent demolitions.

Throughout the 1950s, 1960s, and 1970s, a series of other measures chipped away even more of the remaining residential rights of urban Africans, disqualifying tens of thousands. Those who were caught living in the cities without proper authorization were jailed, fined, or expelled to the reserves. It was exceedingly difficult for Africans to move from one city to another, or to change employers. If they lost their jobs, they could be evicted. Various laws limited the number of African domestic servants allowed to live on the premises of their employers, empowered local authorities to "endorse out" (eject) any African considered "detrimental to the maintenance of peace and order," suppressed most African social activities outside of the townships, and provided for the deportation of any "foreign native." The 1953 Reservation of Separate Amenities Act segregated post offices, railway stations, trains, bridges, buses, public parks, benches, beaches, swimming pools, and libraries. It specifically allowed for the provision of inferior facilities for Blacks.

The key instrument for controlling the African population and enforcing the laws that regulate their daily lives is the pass, popularly known among Africans as the *dom pass* (stupid pass). In 1952 the apartheid regime unveiled the Natives' (Abolition of Passes and Co-ordination of Documents) Act. Despite its misleading name, the act did not abolish passes, but simply consolidated and extended previous pass laws and changed the name of the

8. For a more detailed examination of South Africa's shantytowns, see Ernest Harsch, "South Africa: The Plight of the Urban Squatter," *Africa Report*, May-June 1979.

document from "pass" to "reference book." The new, refurbished pass was a complex document, containing an African's photograph, identity card, registration number, ethnic background description, influx control and labor bureau authorizations, tax receipts, work record, current address of employment, and employer's signature, which had to be updated monthly. In early 1979, the government indicated that it would "simplify" the pass, to make it less cumbersome. Those Africans tied to "independent" Bantustans had their passes replaced with "passports," but, as a circular by an official of the Department of Plural Relations explained, "For purposes of identification there is no difference between a conventional reference book and a travel document issued by Transkei or BophuthaTswana."[9]

The pass is one of the most graphic examples of how the apartheid system tries to dehumanize Africans. All Africans over the age of sixteen must have a pass and carry it with them at all times. Every policeman, and many government officials, can demand to see it, day or night. Failure to produce an up-to-date pass on the spot is punishable by fine or imprisonment. Hundreds of Africans are arrested each day for violation of the pass laws.

Africans consider the pass one of the most odious features of the apartheid system and resent it as a symbol of their inferior status. It has been a frequent target of African protest.

Burdensome as these restrictions are on African men, they are doubly oppressive to women. In the "white" areas of South Africa, not only is the sexist oppression African women suffer as women coupled with the national oppression that all Blacks are subjected to, but women also face special discriminatory measures. They encounter much greater obstacles in moving to the towns, and are liable to immediate expulsion from them upon the death of a husband or the loss of a job. Those African women who work in the "white" cities are barred from many occupations through sexist and racist discrimination and receive wages much lower than those of African men. Abortions are illegal in most cases. Under the Natal Code, virtually all African women are treated as perpetual minors, with no right to own or inherit property, act as guardians over their children, or represent themselves in court. Also in Natal, a commissioner has the power to confine an African woman to her rural home if she is deemed to lead an "immoral life."[10]

9. *Financial Mail* (Johannesburg), June 26, 1979.

10. H. J. Simons, *African Women,* pp. 9, 26, 74, 202, 208, 274, 280.

The white regime's apartheid policies also extend to marriage and sexual relations. As H. J. Simons, a South African Communist, pointed out, "Freedom of choice in marriage is incompatible with rigid social stratifications. When status is closely linked, as in South Africa, to racial type, any assimilation that blurs the obvious physical differences is seen as a threat to the social order."[11] Marriages between whites and Blacks (Africans, Coloureds, and Indians) became illegal under the Prohibition of Mixed Marriages Act. And the misnamed Immorality Act made sexual relations between Blacks and whites a crime, punishable by up to seven years in prison.

To have a standard for enforcing their discriminatory policies, the Nationalists set up a national racial register to classify the entire population as either European, African, or Coloured (which includes Indians). And to prevent any further symbolic blurring of racial distinctions, the act also sought to ensure that no more Blacks would be able to pass themselves off as "white." As J. J. Fouché, a Nationalist legislator, declared during the debate on the bill, if it was impossible to draw a clear line of demarcation between whites and Blacks, "then we have lost or abandoned the struggle to maintain a white race in this country."[12]

Of course, whenever South African officials talk of maintaining the "white race," they usually do not mean its physical survival as such, but the white ruling class's continued dominance.

Though the measures adopted during the National Party's first years in office were significant, they were still by and large relatively minor modifications of the traditional segregationist policies of previous regimes. It was during the mid-to-late 1950s and early 1960s, however, that the apartheid regime began to implement its more far-reaching programs, especially its policies on the Bantustans, labor, education, and the police.

11. Ibid., p. 106.

12. Gwendolen M. Carter, *The Politics of Inequality*, p. 82.

6

Divide and Rule: Pretoria's Bantustan Policy

KwaMashu is less than a half-hour's drive from central Durban. With its small houses of brick or wood or dried earth; with its occasional shacks of corrugated iron or scrap material; with its unpaved and pitted roads running among the trees and along the hilly slopes; with its littered lots, its bus stops, its beer halls and churches, its near-naked children, KwaMashu is very much like other African townships in South Africa. As in Soweto or Mamelodi or Clermont, thousands of KwaMashu's residents stream out of the township early each morning, headed for their jobs in the nearby "white" city, Durban. They return each night in crowded trains to their crowded homes.

As Blacks elsewhere, the people of KwaMashu had very few social or political rights to begin with. Since 1977 they have had even fewer. In that year, a white official in an office somewhere redrew the borders of the KwaZulu Bantustan to include KwaMashu. And with those few marks of a pencil, the township's more than 150,000 inhabitants automatically became "citizens" of an African "homeland."

Their daily lives changed very little. They still had to get up each morning and ride in to work. But now they had lost even those few remaining rights they had in South Africa as a whole. They found themselves foreigners in the country of their birth.

The plight faced by the people of KwaMashu is a common one throughout South Africa. Millions of Africans have already been declared "citizens" of one or another Bantustan, the fragments of territory comprising the 13.7 percent of the country set aside for African occupation. Against their will, they have been deprived of their South African citizenship. Millions more face the same prospect in coming years.

The government in Pretoria claims that it has only the welfare of Africans at heart. Its basic aim, it says, is to enable the various African "nations" to achieve "national self-determination" in their respective "homelands." White officials contend that Africans can best exercise their political rights in one of the ten Bantustans. They point to the elections that are held, the parliamentary debates, the pomp and ceremony of "Black government." When the South African flag is pulled down and the banner of a Transkei or a BophuthaTswana or a Venda is hauled up in its place, millions of dollars are spent trying to convince Blacks that a new African "state" has been born.

Behind this jargon—as with much else in apartheid South Africa—lurks something altogether different: a systematic and determined drive to preserve white capitalist rule. By physically segregating large sections of the African population into a number of small, scattered, and impoverished enclaves and by politically tying the rest of the African population to the Bantustans, the regime is seeking to forestall the emergence of a powerful and united struggle for Black majority rule *over the entire country*. As Prime Minister Malan himself admitted in 1959, "We have the choice of either giving the whites their own territory and the Bantu theirs, or of giving everybody one state and seeing the Bantu govern."[1]

Malan's claim that Africans were getting "their own territory"—besides being untrue—was intended as a justification for denying Africans their rights in South Africa as a whole. From its emergence in the early system of African reserves, through the 1913 and 1936 land acts, the 1951 Bantu Authorities Act, and the 1959 Promotion of Bantu Self-Government Act and its successors, each step in the elaboration of the Bantustan scheme has been marked by further attacks on African rights.

The 1959 act, which introduced the fraud of "self-government," was something of a milestone in this evolution. Even then, there was no mention of ever granting "independence" to the Bantustans. But barely two years later, as a result of domestic upheaval and the international protests that followed the Sharpeville massacre, Prime Minister Hendrick Verwoerd began to talk for the first time of turning the Bantustans into "separate Black states." He apparently hoped that by using the magic word "independence" he could deflect some of the international criti-

1. Monica Wilson and Leonard Thompson, *Oxford History of South Africa,* 2:411.

cisms and divert African nationalist sentiments within South Africa into less dangerous channels. Nevertheless, while the trappings of the Bantustan policy may have changed, Verwoerd made it clear that the aim was still the same, that of "buying the white man his freedom and the right to retain domination in what is his country."[2]

Pretoria advanced yet further on the Bantustan path when it unveiled the Bantu Homelands Citizenship Act of 1970. Under this act, all Africans in South Africa were to be proclaimed "citizens" of one or another Bantustan through a series of arbitrary criteria that were broad enough to cover not only those born in or currently living in a Bantustan, but everyone associated in the remotest way with a Bantustan through language, distant or close relatives, or "cultural" or "racial" background. During the parliamentary discussions on the act, Minister of Bantu Administration and Development Michiel C. Botha stressed that it would serve as a prelude to even more attacks on the rights of Africans in the "white" cities. Referring to their remaining urban residency rights under Section 10 of the Urban Areas Act, he affirmed, "I am going to remove all and every one of them."[3]

The foisting of a phony "independence" on the Transkei in 1976, on BophuthaTswana in 1977, and on Venda in 1979 marked the logical culmination of this process: The more than 6 million Xhosas, Tswanas, and Vendas assigned to those areas were deprived of their basic right to be citizens of South Africa.

An integral part of the entire Bantustan scheme is a conscious effort to weaken African resistance by creating and widening divisions among Africans.

Because of the high level of capitalist development in South Africa and the impact of direct colonial-settler rule throughout most of the country, the various African tribal groupings that existed in precolonial times have lost much of their independent identities and have become closely interrelated. Somewhat identifiable Zulu, Xhosa, Sotho, and other language groups still exist, particularly in the Bantustans themselves, but the social and cultural barriers between them are rapidly breaking down. This is especially true in the cities. Africans from different parts of the country were drawn to the urban centers in search of jobs. They

2. Barbara Rogers, *Divide & Rule*, p. 8.

3. Ibid., p. 21.

lived together, worked together, intermarried, and shared a common experience as an oppressed people and exploited class, often over many generations. Many of them, especially in the more cosmopolitan townships like Soweto, can speak or understand several of the African languages.

A sociological survey of the African population in the Johannesburg area found that "exclusive tribal patriotism seems to have almost died in Soweto. . . . Ideologically, it is race and class oppositions that are claimed to matter, while ethnic oppositions are denied or simply shrugged off."[4]

This process has greatly disturbed South Africa's masters. In 1975, an official government publication noted with alarm that the mass urbanization of Africans had led to "a disquieting collapse of those ethnic values basic to the maintenance of social stability."[5]

It was precisely to reintroduce such "ethnic values" that Pretoria passed the Promotion of Bantu Self-Government Act, which proclaimed the existence of eight "national units": those of the Zulu, Xhosa, Tswana, North Sotho (Pedi), South Sotho, Shangaan-Tsonga, Venda, and Swazi. The Xhosas have been further divided into two Bantustans, the Transkei and Ciskei. In 1972, a South Ndebele "nation" was also officially established.

These "national units" are only loosely based on the precolonial societies. The sharp distinctions drawn between them are artificial, aimed at trying to break down their existing interrelationships. The Zulus, Xhosas, Swazis, and Ndebeles all speak languages in the Nguni-language group, but have been isolated into separate Bantustans. The Sotho-language group has been divided into three main "national units": the North Sotho, South Sotho, and Tswana. In the northern Transvaal, various African peoples, including Tsongas, North Sothos, and Vendas, had been closely intermingled, with no distinct territories that they considered exclusively theirs alone. The regime set out to disentangle them, in the process fostering factional conflicts between the Vendas and Tsongas.

Because of the pattern of the white colonial conquests and the seizure of the best lands by whites, the Bantustans are geographically fragmented and scattered. Keeping them that way has

4. Leonard Thompson and Jeffrey Butler, *Change in Contemporary South Africa,* p. 152.

5. *South Africa 1975,* p. 101.

suited Pretoria's divide-and-rule policies. In some, particularly BophuthaTswana, the pieces of territory are strewn hundreds of miles apart.

In order to extend these divisions to the cities themselves, where firm white control is especially vital, the regime has attempted to link urban Africans to their respective "homelands" as much as possible. Within many townships and in the workers' quarters in the mining compounds, African housing has been segregated according to "national unit." When sections of the Bantustans are close to major cities, as they are around Pretoria, Durban, and East London, some entire African townships have been physically moved into them; others, like KwaMashu, have been made part of a Bantustan by simply redrawing boundaries.

The tying of millions of Africans to the various Bantustans was a completely arbitrary process. Whether they lived in the reserves or in the "white" cities or countryside, they had no say over which "nation" they were to belong to, let alone if they wanted to be assigned to any at all. It was the very opposite of real national self-determination. By focusing on language and cultural differences among Blacks and by physically segregating them on that basis, the apartheid regime hopes to foster petty factional conflicts and divert Blacks' energies from combatting the real enemy—white supremacy.

In this, it has had some limited success. In the Bantustans and in some of the townships there have been occasional factional fights. In Durban in 1949, for instance, 142 persons died in clashes between Africans and Indians that were openly encouraged by white officials. Outbreaks in the mining compounds are not unusual. Within the Bantustans, the government's population resettlement schemes and the maintenance of tribal rivalries have heightened frictions among residents; in 1978 alone, 260 persons were killed in faction fights between Madondas and Majolas in the KwaZulu Bantustan.[6]

Connected with Pretoria's attempts to further fragment the African population geographically and politically was the adoption of a more indirect form of rule. The white authorities resurrected the conservative tribal chiefs to positions of nominal authority and appointed African administrators in the Bantustans with the aim of creating a buffer between the African masses and the regime. "Chiefs and Headmen," a 1955 government report observed, "form an integral and important part of

6. *Financial Mail* (Johannesburg), February 16, 1979.

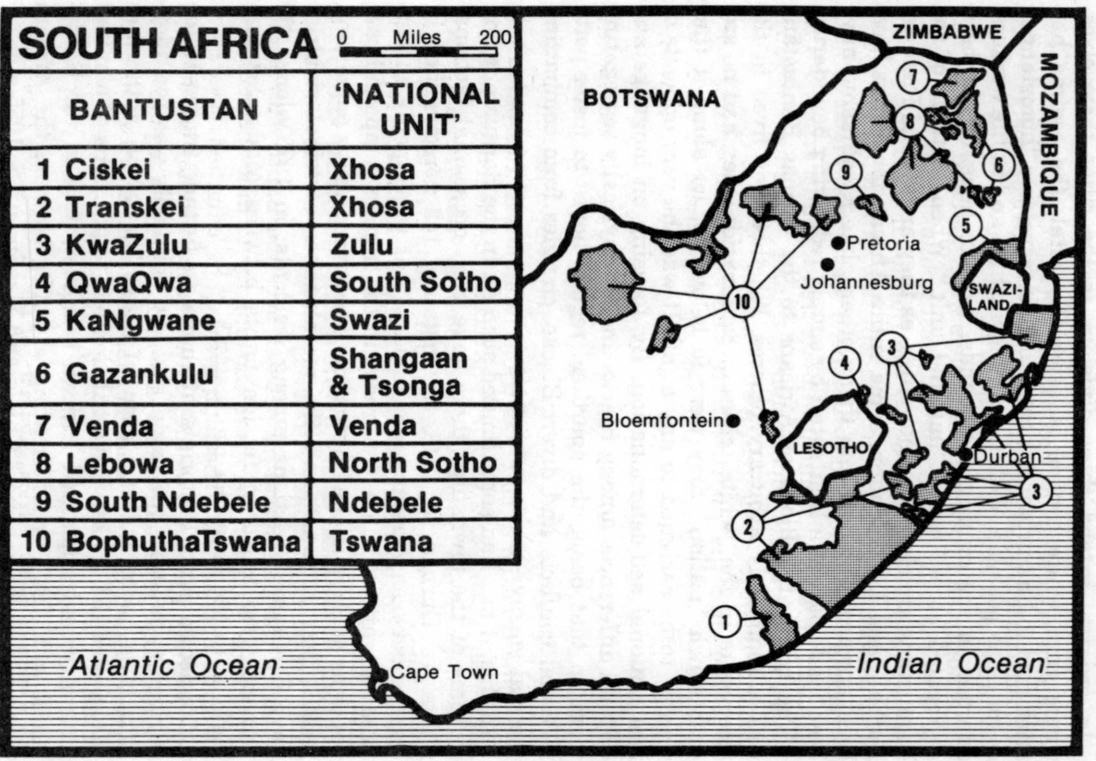

SOUTH AFRICA

BANTUSTAN	'NATIONAL UNIT'
1 Ciskei	Xhosa
2 Transkei	Xhosa
3 KwaZulu	Zulu
4 QwaQwa	South Sotho
5 KaNgwane	Swazi
6 Gazankulu	Shangaan & Tsonga
7 Venda	Venda
8 Lebowa	North Sotho
9 South Ndebele	Ndebele
10 BophuthaTswana	Tswana

the administrative organisation of the Department [of Native Affairs]." It was policy, moreover, to "build up and strengthen the power of the Chiefs. . . ."[7]

The reinforcing of the much-decayed and outmoded tribal institutions was seen by Pretoria as a way of retaining some of the more conservative aspects of traditional African social life in the context of a rapidly industrializing society. In an earlier era, the authority and powers of the chiefs were exercised in consultation with the tribal elders and, at least nominally, in the overall interests of the tribe. But under the Bantustan system they are being wielded arbitrarily on behalf of the white administration. Patriarchal authority, too, has been bolstered, much to the detriment of African women, who are treated under tribal law as minors subject to the supervision of a male "guardian" (father, husband, or other male relative).

To formalize the apartheid regime's "tribal" hierarchy, the Bantu Authorities Act of 1951 set up a pyramid of appointed bodies—called authorities—at the tribal, district, regional, and territorial levels. There is one territorial authority for each Bantustan. Under the act all chiefs hold their office through government sufferance and can be deposed at any time. They are paid by the regime. In most cases, Pretoria appointed chiefs who had some traditional claim as tribal figureheads. If a particular chief was uncooperative, he was either banished or a more cooperative minor chief was promoted to head the authority. Some tribal groupings, such as the Mfengu in the Transkei, originally had no acknowledged chiefs; Pretoria was forced to "find" some.

Sitting at the head of this pyramid is one "supreme chief"—the white president of South Africa.

During the parliamentary debates over the Bantu Authorities Act, Prime Minister Verwoerd did not try to hide the fact that Africans opposed it. "These proposals," he admitted, "were not very warmly welcomed by the Bantu leaders, for they had but one desire—they repeatedly said so—and that was equality and representation in the Union Parliament together with the Europeans."[8]

7. Union of South Africa, *Summary of the Report of the Commission for the Socio-Economic Development of the Bantu Areas Within the Union of South Africa* (hereafter cited as Tomlinson Commission report), p. 66.

8. Rogers, *Divide & Rule,* p. 21.

Indeed, in some Bantustans, especially in the Transkei, the new administrative bodies were imposed only in face of considerable resistance by the African population. Rebellions that broke out in the Transkei in the early 1960s were not put down until after a state of emergency had been declared, five thousand persons arrested, and more than twenty executed. In Zululand (now KwaZulu), widespread opposition to the authorities system forced many chiefs to take their distance from it.

Besides their routine administrative duties, the tribal chiefs were expected to implement apartheid policy and to keep the African population in their areas under control. Emergency powers and repressive laws were given to them. Increasingly, they took on more and more of the policing functions that had previously been carried out directly by the apartheid regime, arresting protesters and political dissidents, implementing anti-labor regulations, and even intercepting Black guerrilla fighters trying to pass through the Bantustans to attack targets in "white" South Africa.

To a limited extent, Pretoria has also sought to use the Bantustan collaborators to oppose or dampen struggles in the urban areas. Chief Gatsha Buthelezi of KwaZulu, for instance, has spoken out against strikes by African workers; during the Soweto rebellions in 1976 he openly condemned the young Black militants who were leading the protests.

Although the chiefs were given a few limited powers, Pretoria made it clear who the real master was. Shortly after the Bantu authorities system was imposed in the Transkei, the white chief magistrate told the chiefs, "We are now giving you the horse to ride (when I say 'we' I mean the Government); but do not forget while you are riding it that the Government will be behind with a big sjambok [a heavy ox-hide whip]. . . ."[9]

Some Bantustan heads, like Chief Gatsha Buthelezi, have made demagogic attacks on Pretoria's apartheid policies and have even rejected its "independence" plans. While this may reflect an effort to broaden their meager bases of support, it does not diminish the collaborationist nature of their positions. In fact, their criticisms lend an aura of credibility to Pretoria's claims that the Bantustan officials are functioning as truly independent African representatives and not as the hired servants they are regarded as by most Blacks. This becomes especially important for foreign consumption, since one of the

9. Govan Mbeki, *The Peasants' Revolt*, p. 57.

duties of the Black Bantustan administrators is to provide political cover for foreign companies investing in South Africa. Buthelezi in particular has made frequent pleas for increased foreign investment on the grounds that it "aids" South Africa's Black population.

Realizing, however, that the chiefs by themselves lack the credibility and social base to keep the Bantustan administrations afloat, Pretoria has consciously fostered the emergence of a relatively prosperous class of Africans in the reserves. It did this partly through the provision of salaried positions in the Bantustan apparatus and partly through the creation of a small layer of African landowners able to exist above the subsistence level, a "self-supporting 'peasant farmers' class," in the words of the 1955 Tomlinson Commission report.[10] In the Transkei, an estimated 8.5 percent of rural households are now "self-supporting," or engaged in production for the market. Together with government-paid African bureaucrats and a small number of African businessmen and traders, this social layer forms the base of Kaiser Matanzima's Transkei National Independence Party, which collaborates closely with the white apartheid authorities.

The opening of administrative, professional, and business positions in the Bantustans simultaneously provided a controlled, though limited, outlet for the aspirations of some petty-bourgeois Africans. In "white" South Africa, the small handful of African professionals quickly become frustrated by the apartheid color bar, leading to disgruntlement and often to active opposition to Pretoria's racist policies. By allowing them to acquire relatively high posts in the Bantustans or to establish small businesses or trading outlets there, the white authorities have tried to open a small safety valve.

Beginning with the Transkei in 1963, most of the Bantustans have been designated as "self-governing." So-called legislative assemblies were set up, in which most of the seats were allocated automatically to government-paid chiefs. Some of the Bantustan constitutions specified that the chief minister had to be a chief or that a certain proportion of the cabinet had to be composed of chiefs. This ensured effective control over the assemblies by the most conservative elements.

Even under the "self-governing" status, Pretoria retained direct control over "defence, foreign affairs, the preservation of peace

10. Tomlinson Commission report, p. 77.

and security, postal, telephone, and related services, immigration of non-citizens, currency and banking, customs and excise."[11] It likewise held the power to veto or supervise any act of the Bantustan legislative assemblies.

After the appropriate preparations had been made and a number of Black lieutenants had been trained, Pretoria began to impose "independence" on the Bantustans in a crude caricature of the decolonization process that had unfolded throughout most of the rest of Africa.

The first to fall victim to this scheme was the Transkei, Pretoria's "showcase" Bantustan. Kaiser Matanzima, the chief minister of the reserve, himself admitted in 1975, "The only practical difference independence will make to the average Transkei citizens is that they will carry Transkei passports instead of Republican passes."[12] Yet the following year Matanzima was more than willing to go along with the whole operation, especially since his position in the administration of an "independent" Transkei brought with it lucrative business opportunities.[13]

On October 26, 1976, the South African flag was lowered in Umtata and replaced by a Transkeian flag—under the watchful eyes of 2,000 South African troops and 650 police. The ceremonies themselves were sparsely attended, and many of the spectators who did show up walked out during the speeches of Matanzima and South African President Nicholaas Diederichs.

Matanzima promised not to allow the Transkei to be used for any "military, subversive or other hostile actions or activities" against Pretoria.[14] The small Transkei army was trained and headed by white officers, though they were eventually to be replaced by Africans. The old South African security laws were repealed, but many of their provisions popped up again in the new Public Safety Act. The Transkei administration added some

11. Muriel Horrell, *The African Homelands of South Africa,* p. 50.

12. Rogers, *Divide & Rule,* p. 48.

13. Kaiser Matanzima and his brother George, the Transkei "foreign minister," owned several companies that were involved in buying up formerly white-owned farms and hotels at a fraction of their real cost. They were bought from the Bantu Trust, a South African government agency that provides assistance to African businesses.

14. *Africa* (London), September 1977.

new repressive twists of its own, such as the General Laws Amendment Act, which made refusal to recognize Transkei "independence" a treasonable crime, punishable by a minimum sentence of five years in prison and a maximum sentence of death.

On December 6, 1977, BophuthaTswana was accorded a similar status, becoming an "independent" state of six unconnected fragments of territory, in which only 700,000 of South Africa's 2.1 million Tswanas actually lived (another 200,000 to 300,000 Africans in BophuthaTswana were of different backgrounds). The widespread opposition to this fraud had been expressed through protest rallies, election boycotts, and even a demonstration in Mafeking in August 1976 that culminated in the burning of the reserve's legislative assembly building.

On September 13, 1979, Venda, the northernmost Bantustan, became the third new tribal "state." Chief Patrick Mphephu, who had previously opposed "independence," got his reward for going along: a $750,000 mansion in the new capital of Thohoyandou.

Pretoria's basic intention of robbing Africans of their South African citizenship was reaffirmed through two amendments enacted in 1978. Under one, anyone who chose to renounce "citizenship" in one of the "independent" Bantustans could not then reclaim South African citizenship as a right. The other stripped urban children born after the "independence" of their parents' Bantustans of any right to reside permanently in the "white" cities. In his first major speech as minister of Bantu administration and development, Cornelius Mulder proclaimed in February 1978 that "if our policy is taken to its full logical conclusion as far as the black people are concerned there will not be one black man with South African citizenship."[15]

In a further refinement of Bantustan policy, Prime Minister Pieter W. Botha began, in 1979, to talk about the eventual establishment of a "constellation of southern African states," a vaguely defined entity that would include at least the South African regime and the ten Bantustans. The apartheid authorities, it appeared, were groping toward some kind of institutional framework for their relations with the Bantustans, one that would maintain the fiction of Bantustan "independence" and at the same time acknowledge the reality of Pretoria's continued domination over them. For the African masses, the results would

15. John Kane-Berman, *Soweto,* p. 239.

be the same: loss of their political rights in South Africa as a whole.

Most Africans recognize the oppressive nature of the Bantustan scheme. A survey of Soweto residents in 1974 found that two-thirds refused to consider the Bantustans as their "real" homes and that there was "nearly universal" opposition to the entire Bantustan policy. That same year, a survey of Bantustan attitudes revealed that only 8 percent of those living in KwaZulu expressed admiration for their chief minister, while the figures for the Transkei were 4 percent and for Lebowa and BophuthaTswana 1 percent. During the "preindependence" elections for BophuthaTswana, only about 500 of the 170,000 Tswanas living in the Johannesburg area bothered to vote. In November 1978, the Transkei Department of Interior revealed that out of an estimated 1.25 million Africans living outside of the Transkei who were considered to be Transkei "citizens" by Pretoria, only *fifty-seven* had actually applied for Transkeian "citizenship" papers.[16]

In addition, every significant Black political organization in the country has put its rejection of the Bantustans on record.

The Bantustans, whatever their official status, are integral—and subordinate—parts of the South African economy. For decades their chief function has been to serve as labor reservoirs for the white-owned mines, industries, and farms in the rest of the country. African migrant workers are confined to the Bantustans in compulsory unemployment until they are needed by the economy. And many of those not required for the immediate purposes of production—such as wives, children, and old people—are exiled to the reserves to live out their lives in squalid poverty.

More than 70 percent of the economically active residents of the Bantustans are involved in the migratory labor system, and at any one time about 35 percent of all employable males (plus a growing number of women) are absent from the reserves and working in "white" South Africa. In 1973, more than 75 percent of the income of all Africans in the Bantustans was earned outside of their borders.

Given the prevalent poverty and high unemployment in the Bantustans, these workers have no choice but to seek jobs

16. Rogers, *Divide & Rule,* p. 31, 51; *Star Weekly* (Johannesburg), August 27, 1977; *Post* (Transvaal), November 16, 1978.

elsewhere. According to one estimate, ". . . the homelands would have to become four to five times more productive merely to reabsorb their *de facto* work forces at constant levels of living."[17]

Besides the absence of any real industries in the reserves, the continual decline of agriculture—caused largely by overcrowding—is a major factor behind increasing unemployment. Most peasants in the Bantustans either have no land or have landholdings that are too small for even subsistence farming.

Because of overcrowding, the land quickly erodes and crop yields decline. In KwaZulu about 86 percent of the land can no longer be cultivated and crop yields per acre are one-fifth of those on white-owned farms.[18]

Per capita income in the Bantustans taken together was a bare R80 a year in the early 1970s. Some 91 percent of all families in the Ciskei and 85 percent in the Transkei live below the semiofficial poverty level. Even with the money sent back by migrant workers, these rural dwellers are incapable of reaching a subsistence level.[19]

As a result, many Africans in the Bantustans become ill and die at an early age. Diseases such as tuberculosis, pellagra, gastro-enteritis, diphtheria, and kwashiorkor (a protein deficiency disease) are rampant. In the Nqutu district of KwaZulu, for instance, it has been estimated that about a quarter of all children five years and younger suffer from malnutrition. In the Transkei, about 40 percent of all African children die before the age of ten as a direct or indirect result of malnutrition.[20]

The poverty in the Bantustans is the product of a conscious government policy to keep them underdeveloped and dependent. Minister of Bantu Administration and Development M. C. Botha stated that "the economy of the homelands is interwoven with that of the republic. And it stands to reason that the development of the homelands cannot be carried out at a pace which would

17. Jeffrey Butler, Robert I. Rotberg, and John Adams, *The Black Homelands of South Africa*, p. 126.

18. Giuseppe Lenta, *Development or Stagnation?*, pp. 1-2, 10.

19. Henry Lever, *South African Society*, p. 220.

20. W. H. Thomas et al., *The Conditions of the Black Worker*, p. 71; Cosmas Desmond, *The Discarded People*, p. 109; Lawrence Schlemmer and Peter Stopforth, *A Study of Malnutrition in the Nqutu District of KwaZulu*, p. 11.

have a detrimental effect on the economy of the country. . . ."[21] In other words, anything more than a very limited level of industrialization in the Bantustans could, by providing alternative sources of employment for Africans, undermine the migratory labor system that much of the South African economy is based on.

Since virtually all of South Africa's natural resources and industries are located in the "white" areas, the Bantustans are dependent on Pretoria for all of their electrical power, transport, telecommunications, and postal services, and for most of their water. The handful of African-owned businesses in the reserves are likewise dependent on the white-owned banks and commercial institutions. All of the Bantustan "governments" rely on Pretoria for an average of 65-85 percent of their revenue.

Aware that many of the Bantustans are becoming increasingly unviable even for Pretoria's own purposes, Prime Minister Botha announced in January 1979 that the Native Land and Trust Act of 1936 would be reviewed. He and other officials subsequently indicated that the Bantustans would be consolidated into less fragmented pieces of territory, possibly including some important towns and some more land. But as the *Financial Mail*, a leading South African business magazine, acknowledged, even if the Bantustans were consolidated—and even if the claims of some Bantustan officials for additional land were granted—"the Bantustans would still be economically dependent on Pretoria," with little chance of "ever developing more than rudimentary economies, and becoming more than the pools of reserve labour for the 'white' areas that they are now. . . ."[22]

As Pretoria intended, the Bantustans also serve as suitable dumping grounds for the victims of one of the largest forced resettlement programs in history. Entire African communities, including some that had been in existence for more than a century, were uprooted. Homes were bulldozed. "Unqualified" African families were kicked out of the "white" cities and off the white-owned farms. They were simply trucked to the Bantustans and dumped at squalid and barren camps.

The resettlement camps are often little more than bare patches

21. C. F. Beyers Naudé and Gatsha Buthelezi, "Foreign Investment in South Africa," *Congressional Record* (Washington), March 17, 1976, p. E1335.

22. *Financial Mail* (Johannesburg), August 19, 1977.

of land, frequently with no water supply or access road. In some the regime rents out tents or small asbestos or tin huts with no floors or ceilings. In others the residents must build their own shelters, from mud or salvaged materials. They are not allowed to keep cattle or plow the land and there is usually no work in the area. Illness and death are a normal feature of camp life.

A 1967 government circular described the rationale behind this forced resettlement program:

> It is accepted Government policy that the Bantus are only temporarily resident in the European areas of the Republic, for as long as they offer their labour there. As soon as they become, for some reason or another, no longer fit for work or superfluous in the labour market, they are expected to return to their country of origin or the territory of their national unit where they fit in ethnically if they were not born and bred in the homeland. . . . It must be stressed here that no stone is to be left unturned to achieve the settlement in the homelands of non-productive Bantu at present residing in the European areas.[23]

The same circular then listed those Africans whom Pretoria considered "non-productive," including the "aged, the unfit, widows, women with dependent children," "Bantu on European farms who become superfluous as a result of age, disability . . . or Bantu squatters from mission stations and black spots which are being cleared up. . . ."[24]

Between 1960 and 1970, an estimated 1.9 million Africans were moved and millions more were slated for resettlement. The majority of those moved in that period were rural "squatters"—Africans who had worked or lived on white-owned farms, particularly in Natal, under informal arrangements that gave them some access to land. With the extensive mechanization of agriculture these families were no longer needed by the white farm owners and could more easily be replaced by migrant laborers. The rest of those resettled were either "endorsed out" of the major cities or were victims of the campaign to rid the country of "black spots," small African-occupied enclaves in predominantly white-owned areas. In 1960, about 36 percent of all Africans were resident in the Bantustans; by 1970 the official figure had risen to 46 percent.

To provide enough land in the Bantustans for the emergence of

23. Desmond, *Discarded People,* pp. 21-22.

24. Ibid., p. 37.

a small African landowning class beholden to the regime, Pretoria has at the same time begun to dispossess many Africans within the reserves of their meager holdings. As a result of various land "rehabilitation" measures, more than 4 million Africans have already been uprooted from their plots of land within the Bantustans.

Altogether, a total of 6 million Africans have been resettled as a result of the Bantustan program. A staggering 7.7 million more are scheduled for similar treatment.[25]

Since there is obviously insufficient land in the reserves to accommodate these uprooted millions, a great many of them have been forced to settle in semiurban ghettos. Their function, similar to that of the African townships around the major cities, is to supply migrant laborers for the mines, farms, and factories in "white" South Africa.

Between 1960 and 1975, the number of Africans living in urban locations within the Bantustans increased by thirty times, to nearly 1 million.[26] Unfortunately for the regime, this growing urbanization has inevitably led to a rise in political militancy and activism within the Bantustans themselves.

The regime has not applied its policy of territorial apartheid to the Coloured and Indian populations in the same manner or to the same degree that it has to the socially more powerful African majority. But neither Coloureds nor Indians have escaped Pretoria's divide-and-rule strategy of "separate development."

Hundreds of thousands of Coloureds and Indians have been evicted from the central cities, especially Cape Town and Durban, to segregated townships on the outskirts. Like Africans, they face numerous racist restrictions.

Just as Pretoria has sought to create divisions among Africans, it is trying to fuel frictions and resentments between Coloureds and Indians on one hand and Africans on the other. Besides physically segregating them, it applies its apartheid policies toward Coloureds and Indians in a slightly different manner. They do not have to carry passes, are allowed to fill some semiskilled and skilled jobs that are barred to Africans, and are able to engage in small-scale commercial activities to a greater

25. Rogers, *Divide & Rule*, p. 28.

26. P. Smit and J. J. Booysen, *Urbanisation in the Homelands*, pp. 19, 41, 42.

extent. The apartheid authorities hope to win some support from the better-off layers of these two communities, while at the same time stirring up African resentments against the "privileged" Coloureds and Indians.

In a move reminiscent of Hertzog's establishment of the Natives' Representative Council in the 1930s, the apartheid regime set up similar powerless advisory bodies for both Coloureds and Indians in 1964: the Coloured People's Representative Council (CRC) and the South African Indian Council (SAIC). Their main function was to win the open collaboration of the so-called leaders of the Coloured and Indian communities and to divert political energies into a carefully controlled "parliamentary" show. Reflecting popular indifference to these bodies, the elections to them have generally met with very low voter turnouts.

Like the African political activists who have condemned Pretoria's Bantustan program, many young Coloureds and Indians reject participation in the CRC and SAIC. They call instead for unity with Africans in a common struggle for Black political rights. Following the big urban rebellions of 1976, in which Coloureds participated in large numbers in the Western Cape, the authorities realized that the CRC and SAIC had failed to achieve their purpose. Something more was needed.

In September 1977, the regime announced a new constitutional plan that projected the eventual establishment of three separate "parliaments," one each for whites, Coloureds, and Indians, the latter two simply being inflated versions of the CRC and SAIC. Though they would have limited legislative authority, these proposed Coloured and Indian bodies would still have to function within the framework of apartheid policy. Real power would rest in a strong, centralized executive composed of a white-dominated "council of cabinets" and a white state president.

Like the CRC and SAIC themselves, this proposed governmental plan met with little enthusiasm. A few Coloured and Indian collaborators expressed an interest, but the most important Black political currents rejected the plan as simply another attempt to perpetuate the regime's decades-old policy of divide and rule.

7

Workers Under Apartheid

The regulation and control of South Africa's Black working class stands at the core of the apartheid system. The police and prisons, the pass laws, the labor bureaus, influx control, the Bantustans, the migratory labor system, segregated townships, even education—all are aimed, in one way or another, at ensuring that Blacks fulfill their assigned role as underpaid and super-exploited laborers.

The extent of the ruling class's dependency on Black labor is evident from its own figures. As of 1977, there were more than 8 million Black workers in South Africa—7 million Africans, 1 million Coloureds, and 221,000 Asians. Africans alone were about 70 percent of the entire work force; all together, Black workers comprised 81 percent. Black workers and their families constitute the overwhelming majority of the Black population.

It was precisely to keep a firm rein on this powerful Black working class and to prevent it from translating its social weight into political power that the white rulers erected the most elaborate and extensive system of labor control in the world. As nowhere else, Black workers in South Africa are reduced solely to their role in the production process, nameless "interchangeable units" who are allowed no political rights in "white" South Africa.

In the words of G. F. van L. Froneman, a Nationalist member of parliament, Africans "only come here to supply labour. They are only supplying a commodity, the commodity of labour. . . . it is labour we are importing and not labourers as individuals."[1]

To banish the specter of "labourers as individuals" settling

1. Ralph Horwitz, *Political Economy of South Africa*, p. 412.

permanently in the towns, demanding their rights, and acquiring a consciousness of their own strength as a class, the apartheid regime acted to greatly entrench and expand the migratory labor system. It sentenced millions of African workers to lives of constant insecurity, of enforced oscillation between the Bantustans and the "white" cities and farms, reducing them to a dehumanized mass of "commodities" available for distribution among the various white employers as needed.

Of the many Africans expelled to the Bantustans, only those who were actually employed were allowed to return to the major cities, to take up their former jobs (or different jobs where they were more needed) as rightless migrants. They were forced to leave their families behind in the resettlement camps in the reserves.

To provide a mechanism for the systematic recruitment and placement of migrant workers, Pretoria established labor bureaus in the Bantustans. All Africans living in the area of a tribal labor bureau have to register for work within one month of reaching the age of fifteen, becoming unemployed, or finishing full-time studies. They are then assigned to a specific category of occupation and must accept whatever job is given to them. A complete employment record of all workers registered with the bureaus is stored in a computer in Pretoria in order to "correlate demand for labour insofar as it affects urban and rural areas . . . with the supply by orderly canalisation."[2] In 1968, the labor bureau arrangement was extended to African townships in the urban areas as well.

When hired, the migrant worker must sign a labor contract that is good for no longer than one year (nine months for workers under eighteen years of age). At the end of the contract period, the worker must return to his or her Bantustan for at least two weeks to await further employment. By forcing migrant workers to return to the Bantustans each year, they are prevented from ever qualifying for permanent legal residency rights in the cities, even if they work for the same boss year after year. In this way, most migrants spend a good part of their adult lives away from their homes and families, with all the misery and corrosive effects on African social life that follow.

All together, there are some 2 million African migrant workers throughout the country, in many urban areas comprising about half of the African work force. The number of commuter work-

2. Rosalynde Ainslie, *Masters and Serfs*, p. 41.

ers—who live in Bantustan townships close to the major industrial centers and commute to work on a daily basis—has also been growing. In 1970 there were 300,000 of them; by 1976 there were 637,000.

Historically, it was the gold mines that first introduced the migratory labor system to South Africa on a large scale. The vast bulk of the nearly 400,000 Black gold miners are still migrants, slightly less than half recruited from beyond South Africa's borders, many of them from Lesotho, Mozambique, Botswana, and other nearby countries.

The migratory labor system also made headway on the white-owned farms. Out of a total of nearly a million African farm laborers, some 570,000 were registered as migrants in 1977. In addition to Africans, about 100,000 Coloureds were employed on white-owned farms, mostly in the Western Cape. (Indian farm workers, in contrast, had largely disappeared by 1970, a majority of them gaining employment in manufacturing and other sectors.)

The migratory labor system in general gives the regime and the employers a much firmer grip over African workers. Suspected "agitators" can be kept from returning to the cities by simply denying them readmission after their contracts have expired. Until 1979, migrant workers were prohibited from organizing unions. They are not allowed to strike. If they strike anyway, they can be quickly deported back to the Bantustans. That happened, for instance, to more than a thousand African dock workers in Durban, who walked off their jobs in 1969 to press for higher wages.

By regulating the flow of African labor from the Bantustans themselves, Pretoria can also keep out "redundant" workers, thus lessening the social impact of Black unemployment in the "white" areas during periods of recession. And since migrant laborers are compelled to leave their families in the Bantustans, the regime is spared the cost of providing additional social services, such as schools, hospitals, and family housing in the urban centers.

The hostels and compounds that migrant workers must live in are designed to hamper political organization, isolate the migrants from other urban Africans, and keep them under strict control. In fact, many of the hostels bear a striking resemblence to prisons. This description of one in the Transvaal, built to house 2,834 women, is probably typical:

At intervals along the corridors were sets of latticed steel doors, electronically operated from a master switchboard in the matron's ground floor control room. It was specifically explained by Mr Kotze [a government official] that these doors were nothing to do with fire control, but were there to enable the matron to seal off the building into 150-person sectors "in the event of unrest."

In addition to the control-board the matron's quarters contained a charge room and a barred cell. There were loudspeakers on all floors both for announcements and "to control disturbances." All floors and corridors were controlled by "secondary matrons" equipped with portable two-way radios.[3]

The social and cultural constraints of the migratory labor system, while less obvious than its more directly repressive aspects, also bear heavily on migrant workers. Though they may spend most of their economically active lives in the cities, the insecurity they face in urban life and the fact that their families are forced to stay behind in the Bantustans prevents them from becoming fully urbanized. The more socially conservative features of rural African society thus continue to retain an influence among many migrants, hampering to some extent the development of their consciousness as a class, although not as much as the employers would like. In fact, those migrants who do acquire a degree of class consciousness often carry new political and social ideas back to the Bantustans with them.

Nevertheless, the fact that migrant workers are largely at the mercy of their employers, the labor recruiting officers, and government officials fosters extreme insecurity among them, obstructing efforts at political or trade union organization. This insecurity, coupled with widespread unemployment in the Bantustans, allows the white employers to pay migrant workers even lower wages than they do to other Black workers. As one migrant commented, the system of influx control "takes away from us the little freedom we had in the choice of job. Nowadays you are liable to be chased out of town if you don't stick to your job, so you have just got to stick to it, even if it is a bad one and underpaid."[4] The low migrant wages, in turn, tend to further depress the wages of all Black workers.

It is in the gold mines that the gap between white and Black wages has traditionally been among the greatest of any sector of

3. *Business as Usual*, p. 14.

4. Philip Mayer and Iona Mayer, *Townsmen or Tribesmen*, p. 59.

the economy, at times reaching a ratio of 20 to 1 (see graph). Since the early 1970s, however, African mine wages have increased substantially, appreciably narrowing the proportional gap between white and African wages. But since white workers also got hefty raises, the *absolute* gap between white and African wages widened even further. In 1978, African miners received an average wage of R119 a month, while white miners earned R840 a month.[5]

In addition, the working conditions for Black gold miners are extremely dangerous. The space on the mining stope, an excavated area providing access to the gold seam, is often so cramped that the worker cannot even sit up. The noise from drilling is ear-shattering. The possibility of rockfalls is constant. In the three decades from 1936 to 1966, no less than nineteen thousand miners, more than nine-tenths of them Black, were killed in the gold mines—an average of three per shift.

Black farm wages (both for Africans and Coloureds) are also extremely low. African farm laborers are often compelled to work fourteen hours a day, seven days a week. They face severe restrictions on movement and have no right to strike. "Disobedience," such as talking back to the *baas* (master) or resisting physical assaults and abuse, is commonly punished. Beatings with a *sjambok,* a whip made of ox hide, are still fairly routine. Forced labor by Black prisoners is likewise a common feature in many farming areas, with the Department of Prisons functioning as a labor recruiter.

Though the migratory labor system has made major inroads into a number of sectors of the South African economy, the rulers are unable to attain their cherished goal of transforming all African workers into "interchangeable units." The very needs of South Africa's modern industrialized economy do not allow it.

The increased technological level of many industries, especially in manufacturing, has produced a demand for skilled and semiskilled workers far beyond the capacities of the white labor force. Coloured and Indian workers could fill some of those positions, but they are also too few in number.

The industrialists are thus forced to employ more and more Africans as clerks, machine operators, lower-level supervisors, blasters in the mines, drivers, etc. From 1962 to 1972, the number of Blacks holding skilled jobs in manufacturing increased by 69 percent for Indians, 51 percent for Coloureds, and 175 percent for

5. *Standard Bank Review* (Johannesburg), February 1979.

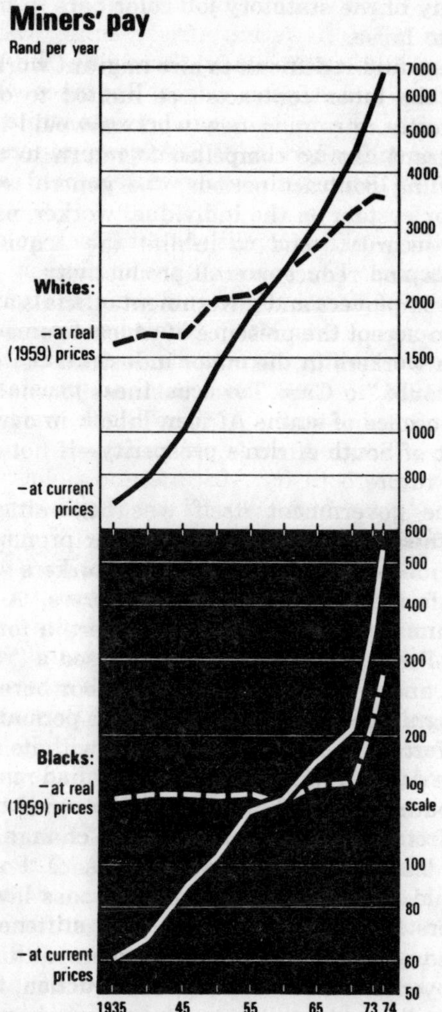

Source: *Economist* (London), March 22, 1975.

Africans.[6] Many of the statutory job color bars in industry have been allowed to lapse.

The employers find it difficult to hire migrant workers for these jobs. Because the labor contracts are limited to one year, the costs of constantly retraining new workers would be very high. Even if a migrant can be compelled to return to the same job during succeeding contract periods, the general effects of the migratory labor system on the individual worker, particularly in terms of job security, tend to inhibit the acquisition of the necessary skills and reduce overall productivity.

So the white employers and government officials are compelled, like it or not, to accept the presence of at least some permanently settled African workers in the major industrial centers. "What is clear beyond doubt," a Cape Town business journal commented, "is that the presence of stable African labour in our urban areas is at the heart of South Africa's prosperity—if not survival—for the forseeable future."[7]

By 1979, the government itself was beginning to publicly acknowledge this reality, despite the earlier pronouncements of the apartheid ideologues that all African workers would eventually be transformed into migratory laborers. A government appointed commission headed by Piet Riekert, a former economics advisor to Prime Minister Botha, proposed a "relaxation" of the pass laws and a refurbishing of the labor bureau system to give legal recognition to the existence of this permanently settled African work force. The government agreed with its recommendation that those African workers who already had residency rights in "white" South Africa be allowed to live with their families and to move from one city to another and change jobs without automatically losing their security of residence. Political rights, of course, would still be denied them, and pass law restrictions against workers from the Bantustans were stiffened even more.

There were some 1.5 million African workers in this category as of 1976, employed in manufacturing, construction, finance, commerce, public utilities, the railways, and other urban occupations. (Another half million Coloured and Indian workers were also employed in these sectors.) Because of their greater level of skills and the fact that they are more or less permanently resident in the cities with their families, the employers have to pay them

6. W. H. Thomas et al., *The Conditions of the Black Worker*, pp. 59-60.

7. *Businessman's Law* (Cape Town), September 15, 1976.

more than Black workers in either mining or agriculture. The approximately seven hundred thousand African workers in manufacturing earned an average of R149 a month in 1978 (which was still far behind the average white manufacturing wage of R661 a month).[8]

Another sign of the relative stability of this sector of the Black work force is the increasing employment of Black women as factory workers. Between 1960 and 1970, the proportion of African women out of the total labor force in manufacturing rose from 2 percent to 7 percent (about seventy-five thousand). A similar number of Coloured and Indian women were employed in manufacturing.[9]

Many African women who are employed in the cities still work as domestic servants, however. Those domestic workers who live in the homes of their employers cannot legally have their families with them; if the husband or child of a domestic worker is caught staying overnight with her (even with the approval of the white employers), they face fine or imprisonment.

Because of their triple oppression—as Blacks, as women, and as workers—Black female employees receive the lowest of all urban wages. In Pretoria, African domestic servants earned an average cash wage of R36 a month in 1978, for working twelve hours a day during the week and somewhat less on weekends.[10]

The apartheid authorities realize that the dependence of the economy upon an urbanized Black working class is the achilles' heel of white supremacy. Because of their greater job security and more social living conditions, these workers are in a better position to organize and struggle for their economic and political rights. So from the ruling class's point of view, the efficient and strict control of industrial workers is particularly vital to the continued survival of the apartheid order.

In its drive to control workers, the regime has followed a dual strategy. On the one hand, it has stepped up its efforts to further divide Black and white workers and forestall any moves toward class solidarity. On the other, it has sought to blunt the organization of effective unions by Black workers.

Despite its earlier successes in turning white worker against

8. Loraine Gordon et al., *Survey of Race Relations in South Africa, 1978*, p. 189.

9. *South Africa 1978*, p. 507.

10. *Rand Daily Mail* (Johannesburg), November 28, 1978.

Black, the ruling class continued to fear the emergence of class alliances among workers. The importance of driving new wedges between them was openly aired and discussed by government officials and supporters. In 1954, G. D. Scholtz, a prominent Afrikaner nationalist, raised an alarm over the fact that Afrikaner workers were disregarding "the dividing line that their nation has drawn between white and nonwhite. . . . The first steps have already been taken toward rapprochement and ultimately toward amalgamation between the white proletariat—which to a great degree exists separately from other Afrikaners—and the nonwhite proletariat."[11]

This concern of the capitalists has a very real material basis: the existence of class divisions *within* the white population. Far from all whites are exploiters. In fact, the white working class is quite large, numbering more than 900,000 in 1970, out of a total of 1.5 million economically active whites. Of the white workers, nearly 360,000 were employed in industry.[12] Because of the extremely low wages of Blacks, white workers appear to be highly privileged. But in reality the living standards of many of them are comparable to those of workers in other industrialized countries like the United States or Britain. The standard of living of a white worker in the Johannesburg area, for example, is roughly equal to that of an industrial worker in the Washington, D.C., region.[13]

Like Blacks, white workers in South Africa are also exploited by the bosses, though to a lesser degree. Their objective class interests do not lie with the white capitalists and the apartheid system, but with the struggles of their Black coworkers.

Because of the *political* backwardness of the vast bulk of the white workers, very few recognize the necessity of allying with Black workers. But there have been some expressions of class solidarity. Despite constant harassment and repression, a handful of white unionists have attempted to aid Black unions. During the 1950s, the South African Congress of Trade Unions (SACTU) was an influential force; though composed largely of Black workers, it included some militant white unionists. As recently as

11. G. D. Scholtz, *Het die Afrikaanse volk 'n toekoms?*, p. 116.

12. Author's estimates, based on employment figures by occupation in *South Africa 1978*, pp. 470-73.

13. F. E. Rädel, *Progress or Exploitation?*, p. 36.

March 1980, a mass meeting in Johannesburg of two thousand white teachers (both Afrikaans and English speaking) condemned the regime's discriminatory wage policies against Black and women teachers.[14]

To prevent such developments from going too far, the apartheid regime has actively intervened. In addition to earlier measures designed to divide Black and white workers, a law adopted in 1956 barred the registration of any new "mixed" unions (with memberships that included whites, Coloureds, and Indians), prohibited nonsegregated union branches and meetings, and barred Coloureds or Indians from holding office in "mixed" unions.

Many of the white trade unionists who were still willing to resist the regime's antilabor policies or who were involved in helping to organize African workers came under attack. By 1955, at least fifty-six key trade union officials had been removed from their posts under the provisions of the Suppression of Communism Act.

Like Coloured and Indian workers, white workers were also fettered by restrictions on their unions, which were kept subservient and tied to the regime's proemployer system of compulsory arbitration, industrial courts, and wage boards. Although whites could legally strike, they could do so only under certain circumstances.

Even more central to Pretoria's antilabor policies was the denial of real trade union rights to Blacks.

Originally, the regime followed a strict policy of not recognizing African unions at all (although Coloured and Indian unions were given legal status). That was the cornerstone of the Bantu Labour (Settlement of Disputes) Act of 1953, which also prohibited all African strikes.

The regime's antilabor policies and its fierce political repression against Black workers were successful by the mid-1960s in destroying the two existing Black-dominated trade union federations, the South African Congress of Trade Unions and the Federation of Free African Trade Unions of South Africa.

Even then, the apartheid regime realized that it was insufficient to just deny African unions legal recognition or simply try to suppress them. The government adopted measures aimed at heading off the formation of African unions and providing a mechanism for controlling African workers on the factory floor.

14. *Star Weekly* (Johannesburg), March 22, 1980.

It set up a system of committees, with some worker participation, that could raise complaints with management. These bodies—known as works and liaison committees—had no real power to represent the interests of workers, and were seen by the employers and government as instruments for ensuring labor discipline and efficiency.

By the late 1970s, it was clear that the committee system had failed to keep African workers under control, preventing them neither from striking nor from forming their own independent unions. Despite the legal restrictions on African strikes, tens of thousands walked off their jobs, beginning with a big strike wave in Natal in 1973. In face of police persecution and employer intimidation, the membership in unregistered Black unions rose from some 40,000 in 1974 to a claimed membership of more than 160,000 workers in thirty-one unions in 1979.[15] (Another 200,000 Coloured and Indian workers belonged to registered unions.) The African-dominated unions operated in some of the most strategic sectors of the economy, including transport, chemicals, automobile assembly, construction, metals, textiles, glass, banking, and commerce. Some had even been successful in winning de facto recognition from the employers and in forcing concessions from them.

Most of the Black unions had class-collaborationist leaderships. Many were indirectly associated with white unions, which, given the current bureaucratic leaderships of those unions, tended to hold back the Black unions. Nevertheless, the ruling class and its government feared that the unions could eventually come under radical leadership and be tranformed into focal points of militant and massive working-class opposition. The 1976 upheavals, in which hundreds of thousands of Black workers struck around political demands, convinced the authorities that something more had to be done to head off such a development within the Black union movement.

In June 1977, just a year after the first Soweto uprising, the government appointed a commission headed by Nicholas Weihahn, an adviser to the Department of Labour, to review existing labor legislation and recommend appropriate alterations. The

15. Official government estimates or figures published in the South African press are generally about half of this number. The author's estimate of 160,000 is based on the claimed membership figures of the Black unions themselves.

commission's report, published in 1979, laid the basis for the most significant changes in labor policy since the National Party came to power.

The Wiehahn Commission report pointed to the "increasing prominence and *de facto* recognition of Black trade unions," which had led to "dissonance" with the "ideal of orderly unionism." The growth of these unregistered Black unions, the "inadequate control" over them, the tendency of some to cut across industrial divisions, their unchecked receipt of funds from other unions and organizations, and the "strong moral support" they received from abroad, all "could well bring extreme stress to bear on the existing statutory system—a development which could within a very short space of time pose a grave danger to industrial peace."[16]

"Black trade unions," the commission noted, "are subject neither to the protective and stabilising elements of the system nor to its essential discipline and control; they in fact enjoy much greater freedom than registered unions, to the extent that they are free if they so wished to participate in politics and to utilise their funds for whatever purposes they see fit."[17]

The Wiehahn Commission was particularly worried about the role that the unions could play in the Black struggle as a whole. Pointing to the "dramatic change" among Black workers since the massive strike wave of 1973, the report warned, "The Black worker and his organisation came to be perceived as a possible means of achieving change in South Africa—not only in the economic conditions of the Black worker himself, but indirectly also in other spheres. . . ."[18]

The commission's proposed solution was not to ban African trade unions—since that would only drive them underground and "add fuel to the flames of radicalism"—but to extend to them the same laws that already applied to white, Indian, and Coloured unions. The reason was that "Black trade unions can no longer be permitted to operate outside the law. . . ."[19]

The government agreed with this recommendation. Shortly

16. Republic of South Africa, *Report of the Commission of Inquiry into Labour Legislation* (hereafter cited as Wiehahn Commission report), pp. 16-19.

17. Ibid., p. 18.

18. Ibid., p. 17.

19. Ibid., pp. 20, 25.

after the report's publication, it rushed through the Industrial Conciliation Amendment Act, extending legal trade union recognition to African workers for the first time in South Africa's history. Initially it excluded migrant workers and commuters, but in September 1979 the authorities modified the act to apply to most of them as well, including migrant workers and commuters from the Bantustans (even the "independent" ones), but not those from other countries.

Labour Minister Fanie Botha called the policy "a new dispensation in the labor history of South Africa."[20] South African government supporters, corporate executives, white opposition parliamentarians, and even some conservative Black union leaders hailed it as a significant "liberalization" of the apartheid system. Africans, they said, now had the same "rights" as other workers to form unions and negotiate with employers; a major segregationist barrier had fallen.

The act *was* significant. It did reflect a notable shift in government policy. But there was very little that was progressive about it. The aim was not to give African workers any new rights, but to *increase* government and employer control over them and to cripple militant Black trade unionism, in particular the existing independent Black unions.

Under the new policy, all unions were required, by law, to apply for official recognition with a newly established "industrial registrar." The registrar could accept or reject recognition of a particular union, according to fairly elastic and arbitrary guidelines. In the words of the Wiehahn report, one key criterion was that a labor organization be "a *bona fide* union" in both "composition and objectives." A bona fide union, as defined by the commission, was one that did not engage in political activities, did not undermine industrial "peace and harmony," and did not threaten the "national interest."[21]

Under such stringent restrictions, any Black union that favored militant action against the employers or participated in struggles for Black political rights could be denied recognition. Nonregistered unions are prohibited from negotiating with employers and face numerous constraints on organizing and recruiting members. Repression against them will be stepped up. Many

20. *New York Times*, May 3, 1979.

21. Wiehahn Commission report, p. 34.

could thus be forced to shut down or to revert to clandestine functioning.

To safeguard against militant activists who may try to use the recognized unions for class-struggle purposes, the government also tightened its control over their day-to-day functioning. The finances of the unions are to be audited annually, their constitutions and memberships kept under "strict control," and the prohibition on political activities or affiliation extended. The unions would formally be allowed to elect their own officers, but under the "surveillance" of a newly established National Manpower Commission. The existing restrictions on the right to strike were maintained. Unions must instead take their disputes before a government- and employer-dominated "industrial court." If a recognized union stepped beyond the bounds of "orderly unionism" set by the regime, it could have its registration withdrawn at any time.

The government's measures drew a mixed response from the Black labor movement. Some of the more class-collaborationist union leaders, such as Lucy Mvubelo of the National Union of Clothing Workers, greeted them wholeheartedly. Others reluctantly agreed to register, either because they felt they had no choice or because they thought it would be possible to use recognition—despite the regime's intentions—to build up large unions that could then press for meaningful concessions. A few of the more militant unions rejected registration entirely.

The employers quickly sought to take advantage of the new policy. In those plants where independent and militant Black unions existed, management actually took the lead in helping to bolster or set up competing "parallel" unions, which are tied to the white unions, in particular to the Trade Union Council of South Africa (TUCSA). Andre Malherbe, the president of TUCSA, explained, "Employers tend to prefer 'parallel' unions because these have good records of co-operation. Many of the so-called independent unions have been involved in confrontations."[22]

Thus rather than making any substantial concessions, the regime's "new dispensation" was actually designed to tighten even further the constrictive web of laws and regulations binding South Africa's powerful Black working class. Like its earlier measures, however, these new shackles could also prove flimsier than anticipated.

22. *Star Weekly* (Johannesburg), November 24, 1979.

8

Education for Servitude

The most potent weapon in the hands of the oppressor is the mind of the oppressed.

—Steve Biko

In a society like that of South Africa, where the overwhelming majority of the population is kept in a constant state of degradation, where basic human values and aspirations are smothered under the weight of a vast apparatus of repression and bureaucratic control, the fundamental rights of everyone to learn and to study the world around them are seen as a deadly threat to the established order.

The white authorities are well aware of their numerical weakness. They realize that it would be impossible for them to keep the Black population in check for long through direct repression alone. That is why they have adopted the Bantustan program and are moving toward other forms of indirect rule in the urban townships. It is also why the control of education, the censorship of ideas, and the stifling of free expression take on a crucial importance in their efforts to maintain white supremacy. From their point of view it is imperative that schools and universities be kept under tight rein and that education itself serve as an instrument of racist domination.

The National Party began formulating its approach toward education several years before coming to power in 1948. Like other aspects of apartheid, the roots of the new education policy lay in the existing system, the goals of which were summarized in a report in 1935-36 by the Departmental Committee on Native Education: "The Education of the White child prepares him for a life in a dominant society and the Education of the Black child for a subordinate society. . . ."[1] Agreeing with this, J. N. le Roux, a Nationalist member of parliament, stated in 1945 that "we should so conduct our schools that the native who attends those schools will know that to a great extent he must be the labourer in this country."[2] But the Nationalists considered the existing school system ineffective in achieving its stated aims. They thought it put too much emphasis on academic pursuits and not enough on the training of Blacks for the workplace. They felt that too many "unhealthy" ideas were still being taught, and that firmer ideological control over the content of education was necessary.

In February 1948, just a few months before the National Party came to power, its supporters published a pamphlet outlining the party's educational principles, which were known as "Christian National" education. Much of it dealt with the education of white children, but it also touched on that of Blacks, who were to be taught from their earliest days that subservience was their lot in life, that the system of apartheid was unquestionable. "Native education," the pamphlet stated, "should be based on the principles of trusteeship, non-equality and segregation; its aim should be to inculcate the white man's view of life, especially that of the Boer nation, which is the senior trustee." Coloured children, the pamphlet added, had to be educated according to similar tenets. "Only when he is christianised can the coloured be truly happy; and he will be proof against foreign ideologies which give him an illusion of happiness but leave him in the long run unsatisfied and unhappy."[3]

In the debate over the National Party's Bantu Education Bill in 1953, Verwoerd stressed the importance of administering African education "in such a way that it should be in accordance with the policy of the state."[4] Accordingly, the Bantu Education Act, passed the same year, transferred control of all African schools from the provincial governments to the central administration of

1. I. B. Tabata, *Education for Barbarism in South Africa,* p. 8.

2. United Nations Educational, Scientific and Cultural Organization (UNESCO), *Apartheid,* p. 27.

3. *Blueprint for Blackout,* p. 43.

4. UNESCO, *Apartheid,* p. 31.

the Native Affairs Department. Five years later a Bantu Education Department was established.

Linking African education to its Bantustan policy, the regime barred African students in rural areas from attending schools in the cities. And in line with Verwoerd's dictum that Bantu Education "should stand with both feet in the reserves and have its roots in the spirit and being of Bantu Society,"[5] the minister of Bantu Education was empowered to establish community schools tied to the various Bantustans. More and more African pupils were pushed toward the reserves. Consequently, by 1977, more than 2.6 million African pupils were enrolled in the Bantustans, compared to 1.4 million in the "white" areas.

In the urban centers, the authorities launched a drive to bring all independently run African schools under government control, or else to shut them down. Many of these schools were run by churches, and the regime moved to eliminate them by withholding, or drastically reducing, state financial assistance. Even those that survived were subject to rigid government control over teaching programs. It became a crime punishable by fine or imprisonment for an unauthorized school to admit students.

Control over Coloured and Indian education was strengthened as well. In 1963, Coloured schools were placed under the administration of the Coloured Affairs Department and two years later Indian schools fell under the control of the Indian Affairs Department.

In modern industry, even unskilled and semiskilled workers require some rudimentary schooling to be able to perform their jobs. So to meet the needs of South Africa's expanding economy, the number of Blacks passing through the first few levels of school was greatly increased. From 1954 to 1977 the enrollment in African schools rose from 860,000 to 4.1 million students. Because of the exceedingly high drop-out rate, however, two-thirds of all African students were in the lower primary school grades and only 13 percent in secondary schools. A miniscule .34 percent reached Form V, the last grade of secondary school. The sharp decline in the number of students in successive grades is the result of a conscious policy by the white authorities to limit African education to the barest minimum needed for the efficient running of industry.

The massive increase in the number of African pupils admitted

5. Heribert Adam, *South Africa,* p. 201.

to the lower grades was coupled with a substantial decline in the quality of education and in school conditions. While more than R654 was budgeted for every white student in 1977, only an average of R49 was allocated for African students in "white" South Africa. White education is free through secondary school, yet African parents must pay special taxes and African students are compelled to make "voluntary" contributions. Until the late 1970s, the burden of paying for textbooks, writing materials, and supplementary teachers' salaries fell on African parents as well. There was a chronic shortage of classrooms, desks, chairs, blackboards, and other facilities. The white pupil-to-teacher ratio is about 20 : 1, but it is closer to 50 : 1 in African schools. Because of the extreme overcrowding, double half-day sessions were introduced in many lower primary schools. The school feeding program that had been introduced in the mid-1940s for African children was dropped by the National Party regime.

The high drop-out rate, the poor quality of education, and the inability of undernourished children to concentrate on their studies has led to a high proportion of functional illiteracy, even among Africans who have attended school. One South African educationalist estimated that 48 percent of all Africans over the age of fifteen were functionally illiterate.[6]

While the white authorities were reluctant to teach Africans how to read and write properly, they were more than ready to instruct them in anything relating directly to their future jobs. Most teaching in the primary grades is done in one or another of the African languages, but both English and Afrikaans are taught as well. According to the 1951 Eiselen Commission report, this was to ensure "that the Bantu child will be able to find his way in European communities; to follow oral or written instructions; and to carry on a simple conversation with Europeans about his work and other subjects of common interest."[7]

Much teaching time is given to manual training, and students learn from a very early age to clean up and use tools. For some of those African students who have been pushed out of the regular school system, but are still too young to find employment, the regime has established "voluntary" labor training camps. Some training centers run by the department are actually located in

6. Freda Troup, *Forbidden Pastures,* p. 33.

7. Monica Wilson and Leonard Thompson, *Oxford History of South Africa,* 2:225.

industrial complexes, to teach machine maintenance, forklift operation, woodworking, and other jobs.

In 1967 Coloured youths became subject to induction into similar labor camps, known as Training Centres for Coloured Cadets. The camps, which are run on semimilitary lines, with court-martial and detention for infractions of the rules, are for the training of Coloureds for any kind of job that employers need done. All Coloured males between the ages of eighteen and twenty-four are required under pain of fine or imprisonment to register for training.

Black schools in South Africa are more than mere labor training institutions. They are also indoctrination centers designed to stunt the minds and critical capabilities of Black children, who are expected to docilely submit to all the barbarities of apartheid when they become adults.

The courses, syllabi, and textbooks used in South African schools are thoroughly retrograde. Besides the teaching of manual labor, there is a heavy emphasis on religious instruction, with conservative Christian dogma tainting virtually all subjects. In the Transvaal, the theory of evolution is not included in the biology syllabus. History courses perpetuate the myth that the early white settlers occupied an unpopulated land, some referring to Afrikaners as a "chosen people" who had been planted by God on the southern tip of Africa. White supremacy is at times presented as a product of divine predestination.

The most important form of brainwashing from Pretoria's viewpoint involves instilling in African children the belief that they belong to separate Zulu, Xhosa, Sotho, or other African "nations." To pass their social studies courses, African students must say that they accept the legitimacy of the Bantustan system.

To counteract the tendency toward social and political unity among Africans, the regime imposed "mother tongue" instruction, that is, the compulsory use of various African languages as mediums of instruction throughout the primary grades, which account for nearly 90 percent of all enrollment. By doing so, Pretoria sought to push African children toward cultural identification with one or another of the Bantustans, turn them against each other, isolate them from Indians and Coloureds (who tend to speak either English or Afrikaans), and cut them off from much of the outside world.

Another effect of "mother tongue" instruction is to further inhibit African education, since there is a limited range of scientific, political, historical, or other literature published in the African languages. After six years of school, both English and Afrikaans are introduced as additional mediums of instruction, greatly burdening students who had been taught through most of primary school in an African language.

Pretoria's language policy in the schools has generated some of the most vociferous opposition among students and parents. In 1972, Dr. Melville Edelstein, a South African sociologist, found that 88.5 percent of African pupils prefer English as the main language of instruction, rather than Afrikaans or any of the African languages.[8] This is largely because of the hatred Africans have not only for the Bantustans, but also for the predominantly Afrikaans-speaking police, judges, and government officials. In addition, English, unlike Afrikaans or the African languages, is an international language and thus provides a cultural bridge to other countries in Africa and in the rest of the world. In fact, it was Pretoria's imposition of the compulsory use of Afrikaans as the language of instruction in half the courses in Soweto secondary schools that prompted Black students there to stage a protest on June 16, 1976, setting off the massive upsurge in the Black townships.

Black students were not the only victims of apartheid education. Pretoria could never have begun to put its education policies into practice without first breaking the resistance of Black teachers, who had a long tradition of opposition to white supremacy.

One of the National Party regime's first acts was to take over the teacher training schools to begin the process of turning out a new corps of Black teachers willing and able to carry out the Bantu Education policies. As Verwoerd bluntly declared, "People who believe in equality are not desirable teachers for Natives."[9]

To terrorize the African teaching staffs, members of the Criminal Investigation Division raided schools and interrogated teachers in front of their classes, dismissing many who were considered unsuitable for Bantu Education. The executive members of the Cape African Teachers Association were driven out of the profession for their opposition to the new education policies. A code of conduct was introduced for teachers, warning

8. Melville Leonard Edelstein, *What Do Young Africans Think?*, p. 114.

9. J. F. Bosch, "Control of the Teacher," *Educational Journal* (Cape Town) 27, no. 2 (August 1955): 29.

them, under pain of dismissal, not to "contribute to the Press by interview, or in any other manner, or publish letters or articles criticizing or commenting on the Department of Native Affairs, or any other State Department, or school committee, school board, or any Bantu Authority, or any official connected with one or more of the above-mentioned bodies."[10]

Many of the teachers who were not dismissed outright for political reasons were gradually replaced anyway, as new layers of government-trained instructors emerged from the teachers' schools. The educational level of these new teachers was generally quite low. In 1963, no more than 31 percent of those employed in secondary and training schools were themselves graduates. They receive salaries well below the official poverty level.

Having totally transformed primary and secondary education, the apartheid authorities tightened their grip over the universities with the passage in 1959 of the Extension of University Education Act. Before the act, some Black students had been admitted to the two "open" universities, the University of the Witwatersrand and the University of Cape Town, but Black admissions were largely eliminated after its passage. Instead, five segregated Black universities were established: the University of the Western Cape for Coloureds; the University of Durban-Westville for Indians; the University of the North, at Turfloop, for Sothos, Tswanas, Ndebeles, Vendas, Shagaans, and Tsongas; the Univeristy of Zululand, at Ngoye, for Zulus and Swazis; and the University of Fort Hare for Xhosas. In addition, the medical facility at the University of Natal admits Blacks, and many Blacks study through correspondence courses with the University of South Africa. In 1978 there were only about 30,000 Black university students, compared to 118,000 whites.

Fort Hare, originally founded in 1916, had long been one of the most important centers of African learning in South Africa. Many prominent Black political figures, such as Oliver Tambo, Robert Sobukwe, Govan Mbeki, Dennis Brutus, and Z. K. Matthews, had studied there. Its transformation into a predominantly Xhosa university oriented toward the Transkei and Ciskei Bantustans was designed to break that tradition.

In the new segregated universities, students are not allowed to leave the area of the campus or belong to any student organization without permission by the rector or white administrative

10. Tabata, *Education for Barbarism*, p. 63.

council. They cannot hold unapproved meetings, distribute or display magazines, pamphlets, or notices, or give statements to the press. Anyone from outside the campus must get official approval to visit. At the beginning of each school year, students must hand in a testimonial of "good conduct" from a religious minister. The two newer African universities, the one at Turfloop and the one at Ngoye, are located in remote areas of the countryside to further isolate the students from the rest of the Black population.

In 1978, the regime revealed its intention to tighten control over African education even further, issuing a draft of a new Education and Training Bill. While it introduced the principle of compulsory education through the primary grades for all African students, it adhered to the standard policy of segregated schooling and made no provision for ending the vast gap in per capita expenditures between white and Black students. It projected stiffer penalties for various infractions. Boycotts by students or teachers were to be outlawed, punishable by fines of R200. Anyone caught teaching African students without official authorization would be subject to a R500 fine or a one-year jail term.[11]

As with a number of other aspects of apartheid, whites, too, are victims of the regime's educational policies. For the ruling class, it is imperative that the bulk of the white population remain enslaved to the concepts of white supremacy, that whites do not question the unjust basis of South African society. One Afrikaans writer has noted that with the proletarianization of a section of the white population, there has been a corresponding "disappearance of nationalist sentiments and a rise of class sentiments among many Afrikaners."[12] To counteract that tendency, education in white schools stresses religious instruction and the glorification of white "civilization," in particular of the Afrikaner *volk*. It tries to indoctrinate white students into a firm belief in the righteousness of apartheid and the necessity of keeping Blacks in their allotted place. It seeks to stifle all independent thought and produce a population of bigoted and narrow-minded whites. It attempts to ensure, in the words of a leading apartheid ideologue, that "there will be no propagation in South Africa of any antinational spirit or tendency in any school."[13]

11. *Post* (Transvaal), November 14, 1978.

12. G. D. Scholtz, *Het die Afrikaanse volk 'n toekoms?*, p. 113.

13. E. Greyling, *Christelike en nasionale onderwys* [Christian-national education], 2:107.

The regime's restrictions on learning in the schools and universities are also applied to the population as a whole, both Black and white, through heavy censorship of books, periodicals, plays, films, records, photographs, and almost any other means of communication. The Publications Act of 1974, just one of many laws hampering freedom of the press and expression, provides for the banning of any "undesirable" publication, object, film, or public entertainment deemed to be "indecent or obscene," "blasphemous," "harmful to the relations between any sections of the inhabitants of the Republic," or "prejudicial to the safety of the State."[14] Over the past few decades tens of thousands of publications have been banned.

With their extensive resources, the apartheid planners have set up a vast bureaucratic apparatus for the suppression of ideas and the indoctrination of minds. Yet no amount of proapartheid propaganda or Bantu Education has been able to convince Blacks that they are not oppressed or that the white regime is not their enemy. The young Black students of Soweto and other townships who led the spirited rebellions of 1976 had all passed through the apartheid school system. They are the best example of the basic failure of Bantu Education to keep Black thought and aspirations under lock and key.

14. Muriel Horrell et al., *Survey of Race Relations in South Africa, 1974*, p. 78.

9

The Profits of Racism

My policy is this, to get the Native under the European and push the European up.

—Ben Schoeman,
minister of labor

For the rulers of South Africa, the fruits of apartheid have been plentiful. Since the early 1930s, the capitalist economy has grown and expanded beyond all their expectations. While Blacks were kept "under the European" in a state of impoverishment and exploitation, corporate profit rates were pushed upward to levels among the highest for any advanced industrialized country. Michael O'Dowd, a senior official of the giant Anglo American Corporation, accurately termed it a "fierce class system."[1]

While some South African businessmen claim to chafe at certain aspects of apartheid policy, they are almost universally in favor of maintaining white supremacy as such and appreciate the central role played by the apartheid state in keeping the Black working class under strict control. Heribert Adam, who conducted a survey of South African business opinion in 1966-67, found, "The entrepreneurs on their part are aware that only the Apartheid order, especially the prohibition of effective non-white unions, ensures a relatively cheap labor force. Any political advance of the non-whites would enable them to force economic concessions to the detriment of white profit rates. Thus far,

1. Charles Harvey et al., *The Policy Debate*, p. 199.

Apartheid has not been an obstacle to the present [economic] boom, but one of its important prerequisites."[2]

Some of the so-called critics of apartheid—especially the self-described "liberal" or "moderate" academics, politicians, businessmen, and writers—are less forthright than the government and the business community as a whole concerning the close interrelationship between capitalism and white supremacy in South Africa. They try to explain away the regime's apartheid policies as an aberration, a violation of the principles of the "free enterprise system," a constraint on the "market economy." Against all the evidence, they portray capitalism as a "progressive" force capable of breaking down social barriers and improving the lot of the entire population, Black and white.

Similar views have been expressed by American officials. While visiting South Africa in May 1977, Andrew Young, at that time American ambassador to the United Nations, told a gathering of South African businessmen in Johannesburg, "My argument boils down to my conviction that the free market system can be the greatest force for constructive change now operating anywhere in the world."[3]

The entire history of South Africa belies such arguments. As the capitalist mode of production extended its reach throughout South Africa—from the time of the early gold and diamond mines, through the commercialization and mechanization of agriculture, to the emergence of numerous manufacturing industries—the political and economic hold of the white ruling class on the Black majority grew ever tighter. Rather than being weakened, national oppression was intensified. And since national oppression ensured that Blacks were compelled to work as laborers for the white employers for the barest minimum wages, capitalism in turn was strengthened; it could benefit from high profit rates and a rapid accumulation of capital.

There is no contradiction whatever between capitalist development and national oppression, in South Africa or in the rest of the world. Everywhere that capitalism exists, including the United States, employers use racial, national, or sexual discrimination to one degree or another to divide the working class, push down wages, and boost profits.

2. Heribert Adam, *Modernizing Racial Domination*, p. 148.

3. *New York Times*, May 22, 1977.

To Blacks in South Africa, capitalism is no "liberating" force. It is a prison house from which they are struggling to escape.

Real wages of Black workers have risen somewhat in recent years, but that has not lessened the rate of exploitation that they are subjected to, nor has it appreciably improved the position of the Black population as a whole. In 1917-18, Blacks comprised about 62 percent of the entire population, but received only 28 percent of the national income. By 1977 the number of Blacks had risen to 83 percent of the entire population, but their share of the national income had edged up to only 32 percent.[4]

The average white per capita income (combining figures for both white workers and capitalists) was about fourteen-and-a-half times greater than the average African income in 1975. It was five times greater than that of Coloureds and three-and-a-half times greater than that of Indians.[5]

Under capitalism, the level of workers' wages—and consequently of the bosses' profit rates—is determined by the class struggle between the workers and the employers. The latter constantly try to drive down workers' living standards. They also seek to increase their rate of profit by raising productivity, without a corresponding rise in wages.

Because of South Africa's historical development as a colonial-settler state, the government takes part in this struggle openly on the side of the ruling class. It makes no pretense of being "neutral," of representing the interests of all South Africans. It uses its vast repressive apparatus to prevent Blacks from struggling for their rights or to improve their conditions. It employs its elaborate system of national oppression to keep Black living standards as low—and profits as high—as possible.

It was because of the profound economic and social changes during and after World War II that the apartheid regime was impelled to intervene even more forcefully than before on behalf of the capitalist class.

On the one hand, the agricultural conditions in the African reserves, which had previously helped to subsidize part of the migrant workers' wages, were deteriorating rapidly. More and more Africans were unable to subsist on the land, even for part of

4. Lawrence Schlemmer and Eddie Webster, eds., *Change, Reform and Economic Growth in South Africa*, p. 152; *Financial Mail* (Johannesburg), September 16, 1977.

5. *South Africa: An Appraisal*, p. 63.

their needs; they became largely dependent on cash incomes.[6] If left unchecked, this process would have resulted in massive struggles by Black workers for higher wages, seriously threatening the cheap-labor basis of the South African economy.

On the other hand, the significant rise in industrialization and the rapid influx of Blacks into the urban areas placed severe strains on the old mechanisms of social control. A major overhaul was required if the rulers were to contain the growing social strength of the Black working class.

The apartheid policies introduced by the National Party were a response to these conditions, aimed at shoring up the capitalist system and providing the conditions for it to flourish.

Attempts were made, through the Bantustan program, to freeze the situation in the reserves and prevent their complete breakdown. Political and social repression were stepped up to keep Blacks from effectively using their greater social power. Most significantly, the system of strict labor control that had already existed in the mines was extended to urban industry. In effect, the apartheid regime became the main regulator of labor for the entire capitalist economy, ensuring a smooth and steady flow to wherever it was needed.

All this directly benefitted profit levels. In the gold mining industry, for example, the working profit per ton of mined ore increased by more than seven times between 1960 and 1974; in the latter year, company profits totalled $2.34 billion, while the Black wage bill for the gold mines stood at only $302 million.[7]

Real Black wages, even when they have increased, have consistently lagged behind rises in productivy. The Johannesburg *Financial Mail* admitted in 1971 that "the relatively high returns on capital invested are due, at least in part, to South Africa's discriminatory non-White labour policies, which . . . perpetuate wage levels well below those justified by productivity."[8]

One study of a typical large South African company found that

6. Between 1936 and 1951, the proportion of Africans officially classified as "peasants," out of the total economically active African population, declined from 51 percent to 8 percent.

7. *South Africa: An Appraisal*, p. 207; Ann and Neva Seidman, *South Africa and U.S. Multinational Corporations*, pp. 47-48.

8. Barbara Rogers, *White Wealth and Black Poverty*, p. 40.

if the wages of its Black workers were raised to the Poverty Datum Line, the bare subsistence poverty level, after-tax profits would fall 8 percent; if the wages were raised to a higher, more "humane" poverty level, profits would drop by 21.9 percent.[9] Reason enough, from the employers' standpoint, to keep Blacks impoverished.

Thanks to the labor of millions of underpaid Black workers, the South African economy achieved a growth rate for many years that was among the highest of any advanced capitalist country, nearing even Japan's postwar "economic miracle." The 1960s was a period of virtually uninterrupted expansion, in which the real gross domestic product (GDP) rose by an average of 6.3 percent a year. (By the early 1970s, however, the growth rate had slowed down appreciably; in 1975-77 it was brought to a crawl by a serious recession.)

The mining industry remains a central pillar of the economy. Though it has been overtaken in recent years by manufacturing, it still accounted for 12.5 percent of the GDP in 1976.

Within the industry, gold has retained its traditional dominance. Aside from the attractive profits the gold mining companies have been able to skim off, gold continued to serve as a catalyst to the economy as a whole, directly stimulating a number of other industries. The massive foreign exchange earnings from gold sales, moreover, made it possible for South Africa to afford the expensive capital equipment imports it needed for the expansion of manufacturing. The rise in the world price of an ounce of gold to around $400 in 1979—bringing in record gold earnings of $7.5 billion to South Africa that year—did much to pull the South African economy out of its slump, compensate for the serious capital outflow of the previous few years (caused partly by the political turmoil), and push South Africa's balance of payments into an unprecedented surplus.

The mining companies have also increasingly diversified into other minerals, including uranium, asbestos, copper, iron, nickel, zinc, platinum, and manganese. As in the case of gold, South Africa is among the world's top producers of many of these minerals; in fact, it has the largest known deposits of platinum, vanadium, manganese, chrome, and fluorspar. Together with gold, these minerals give South Africa an immense strategic

9. S. Biesheuvel, *The Black-White Wage Gap*, p. 16.

importance in the eyes of Pretoria's imperialist allies.

Agriculture, meanwhile, has declined greatly in significance since the early days of white colonization. It now lags behind both manufacturing and mining in terms of total output, contributing only 7.5 percent to South Africa's GDP in 1976. Much of this sector is dominated by large white-owned commercial farms, some of them highly mechanized.

The most important facet of the economy's expansion has been the development of a sophisticated and diversified manufacturing sector, which grew at an even faster rate than the economy as a whole. The contribution of manufacturing to the GDP rose from just over 15 percent at the end of World War II to nearly 25 percent by 1976.

Manufacturing industries range from textile mills, food canning factories, and rubber processing plants to automobile companies, steel foundries, and chemical concerns. By 1965, heavy engineering had developed to the stage where almost any type of plant or machinery could be designed and produced within the country; it is estimated that domestic manufacturers now supply about 80 percent of South Africa's industrial plant.

By 1977, South Africa's GDP had reached R34.6 billion, ranking the country's economy as the twenty-fifth largest in the world.[10]

Although it accounts for only 6 percent of Africa's total population, South Africa's gross national product is the largest on the continent, equaling the combined gross national products of the rest of the countries of southern, central, and eastern Africa. It produces 43 percent of Africa's mineral output, generates half of its electricity, and manufactures six times as much steel as the other countries of Africa put together. Employment in South Africa's nonagricultural sectors is almost equal to nonagricultural employment for all the rest of Africa south of the Sahara Desert.

This powerful economic position on the continent is not the accomplishment of "white skill and ingenuity," as the apartheid propagandists are so fond of claiming. It is the product of an unparalleled degree of exploitation and oppression stretching over many decades. Because control over the economy gradually came into the hands of South African businessmen, and out of

10. United Nations, *Monthly Bulletin of Statistics / Bulletin Mensuel de Statistique*, March 1979, pp. 188-92.

the hands of foreign investors, most of the capital generated within the country was not funnelled abroad as in the case of other African states, but retained for the benefit of local capitalist expansion.

South Africa, in the words of one government official, is clearly a "treasure house."

A "treasure house," that is, for the white ruling class. While the economy expanded, while profit rates soared, the Black majority was kept impoverished.

In 1976, the average urban African family had a monthly income of just R73, far below the estimated R120 a month needed in that year to reach the admittedly conservative Poverty Datum Line. A study by the Bureau of Market Research in 1971 estimated that the incomes of *three-quarters* of all African families fell below the PDL; another survey in March 1978 found that a similar proportion of urban African households were still below the rough poverty level.[11]

Most Coloureds and Indians are not much better off. About half of all Coloured wage earners in the country and two-fifths of all Indian households in Durban have incomes below the poverty levels for those communities.[12]

Although the rest of Africa is much poorer than South Africa in terms of productive output, there are a number of African countries that have higher per capita incomes than Africans have in South Africa. In the desolate Bantustans, the income per person is less than 40 percent of the average on the continent as a whole.[13]

While white workers in South Africa are virtually assured of full employment, Africans suffer from endemic unemployment and underemployment. In 1960, some 1.2 million African workers, or about 19 percent of the African work force, were unemployed; by 1977 the number doubled to 2.3 million, the proportion rising

11. *Financial Mail* (Johannesburg), April 23, 1976; Peter Randall, ed., *Power, Privilege and Poverty*, p. 19; Loraine Gordon et al., *Survey of Race Relations in South Africa, 1978*, p. 161.

12. Hendrik W. van der Merwe and C. J. Groenewald, eds., *Occupational and Social Change Among Coloured People in South Africa*, p. 61; Henry Lever, ed., *Readings in South African Society*, p. 139.

13. Barbara Rogers, *White Wealth and Black Poverty*, p. 29.

to 22 percent.[14] Thus even during the boom years of the 1960s, roughly one out of every five African workers could not find a job. This large-scale African unemployment is a built-in feature of South Africa's capitalist economy, and helps to depress African wages in general.

Unemployment benefits are virtually nonexistent for Africans. Other social benefits, such as old-age, blindness, and disability pensions, are much lower for Blacks than for whites. Despite the smaller size of the white population, there are more than five times as many whites in homes for the aged than there are Blacks. Blacks, however, are taxed at a higher rate than whites.

Most Black townships are afflicted with serious housing shortages and overcrowding. A survey of ten urban areas covering 2.8 million Africans (nearly half the urban African population) found that the average number of persons per house jumped from thirteen in 1970 to seventeen in 1975.[15]

Hunger among Blacks is widespread. According to one estimate, around 1 million African children between the ages of one and four years are malnourished. In some urban areas, up to 80 percent of school-age children suffer from malnutrition or undernourishment.[16]

Given the poverty, hunger, overcrowding, and inadequate social services for Blacks, it is not surprising that diseases such as tuberculosis, kwashiorkor, typhoid, beriberi, and others are extremely common. The incidence of tuberculosis is twenty times higher for Africans than for whites. In 1965, the incidence of typhoid was seventeen times higher and for kwashiorkor, a protein-deficiency disease, 332 times higher.

In 1972, there was one doctor for every 400 whites, but only one for every 900 Asians, 6,200 Coloureds, or 144,000 Africans. The absence of adequate medical care for Blacks, together with the unsanitary and impoverished surroundings they are forced to live in, is also reflected in the wide racial differential in infant mortality rates. According to official health statistics, the rate in 1971 was 19.4 per thousand for whites, 38.3 for Asians, and 121 for Coloureds. Infant mortality figures for Africans are not

14. Charles Simkins and Duncan Clarke, *Structural Unemployment in Southern Africa,* pp. 33, 41.

15. George Ellis et al., *The Squatter Problem in the Western Cape*, pp. 17, 103; John Kane-Berman, *Soweto*, pp. 50-51.

16. J. V. O. Reid, *Malnutrition*, p. 13.

officially published, but a United Nations report estimated in 1970 that it stood at 200 to 250 for every thousand live births.[17]

Official government sources estimated that average life expectancy in 1970 was about 68 years for whites, 62 years for Indians, 53 years for Coloureds, and 55 years for Africans.

The white South African capitalists are the major beneficiaries of this system. But they are not alone. In industry after industry, they are in league with foreign investors eager to take advantage of South Africa's high profit rates. In many companies, in fact, the senior partners are not South Africans at all, but corporate chiefs in New York, London, Paris, Frankfurt, Rome, Tokyo, and other financial centers around the world. They sit on the boards of General Motors, IBM, Mobil Oil, British Leyland, Krupp, Kawasaki.

According to the South African government's own figures, the book value of all direct foreign investments in 1976 stood at R8.14 billion. Indirect investments, largely in the form of loans and credits, amounted to another R11.79 billion, bringing the total to R20 billion (nearly $23 billion).[18] The vast majority of these investments have been made over the past two-to-three decades, the period of the economy's most sustained and extensive growth.

Although Britain's traditionally paramount position among foreign investors has been eroded since the 1960s by other powers, it still remains Johannesburg's most important economic partner by a wide margin. As of 1974, British capital accounted for about 60 percent of all foreign investments in South Africa. Reflecting the importance that its former colony still holds in British imperialism's worldwide interests, South Africa takes about 10 percent of all British overseas investments. Out of South Africa's top one hundred companies, twelve are direct subsidiaries of British companies and another twenty-five are partially owned by British interests. They include many of the leading names of British capitalism: Imperial Chemical Industries, Unilever, British Steel, Slater and Walker Securities, Lonrho, Leyland Motors, Rio Tinto Zinc, Courtaulds, Cadbury Schweppes, and Barclays Bank.

Next in importance are American direct investments, which by 1977 had reached nearly $1.8 billion, or 17 percent of total direct

17. Paul Lowinger, "South African Health Care," *Congressional Record* (Washington), August 9, 1974, p. E5396.

18. *South Africa 1978*, p. 550.

foreign investment in South Africa.[19] Nearly three-quarters of this American stake is held by just a dozen firms: General Motors, Ford, Goodyear, IBM, Firestone, 3M, Mobil, Caterpillar, Chrysler, ITT, Caltex (jointly owned by Texaco and Standard Oil of California), and General Electric. But scores of other companies are also involved; out of the top one hundred American companies, fifty-five have South African investments. In addition, outstanding loans to South Africa by American banks and their subsidiaries surpassed $2 billion as of 1976.

Some three hundred West German companies operating in South Africa accounted for about 10 percent of all foreign investments there in 1977, their share having doubled in just four years. Although the French alliance with Pretoria has been the closest in the field of arms sales, French economic interests in South Africa have also become increasingly important, reaching $900 million in investments as of 1976, twice the figure of 1970. Officially, Japan does not have any direct investments in South Africa, but it does have indirect ties through the establishment of more than seventy franchised Japanese subsidiaries in the auto, electrical appliance, electronics, rubber, and other industries; Japan has also become one of South Africa's top foreign customers, importing much of its chrome, iron ore, coal, manganese, and agricultural products.

Many of the foreign companies operating in South Africa claim that their economic involvement will lead to improvements for South Africa's Black majority. But their practice exposes the worth of their preaching. A 1979 survey conducted by the Washington-based Investor Responsibility Research Center found that 95 percent of U.S. companies responding to its questionnaire paid their Black workers a minimum wage under $238 a month, a figure well below the 1978 Minimum Effective Level, one of the more "humane" poverty levels. A U.S. State Department survey released that same year found that 40 percent of all American firms in South Africa paid Blacks wages of less than $192 a month.[20]

Like local industrialists, foreign investors benefit from the superexploitation of Black workers, using Pretoria's system of national oppression to squeeze extra profits from the labor Blacks perform.

19. Gordon et al., *Survey of Race Relations, 1978*, p. 141.

20. *Southern Africa* (New York), September 1979.

The overall profit rate for American companies in South Africa averaged 18.6 percent from 1960 to 1970, compared to 11 percent worldwide; in 1974, the rate of return still averaged 17.9 percent, although it has declined slightly since then. The profits of U.S. firms in South Africa are also consistently higher than those of U.S. companies in the rest of the continent; in 1973-74, mining firms and financial institutions had profit rates three times higher and manufacturers reported average profit rates nearly six times higher.[21]

Profits for British investors in South Africa are not as great as those enjoyed by their American counterparts, but are still about 50 percent higher than in the rest of the world. Rio Tinto Zinc, one of the most successful mining and mining-finance houses in the world, has only 7.7 percent of its assets in South Africa; yet in 1970 about 42 percent of the British company's profits came from its Phalaborwa copper mine in the Transvaal.

Whatever they may say publicly, the foreign companies operating in South Africa know that their profits are dependent on the maintenance of white supremacy and the suppression of Black rights. They are therefore keen on upholding the status quo. Their attitude toward Black workers does not differ significantly from that of local South African firms. The wages they pay are usually just as low, and the benefits they provide just as meager. They are equally hostile to the development of independent Black trade unions.

The role of foreign firms in South Africa explains a lot about the political and diplomatic policies of the American, West European, and Japanese governments toward Pretoria. Despite occasional criticisms of apartheid, their basic approach is to try to help the white supremacist regime survive, in order to protect the substantial imperialist investments and other vital economic and political interests in the region. Washington does not favor real advances for the Black liberation struggle—not in southern Africa, and not in the United States itself.

For its own reasons, the apartheid regime is eager to attract foreign investors and goes to great lengths and considerable expense to encourage them to sink their money into South Africa. This stems to an extent from the continued weakness of South African capitalism. To build up certain key sectors of the

21. Donald McHenry, *United States Firms in South Africa*, pp. 15-16; Desaix Myers III, *Labor Practices of U.S. Corporations in South Africa*, p. 12; Ann and Neva Seidman, *U.S. Multinational Corporations*, pp. 87, 96, 111-12.

economy, foreign firms are invited in. As a result, the automobile industry, is almost totally dominated by foreign firms: General Motors, Ford, Chrysler, Volkswagen, Toyota, and others. In the early 1970s the first three controlled 60 percent of the South African auto market. Foreign oil companies, particularly American ones, dominate oil refining and exploration. American and British firms have a complete monopoly on computer sales, with IBM alone controlling about half of the market. As of 1970, foreign banks held just over half of all South African bank deposits. Foreign capital is also heavily involved in rubber and tires, chemicals, electronics, heavy engineering, photography, and mining. An official South African government report issued in 1970 found that about 40 percent of the country's industry was controlled from overseas.

Since South Africa is already an industrialized power, with a strong South African capitalist class in control of a powerful state apparatus, such heavy foreign investment does not hinder the country's overall capitalist economic development, as it would in a nonindustrialized colonial or semicolonial country. Through its control of the state, the South African bourgeoisie is able to utilize the presence of foreign capital to strengthen its own base. By filling the gaps that South African capital is not yet able to fill on its own, foreign investors play an invaluable role in helping Pretoria realize its aim of building up a highly developed and diversified industrial economy, one that can provide greater resources for the white supremacist regime's apparatus of national oppression and that can offer more favorable opportunities for the strengthening of South African capitalism itself.

The auto industry, to take one of the more prominent examples, has had a very stimulating effect on manufacturing in general. Following the introduction of the government's "local content" program in the 1960s, which required foreign auto manufacturers to use a certain percentage of locally made parts, a whole series of ancillary industries began to flourish.

The auto industry also shows how foreign firms can provide openings for South African capitalists to enter new fields through partnership arrangements. In late 1976, a South African company, the Anglo American Corporation, merged one of its subsidiaries with Chrysler to form the Sigma Motor Corporation. Since Anglo American owned more than 75 percent of the new firm, Sigma became the first South African dominated auto manufacturer. It then quickly took over the French auto firm Peugeot-Citroën, and merged with British Leyland's local subsidiary, acquiring a majority holding in the new company.

Another important feature of the foreign economic involvement in South Africa is the direct access it gives South African firms to the most advanced technology and manufacturing methods in the world. It has been estimated that some two-thirds of the "technological change" in South African industry between 1957 and 1972 resulted from new technology entering the country via foreign investment.[22] This is especially obvious in many of the more technologically advanced industries, such as electronics, synthetic fibers, chemicals, auto, engineering, and nuclear power. A study of Japanese economic involvement in South Africa noted that "Japanese expertise and technology in the shape of patents, blueprints, management skills, personnel training, direct advice from Japanese business partners, new methods for improving plant production, all are available and contributed."[23]

Foreign financing, too, has been vital to the expansion of South African capitalism, and has become increasingly important in comparison to direct foreign investments. In 1962, the proportion of total foreign investment in the form of loans and credits stood at 21.3 percent; by 1976 it was 59.2 percent. Among the major lenders to South Africa have been the American-dominated World Bank; Citibank, Chase Manhattan, and Morgan Guaranty Trust of the United States; Barclays National Bank of Britain; Deutsch Bank of West Germany; Toronto Dominion Bank of Canada; and the Société Générale of France. Most of their funds have gone to the South African state corporations, as well as directly to the government itself.

The South African authorities have been able to take advantage of the prominent involvement of foreign firms for directly political purposes as well. Pointing to the support and solidarity of their allies in Europe, North America, and Japan, they have sought to foster an image of stability and strength, to convince Blacks that Pretoria's foreign backers will not allow their vital stake in South Africa to be threatened by an overthrow of the white minority regime.

Because of the massive involvement of foreign companies in bolstering and profitting from Pretoria's apartheid system, virtually every Black political organization fighting against white

22. John Suckling, Ruth Weiss, and Duncan Innes, *The Economic Factor*, p. 23.

23. Yoko Kitazawa, *From Tokyo to Johannesburg*, p. 25.

supremacy has gone on record in opposition to foreign investments, from the African National Congress and Pan Africanist Congress to the South African Students' Organisation, Black People's Convention, Soweto Action Committee, and others. They have done so despite provisions in the Terrorism Act outlawing calls for boycotts of investment and trade.

Supporters of the South African freedom struggle in other countries, including the United States, have taken up these appeals. They have organized to oppose the participation of foreign firms in the exploitation of South Africa's Black population. They have mobilized to demand a withdrawal of foreign investments and an end to all other forms of assistance to the apartheid authorities. In many countries, students have taken a prominent place in these campaigns, but the active involvement of organized labor has been growing and is potentially even more significant; unions in the United States, Britain, Australia, and a number of other countries have carried out actions in solidarity with Black workers in South Africa. Whatever the immediate results of such campaigns in limiting the support of foreign companies and governments to Pretoria, they have had an important political impact by showing Blacks in South Africa that they are not alone.

The considerable growth and expansion of industry in the three decades after World War II naturally led to a strengthening and consolidation of the South African capitalist class. With the opening of new mines, the establishment of new manufacturing concerns, and the formation of new financial institutions, the white mining barons, industrialists, and bankers greatly augmented their assets and holdings.

There was at the same time a marked trend toward greater and greater concentration of wealth, with more than three hundred corporate mergers consummated in the period from 1964 to 1969 alone. A government-appointed commission reported in 1977 that in about a third of all manufacturing industries the top three companies controlled 70 percent or more of the total turnover in those industries.[24] One factor reinforcing this trend toward monopolization has been the need of the South African capitalists to strengthen their position at home, so as to be on a better

24. *Times* (London), October 27, 1969; *South Africa: An Appraisal*, pp. 146-7.

footing to penetrate export markets in competition with their imperialist rivals.

Despite the common belief that South African capital remains a largely English-speaking preserve, Afrikaner capitalists have taken advantage of the period of industrial growth since World War II to extend their economic interests and firmly entrench themselves as a major wing of the South African bourgeoisie.

In 1950, Afrikaners controlled just 11 percent of the private sector; by 1975, their share had jumped to 27.5 percent. The two main Afrikaans banks, Volkskas and the Trust Bank, had grown respectively into the third and fourth largest banks in South Africa, with combined assets in 1978 of R3 billion. Sanlam, the Afrikaans insurance company originally established in 1918, developed into a major financial power, setting up its own banks and growing into one of South Africa's largest conglomerates. Federale Volksbeleggings, the Afrikaans investment company, had become the fourth largest industrial conglomerate by 1974.

Particularly striking has been the tendency of many Afrikaans companies, like their English counterparts, toward greater financial and industrial concentration. One of the most successful monopolies is the Rembrandt Tobacco Corporation, headed by Anton Rupert, which is among the top five cigarette manufacturers in the world. With assets of R2.4 billion in 1977, the company has also acquired interests in mining and is forging close ties with the Federale Mynbou mining finance house.

With the complete commercialization of white-owned agriculture—and its extensive mechanization—there has been a corresponding concentration of wealth in the rural areas. Only one-quarter of all white landlords, most of whom are Afrikaners, own farms of more than 901 hectares each, but they produce no less than 77 percent of total commercial agricultural production.

Perhaps the most significant Afrikaans monopoly, considering the traditional domination of mining by English-speaking capitalists, is Federale Mynbou, a mining finance house set up in 1953 by Federale Volksbeleggings with a capital of only R120,000. By 1976 it had assets of more than R1 billion and had taken over two other major gold mining houses, General Mining and Finance (Genmin) and the Union Corporation. Among mining companies, Federale Mynbou now ranks second. It produces one-fifth of South Africa's gold output and is the largest coal producer in the country. It dominates the asbestos market, is the biggest producer of chrome and ferrochrome, and has substantial interests in platinum, manganese, fluorspar, and a wide range of industrial enterprises.

Of the seven gold mining monopolies in South Africa, Anglo American, a South African firm, is still by far the largest. As of 1969, the gold mines controlled by it accounted for more than 40 percent of all gold production.

Through a series of interlocking directorships, cross holdings, and management contracts, the Anglo American group's influence extends into virtually all sectors of the South African economy, from diamond, copper, uranium, and other mining ventures to agriculture, real estate, automobile assembly, construction, chemicals, and computers. It directly controls more than nine hundred companies. By the time Harry Oppenheimer became the chairman of Anglo American in 1958, he controlled "40 per cent of South Africa's gold, 80 per cent of the world's diamonds, half of Southern Africa's coal, almost a sixth of the world's copper."[25]

In 1975, the Anglo American group's holdings stood at R5.3 billion (about $6 billion).[26] Its companies account for fully one-tenth of South Africa's gross national product and about one-third of its exports.

The different wings of the South African bourgeoisie—English and Afrikaans, mining and manufacturing, commercial and agricultural—still have their own particular interests. But the old conflicts between them have been largely blurred and ameliorated. They are now cooperating to a greater degree than ever in their drive to exploit the Black working class and uphold the entire system of white supremacy.

Despite the significant economic advances scored by the South African capitalist class over the past decades, it has nevertheless been compelled to rely heavily on its control of the state apparatus, not only to maintain the superexploitation of Blacks, but also to ensure that the country's industrialization is as diversified as possible. While only 35 percent of all gross domestic fixed investments came from state-controlled sources in 1950, the share had risen to 46 percent two decades later.[27]

The main vehicles through which the apartheid regime inter-

25. Anthony Hocking, *Oppenheimer and Son*, p. 337.

26. *Financial Mail* (Johannesburg), April 30, 1976.

27. D. Hobart Houghton, *The South African Economy*, p. 204.

venes in the economy are the powerful state-controlled corporations, which dominate steel, railways and harbors, electricity, armaments, and aircraft, and are involved in numerous other industries. The investments of these state corporations are enormous; by the 1960s, their total invested capital had already reached a figure equivalent to that of all foreign investments in South Africa combined.

One aspect of the operations of these state-controlled corporations has been to specifically aid private Afrikaans companies through contracts, subsidies, and assured markets. This state aid and protection was an important element in the ability of Afrikaner capitalists to strengthen their position in relation to their English-speaking counterparts. The roles of Afrikaner businessmen and government officials, moreover, often overlap.

Because of the direct ties between the government administration and business circles and because of the sheer weight of the state corporations, the apartheid regime is able to influence the overall direction of the economy, inducing both foreign and South African investments into those areas deemed vital for the continuance of white prosperity and privilege.

The industrial expansion since World War II has also been accompanied by further shifts in the relative weight of domestic and foreign capital. While foreign interests still have billions of dollars invested in South Africa, there has been an even further decline in their influence over the economy. During the early 1970s, foreign capital inflows accounted for only 3.6 percent of South Africa's gross domestic product, while foreign investment provided only 13 percent of annual gross capital formation. Conversely, as indigenous South African industry matured, the rate of domestic fixed capital formation skyrocketed, from a mere R284 million in 1945, to R3 billion in 1970, or about a quarter of the gross domestic product.[28]

South African capital continued to move into mining. While just 40.5 percent of total mining dividends were paid within the country in 1935, this figure had risen to 70.9 percent by 1964. Even in the gold industry, where foreign investment has traditionally been higher than in other mining sectors, South Africans held 62 percent of all shares in 1977. According to an official

28. *Standard Bank Review* (Johannesburg), June 1977; Schlemmer and Webster, *Change, Reform and Economic Growth*, p. 20; Houghton, *South African Economy*, pp. 40-41.

government study in 1971, about 60 percent of all industry was under the control of South African firms.[29]

South African finance capital has also gained in strength. The British Barclays and Standard banks, which have traditionally dominated commercial banking, have faced increasing competition from South African commercial banks and new government policies encouraging them to turn over at least 50 percent of their shares to South Africans. Merchant banking, which specializes more in industrial and other business transactions than does commercial banking, came under the domination of an Afrikaans banking conglomerate in the early 1970s. Life insurance companies have long been dominated almost exclusively by South African interests, as have building societies, whose financial assets are enormous, equaling three-quarters of the total assets of all commercial banks.

Though still quite weak by European or North American standards, the emergence of an "indigenous" white capitalist class in South Africa meant that the colonial-settler state could enjoy much greater political and economic independence from its imperialist partners. The last formal political ties with Britain were cut in 1961 when Pretoria proclaimed itself a "republic" and withdrew from the British Commonwealth. In the same year, the free transfer of securities between the London and Johannesburg stock exchanges was ended and strict controls were clamped on foreign investors seeking to pull their capital out of South Africa.

The considerable weakening of British economic and political influence over South Africa was a chief element in the country's rapid industrialization (together, of course, with the superexploitation of Black labor). Without such independence, South African business and financial circles would have been unable to reduce the flow of profits abroad and retain large amounts of capital within South Africa.

The increased independence on the part of the South African bourgeoisie is likewise a reflection of the development of the colonial-settler state into a junior imperialist power.

In the process of forging themselves into a cohesive ruling class, the white capitalists conquered the country's internal market, largely destroyed the precapitalist forms of property ownership and production, mechanized agriculture, established a

29. Houghton, *South African Economy*, p. 115; *Star Weekly* (Johannesburg), March 5, 1977; Rogers, *White Wealth and Black Poverty*, p. 97.

modern industrialized economy on the backs of Black workers, moved into the most profitable and highly technological sectors of the economy, achieved a high degree of monopolization, provided a leading role for finance capital, and began to invest abroad. Initially an outpost of the British Empire, South African capitalism developed along its own course and established its own independent state. It now exploits the Black millions of South Africa—and other countries—essentially for its own profit, although in close alliance with the other imperialist powers. At the same time, the South African state continues to rest on the old colonialist foundations, in which the indigenous Black population is denied all political rights and is nationally oppressed by a settler ruling class.

The very logic of South Africa's capitalist economy, like those of other imperialist powers, demands that it continually expand beyond the country's borders (as well as internally) in search of new trade and investment outlets.

Unlike other imperialist economies, however, South Africa's has an additional compulsion toward geographical expansion because of the constrictions on its domestic market caused by the extremely low purchasing ability of the Black population. Often South African capitalists seeking to reinvest their earnings must either develop foreign markets large enough to make further expansion of their interests within the country profitable or they must export their capital abroad.

The drive toward economic (and political) expansion outside of South Africa was already evident in the early part of this century, with Pretoria's acquisition of South West Africa (Namibia) as a direct colony and its attempts to annex Bechuanaland (Botswana), Basutoland (Lesotho), Swaziland, and Southern Rhodesia. As early as 1924, General Smuts explicitly gave voice to this expansionist drive when he wrote that the East African highlands, between South Africa and Ethiopia, was "one of the richest parts of the world and only wants white brains and capital to become enormously productive."[30]

The actual export of capital, however, did not taken on any real significance until after World War II and the beginning of the country's rapid industrial growth. In 1958, the amount invested by South Africans in other countries stood at R846 million. By 1977, it had risen substantially, to R5.36 billion (about $6.16

30. Martin Legassick, "Forced Labor, Industrialization, and Racial Differentiation," p. 253.

billion),[31] equivalent to nearly 20 percent of South Africa's GDP for that year.

Of all the South African monopolies, the Anglo American Corporation has been the most energetic in its outward drive. Its holdings are extremely varied, scattered across the entire globe. They range from copper and diamonds in Africa, North America, and Australia to chemical sales in East, Central, and West Africa. Anglo American's Mineral and Resources Corporation, based in Bermuda, has a 30 percent stake in the American company in Engelhard Minerals and has interests in copper in Zambia, oil in Indonesia, and gold and other minerals in Brazil. Besides investments in gold exploration in Brazil's northeast province of Bahia, Anglo American owns a 49 percent share in Brazil's oldest gold mining firm, Mineração Morro Velho, through its Brazilian subsidiary. The group's holdings also include interests in an Italian finance and investment company, tungsten mining in the French Pyrenees, "prospecting operations in the Yukon, the Amazon basin and the sea off Thailand; nickel in Australia, potash in Yorkshire, tin in Malaysia, oil in Canada; diamond sales in London, the bullion market in Zurich, citrus farming in Rhodesia, beer brewing in Zambia. . . ."[32]

Nor have other South African monopolies been far behind. The Rembrandt Tobacco empire of Anton Rupert has interests in about seventy countries. The Iron and Steel Industrial Corporation, Pretoria's state-controlled steel enterprise, has acquired a 49 percent holding in Israel's largest steel processing group, Koor Metal Industries. Other South African interests have moved into Israel too, their operations including a cotton-print factory specifically aimed at the export market to Black-ruled Africa.

In recent years Latin America has become a potentially significant outlet for South African investment and trade. In addition to Anglo American's interests in that part of the world, South African companies are involved in a hydroelectric scheme in Paraguay, tobacco growing in Brazil, sugar processing in Venezuela, and mining in Bolivia. The Union Corporation, one of the Afrikaans-owned mining houses, owns 30 percent of Minera Frisco, a Mexican mining firm.

Although their economic interests are far-ranging, the South

31. *South Africa 1975*, p. 529; *Financial Mail* (Johannesburg), December 15, 1978.

32. Hocking, *Oppenheimer and Son*, p. 467.

Africans are particularly keen to expand into the rest of the African continent itself, most notably into those countries immediately north of South Africa's borders. Perhaps the clearest expression of their ambitious aims was given by Prime Minister Vorster in a 1966 interview, in which he said, "In many ways we have, with respect to much of Africa south of the Sahara, a responsibility for assisting in development—comparable to the responsibility which the United States had undertaken on a much larger scale with respect to the underdeveloped areas of the world as a whole. Although we do not publicize it, we are in fact already doing quite a lot in this field."[33]

Despite the secrecy involving South African involvement abroad, it is known that Johannesburg's industrialists, bankers, and mining barons have investment and trade ties with more than a dozen African countries (see chart).

Out of all of them, Namibia is the most directly under Pretoria's thumb. It was first seized by the South Africans in 1915, during World War I, when South African troops under General Smuts invaded the territory on behalf of the Allied powers and defeated the forces of Germany, which had colonized South West Africa several decades earlier. As a reward for loyal service to the Allies, the South Africans were given a "mandate" to rule Namibia by the newly formed League of Nations. (After the dissolution of the League, Pretoria refused to yield its mandate, even after it was formally revoked by the United Nations in 1966.)

A large, sparsely populated territory, Namibia has extensive deposits of copper, zinc, diamonds, uranium, tungsten, cadmium, iron, manganese, vanadium, and other minerals, as well as valuable fishing off the coast and ideal conditions for livestock husbandry. To exploit these resources, the South Africans denied Namibians their political rights and imposed a migratory labor system similar to that operating in South Africa.

Other foreign concerns, especially British and American, are also involved in the exploitation of Namibia, but the South Africans account for the largest share of foreign investments, nearly half. Although this includes fishing, animal husbandry, and a minimal amount of manufacturing, most of the investment is in mining. Consolidated Diamond Mines, the Namibia subsidiary of Anglo American's De Beers interests, has a monopoly of the production and sale of diamonds in the territory, netting R500

33. *U.S. News and World Report* (New York), November 14, 1966.

Some South African Economic Interests in Africa

Namibia	holds 47% of all foreign investments majority stake in Cunene River project dominates trade
Lesotho	De Beers 75% stake ($30 million) in diamond fields 100,000 migrant workers employed in SA member SA customs union
Botswana	extensive investments in copper, nickel, coal, diamonds member SA customs union
Swaziland	investments in iron ore, kaolin, diamonds, sugar, tobacco, timber, manufacturing, land member SA customs union
Zimbabwe	$800 million in investments (1976) extensive trade relations
Zambia	Anglo American minority holding in copper mines trade ($54 million, 1975)
Malawi	$30 million financing for Chikwana sugar mill, railways, Lilongwe capital project $17 million investment in Dwangwa sugar refinery provides 35% of Malawi's imports (1977) 30,000 migrant workers employed in SA (1977)

Mozambique	75% stake in Cabora Bassa hydroelectric project trade routed through Mozambican ports 70,000 migrant workers employed in SA (1977)
Angola	De Beers minority holding in Diamang diamond firm majority stake in Cunene River project
Zaïre	trade (exported $46 million to Zaïre, 1976)
Tanzania	Anglo American 50% stake in Mwadui diamond fields
Central African Republic	credits for housing construction mineral surveying
Mauritius	$11-17 million in investments (1977) trade ($47 million, 1976) serves as base for SA reexports to Africa
Réunion	trade (exported $26 million to Réunion, 1976)

Sources: *Africa Research Bulletin* (London), *Africa South of the Sahara, 1978-79* (London: Europa Publications, 1978), *Financial Mail* (Johannesburg), *Star* (Johannesburg), other.

million in gross profits in the decade from the early 1960s to the early 1970s.[34]

The trade relations between South Africa and Namibia are a clear reflection of the near-total domination of the territory by South African imperialism. About half of Namibia's exports go to South Africa and about 80 percent of its imports come from there. In 1965, Namibia's exports were equivalent to more than 90 percent of its gross domestic product, highlighting the extremely lopsided development of the Namibian economy resulting from its role in the capitalist system as a colonial supplier of raw materials.

Even the South African *Financial Mail* was forced to admit that Namibia "is operated in colonial-style, with [South Africa] the 'imperial power' and most of the spoils of fishing and mining sucked out by 'foreign' concerns."[35]

Much the same could be said about Zimbabwe, where South African companies had some $800 million invested as of 1976 (with British imperialism holding a roughly equal stake). South African dominance has grown considerably since the mid-1960s, when the Rhodesian settler regime declared its "independence" from Britain. As early as 1970, five of the ten largest firms were totally or partly South African owned. South African capital is involved in the mining of platinum, copper, nickel, and coal; in the manufacture of fertilizer, cement, glass, and beverages; in hotels; in agriculture; in retail trade; and in banking.[36]

Also largely under South African domination are the three former British High Commission territories—Botswana, Lesotho, and Swaziland. All three are members of the South African Customs Union, which provides for relatively free trade among the states, assuring the South Africans of virtually captive markets. Since Pretoria also collects the customs duties for the trade of the three states, and then pays them a negotiated amount each year, it has a strong economic and political handle that it can use to its advantage.

34. *Financial Mail* (Johannesburg), March 2, 1973.

35. Ibid.

36. Colin Stoneman, "Foreign Capital and Zimbabwe," *Review of African Political Economy* (London), no. 11 (January-April 1978), pp. 69-71; John Sprack, *Rhodesia*, p. 56.

Like other imperialist investments in Africa, those by South African firms help perpetuate and exacerbate the economic underdevelopment of much of the continent. Despite the claims that such investments bring economic benefits to Africa, they in fact help heighten the unequal economic relationships between the imperialist and the neocolonial countries, siphoning off enormous profits toward Johannesburg. Fearing that the development of indigenous industry in the rest of southern Africa could later compete with their own manufacturing interests, South African businessmen and government officials have consciously sought to block industrial growth in countries like Lesotho, Botswana, and Swaziland. Instead, its foreign investments tend to concentrate on the extraction of raw materials, resulting in an extremely lopsided and export-oriented growth of the African economies, one that does little to improve overall economic development and that leaves those countries vulnerable to sudden fluctuations in the prices of their export products on the world market.

South Africa's trade relations with the rest of Africa are also unequal, exchanging high-priced manufactured and consumer goods for undervalued raw materials. While South Africa's direct trade with Africa is much less than that with its major trade partners in North America, Europe, and Japan, it is nevertheless significant. Because of political opposition to Pretoria, trade with Africa dropped considerably during the mid- and late 1960s, but by 1970 South African exports to Africa rose to 17 percent of its total exports.

The bulk of this trade was with other countries in southern Africa, but a South African publication reported in 1976 that "While the South African Government does not disclose information about trade with Africa, it is known that the country does trade directly or indirectly with about 19 African states. . . ."[37]

Because of South African imperialism's relative weakness, however, it frequently engages in joint operations abroad with other foreign capital, sometimes as a minority shareholder, sometimes as the controlling interest. In Namibia, for instance, this includes joint mining ventures with British, American, Canadian, and French interests. In Botswana, American Metal Climax has gone into partnership with South Africa's Roan Selection Trust to exploit nickel and copper deposits. The Anglo

37. *South African Digest* (Pretoria), November 5, 1976.

American Corporation and two British companies are jointly involved in the mining of iron ore in Swaziland.

A strong alliance between Pretoria and other imperialist powers has been forged. Arm-in-arm, they are engaged in exploiting southern Africa's resources and Black labor power.

Above, Soweto, with Johannesburg in background. Below, Johannesburg skyline.

Above, farm worker's shack, southern Transvaal. Below, workers in KwaMashu township, Durban.

Crossroads squatters' camps, near Cape Town.

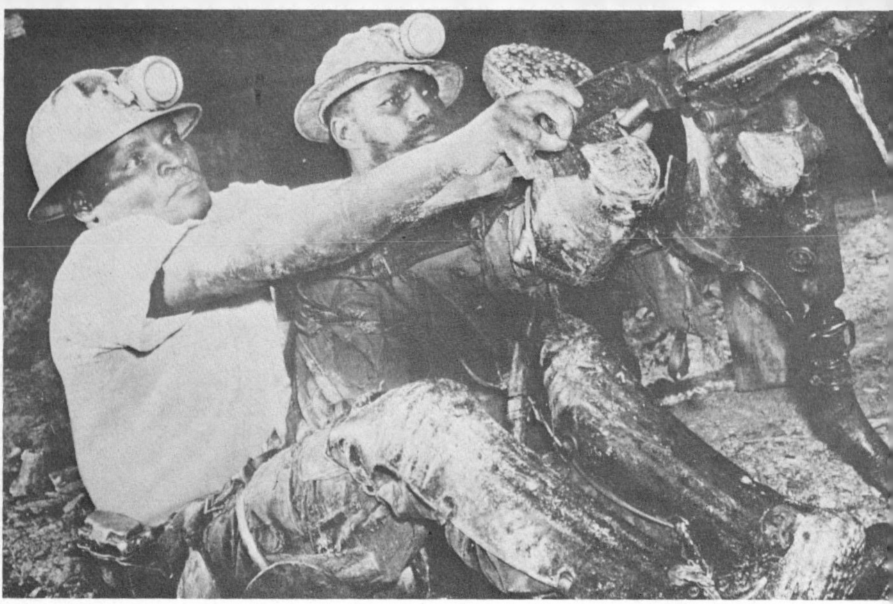

Above, gold miners. Below, an African's passbook.

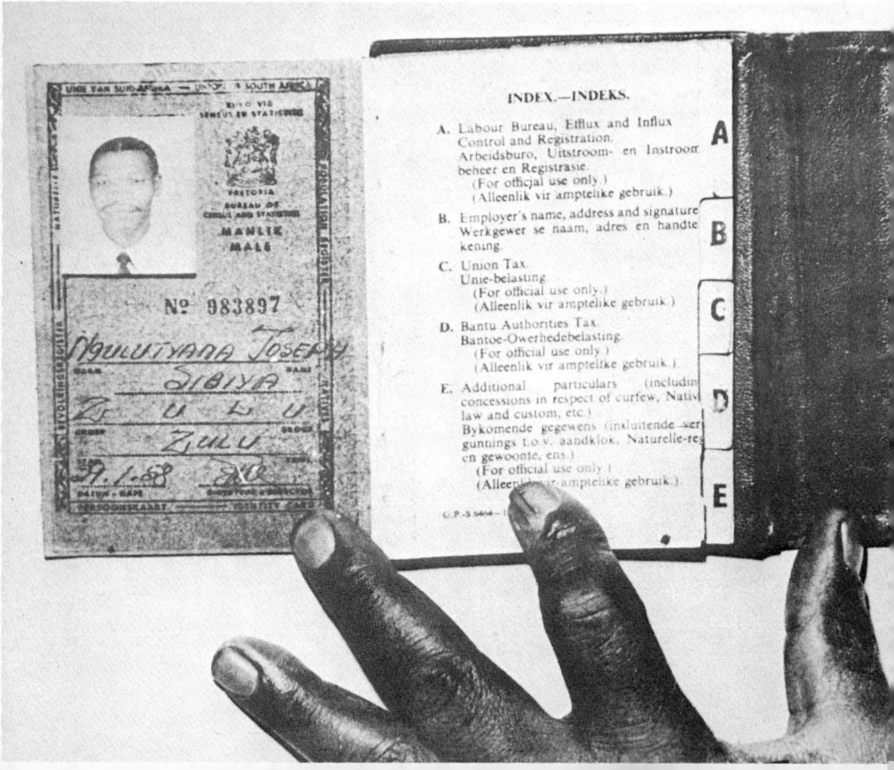

Segregated facilities.

Above, prisoners breaking rocks on Robben Island. Below, from left, Jan Christian Smuts, D. F. Malan, Hendrick Verwoerd.

Above, students demonstrate in Soweto, June 16, 1976. Below, Soweto students protest rent hikes, April 1977.

Above, John Vorster meets wit
Henry Kissinger in Zurich, Sep
tember 4-6, 1976. Left, Sout
African troops in Namibia.

10

Rule by Sjambok

Rimmed by trees and luxuriant green foliage, with a clear view of the southeastern slopes of Cape Town's stunningly beautiful Table Mountain, Pollsmoor could seem to an outsider like an idyllic retreat. But to Pollsmoor prison's hundreds of Black inmates, the view from inside its walls is exceedingly bleak.

Fred Carneson, a white former political prisoner who spent some time at Pollsmoor, described what life was like there: "Men in chains. Men with their buttocks raw and bloody from whippings. Yells and screams—these were commonplace sights and sounds in the isolation section." He wrote that he saw "enough of conditions at Pollsmoor to convince me that the possibility of death, the possibility of physical assault, of arbitrary and unjust punishment, is ever-present in the consciousness of black prisoners. . . ."[1]

Pollsmoor is just one of 230 similar prisons scattered around South Africa. It is part of a vast and extensive network of repression set up to protect white supremacy and profits and to keep Blacks (and a few whites like Carneson) under tight rein. Confronted with frequent and active opposition to its oppressive policies, the apartheid regime needs institutions like Pollsmoor. Without its prison system, its tear gas and clubs, its gallows, without the constant threat and periodic demonstration of its armed might, Pretoria could never have maintained its rule for so long.

Repression in South Africa, however, is not something that is experienced only by those who stand up to fight for their rights or who speak out against the regime. It is a part of daily life for the overwhelming majority of the Black population. Because of the

1. Allen Cook, *South Africa: The Imprisoned Society*, p. 40.

extreme complexity of the apartheid laws, it is virtually impossible for any Black to live in "white" South Africa without breaking them at some point or another. In an extensive study of the legal system in South Africa, Albie Sachs estimated that one African adult male in every three could expect to be convicted and serve a prison sentence sometime during the 1970s. If pretrial prisoners who were not subsequently convicted were included, the ratio would rise to one in every two.[2]

From the time of Union in 1910 until 1970, the number of prosecutions of Blacks under specifically racial laws increased by more than ten times, from ninety thousand a year to more than a million a year. About a third are for pass law violations. Others are for such crimes as being in "white" areas after curfew hours, failing to pay the various taxes Blacks are subjected to, and trespassing, that is, living on white-owned land without official approval. In addition, as many as twenty thousand persons a year are prosecuted on various charges relating to their jobs, such as "desertion, disobedience, being unfit for work due to liquor, etc., negligence and noncompliance with service contracts."[3]

Nighttime police sweeps through the central cities and Black townships in search of pass law violators and curfew breakers are common occurrences, designed to spread terror and insecurity throughout the Black community.

The average prison population at any one time is about a hundred thousand. The ratio of prisoners to total population is among the highest in the world.

As in the rest of society, Blacks who are brought to court have few, if any, rights. There have been no jury trials in South Africa since 1969, but even before then Blacks were not judged by their peers, since juries were all-white. Blacks usually cannot afford proper legal aid, their testimony is given less weight than that of whites, and as a general rule they receive stiffer sentences than whites for the same offenses. In short, they appear in court as members of a conquered people, tried and sentenced by white judges who officiate on behalf of white rule.

What happens in South African prisons has a wide impact, since so many Blacks pass through them at some point in their lives. The apartheid regime generally denies that conditions are

2. Albie Sachs, *Justice in South Africa*, p. 188.

3. Leonard Thompson and Jeffrey Butler, *Change in Contemporary South Africa*, p. 244.

bad; in 1959 it passed the Prisons Act to prevent the publication of "false information" about prisons and the treatment of prisoners. Nevertheless, enough evidence has surfaced to paint a revealing picture of what life is like behind bars in South Africa.

In 1944, F. E. T. Krause, a former judge, described conditions at that time. "In our prisons," he said, "you will still hear the clank of leg irons, you will see a caged human being, half-starved, marching up and down a narrow isolation cell, with a hard and cold cement floor and no furniture, with hardly any ventilation, in a foetid atmosphere, with a minimum of light . . . ; you will still hear cries of pain and distress as the skilled operator, with a cat or the cane, takes a sadistic delight in hacking dead human flesh to shreds."[4]

Not that much changed in subsequent years. In 1959, an epidemic of typhoid broke out in the "Fort," a prison in Johannesburg's Hillbrow district. Fearing that the epidemic might spread to the city itself, the public health authorities went into the prison to inspect it. "They found that cells measuring about 12 feet by 30 feet held as many as 100 men; sanitary facilities consisted of open buckets which stood next to buckets of drinking water. Prisoners ate and slept in these cells although they were frequently too crowded to allow them to lie down. Prisoners often slept body to body in a squatting position."[5] These revelations led to a few minimal improvements in the sanitary conditions of the "Fort."

In 1965, Harold Strachan, a white former political prisoner who had been jailed for three years, exposed the conditions in four prisons that he had been in. In Port Elizabeth North End, prisoners were sometimes packed twelve to a cell and were forced to brush their teeth in the common toilet bowl. At Pretoria Local he heard "the most terrible and prolonged screams you have ever heard" coming from the African section of the prison. Also at Pretoria Local, Black prisoners who wanted to see the prison doctors were forced to strip naked and wait for hours outside in the winter cold. "They had to stand with frost thick on the ground," he wrote, "barefoot, clutching each other to try to keep warm. Shivering." Black prisoners were frequently beaten, brutalized, and publicly humiliated.[6]

4. Cook, *Imprisoned Society,* p. 29.
5. *Brute Force,* p. 6.
6. Cook, *Imprisoned Society,* pp. 31, 67, 70.

The regime responded to these exposures by serving Strachan with a five-year banning order, to prevent anything further he said from appearing in the press, and sentencing him to another jail term, of two and a half years. The public outcry aroused by the Strachan revelations, however, did force the Prison Department to introduce a few minor improvements in the treatment of prisoners, including political prisoners.

Prisoners still have no real rights. Although the regulations provide for opportunities to read, to get some exercise, and to receive and send letters, these "privileges" are generally dispensed as rewards for "good behavior." Prison diets are inadequate, both in quantity and nutritional value, with Black prisoners as a rule receiving less than white prisoners.

In addition to jail terms, Black prisoners are often sentenced to lashings. One of the National Party's earliest acts was the adoption of the "Whipping Bill," which provided for compulsory lashings for certain offenses. On the day he introduced the bill, Justice Minister C. R. Swart, later to become a president of South Africa, walked into parliament carrying a cat-o'-nine-tails. According to the Department of Justice, lashings were administered to 45,233 persons, including juveniles, in the one-year period from July 1972 to June 1973.[7] Whippings have even been administered to persons found guilty of traffic offenses or of fishing illegally.

Judges are likewise generous in dispensing death sentences. While there were only three crimes punishable by death in 1955, the number has since been upped to nine. South Africa has one of the highest rates of legally-sanctioned executions in the world. Nearly half of all known judicial executions in the early 1960s were carried out in South Africa. During the decade of the 1960s, an average of ninety-five persons were hanged each year, for a total of 948, the overwhelming majority of them Black. After a somewhat lower number for several years in the early 1970s, the rate again started to pick up following the 1976 rebellions, reaching an all-time high in 1978, when 132 persons—all but one of them Black—were sent to the gallows. This amounted to an average of one hanging every three days.[8]

The gallows at Pretoria Central Prison hold a number of

7. Ibid., pp. 10-11.

8. Sachs, *Justice in South Africa,* p. 192; *Rand Daily Mail* (Johannesburg), January 23, 1979.

nooses, to allow multiple hangings. Strachan described how the condemned prisoners there were kept in a special section, but surrounded by regular prisoners, who could hear the condemned prisoners sing through the night to calm their nerves. They could even hear the sound of the trap-door dropping open as a prisoner was being hanged.[9]

For the millions of Blacks who pass through the apartheid jails, bad as they are, prison life may not seem all that different from the lives they are forced to live on the outside. The African townships are designed to facilitate police control,[10] Blacks cannot travel about freely, the migrant labor hostels are built like cell blocks, and the Bantustans themselves are like huge outdoor prison camps from which it is difficult to escape. And Blacks do not have to be in prison to be beaten or shot; police kill several hundred Blacks each year in the course of their routine activities. Indeed, for South Africa's twenty-two million Blacks, the country itself is one vast prison house.

Though all Blacks in South Africa are candidates for possible imprisonment, the government's fire is directed against political activists in a much more concerted and brutal manner. Since coming to power, the National Party has added greatly to South Africa's armory of repressive laws, covering virtually all forms of political action and expression.

In 1950, the apartheid regime adopted the notorious Suppression of Communism Act. Under it, communism was defined in extremely broad and vague terms, giving the authorities a convenient weapon against a wide spectrum of political activity. Communism, according to the act, meant not only "the doctrine of Marxian socialism as expounded by Lenin or Trotsky, the 3d Communist International or the Communist Information Bureau," but also any doctrine "which aims at bringing about any political, industrial, social or economic change within the Union by the promotion of disturbance or disorder by unlawful acts" or

9. Cook, *Imprisoned Society*, pp. 66-67.

10. The newer townships are laid out in regular geometric patterns, with wide streets, to allow unobstructed fields of fire and the easy passage of police vans, armored cars, and tanks. They are dotted with strategically located police stations. They are often surrounded by a *cordon sanitaire* of bare land to enable the authorities to isolate them in times of unrest. Some townships even have barbed wire fences around them.

which "aims at the encouragement of feelings of hostility between the European and non-European races."[11]

In other words, trade unionists could be found guilty of being communists if they favored African strikes for higher wages and Black activists could be painted with the same brush for simply advocating opposition to any apartheid regulation.

The act provided sentences of up to ten years' imprisonment for such minor acts as possessing a communist button or publication. More serious "crimes" could draw the death penalty. The minister of justice was empowered to issue banning orders against any individual. These orders impose a number of restrictions, such as barring a banned person from attending gatherings, communicating with all but a few select individuals, or publishing anything in any form. Banned persons are frequently placed under a form of house arrest as well or confined to a particular township, city, or part of the country and required to report to the police on a daily or weekly basis.

Under the Suppression of Communism Act, the regime outlawed the South African Communist Party, shut down publications, dismissed dozens of trade union leaders from their posts, convicted thousands of political activists, and banned hundreds of others, many of them active members of such groups as the African National Congress or the South African Indian Congress.

A series of other measures during the 1950s gave the regime powers to declare a state of emergency throughout the country or in a particular area and to ban any public gathering of twelve or more persons. Police were empowered to use force, including gunfire, to disperse unlawful meetings. Picketing of any kind was prohibited.

During the Black upsurge of the late 1950s and early 1960s, the regime outlawed the African National Congress and the Pan Africanist Congress, the two principal Black groups at that time. Penalties ranging from five years in prison to death were laid down for a wide range of activities characterized by the regime as "sabotage," including simple trespass. Incommunicado detention without trial was sanctioned for "any person likely to give material evidence for the State" in a political trial; any such witness who refused to turn state's evidence could receive a year at hard labor.

In 1967 came the far-reaching Terrorism Act. It defines "terror-

11. Robert W. Peterson, ed., *South Africa & Apartheid*, p. 16.

ism" as "any act" that could "hamper or . . . deter any person from assisting in the maintenance of law and order," "promote, by intimidation, the achievement of any object," "cripple or prejudice any industry or undertaking," "endanger the safety of any person," "obstruct or endanger the free movement of any traffic," or "embarrass the administration of the affairs of the State."[12]

This concept of terrorism applies not only to physical actions, but also to speeches and writings; in 1975 Minister of Justice, Police, and Prisons James T. Kruger even referred to something he called "terrorism of the spirit."[13] Section 6 of the act provides for *indefinite* detention without trial, in solitary confinement, of anyone suspected of terrorism or of having information about it. No court can intervene and no one, not even a lawyer or relative, can have access to the suspect. Section 6 thus offers ideal conditions for the mistreatment and torture of political prisoners. In court, the onus is on the accused to prove that he or she did not intend any of the results specified in the act. Conviction brings sentences ranging from five years in jail to death.

The Prohibition of Political Interference Act, passed in 1968, sought to segregate all political organizations, making it a criminal offense for Blacks and whites to engage in any joint political activity or to belong to the same political party.

In May 1976, one month before the beginning of the massive Black protests that year, the apartheid regime took a further step toward strengthening its already bulging stockpile of repressive laws, introducing the Promotion of State Security Bill. Embarrassed by its opponents' labeling of the measure as the "SS Bill," the regime renamed it the Internal Security Act when it was adopted several weeks later. The act incorporated and expanded the already broad provisions of the Suppression of Communism Act, empowering police to detain anyone suspected of "endangering the security of the State or the maintenance of public order" for up to a year without bail, trial, or legal aid. It likewise extended the regime's banning powers and deleted a provision of the Terrorism Act that had allowed suspects to be released on bail. The Internal Security Act in addition gave the regime powers to ban any publication containing information deemed to endanger "the security of the State," thus adding one more clause

12. "The Terrorism Act of South Africa," *Current History* (Philadelphia), no. 333 (May 1969): 299.

13. Thoko Mbanjwa, ed., *Black Review 1974/75,* p. 96.

to the long list of measures restricting freedom of the press.

Geoff Budlender, a South African lawyer, commented at the time, "The remarkable feature of the Act is that it creates no new criminal offences. . . . It is aimed at lawful activities, and the aim is not to make these activities unlawful, but to give the State arbitrary power to stop them, and to punish the individuals concerned."[14]

This was confirmed in practice in October 1977. In the most drastic crackdown since the early 1960s, Pretoria used its newly acquired powers under the Internal Security Act to ban eighteen Black and antiapartheid organizations.

Between 1960 and 1967, about 4,000 persons were convicted and sentenced under the four main security acts. In addition, another 120,000 political activists were convicted under seventeen other repressive laws. In the subsequent decade, many hundreds more were found guilty and sentenced under these, as well as more recent, acts; in the year following the outbreak of the large-scale urban revolts in June 1976, more than 13,500 Blacks were prosecuted on charges stemming from the unrest and another 2,430 persons were detained under the Internal Security Act, Terrorism Act, and other similar measures.

In general, political prisoners, especially Blacks, face considerably worse treatment in jail than do other prisoners. Those who have been convicted and sentenced are held in three main prisons: Robben Island for Black men, Barberton for Black (and a few white) women, and Pretoria Local for white men. Political prisoners are not eligible for remission of sentence, amnesty, or parole. That means that those who are sentenced to life terms are meant to die in prison. As a general rule, political prisoners are not allowed any newspapers or radios. Guards and other prison officials frequently victimize them by denying them "privileges" that other prisoners sometimes receive, cutting back on meals, and withholding medical attention.

The more prominent prisoners on Robben Island are usually confined to small individual cells, but for the majority the conditions are more cramped. Amnesty International reported in 1965 that cells "designed for up to 50 prisoners, are accommodating between 80 and 90 prisoners; the approximate measurements given are 80' x 20', thus giving each prisoner something under 20 square feet. Floor space is said to be only enough for prisoners to

14. *South Africa—A "Police State"?*, p. 3.

lie down side by side for sleeping. As washing, eating and excretory functions usually take place in the cells, the problems caused by over-crowding are increased."[15]

In a letter smuggled off of Robben Island, a Namibian political prisoner explained that the inmates are often victimized by confinement to isolation cells and subjection to dietary punishment. "Maltreatment is an everyday thing," he wrote. "We are assaulted by warders and officers alike, then left in isolation cells until we no longer bear the marks, then taken to the hospital so the doctors can 'prove' we have not been beaten. Sometimes they come and beat us with handles in the night."[16]

With the sentencing of more than 130 additional political prisoners to Robben Island after the Soweto protests, the total inmate population there rose to more than 400 by the end of May 1977.

In numerous political trials, the defendants have told in detail of the tortures inflicted on them during their detention and interrogation. The police, naturally, deny these charges and claim that the bruises, cuts, and other visible signs of mistreatment on many prisoners are the result of "falls" or other "accidents," or even that they were self-inflicted so as to embarrass the police.

After reviewing much of the evidence on torture in South African prisons, the United Nations Special Committee on Apartheid stated in a 1973 report, "The conclusion is inescapable that cruelty against opponents of *apartheid* is the application of a deliberate and centrally directed policy, and that torture by the Security Police is condoned, if not actually encouraged, by the Government."[17]

The torture methods employed by the apartheid inquisitors are extremely brutal and varied, some of them dating from the days of slavery, some more modern and sophisticated. They range from the standard beatings and the increasingly common application of electric shocks to the driving of nails through men's penises and the suspension of prisoners from rafters for prolonged periods.

In one trial alone in 1971, twelve defendants belonging to the Unity Movement of South Africa and the African People's

15. *Prison Conditions in South Africa,* p. 13.

16. *Namibia News* (London), September 1976.

17. *Amnesty International Report on Torture,* p. 126.

Democratic Union of South Africa charged that among the tortures inflicted on them were:

> Electric shock treatment;
> Forcing people to stand barefoot on the edges of bricks for hours at a time;
> Compelling them to lift weights while wearing shoes containing pebbles;
> Making them hold weights above their heads for long periods;
> Handcuffing them to trees all night;
> Forcing them to sit on imaginary chairs until their muscles collapsed;
> Kicking and punching.[18]

Women activists, too, are subjected to harrowing "interrogation" sessions. Oshadi Jane Phakathi, a prominent member of the Christian Institute of Southern Africa, was held for four months in late 1976, during which she was forced to sign a statement by the police. "The actual pressure was applied by means of assaults, electric shocks applied around my waist and on my breasts whilst I was blinded with a thick cloth around my eyes," she later revealed. "I was also put in an electric frozen bag and suspended in the air by means of a heavy iron until I was suffocating."[19]

The brutalities carried out in the regime's torture chambers have all too frequently resulted in death. Between 1963 and 1979 about fifty political prisoners are known to have died in pretrial detention under suspicious circumstances, about half of them during and after the massive Black protests that began in June 1976. Steve Biko, a young leader of the Black Consciousness movement who was killed in police custody in September 1977, was the most prominent. If it bothered to list a cause of death at all, the regime claimed that the prisoners had "committed suicide," died of "natural causes," or fallen down stairs or out of windows.

However, the available evidence and what is generally known about the treatment of Black political prisoners suggests that many, if not all, of those who died in detention were the victims of police brutality. During the occasional public inquests into such deaths, the police have often been unable to explain away the numerous bruises, fractures, cuts, strangulation marks, brain contusions, and other injuries cited in the autopsy reports.

18. *Torture in South Africa?*, p. 18.

19. *Political Imprisonment in South Africa,* p. 63.

Political killings outside of the jail cells are even more common. In the sixty years *before* the Soweto uprisings, police fired on protesting crowds on about thirty occasions, killing approximately five hundred Blacks. The most famous of these massacres was at Sharpeville in March 1960, where sixty-seven Blacks were killed, more than half of them shot in the back. But beginning with the June 16, 1976, student protests in Soweto, the police surpassed themselves. According to the South African Institute of Race Relations, more than six hundred Blacks, many of them still in their teens, were known to have been shot down in the streets by police and white vigilante squads during the 1976 upheavals.[20] Black community leaders estimated that the real death toll was much higher.

Pretoria's steadily expanding police and military capabilities are an index of its increasing reliance on rule by force.

The main armed wing in charge of day-to-day enforcement is the South African Police (SAP), which is largely paramilitary in nature. It is the police, not the army, that usually moves in to suppress Black political opposition. This was the case during the ferment of the early 1960s, as well as during the Soweto protests. As of 1977, the number of authorized regular police was 35,000, but this force is supplemented by a large corps of traffic police and location police, who patrol the African townships, as well as a police reserve of 20,000 created after the Sharpeville events. Some police units are trained in counterinsurgency techniques.

In the 1920s, a "special branch" of the SAP was established to deal specifically with political dissent. This later evolved into the present Security Branch. It keeps political activists under surveillance, raids homes and offices for information, opens mail, taps phones, and operates an extensive network of police informers. There are estimated to be about fifteen thousand informers in the Transvaal alone.

In mid-1968, Prime Minister Vorster moved to establish an even more powerful secret police apparatus in charge of overall political repression and of coordinating the activities of the Security Branch, Military Intelligence, and other units. In May 1969 this body was officially established as the Bureau of State Security (BOSS), with Gen. H. J. van den Bergh, a former Nazi sympathizer, as its first head. Through infiltration, informers, electronic surveillance, and other means, BOSS collected

20. *Political Imprisonment in South Africa,* p. 99.

information on groups or individuals, both within South Africa and abroad, thought to be a present or potential threat to the regime. It worked in close collaboration with intelligence services in several other countries and had an agreement with the American Central Intelligence Agency for an exchange of information. BOSS is also suspected of having conducted a number of kidnappings of South Africans living abroad, as well as several assassinations.[21] In 1978, BOSS was renamed the Department of National Security.

Besides the regular activities of the police and the intelligence services, which help protect the apartheid system on a daily basis, Pretoria has developed an extensive military and paramilitary strength capable of assisting the police forces when necessary. The regular army had 38,000 troops in 1975-76, the overwhelming majority of whom were white. There is a Cape Coloured Corps, composed exclusively of Coloureds. A few hundred Africans have been recruited as well, with the aim of setting up a similar segregated unit. In addition, there is an active reserve, called the Citizen Force, of 138,000 white troops.

Much of Pretoria's conventional military might is designed for the maintenance of internal "order." As early as 1961, Minister of Defence J. J. Fouché stressed that "our armed forces have to be prepared to combat internal subversion as well as outside aggression."[22] In March 1975 the Ministry of Defence revealed that it was planning to reorganize the army to include both a conventional force and a counterinsurgency force. At least five special "antiterrorist" training camps have been established and both land and air troops have conducted mock counterinsurgency operations in the northern Transvaal.

In addition to the regular troops is a 90,000-member paramilitary commando force, composed of armed civilians organized into battalion-type units that are responsible for patrolling local urban and rural areas in times of unrest. There are several squadrons of air commando units, made up of private pilots and planes.

Altogether, it is estimated that Pretoria is capable of fielding a military force of 200,000 whites within about ninety days. Military expenditure is the largest item in the government budget. It increased by 250 percent from 1973 to 1978.

21. *BOSS,* pp. 11, 22, 29, 32, 36.
22. Pierre van den Berghe, *South Africa,* p. 137.

A large part of Pretoria's military budget, in some years as much as two-thirds, has been used to purchase major weapons systems from abroad. The arms flowed easily into South Africa. The "voluntary" United Nations-sponsored arms embargo in effect against South Africa since 1963 and the "mandatory" embargo imposed in November 1977 did little to impede the flow.

With access to the world's arms trade, the South African regime has been able to build up one of the most powerful armed forces on the African continent. The South African military now has in service well over a thousand aircraft, more than five hundred tanks, more than a thousand armored cars, nearly a thousand armored personnel carriers, and numerous medium and heavy artillery pieces. Although some of the equipment is old or refurbished British and American hardware dating from before the 1963 UN arms embargo, a large portion was obtained *after 1963*.

The French government and industry were the most open in their violations of the 1963 arms embargo, directly providing tanks, jet fighters, helicopters, armored cars, and other equipment. International protests against this blatant trade were ignored. It was only after the "mandatory" embargo was imposed in 1977 that the French even bothered to claim that they would no longer sell arms to South Africa.

Because of the openness of the French arms trade with South Africa, it was widely thought that Paris had served as Pretoria's main foreign quartermaster. But both the United States and Britain have played equally important roles as South African arms sources, with countries such as Italy, Portugal, Switzerland, and Canada filling the gaps (see chart, pp. 142-43).

Washington was especially adamant in its claims that it was abiding by the embargo. Because of the political embarrassment that revelation of American arms sales to South Africa would cause, hardly any of the weapons systems (as far as is known) were sold directly by American corporations. The favored method was to have the American arms manufactured under license by foreign companies, who then sold them to South Africa. No known attempt has been made by the American government to stop this arms traffic. And government officials still maintain that they know nothing about it. But given the extent of American intelligence surveillance of world arms traffic, that is difficult to believe. In fact, in February 1978 Donald McHenry, then the U.S. deputy representative to the United Nations, revealed that the Ford administration had consciously *relaxed*

Foreign Weapons Systems in Service with South African Armed Forces (as of 1976)

Item	Country of Manufacture or License	Number Delivered
Lockheed F-104G Starfighter fighter-bomber	U.S./W. Germany	40
North American F-51D Cavalier counterinsurgency strike aircraft	U.S.	50
Agusta-Bell 205A Iroquois helicopter	U.S.	25
M-47 Patton main battle tank	U.S./Italy	100
M-41 Walker Bulldog light tank	U.S.	100
Lockheed P-2 Neptune antisubmarine patrol boat	U.S.	12
M-7 105mm self-propelled artillery gun	U.S.	200
M-109 155mm self-propelled artillery gun	U.S./Italy	(50)
T-17 E1 Staghound armored car	U.S.	450
M-3A1 White armored personnel carrier	U.S.	400
Commando V-150 armored personnel carrier	U.S./Portugal	(300)
M-113A1 armored personnel carrier	U.S./Italy	(400)
Mirage III fighter-bomber	France	95+
Mirage F-1 jet fighter	France	48+
Aerospatiale Alouette III armed attack helicopter	France	115+
Aerospatiale/Westland 330 Puma assault helicopter	France/Britain	40+
Aerospatiale/Westland 341 Gazelle helicopter	France/Britain	2 ?

AMC-13 light tank	France	80
Centurion Mk 7 heavy tank	Britain	150
Centurion Mk 10 heavy tank	Britain	240
Daimler Ferret Mk 2 scout car/ anti-tank armored car	Britain	450
Saracen FV603 and FV610 armored personnel carrier	Britain	700
Short SB 301 armored personnel carrier	Britain	(300)
Shorland Mk 3 armored car	Britain	(200)
Aermacchi MB-326M Impala I strike/trainer aircraft	SA/Italy	300
Aermacchi MB-326K Impala II	SA/Italy	100
Piranha armored personnel carrier	Switzerland	(100)
Sexton 25 pdr self-propelled artillery gun	Canada	200

Note: Figures in parentheses indicate orders on which deliveries were still continuing as of late 1976.

Source: Sean Gervasi, "Breakdown of the United States Arms Embargo," in *U.S. Military Involvement in Southern Africa*, pp. 144, 146.

the official American arms embargo against South Africa at the very time when Pretoria was suppressing the 1976 youth uprisings. "We were making changes in our arms embargo," he said, "being more lenient with South Africa, while 600 children were being killed in Soweto."[23]

Besides the clandestine funneling of American arms to Pretoria by indirect means, American companies openly sold some equipment—with Washington's official approval—on the grounds that it was not for military use. This included "dual purpose" aircraft, such as "civilian" Bell helicopters, Lockheed L-100 and Starlifter C-141 transport planes, twin-engine Lear jets, and small Piper and Cessna aircraft. The helicopters, however, are capable of police and military service, the transport planes have been used by the air force to ferry troops and military supplies, and small aircraft like the Cessnas find their way into Pretoria's air commando squadrons. *Paratus,* a South African military journal, commented that "without these aircraft, the helicopter, Cessna and Dakota, problems of supplies and communications would be insurmountable."[24]

In addition, between 1967 and 1972, more than $22 million worth of American communications equipment, including radar and electronic search-and-detection equipment, was exported openly to South Africa. At least four IBM computers were supplied directly to the South African Department of Defence.

In November 1977, the international outcry over the killing of Steve Biko and the banning of the major Black Consciousness organizations compelled Pretoria's Western allies to formally approve the adoption of a new, supposedly more stringent, arms embargo. Although it was presented as a "mandatory" embargo, no provision was made for enforcement, nor even for systematic monitoring of the arms flow into South Africa; compliance rests entirely on whether the member governments of the United Nations choose to obey the embargo.

Less than six weeks after the UN resolution was adopted, the Carter administration approved the sale of six Cessna reconnaissance planes to South Africa, and in March 1978 gave the go-ahead for the sale of seventy to eighty additional light aircraft,

23. *U.S. Military Involvement in Southern Africa,* p. 135.

24. Jennifer Davis, "The U.S. Role in South Africa's Military Build-up," testimony presented before the U.S. Senate Foreign Relations Committee, July 24, 1975 (New York: Africa Fund, 1975), p. 5.

including Pipers and Cessnas. J. F. Clarke, the IBM general manager in South Africa, declared that his company would continue to provide maintenance service for the computers being used by the military and police.[25]

One indication of Pretoria's continued ability to purchase arms abroad came through an analysis of South Africa's 1978 trade statistics. According to Howard Peerce, a South African financial editor, "South Africa is still spending more than R300-million a year on arms imports in spite of the widespread restrictions on sales of military equipment to this country."[26]

The loopholes in the arms embargo and the continuing clandestine arms sales to South Africa notwithstanding, the UN measure does make it more difficult for Pretoria's allies to supply it with large quantities of sophisticated weaponry. However, this is less of a problem today than it would have been in the 1960s. With Western help, Pretoria has managed to build up its own extensive arms industry, now manufacturing within South Africa much of the equipment it previously had to import.

The establishment in 1968 of the Armaments Development and Manufacturing Corporation (Armscor) stimulated domestic production of a growing variety of weapons, including rifles, submachineguns, more than a hundred kinds of ammunition, explosives, cannons, armored vehicles, electronic equipment, aircraft, and missiles. Some of these arms are produced under foreign license, such as the French-designed Panhard and Levasseur armored cars, of which Pretoria has built more than a thousand, and the French F-1 Mirage fighter planes. Others involved foreign financing or technology, such as the joint French–South African scheme to develop the Cactus ground-to-air missile system. It was two West German companies that originally helped initiate Pretoria's missile industry, through construction of a missile base near Tsumeb, Namibia, in the early 1960s; in 1964 it was revealed that the project was directly financed by the West German Defense Ministry.

The development of the South African nuclear industry—and with it Pretoria's ability to produce nuclear weapons—is another area where foreign assistance was vital. Shortly after the South African Atomic Energy Board was set up in 1949, the U.S. Atomic Energy Commission opened its facilities to South African

25. *Southern Africa* (New York), May 1978.

26. *Rand Daily Mail* (Johannesburg), December 18, 1978.

engineers and nuclear scientists. In 1957, Washington and Pretoria signed a fifty-year bilateral nuclear energy cooperation agreement. The Allis-Chalmers Corporation provided a research reactor to South Africa in 1961 at a cost of $450 million. Following the imposition of the 1977 arms embargo, the Carter administration specifically rejected demands for a break in all American nuclear collaboration with South Africa, although the political climate did compel it to make a limited gesture by halting shipment of enriched uranium fuel.

In 1970, Prime Minister John Vorster announced that the regime had developed its "own" uranium enrichment process, and five years later, in April 1975, the first pilot enrichment plant went into operation at Valindaba, near Pretoria. Documents taken from the South African embassy in Bonn later revealed that the enrichment process had been developed with the assistance of Dr. Erwin Becker of the West German Steinkohlen Eliktrizität AG (STEAG), a state-controlled company, and in collaboration with high West German military officials.

The military potential of South Africa's nuclear industry was so central to Pretoria's plans that in August 1965 Prime Minister Verwoerd had to remind South African officials that it *also* had an economic value. Speaking at the inauguration of the country's first reactor, he said, "It is the duty of South Africa not only to consider the military uses of the material, but also to direct its uses to peaceful purposes."[27] Shortly after India exploded a nuclear device in 1974, Louw Alberts, the vice-chairman of the Atomic Energy Board, remarked that "our nuclear program is more advanced than that of India."[28]

That boast may have become a reality on September 22, 1979. At 3:00 a.m. that day an American nuclear detection satellite recorded two bursts of intense light originating in an area of the Indian Ocean and South Atlantic around South Africa. The flashes, a short one immediately followed by a longer burst, are an unmistakeable sign of a nuclear explosion. Scientists in New Zealand later picked up traces of radioactive material. Pretoria refused to take official responsibility for the blast, but the evidence was incriminating.

South Africa not only has the economic and technological capacity to produce nuclear weapons, but the bombers and

27. Alex La Guma, ed., *Apartheid,* p. 127.

28. *Africa* (London), November 1975.

missile systems required to deliver nuclear warheads to their targets. While nuclear weapons would be worthless in face of domestic political upheavals, Pretoria's *capability* of "going nuclear" (whether or not it actually does so publicly) gives it greater leverage in its dealings with other states. In the event of a serious conflict beyond South Africa's borders, nuclear weapons could serve as a direct threat to the populations of other African countries.

11

The Gendarme of Southern Africa

At a military ceremony in Langelbaanweg, north of Cape Town, in late 1978, South African Air Force Chief Lt. Gen. R.R.D. Rogers told his listeners that a strong military force was more than ever necessary, "not only to defend the fatherland but to establish stability in Southern Africa and to establish ourselves as guardians of peace and freedom in this subcontinent."[1]

The demagogy about "peace and freedom" aside, Rogers was simply reaffirming Pretoria's wider role as an imperialist policeman for all of southern Africa. While its acquisition of a sophisticated and bristling arsenal is most immediately aimed at upholding capitalism and white colonial-settler rule within South Africa itself, its substantial economic and political interests beyond South Africa's borders propel it to function as a regional gendarme, a guardian of "stability" in Namibia, in Zimbabwe, in Angola, or in any other country within its reach. The rulers of South Africa are aware that events in the rest of southern Africa soon reverberate directly or indirectly at home, that any advance of the Black liberation struggle, anywhere in the region, tends to loosen their own hold on power.

So with the backing and close collaboration of their allies in North America and Europe, the authorities in Pretoria have sought to meet aggressively such challenges to white supremacy, however far-flung, employing whatever means necessary: economic inducement and pressure, diplomatic overture, or military force.

Pretoria's concern over the impact of events in the rest of

1. *Argus* (Cape Town), November 30, 1978.

Africa dates back to the earliest days of the anticolonial struggle. It was evident in the public pronouncements of government officials and in such acts as the sending of tear gas to Northern Rhodesia (now Zambia) in 1935 to help the British colonialists there put down a strike by African workers in the copper mines. "South Africa's aim," Prime Minister Malan commented in 1951, "is to take responsibility, in so far as agreement can be reached with other countries, for territories to the north of South Africa. We want to help in the protection of our neighbours."[2] But so long as the bulk of Africa continued to lie under direct colonial rule, the South African regime remained more or less content to let the European colonial powers police their own empires.

It was not until many African countries began to attain their formal political independence in the late 1950s and early 1960s that Pretoria adopted a more active foreign policy toward the continent. To an extent, this involved diplomatic overtures to the newly emergent states, in the hopes of eliciting friendly responses from some of the Black neocolonial rulers. South African Foreign Minister Eric Louw explained at the time that the overall goal of such overtures was "to maintain a white civilization at this southern end of the African continent."[3] But at a time of heightened political militancy among Blacks throughout Africa, especially in the wake of the March 1960 Sharpeville massacre, these diplomatic bids withered in the face of widespread Black hostility and boycott campaigns.

As the real drive of the anticolonial struggle built up momentum in the 1960s, the more openly aggressive side of Pretoria's policy came to the fore in a series of military interventions designed to stem the tide of radical change as far from South Africa's borders as possible.

The first major battlefield lay in the former Belgian Congo (now called Zaïre). Geographically one of the largest African countries, strategically straddling the center of the continent, laden with considerable mineral wealth, the Congo had gained its independence in June 1960 under the leadership of Patrice

2. James Barber, *South Africa's Foreign Policy, 1945-1970*, p. 82.

3. Eric H. Louw, *Die toenemende belangrikheid van Afrika op die internasionale terrein en samehangende daarme die Unie se belange in Afrika, meer bepaald in Afrika Suid van die Sahara* [The growing importance of Africa in the international sphere, and as a corollary the Union's interests in Africa, in particular in Africa south of the Sahara], New Series No. 3 (Pretoria: Universiteit van Pretoria, 1957), p. 14.

Lumumba, the most outstanding of the Congolese nationalist leaders. Fearing that Lumumba could become "another Castro," the American CIA laid plans for his overthrow and assassination (he was eventually killed in February 1961). Meanwhile, the South Africans established close ties with the reactionary Moïse Tshombe, and helped recruit South African mercenaries to fight alongside him. In the mid-1960s, after the pro-American Mobutu Sese Seko was brought to power, Pretoria cooperated closely in the CIA's efforts to crush a massive peasant rebellion in the eastern Congo. According to John Stockwell, who supervised the CIA intervention in Angola in 1975-76 and who had previously been based in Zaïre, "the South Africans had facilitated the agency's development of a mercenary army to suppress the Congo rebellion."[4]

Pretoria's still-limited experience in covert intervention was broadened a few years later in a different sort of conflict—the civil war in Nigeria. The secession of Biafra in 1967 and the consequent war, which threw Africa's most populous country into two-and-a-half years of turmoil and devastation, provided Pretoria with an irresistable opportunity to play the role of spoiler. With the aim of weakening Nigeria—a large financial contributor, through the Organization of African Unity, to southern African liberation movements—the apartheid regime quietly provided the Biafran forces with aircraft, pilots, and supplies, and allowed South African-based mercenaries to offer Biafra their services.[5] This episode was brought to an abrupt close in 1970 with the collapse of Biafra, but by then the civil war had already claimed many thousands of lives on both sides.

From the early 1960s, Pretoria had forged close military and intelligence ties with the Portuguese colonialists in Mozambique and Angola and with the Rhodesian settler regime. Whatever frictions existed with the Portuguese and whatever doubts Pretoria had about Ian Smith's 1965 unilateral declaration of independence from Britain, the South Africans nevertheless saw them as valuable buffer states that could hamper the tide of national liberation that was sweeping southward.

Some of these countries were also valuable outlets for South African investment. Between 1963 and 1970, South African

4. John Stockwell, *In Search of Enemies*, pp. 187-88.

5. John de St. Jorre, *The Brothers' War: Biafra and Nigeria* (Boston: Houghton Mifflin Company, 1972), pp. 219, 315, 325; *Elsevier's Magazine* (Amsterdam), August 1979.

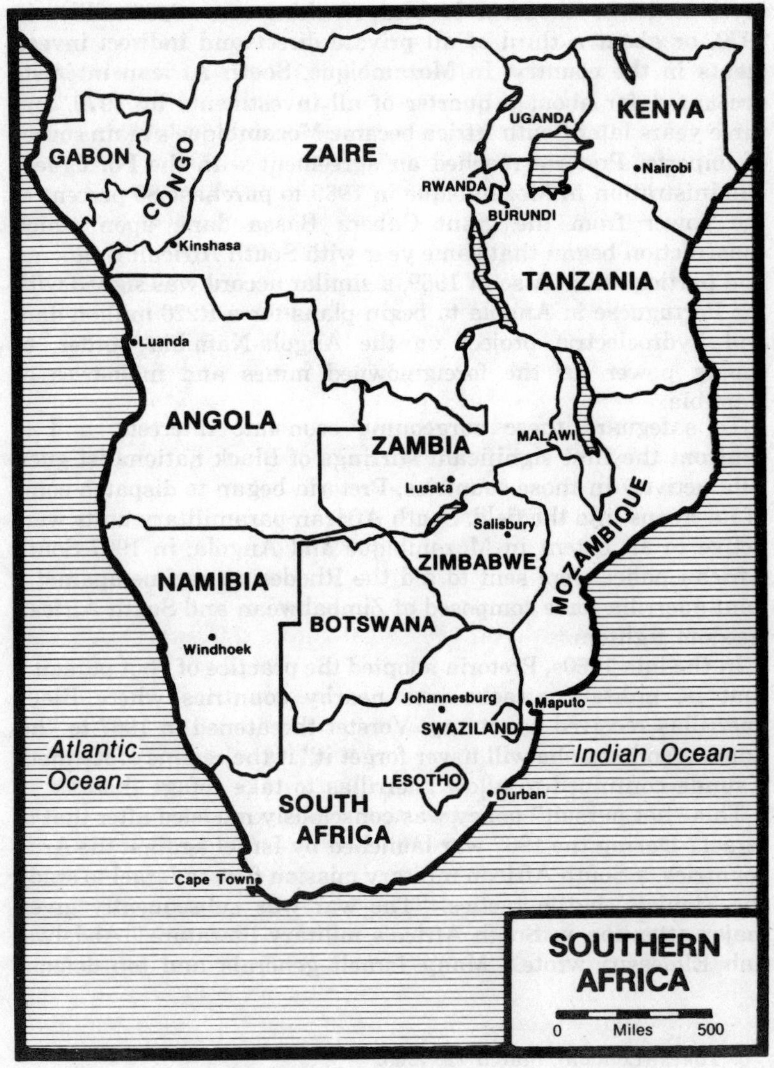
GABON
CONGO
ZAIRE
UGANDA
KENYA
Nairobi
RWANDA
BURUNDI
Kinshasa
TANZANIA
Luanda
ANGOLA
ZAMBIA
MALAWI
Lusaka
Salisbury
ZIMBABWE
MOZAMBIQUE
NAMIBIA
BOTSWANA
Windhoek
Johannesburg
Maputo
SWAZILAND
Atlantic Ocean
Indian Ocean
LESOTHO
Durban
SOUTH AFRICA
Cape Town
SOUTHERN AFRICA
0 Miles 500

investments in Rhodesia doubled, reaching some $480 million in 1970, or about a third of all private direct and indirect investments in the country. In Mozambique, South African interests accounted for about a quarter of all investments by 1970, and three years later South Africa became Mozambique's main source of imports. Pretoria reached an agreement with the Portuguese administration in Mozambique in 1969 to purchase 80 percent of the power from the giant Cabora Bassa dam, upon which construction began that same year with South African financing and participation. Also in 1969, a similar accord was signed with the Portuguese in Angola to begin plans for a R220 million dam and hydroelectric project on the Angola-Namibia border, to supply power for the foreign-owned mines and industries of Namibia.

To safeguard these burgeoning economic interests, and to confront the first significant stirrings of Black nationalist guerrilla activity in those countries, Pretoria began to dispatch some of its troops into the field. South African paramilitary units were active to an extent in Mozambique and Angola; in 1967 South African police were sent to aid the Rhodesian regime against a joint guerrilla force composed of Zimbabwean and South African freedom fighters.

In the late 1960s, Pretoria adopted the practice of "hot pursuit," that is, military attacks into nearby countries where Black guerrillas received sanctuary. Vorster threatened in 1967 to "hit Zambia so hard she will never forget it" if the regime of Kenneth Kaunda continued to allow guerrillas to take refuge there.[6]

This "hot pursuit" policy was consciously modeled after that of Israel.[7] During the 1967 war launched by Israel against the Arab countries, a South African military mission flew to Israel to study the Zionists' battle tactics. "The war was subsequently given major attention in South Africa's military literature," Abdelwahab Elmessiri wrote. "Many Israeli generals and top defense

6. *Times* (London), March 12, 1968.

7. Since Israel, like South Africa, is a colonial-settler state, the two regimes have long had a strong affinity toward each other. Louis Botha and Jan Christian Smuts maintained close relations with the early Zionist movement and Prime Minister Malan was the first foreign head of state to visit Israel. Many South African volunteers fought on the side of Israel in the Middle East wars of 1948, 1956, 1967, and 1973. Since the early 1970s, investment, trade, technical, military, and political ties between the two countries have been increasing rapidly.

officials, such as General Mordechai Hod, Commander of the Israeli Air Force, and Defense Minister Shimon Peres visited Pretoria."[8]

The South Africans carried a few minor attacks into Zambia in 1967 and 1968, largely as warnings to the Kaunda regime. And challenged by the first outbreaks of Namibian guerrilla activity, Pretoria also staged regular helicopter patrols over southern Angola, where some of the Namibians had set up guerrilla bases.

Nevertheless, the South Africans realized that military bluster alone was insufficient for advancing and protecting their interests. In particular, trade with Black-run states had suffered considerably and would continue to suffer so long as the apartheid regime remained isolated on the diplomatic level. So with an eye toward breaching the virtually solid front of rejection that Pretoria met throughout the continent, Vorster launched his "outward" policy, directed at establishing open—and covert—political and economic ties with some of the Black regimes.

On the African side, a few states, especially the regime of Félix Houphouët-Boigny of the Ivory Coast, responded favorably to Pretoria's overtures, under the guise of engaging in a "dialogue" with it. However, Pretoria was rebuffed by most states, and a 1971 summit conference of the Organization of African Unity adopted a resolution that spurned "any dialogue with the minority regime of South Africa which is not designed solely to obtain for the enslaved people of South Africa their legitimate and inherent rights. . . ."[9]

Despite this setback, the South Africans took advantage of the opening provided by Houphouët-Boigny and a few other African rulers to expand their investments and trade. Between 1970 and 1978, South African trade with other African countries rose from R264 million to R539 million.

One of the African states in which the South African stake had grown significantly was Malawi. From a negligible beginning at the time of Malawi's independence in 1964, South Africa soon became one of the country's major suppliers; a formal trade pact was signed in 1967. A South African military attaché was posted to Malawi that same year. President Hastings Kamuzu Banda appointed South Africans to run the National Malawi Airways,

8. Richard P. Stevens and Abdelwahab M. Elmessiri, *Israel and South Africa*, p. 78.

9. Colin Legum, ed., *Africa Contemporary Record, 1971-72*, p. C3.

the Board of Censors, and the Department of Information.

Lesotho, which is completely surrounded by South African territory, has long been under Pretoria's economic and political influence. This was reaffirmed in 1970, when Chief Leabua Jonathan, after having been voted out of office in elections that year, forcibly seized power, relying on the South African-trained Police Mobile Unit.

In recognition of the valuable role Pretoria was playing in defense of imperialist interests in southern Africa, Washington and some of the Western European powers provided greater assistance to Pretoria and coordinated their own activities more closely with the South Africans.

A tightening of the partnership between Pretoria and Washington ensued. In April 1969, President Nixon ordered his national security adviser, Henry Kissinger, to draw up a secret policy study of southern Africa, entitled National Security Study Memorandum 39. Based on Kissinger's recommendations, Nixon adopted Option 2 of the secret study—nicknamed "Tar Baby" by White House advisers—tilting Washington toward more open support for the white minority regimes. Among the several policy steps suggested by Kissinger under this option were:

—Enforce arms embargo against South Africa but with liberal treatment of equipment which could serve either military or civilian purposes. . . .

—Retain tracking stations in South Africa as required.

—Remove constraints on EXIM Bank facilities for South Africa; actively encourage US exports and facilitate US investment consistent with the Foreign Direct Investment Program.

—Conduct selected exchange programs with South Africa in all categories, including military.

—Without changing the US legal position that South African occupancy of South West Africa is illegal, we should play down the issue and encourage accommodation between South Africa and the UN.[10]

In practice, this policy meant greater American investment and trade ties, and an increase in open sales of aircraft that could be used for military purposes. More quietly, other American arms found their way into Pretoria's stockpiles.

In concert with the Nixon administration, the North Atlantic Treaty Organization (NATO) as a whole moved toward more direct collaboration with Pretoria. In November 1972, NATO initiated contingency planning for the South Atlantic, ostensibly

10. *The Kissinger Study of Southern Africa*, pp. 67-68.

to protect Europe's shipping lanes. One NATO official stated that the planning was designed to make it possible "to go to the aid of our potential allies in southern Africa if the need should arise."[11]

The April 1974 coup in Portugal that brought down the Caetano dictatorship and undermined Lisbon's African empire provided a new impetus to the African liberation struggle—and to expansion of the network of collaborative alliances being woven among Washington, Pretoria, Bonn, Paris, London, and other powers.

A month after the coup, Adm. Hugo H. Biermann, commander in chief of the South African military, visited Washington, where he met Gen. Thomas H. Moorer, chairman of the Joint Chiefs of Staff, and other American military officials. By the end of the year, the NATO contingency planning had been completed, and a South African journalist reported from a meeting of NATO defense ministers that "the defence of the Cape sea-route is 'well covered' in a contingency plan, and that South Africa would receive naval assistance if the oil route was threatened."[12]

Another signpost of more direct NATO involvement in South Africa is Silvermine, located at the foot of Cape Town's Table Mountain. From the outside, Silvermine looks relatively inconspicuous, with only a few buildings and antennas jutting out. But built into the mountain is a highly sophisticated and far-ranging communications network, with a surveillance radius of some five thousand miles. Using aerial reconnaissance, radio monitoring, and other sources of information, the computerized center can plot the course, size, armament, number of personnel, and other characteristics of virtually any ship or plane within that radius. South African officials have used NATO computers to calculate the types and quantities of spare parts needed for Silvermine's maintenance and have used NATO purchasing codes to buy equipment from such countries as Denmark and the Netherlands, which have publicly refused to sell arms to Pretoria. Silvermine's surveillance system is hooked up to outlets in Britain, the United States, and NATO headquarters in Brussels.

The 1974 coup in Portugal had toppled one of Pretoria's closest allies and threatened to strip away the buffer states of Angola and Mozambique. So in a calculated bid to soften or stave off the impact that this sudden change would have on the apartheid

11. New York *Post*, May 10, 1974.

12. *Star Weekly* (Johannesburg), December 14, 1974.

regime's own position, Vorster resurrected the old "outward" policy under a new name: "détente."

Little-publicized meetings were held between Vorster and presidents Houphouët-Boigny of the Ivory Coast, Léopold Sédar Senghor of Senegal, and William Tolbert of Liberia. Lower-level contacts were established with Mobutu Sese Seko of Zaïre, James Mancham of the Seychelles, and Jean-Bedel Bokassa of the Central African Republic. In late 1974, Vorster and Zambian President Kaunda sent diplomatic feelers out to each other, both publicly calling for an end to the armed conflict in Zimbabwe through a negotiated settlement. Vorster applied some pressure on Rhodesian Prime Minister Ian Smith to compromise, while Kaunda temporarily turned the screws on the more militant wings of the Zimbabwean nationalist groups. But despite ensuing negotiations, the pace of the Zimbabwe struggle was beyond either Vorster's or Kaunda's control, and the fighting soon resumed.

Mozambique presented a somewhat different case. Concerned about the apparent militancy of the victorious Frelimo (Frente de Libertação de Moçambique—Mozambique Liberation Front), Vorster sought to use Mozambique's severe economic difficulties and dependency on South Africa to try to keep the new rulers from doing anything rash. Economic inducements were offered to that end, including the routing of South African trade through Mozambican ports (from which Mozambique received higher transport fares and customs duties) and the direct payment in gold bullion to the Mozambican government of part of the wages of Mozambican miners working in South Africa (which could then be sold at a higher price on the world market). In November 1974, shortly after Lisbon agreed to grant Mozambique its independence, Vorster stated, "The question has been asked whether Mozambique could possibly be used as a launching pad for people wanting to sabotage South Africa. In this regard, I have asked for and received assurances from Mozambique."[13] But Pretoria's continued ill-disguised hostility toward the Frelimo regime betrayed a certain lack of confidence in any such assurances.

Behind these South African bids to various Black states lay Pretoria's ever-present trump card: the specter of direct military intervention. While introducing the military budget in March 1975, Minister of Finance Owen Horwood affirmed, "Although

13. John de St. Jorre, *A House Divided*, p. 68.

the government hope to achieve *detente* with black Africa, until it is achieved it is imperative to enable the defence forces to defend the republic's borders effectively."[14] President Nicholaas Diederichs later added, "Our policy of détente and the maintenance of a strong national defense are complimentary and in no way contradictory."[15]

Just what the South African authorities meant was spelled out by the South African military invasion of Angola. Both in its scope and character, the intervention of the regular South African armed forces into Angola was unprecedented.

The South African aggression developed in two stages. The first, preliminary stage started in August 1975, when troops occupied the construction sites of the Calueque hydroelectric station on the Cunene River in southern Angola (part of the South African-financed Cunene power project) and carried out attacks against the Angola guerrilla bases of the South West Africa People's Organisation (SWAPO), the main Namibian nationalist group. The second stage began in October, when several thousand additional South African troops flooded in to take direct part in the Angolan civil war against the MPLA (Movimento Popular de Libertação de Angola—People's Movement for the Liberation of Angola). South African mechanized units linked up with the FNLA (Frente Nacional de Libertação de Angola—Angolan National Liberation Front) and the UNITA (União Nacional para Independência Total de Angola—National Union for the Total Independence of Angola). Within just three weeks the South African-FNLA-UNITA alliance captured about twenty cities and towns in central and southern Angola and drove precariously close to Luanda, the MPLA's strongest base.

Pretoria had reason enough for intervening. The Angolan independence struggle and the mobilizations of the Angolan workers and peasants potentially threatened South African and other imperialist interests in the country. "The R100m already invested in the Cunene hydroelectric scheme is at stake," the Johannesburg *Financial Mail* warned, "as well as exports that last year [1974] approached R44m, and substantial investments in mining."[16] Although the MPLA made repeated overtures and

14. *Africa* (London), October 1975.

15. *Le Monde* (Paris), January 25-26, 1976.

16. *Financial Mail* (Johannesburg), October 31, 1975.

conciliatory gestures to foreign investors, Pretoria did not trust the organization, preferring the blatantly proimperialist FNLA and UNITA (which also happened to be backed by two of Pretoria's closest "détente" partners, Mobutu of Zaïre and Kaunda of Zambia). Pretoria was likewise concerned that the MPLA would provide increased assistance to the Namibian freedom fighters; by invading Angola, the South Africans could thereby strike a blow at the Namibian independence struggle as well.

Perhaps the most persuasive element in the South African decision to go into Angola on such a large scale was the encouragement Pretoria received from Washington, which at that time was sharply stepping up its own intervention against the MPLA. The American government continues to publicly deny any role in the South African invasion, but in April 1978 South African Defence Minister Pieter Botha (soon to become prime minister) declared before parliament that Washington had urged the South Africans to intervene and that American planes had even flown supplies into South African-held bases in southern Angola. "I was there myself," he said, "and I saw how the arms were offloaded."[17]

Confirmation of this direct collaboration also came from John Stockwell, who directed the CIA operations in Angola during that period. "To the CIA," Stockwell later revealed, "the South Africans were the ideal solution for central Angola." The CIA transferred arms to South African planes in Zaïre, for shipment into central Angola. CIA officials met regularly with BOSS agents in Kinshasa, Zaïre. On at least two occasions a top BOSS official visited Washington and secretly met with the chief of the CIA's Africa Division; on another occasion he met with the CIA station chief in Paris. "Thus, without any memos being written at CIA headquarters saying 'Let's coordinate with the South Africans,' coordination was effected at all CIA levels and the South Africans escalated their involvement in step with our own."[18]

However, both Washington and Pretoria ran up against an unexpected contender in the war: the revolutionary government of Cuba. In response to the American-South African aggression against Angola, Fidel Castro had quickly answered an MPLA plea for help by sending thousands of Cuban troops. The Cuban-

17. *Star Weekly* (Johannesburg), April 22, 1978.

18. Stockwell, *In Search of Enemies*, pp. 187-88.

MPLA forces were successful in checking the South African advance by mid-November, and a month later started to turn the tide back.[19]

This bold and decisive Cuban move immediately forced Washington and Pretoria to choose between withdrawing or sharply escalating their intervention. The widespread antiwar sentiment in the United States made the latter choice politically unfeasible for the White House, and it was forced to pull back. The South Africans, complaining that Washington had "left us in the lurch" (Botha's words),[20] had little option but to do likewise. Their troops were withdrawn from the frontlines in central Angola in January 1976, and the last of them formally left Angola in late March. This pullback revealed that Pretoria was still basically dependent on Western backing for any large-scale or long-term military operations beyond its borders.

The disastrous outcome of the Angola invasion was a severe political setback to the apartheid regime. It shattered the myth of white invincibility, compelled Pretoria's détente partners to be much more circumspect in their dealings with it, injected a sudden dose of adrenalin into the veins of the Namibian and Zimbabwean freedom fighters, and fired the imaginations of Black youths in South Africa's townships. The image of well-armed white South Africans retreating before Black and Latino troops did much to hasten the coming explosion in South Africa.

The apartheid authorities had been painfully stung by Angola, but they could not afford to back down from their aggressive stance. To do so would have been political suicide. Their only real option, as they saw it, was to continue along the same path, perhaps with a few tactical detours.

Even while pulling back from Angola, the officials in Pretoria were publicly promising even bigger engagements in the future. "In the past we hit back with small forces," Botha stated in January 1976. "If necessary, we will retaliate with greater force."[21]

Two days after Botha spoke, the Defence Amendment Bill was introduced, authorizing the government to use troops for the

19. Nelson P. Valdés, "Revolutionary Solidarity in Angola," in Cole Blasier and Carmelo Mesa-Lago, eds., *Cuba in the World* (Pittsburgh: University of Pittsburgh Press, 1979), pp. 87-113.

20. *Star Weekly* (Johannesburg), April 22, 1978.

21. *New York Times*, January 27, 1976.

"prevention, or suppression of any armed conflict outside the Republic which, in the opinion of the State President is, or may be, a threat to the security of the Republic." The sphere of South African military operations, according to the act, was extended to the equator, covering Namibia, Zaïre, Tanzania, Zambia, Angola, Mozambique, Zimbabwe, Malawi, Lesotho, Swaziland, and Botswana. When the act was finally passed, its provisions were made retroactive to August 9, 1975, thus sanctioning (in terms of South African law) the intervention in Angola.[22]

As part of the groundwork for further interventions, Pretoria continued to beef up its ground forces and air-strike capabilities. A site near Hoedspruit was selected for a new airbase; located in the eastern Transvaal, it is within easy striking distance of both Mozambique and Zimbabwe.

Relations were maintained—and in some cases strengthened—with several Black regimes, all with as little publicity as possible. With Zaïre beset by serious economic difficulties in the wake of the Angolan war, Pretoria acted to help prop up the Mobutu regime, providing an outlet for Zaïrian copper exports and shipping food and fuel to Zaïre. South African exports reached R40 million in 1976 alone. The following year, when Mobutu faced a serious uprising in the mineral-rich province of Shaba, a top BOSS official flew to Kinshasa to meet with Mobutu and arrange for the provision of even more South African fuel and funds.[23]

The apartheid regime's biggest headache remained in southern Africa, however, just beyond its borders. Zimbabwe and Namibia were the main flashpoints.

Despite all the efforts by Washington, London, and Pretoria to "settle" the Zimbabwean conflict, the pendulum continued to swing increasingly in favor of the liberation movements, a process that made the installation of a new regime acceptable to Pretoria that much more difficult. In an effort to break out of the impasse, Smith agreed to bring some Black figures into the government, with Bishop Abel Muzorewa becoming prime minister in 1979.

As the struggle on the ground sharpened, the major imperialist powers increasingly looked toward the Muzorewa-Smith forces as

22. Muriel Horrell et al., *Survey of Race Relations in South Africa, 1976*, p. 37.

23. *Financial Mail* (Johannesburg), April 8, 1977; *Washington Post*, April 9, 1977.

their most reliable bulwark against the Zimbabwean revolution. While pressuring the Patriotic Front to compromise, London, Washington, and Pretoria moved in behind the regime in Salisbury in the hope that it could serve as a counter to the insurgent forces. During the negotiations in London in late 1979, which resulted in the temporary resumption of direct British rule over Zimbabwe, the British government's sympathies for the Salisbury administration were evident. Although an agreement was reached with the Patriotic Front on a new constitution, a ceasefire, and the holding of fresh elections, London and its allies continued to prepare for further war, while seeking to deny the Patriotic Front an electoral victory.

Pretoria in particular was concerned that the Zimbabwean struggle could escape control and threaten "stability." According to Eschel Rhoodie, the former head of the South African Department of Information, Pretoria had given hundreds of thousands of dollars to Muzorewa's party in early 1979 to help him win the April elections.[24] By the end of the year, it was estimated that South Africa was providing 40 percent of the Rhodesian war budget. The bishop thanked his benefactors, stating that he would accept aid even from "the Devil."[25]

Behind the scenes, the "devil" had already started to move in directly. As many as a thousand regular South African troops and police were reported to have taken up positions within Zimbabwe to guard key rail installations. Regular officers of the South African Air Force were piloting helicopters and planes in many of the Rhodesian counterinsurgency operations. South African gunners, technicians, artillery officers, and armored car units were dispatched to bolster Salisbury's war drive. New Mirage jet fighters from South Africa, many piloted by South Africans, appeared in the Rhodesian air force, proving particularly useful in the savage bombing raids into Zambia, Mozambique, and Angola. By late 1979, at least one South African Puma helicopter had been shot down during a raid into Mozambique, and its three-man South African crew killed.[26]

As news of South African military intervention into Zimbabwe began to leak out, Prime Minister Botha admitted for the first

24. *Elsevier's Magazine* (Amsterdam), August 1979.

25. *New York Times*, April 30, 1979.

26. *Washington Post*, December 1, 1979; *Guardian* (London), December 3, 1979; *New York Times*, December 23, 1979.

time on November 30, 1979, that South African military forces were indeed stationed there. A week earlier he had hinted at a massive military intervention into Zimbabwe, stating that Pretoria would not tolerate "chaos" on its borders.[27]

The South African threats and the harassment, intimidation, and repression carried out by the British colonialists and the Rhodesian forces were to little avail. In February 1980, during the first relatively free elections in the country's history, the Black majority of Zimbabwe made its aspirations known. In massive numbers, Blacks lined up at polling stations and cast their ballots for the parties of the Patriotic Front, giving Robert Mugabe's Zimbabwe African National Union (ZANU) an absolute majority in the new parliament and Joshua Nkomo's Zimbabwe African People's Union most of the remaining seats reserved for Africans. It was a stunning setback to the apartheid regime and its imperialist allies and a major victory for the liberation forces. ZANU—the very party that the imperialists most feared—was now able to establish the first independent government of Zimbabwe.

Like the collapse of the Portuguese empire in 1974-75, Zimbabwe's attainment of independence in April 1980 opened a new stage in the southern African liberation struggle. Another bastion of colonialism and white supremacy had fallen. Pretoria was more isolated than ever. The reverberations of the Zimbabwean victory were immediately felt in Soweto, where Black youths joyfully celebrated Mugabe's election.

In Windhoek, the capital of Namibia, Blacks also greeted the results of the Zimbabwean elections. Zimbabwe's independence promised to make it even harder for Pretoria to maintain its hold over the mineral-rich territory.

Even before the breakthrough in Zimbabwe, the problem that the apartheid regime faced in Namibia was a difficult one: how to grant the appearance of independence to its colony (only the most shortsighted sectors of the ruling class were still holding out for indefinite direct South African rule), while safeguarding its lucrative exploitation of Namibia's mineral resources and preventing Namibian independence from having immediate political repercussions on Blacks within South Africa itself. Pretoria's difficulties began with the fact that there was another leading contender in the drama—the South West Africa People's Organisation, which had widespread support among Namibia's more

27. *New York Times*, November 20, 1979.

than one million Blacks and was fighting for more than just a facade of political independence.

Pretoria put little faith in the occasionally conciliatory statements of the SWAPO leaders, and preferred to install a more subservient administration to run Namibia when the time came. This it attempted to do by grooming and building up the Democratic Turnhalle Alliance, a grouping of white settlers and conservative tribal chiefs who favored continued South African domination of the Namibian economy. Pretoria at the same time saw nothing to lose by engaging in long and drawn-out negotiations with SWAPO through the intermediary of the United Nations, on the chance that it might be possible to divert the liberation group from more direct action against South Africa and even entice it into making major concessions.

The apartheid regime had few illusions, however, in the power of talk. It maintained a large and active force of thousands of South African troops in the territory, to harass and detain SWAPO activists, to combat the ever greater flow of guerrillas coming from across the border, and to terrorize the rural inhabitants of the densely populated northern regions, where SWAPO drew extensive support.

Just as the conflict in Namibia had originally been a factor in the South African invasion of Angola, so now Angola remained an element in the Namibian war. To strike out at SWAPO forces based in Angola and to inflict casualties on SWAPO's allies—the MPLA and the Cubans—South African troops and planes staged repeated raids across the border, bombing villages and installations, laying mines, and gunning down Namibian refugees. In one particularly heavy attack, jets and troop-laden helicopters descended on a Namibian refugee camp at Cassinga, 155 miles inside Angola, in May 1978. When they pulled out, they left behind more than six hundred dead refugees. The remnants of UNITA also were useful in Pretoria's war of attrition against Angola. Provided sanctuary and training in Namibia, armed and fed by the South Africans, the UNITA bands likewise struck across the border, attacking MPLA, SWAPO, and Cuban targets and gathering intelligence for Pretoria's own incursions.

As in the Angola war, Pretoria was forced to take into account the continuing—and expanding—role of revolutionary Cuba in southern Africa. Not only were the Cubans still helping to defend Angola from foreign aggression, but they were now using Angola as a base from which to aid SWAPO and other southern African liberation movements. A seminar held in Pretoria in June 1979 under the auspices of the Security Association of South Africa took due note of this development. One speaker, John Barratt of the South African Institute for International Affairs, warned his select audience that the link between the national liberation movements and Cuba "has become very close, especially since the Angolan War, and Cuba is now the major source of training and advisers for these movements in Southern Africa."[28]

In a candid examination of Pretoria's overall "security" predicament in southern Africa, Barratt also drew attention to a particularly vexing facet of the struggles in Zimbabwe, Namibia, Angola, and Mozambique, telling his audience that "we must appreciate that many Blacks in South Africa identify with the liberation movements of Southern Africa."[29]

Like many other apartheid ideologues and administrators, Barratt understood full well that what happened in the forests and cities of Zimbabwe or in the savannahs of Namibia could quickly echo thousands of miles away through the streets of South Africa's own Black townships. The struggles are the same. That is why Pretoria is repeatedly impelled to strike out beyond its borders. That is why the apartheid state is a deadly threat to Blacks throughout the continent.

28. John Barratt, "Political and Strategic Origin of Security Threats to South Africa," paper delivered before a seminar of the Security Association of South Africa, Pretoria, June 27, 1979, p. 8.

29. Ibid., p. 10.

12

Apartheid in Crisis

With an influence that extends thousands of miles beyond its borders, with the biggest industrial base in Africa, with a powerful military machine that has so far withstood all internal opposition, the apartheid regime is seemingly at the peak of its power.

Yet behind this apparent invincibility and omnipotence, apartheid is in deep trouble. The administrators and theorists of white supremacy are themselves aware of that, and are busy seeking "solutions" to the increasingly persistent challenges that face them.

On an international level, South Africa today finds itself in a political environment radically different than before. The world capitalist system, of which South Africa is an integral part, has been considerably weakened over the past decade. It has suffered major political reverses. Washington's defeat in Vietnam, the Ethiopian revolution, the overthrow of the shah of Iran, the growing world role of revolutionary Cuba, the revolution in Nicaragua, the fight for Black rights in the United States, all have left Pretoria more isolated internationally and thus more politically vulnerable at home.

In its own immediate vicinity, the collapse of Portuguese colonialism and the victory in Zimbabwe not only deprived Pretoria of valuable allies, but inspired a resurgence of national liberation struggles throughout southern Africa, challenging South Africa's grip on Namibia and contributing to the resistance in South Africa itself.

In the rest of Africa, the European imperialists had met the challenge of the African independence struggle by altering the forms of domination. They relinquished direct political control to indigenous bourgeois or petty-bourgeois social forces and helped establish neocolonial capitalist states, preserving, and even strengthening, their economic stranglehold over those countries. While a small African elite could bask in the privileges of political power, nepotism, corruption, and economic favors from their former colonial masters, the bulk of the populations—the workers and peasants—were often consigned to an economic and social position little different from before. Hunger, unemployment, poverty, disease, all remained day-to-day realities. Foreign firms continued to exploit cheap African labor and drain off valuable natural resources and profitable dividends. This meant that the African countries lacked the capital to industrialize or even to boost agricultural production enough to match the needs of their populations. Thus, the tide of "decolonization" that swept most of the continent did not end imperialist domination.

The apartheid regime, however, is by its very nature incapable of following a similar course within South Africa. It cannot seek to contain the freedom struggle by granting formal political control to Blacks and still hope to safeguard the class dominance of the white capitalists. Unlike the rest of the continent, the imperialist rulers of South Africa are based within the country itself. The South African bourgeoisie has little margin for any fundamental concessions in its overall policy of white supremacy, because the struggle against national oppression and class exploitation are completely intertwined since South Africa's subjugated Black majority simultaneously forms the bulk of the country's industrial work force. The white ruling class needs direct control of the state apparatus to enforce the extreme degree of exploitation of Blacks upon which South African capitalism rests.

Even if Pretoria wanted to attempt it, there is no Black capitalist class to which it could delegate the trappings of formal political power; South Africa's development as a white-controlled industrial power, with a strong white bourgeoisie, precluded the emergence of such a class (although there are a few individual Black capitalists). Pretoria, therefore, cannot grant the one basic demand around which most other Black grievances revolve: political power.

Conversely, since Blacks cannot attain even formal self-rule in South Africa without challenging the capitalist system on which white supremacy rests, the struggle for Black majority rule, upon its victory, will lead to the dethroning of the white capitalist class *as a class.*

Closely linked to this dilemma facing the apartheid regime is another. The very same industrialization that the white rulers rhapsodize over is also the source of their worst nightmares: It has given birth to a large Black working class, comprising the vast majority of the Black population. Given the nature of South African society, the fight of Black workers against their employers leads inevitably in the direction of political action. It cannot be separated from the broader struggle for majority rule. Black workers have the social strength to lead all the oppressed and exploited forward. They have the potential power to bring the economy to a standstill, overthrow the white supremacist state, and take the reins of society into their own hands.

As elsewhere, capitalism in South Africa is producing its own gravedigger.

Some supporters of apartheid have clearly recognized this. In the words of *Die Burger*, a leading Afrikaans newspaper, "What many people, unfortunately, do not realize . . . is that increasing dependence on Black labour carries its own germs of destruction."[1]

The whole apartheid structure, the entire system of labor control, was devised to help the rulers contain this threat. Basically, it aimed at attaining industrialization without permanent Black urbanization. But the fetters imposed on Blacks have proved less effective than the white employers and authorities originally hoped. Some have snapped and others have been weakened by the growing proletarianization of Blacks. The steady economic deterioration of the Bantustans and the needs of an increasingly capital-intensive economy in the rest of the country placed severe limitations on how far the regime could push ahead with the extension of the migratory labor system, the keystone of its policy of cheap, controlled labor. That in turn made it even more difficult to convince Africans to look to the Bantustans for their political rights. Thus no amount of legislation or police action could hope to seriously stem Black urbanization and prevent Black workers from becoming aware of their class strength.

The rise of the militant Black Consciousness movement in the early 1970s, the repeated strikes by Black workers and their efforts to form unions, and the unprecedented uprisings, demonstrations, and general strikes of 1976 were the clearest reflections of the inherent weakness of the apartheid system and its failure to keep the Black majority in continual subjugation. Especially

1. Ralph Horwitz, *Political Economy of South Africa,* p. 399.

noteworthy were the leading roles played by township youths (who were supposed to have been tranquilized by Bantu Education); the displays of solidarity among Africans, Coloureds, and Indians; the participation of Black workers in explicitly political strikes; and the spread of the political ferment into the Bantustans themselves.

Though the white supremacists had been prepared for the eventuality of renewed Black resistance, the immensity of the uprisings took them by surprise and shook their confidence. By sharply illuminating the cracks in the apartheid edifice, the rebellions also impelled the authorities to initiate some modifications in the white supremacist system with the aim of better containing and deflecting the struggle for Black majority rule. Changes were introduced not to meet Black aspirations, but to protect the basis of South African capitalism.

Clive S. Menell, vice-chairman of the Anglo-Transvaal Consolidated Investment Company, one of the major mining houses, commented, "We became involved [in urging reforms] because we were scared. There was a concern for the country, of course, but there was also a selfish concern for our assets."[2]

Pressure by sectors of the ruling class for minor reforms or even major overhauls of the white supremacist system had been evident for some time. For years, the white "opposition" parties, particularly the United Party and the Progressive Party (now the New Republic Party and the Progressive Federal Party, respectively) had put forward various proposals to modify the administration within the broad framework of white supremacy. In the 1960s, a loose "reformist" tendency emerged within the National Party, calling itself the *verligte* (enlightened) wing, as opposed to the *verkrampte* (narrow-minded or dogmatic) wing that was against any change in apartheid policy.

It was the jarring impact of the Soweto protests, however, that brought new calls for adjustment and reform from the most important ruling-class circles and from the top echelons of the National Party itself.

Jan Marais, a millionaire banker and former head of the South Africa Foundation, a progovernment body, declared shortly after the rebellions, "The separate development concept has got to be redesigned and redefined. . . . We have to find peaceful ways to head off bloodshed." Stressing the need for flexibility, Gerrit Viljoen, the *verligte* chairman of the powerful Afrikaner society

2. *New York Times,* June 10, 1977.

the Broederbond, stated that apartheid "is not an ideology nor a dogma. It is a method, a road along which we are moving."[3]

Prime Minister Vorster initiated a few minor, peripheral changes in the immediate wake of the Soweto rebellions, such as the scrapping of the compulsory use of Afrikaans as a medium of instruction in African high schools, the easing of African home ownership restrictions, a very limited desegregation in sports and public facilities, and the dropping of some of the more offensive racist terms, such as *Bantu,* from official usage.

It was Pieter W. Botha, however, who developed a more coherent and long-range strategy of adjustment. As defense minister, with the backing of the more "political" generals, Botha chaired a commission set up after the Soweto upheavals to hammer out a "total strategy" for the long-term preservation of white supremacy.

Although Botha himself had not been previously identified as a *verligte,* his ascension to the post of prime minister in September 1978, after Vorter's resignation, gave the *verligte* wing of the party much greater influence and legitimacy, with some its most prominent exponents, such as Piet Koornhof, named to key cabinet posts. The rise to authority of Koornhof and other *verligtes* was a product of the crisis facing the apartheid system, and the white supremacists' need to try some new "solutions."

To an extent, their rise was smoothed along by the "information scandal," also known as "Muldergate," after former Minister of Information and Plural Relations Cornelius P. Mulder, who until then had been considered Vorster's most likely successor. The scandal broke out in mid-1978 with revelations of corruption in the Department of Information and spread to include exposures of secret government influence-peddling operations abroad, such as attempts to buy foreign newspapers and bribe foreign officials to get them to adopt a pro-South African line. Although not directly implicated in the scandal initially, Vorster was nevertheless compelled to resign as prime minister and retreat to the largely ceremonial post of president; later, when he was implicated, he had to resign the presidency as well in June 1979. Mulder was dropped from the cabinet and kicked out of parliament and the party. Gen. Hendrik van den Bergh, the head of the powerful Bureau of State Security, was booted into retirement.

Botha and his *verligte* allies took advantage of the scandal's fallout to press forward with their answers to the crisis, although

3. *Washington Post,* January 11, 1977.

they continued to face stiff resistance within the party from the more traditionalist *verkrampte* wing, which feared that any changes in established apartheid policy could loose uncontrollable social forces.

Despite the short-sighted obstinacy of some party circles, the regime began in late 1978 and early 1979 to move in a much more concerted way than before to try to streamline apartheid and bring it more into accord with the changing requirements of South African capitalism and the need to maintain control over a growing and increasingly urbanized Black population. Botha told his right-wing critics, "We must adapt or die."[4]

The most ambitious changes were in the system of control over urban Blacks, in particular Black workers. Industry's need for an increasing number of semiskilled and skilled Black workers compelled the regime to pull back from its earlier plans of turning virtually all Black workers into migrant laborers. Grudgingly, it had to acknowledge the fact that at least a sector of the Black working class would have to be based permanently in the major urban centers. That had already been obvious for several years, but the economic recession of the mid-1970s and especially the political crisis symbolized by Soweto now made it necessary to bring the legal code into accord with social practice and to make the corresponding political adjustments.

In May 1979, the government-appointed Riekert Commission recommended easing residency restrictions on those Africans deemed fully "qualified" to live in the urban areas (only about 1.5 million persons out of a total African population of nearly 20 million). African workers in this category could travel more freely to other cities to take jobs, would not have to report regularly to labor bureaus for registration, and could live with their families—as long as housing was available. None of this would be by right, however. These "privileges"—subject to the specific requirements of the labor market—could be withdrawn at any time by the authorities.

The Riekert Commission also emphasized the establishment of training facilities for African workers, so that they could fulfill the growing number of semiskilled tasks demanded of them.

In a further extension of the divide-and-rule strategy behind the Bantustan policy, the Riekert report likewise projected a plan to deepen the divisions between the various sectors of the African working class: between the fully urbanized and the migrant

4. *Economist* (London), September 8, 1979.

laborers, between the employed and the unemployed. While "qualified" Africans would have greater security of residence in the cities, it would become even more difficult for workers from the Bantustans to enter "white" South Africa, unless specific jobs were waiting for them; the labor bureaus, the commission recommended, "should exercise strict control over the admission of contract workers."[5] Deportation to the Bantustans of all those illegally in the cities would be compulsory. The unemployed would find themselves quickly ejected.

Botha and his colleagues realized too that if a permanently urbanized layer of Africans was permitted, then new methods of control over them would have to be developed.

In industry, this involved the government's acceptance in May 1979 of the major recommendations of the Wiehahn Commission, leading to an extension of limited and carefully scrutinized trade union rights to African workers. While on the surface a major departure from past policy, its central goal remained the imposition of labor discipline through the suppression or curtailment of militant Black trade unionism, while simultaneously establishing a framework for the nurturing of a house-broken Black union "leadership."

On the political and administrative level, at least within the confines of individual African townships, the regime introduced new forms of indirect rule. Originally Pretoria had tried, in a mechanical manner, to extend the authority of the Bantustan representatives to cover Africans in the urban areas through the intermediary of the Urban Bantu Councils. After the failure of that policy became clear in 1977 with the collapse under mass pressure of the Soweto UBC, the regime introduced the new Community Councils, which were not formally linked to the Bantustans at all.

With the new councils came a much greater emphasis on the creation of a collaborationist layer of petty-bourgeois Blacks *in the urban areas themselves,* a stratum that was not directly identified with the unpopular Bantustans but that would nonetheless preserve the status quo and serve as a buffer between the Black masses and the white regime.

As early as 1976, shortly after the initial Soweto rebellions, Botha declared that the regime would be able to protect itself only if it could "succeed in establishing a strong middle class—not

5. *Star Weekly* (Johannesburg), May 26, 1979.

only among Whites, but Black and Brown people as well."[6]

A number of restrictions on the setting up of African businesses and professions in the townships were lifted. The authorities dropped a requirement that applicants for new trading sites, shareholders, and members of partnerships produce Bantustan "citizenship" papers. All restrictions were scrapped on the types of trading and professional work allowed, except that African-owned manufacturing enterprises were still barred outside the Bantustans. The maximum authorized size of businesses was more than doubled. The Riekert Commission proposed granting trading rights to Blacks in certain "free trade" areas in the central cities. Those Africans who could afford to buy or build their own homes in the urban townships were granted limited leasehold rights, allowing them to own, sell, or bequeath their homes over a period of ninety-nine years; only a small minority of urban Africans had incomes high enough to be able to take advantage of this measure.

Speaking before a conference of the National African Federated Chambers of Commerce on July 5, 1979, Minister of Cooperation and Development Piet Koornhof promised that, "By 1982, the Black businessman will have arrived in South Africa, and he will have taken his rightful place in the economic set-up of the country."[7]

The regime gambled that such moves, while very limited in terms of the needs of the Black community as a whole, would at least be successful in retaining the acquiescence of some Black figures and enticing them into more active cooperation with the white authorities.

The Community Councils were to provide the mechanism for such collaboration. Although few Blacks bothered to turn out for the elections to them, about 130 councils had been set up in townships around the country by the end of 1978. To give them the appearance of having more power than the old councils, the new ones were assigned administrative tasks. They were also to take on certain policing functions, including responsibility for setting up "community guards" to maintain "law and order," a particularly contentious issue in politicized townships like Soweto, where residents were painfully aware that the guards would be nothing more than extensions of the white-run police

6. *Africa Research Bulletin* (London), October 15, 1976.

7. Radio RSA, Johannesburg, July 6, 1979. Monitored by the author.

apparatus. In November 1979, Soweto was elevated to "municipal status," with the Soweto Community Council taking over local administration from the West Rand Administration Board.

While real overall control remained in white hands, these councils made it possible for the government to delegate some of the day-to-day footwork to Black subordinates. To give this some credibility, more funds were promised for township development, such as the construction of new housing, the building of shopping centers, and the provision of electricity.

Important figures in the government and National Party also raised the possibility of including the Community Councils, or some variant of them, in Pretoria's evolving plans to restructure the entire governmental apparatus and rewrite the constitution, giving the councils a place, as "cantons" or "city-states," alongside the proposed Coloured and Indian "parliaments." Although a heretical concept to the *verkrampte* Nationalists, the simple raising of the idea was an indication of how seriously the rulers viewed the impending crisis and the kind of steps necessary to try to head it off.

For the rest of the African population, the Bantustans remained the bedrock of apartheid policy. Like his predecessor, Botha pressed ahead with the plans to foist "independence" on the Bantustans, and even accelerated the drive to deprive most Africans of their South African citizenship. But even the Bantustans were now subject to change. The plans for territorial consolidation and the possible provision of additional land to make them less fragmented geographically revealed a recognition of their current inadequacy. Clearly, if Pretoria's attempts to buy more time were to have even a chance of success, the Bantustan administrations would have to be made more viable.

Linking the apartheid regime's Bantustan policy to its broader imperialist aims in southern Africa, Botha proposed in May 1979 the establishment of a "constellation" of states in southern Africa, drawn together into a "sphere of common interest."[8] In November of that year, a conference of 250 top government officials and businessmen was held in Johannesburg to help swing the capitalist class as a whole behind the proposal. Pretoria's aim was to group around itself a whole series of quisling, Black-administered entities, including the ten Bantustans and any of the neocolonial regimes in neighboring countries that would be willing to go along. In the center of this "constella-

8. *New African* (London), June 1979.

tion," of course, would be Pretoria, a fortress of white colonial reaction, seeking to dominate a region of forty million people and hold back the liberation struggle in southern Africa for as long as possible.

Botha's "constellation" proposal exhibited a stubborn determination by the white supremacists to hang onto power at all costs. It underscored the fact that Pretoria's changes in policy, rather than being real concessions to mounting Black pressure, were in actuality part of a carefully calculated counterattack.

Botha, Koornhof, and other leading figures at the same time consciously tried to present their new measures as proof of the regime's "reasonableness" and its willingness to meet Black aspirations. Botha became the first prime minister to personally visit Soweto, as a display of his "concern" for the well-being of its inhabitants. Koornhof sought "consultations" with Black figures and promised to get rid of the hated passes, although it soon became clear that they would merely be replaced by simplified identification documents. Particularly offensive names and terms were dropped. Figures were released to show that expenditures on Black education, housing, and other services had gone up. Apartheid, many officials declared, was "dead."

Pretoria's foreign allies eagerly seized on this public relations ploy to try to justify continued links with the regime—and to invest even more money in South Africa.

But to Blacks themselves it was painfully evident that apartheid was still very much alive. Despite all the talk about a "new deal," the ruling class's intention of actually solidifying its overall control over the Black majority could scarcely be missed. It was especially obvious in the stepped-up repression: the outlawing of the major Black Consciousness organizations, the detention or banning of hundreds of leaders, the holding of scores of political trials, the murder in police custody of dozens of activists, the placing of new repressive laws on the books, the extension of press censorship.

In fact, a number of declarations by leading *verligtes*, despite the seemingly "moderate" image they have sought to foster, expressed a determination as ruthless as that of the most arch-reactionary racists to uphold white political and economic domination.

Roelof "Pik" Botha, the *verligte* minister of foreign affairs, affirmed that the government would "never in a hundred years" agree to share political power with Africans. He maintained that whites would "fight to the last man" rather than abandon the policy of imposing "independence" on the Bantustans.[9]

Willem de Klerk, the editor of the influential *Die Transvaler* and also an outspoken *verligte,* issued a warning to Blacks to be satisfied with the new reforms—or else. "If black spokesmen continue to spit on the ground when whites make proposal after proposal," he wrote; "if every white attempt to make progress simply elicits another black protest and demand; . . . if black leaders simply laugh at us and amuse themselves with our fear and tell us that the day of liberation and of reckoning is at hand . . . if it goes on building up . . . then the cord will snap. . . ." What would then follow, he explained, would be a "great counter-revolution."[10]

Under the impact or threat of future Black protests, strikes, and uprisings, the white rulers of South Africa could be impelled to initiate even more drastic adjustments in their methods of domination and control, as they cast about for some way of prolonging white supremacy. They are capable of remolding their system of class and national oppression to meet changing circumstances. They are willing to implement apartheid in a flexible manner, to confront new conditions and challenges.

But the regime cannot display any real flexibility on the fundamental question of political domination. The white "masters" know that if Blacks acquire any basic political rights they will immediately use them to try to strengthen their position and sweep away the remaining political constraints. They know what would come with that: a flood of economic and social struggles that would threaten the entire basis of South African capitalism. And never in history has a ruling class voluntarily abandoned its power and privileges.

The agents for real social change in South Africa are the Black masses themselves. The white supremacists may be able to obstruct and delay the freedom struggle, but Blacks have numbers—and history—on their side.

9. John Kane-Berman, *Soweto,* p. 179.

10. Ibid., p. 176.

II

The Struggle for Freedom, 1488-1980

13

The Roots of Resistance

Bartolomeu Dias, the Portuguese navigator and explorer who was to become famous for opening up the colonial trade routes to Asia, landed at a bay on the southern tip of Africa in 1488. He was the first European to do so. With a group of sailors, Dias went ashore, believing that his position as an emissary of Western civilization gave him the unquestioned right to set foot wherever he pleased. The Khoikhoi cattle herders who inhabited the area, however, became alarmed at the sight of the strange ships and the unexpected intrusion onto their grazing lands. When they pelted the white intruders with stones, seeking to drive them away, Dias picked up a crossbow and shot a bolt through one of the Africans.

That anonymous Khoikhoi was the first martyr in a centuries-long war of resistance by the indigenous peoples of South Africa against the European invaders and conquerors, a struggle that still continues.

Though the Khoikhoi, San, Xhosa, Zulu, Sotho, Pedi, and other peoples of the region fought long and hard to retain their independence, land, and way of life—and at times were successful in inflicting stinging defeats on the colonialists—the struggle was an unequal one. On one side stood precapitalist societies of a relatively simple and egalitarian nature, composed of hunter-gatherers, pastoralists, and agriculturalists; on the other side stood the most socially and economically developed powers on the globe at the time, ruled by rising capitalist classes whose rapacious drive for world conquest and plunder was unmatched in human history. On one side, a number of small and separate tribes and nations; on the other, states with large populations and vast resources that could be pitted against each of the

African peoples one at a time. On one side, the arrow, spear, and *assegai*; on the other, the cannon and the gun.

The African resistance faced tremendous odds, but the struggles were not in vain. In some areas they slowed the pace of conquest appreciably. They also left an inspiring legacy for future generations; the heroes of those wars are among the heroes of today's freedom fighters.

Though the Khoikhoi suffered the first casualties in the struggle against colonization, they also scored the first victories. Following Dias, other Portuguese mariners attempted to encroach on Khoikhoi land—unsuccessfully. Vasco da Gama was wounded in 1497 while attempting to land at what is now St. Helena Bay. Francisco de Almeida, the first Portuguese viceroy of the Indies and the victor in a series of colonial wars on the eastern coast of Africa, was killed near the Cape in 1510 along with sixty-five of his troops. The Portuguese got the message. They subsequently avoided the Cape, even though it had the best harbor between their colonies of Angola and Mozambique.

The Khoikhoi victory in 1510 won them a respite from further colonial intrusions for nearly a century and a half—until the arrival in 1652 of Jan van Riebeeck. Mindful of the earlier Portuguese misfortunes, van Riebeeck was cautious and initially avoided antagonizing the Khoikhoi. Believing that van Riebeeck and his handful of colonists had peaceful intentions, some Khoikhoi chiefs gave them permission to graze cattle and raise crops on traditional Khoikhoi land. Since the Khoikhoi had no concept of private ownership, all they were granting was temporary *use* of the land. But once the colonists had gained a toehold, they quickly consolidated their presence, claimed the land as their exclusive property, and started to expand further afield. This inevitably led to war.

Now militarily stronger, the colonists embarked on a series of armed raids and wars against the Khoikhoi beginning in 1659—just seven years after their arrival. Conscious that they could defeat the Khoikhoi only if the various tribes did not unite, the Dutch colonists made treaties with some chiefs while they directly attacked others. Through this divide-and-conquer strategy, they finally defeated the Khoikhoi in 1677, despite some fierce resistance, especially by the Khoikhoi leader Gonnema.

During a round of negotiations in the midst of the wars, both sides explicitly spelled out the social and economic conflicts that lay beneath the clash of arms, the same conflicts that underlay all the subsequent colonial wars. Writing to his company directors in Holland, van Riebeeck said that one Khoikhoi, "having been asked the reason why they caused us this trouble, declared for no other reason than that they saw that we kept in possession the best lands, and grazed our cattle where they used to do so, and that everywhere with houses and plantations we endeavoured to establish ourselves so permanently as if we intended never to leave again, but take permanent possession of this Cape land for our sole use. . . ." When van Riebeeck pointed out that there was not enough grazing land for both the white settlers and the Khoikhoi, another Khoikhoi retorted, ". . . who should by right give way, the rightful owner or the foreign invader?" Van Riebeeck ended the talks by bluntly asserting that the land now belonged to the settlers by the "rights of war."[1]

Following the Khoikhoi defeat, the colonialists turned their attention toward the San. Since the San were organized in small mobile hunting parties, they could not be defeated through a few major battles as were the larger Khoikhoi tribes. So the settlers adopted a policy of physical extermination. Hundreds of San were hunted down and slaughtered, the massacres becoming particularly intense after 1715. Some of the surviving San children were captured and made virtual slaves. Though the San, with their poisoned arrows, could put up deadly individual resistance, the very nature of their loosely organized hunting society precluded any united or coordinated response to the invaders. The few survivors could only flee for their lives into the Kalahari Desert, where most of their descendants now live in present-day Namibia and Botswana.

With the expansion of white colonization eastwards in the eighteenth century, it was not long before the settlers came into contact with another African people, the Xhosas. Their society, based on an economy of cattle herding and agriculture, was more organized and complex than those of the Khoikhoi and San. The Xhosa tribes were also much larger.

The Dutch settlers first encountered large numbers of Xhosas east of the Gamtoos River, near the present city of Port Elizabeth. The whites' encroachments on African land and theft of cattle soon led to armed clashes. In 1779 the first war of a century of armed conflict between the Xhosas and the white invaders—both Boer and British—began.

1. Leo Marquard, *A Short History of South Africa,* pp. 38-39; E. A. Benians et al. (eds.), *Cambridge History of the British Empire,* 8:125.

The larger tribes and more developed character of Xhosa society meant that the colonialists had a tough fight on their hands. Despite their vastly superior resources and armaments, they were able to make only gradual territorial advances. Driven eastward as a result of major battles, the Xhosas would trickle back to their former lands once the fighting had stopped. At times they fought combined forces of British and Boers to a standstill.

Perceptibly, the extended wars forged closer ties of unity, both among the various Xhosa tribes themselves, and with other Blacks. During the war of 1798-1802, the Khoikhoi and Coloureds who worked on the Boer farms or served as auxiliaries with the British military forces rose up and rallied to the Xhosa side; they realized where their real interests lay. The result of this first display of Black unity was immediate: The colonialists lost the war and the Xhosas temporarily regained some of their land.

The whites quickly recognized that if they were to make any further headway, they would have to break this unity. Calculated concessions were made to the Khoikhoi and Coloureds to wean them away from any lasting alliance with the Xhosas. Through the medium of Christian missionaries—who acted as spies and colonial agents—factional disputes among the Xhosa tribes were fostered and heightened; the British were able to win the allegiance of some chiefs against the others.[2] Having thus undermined and weakened the opposition, the colonialists renewed their military drive.

The Xhosas were still capable of fierce resistance, and even launched two spectacular counterattacks. In 1819, Makana, a religious leader and military commander who was seeking to unite the western Xhosa tribes against the settlers, led ten thousand troops into the Cape colony and laid siege to the city of Grahamstown. They suffered heavy losses, however, and were driven back. Makana was captured and sentenced to life imprisonment on Robben Island, where he drowned a year later while trying to escape. In 1834-35, Maqomo led an even bigger force of twenty thousand Xhosa troops into the colony, attacking the

2. The most important Xhosa chief to ally with the British, Ngqika, later realized his mistake when it was already too late. After the British seized three thousand square miles of his people's land, he told a British official, "When I look at the large piece of country which has been taken from me, I must say that, though protected, I am rather oppressed by my protectors." (Edward Roux, *Time Longer Than Rope*, p. 16.)

settlers on a broad front from Algoa Bay to Somerset East. Maqomo, too, was defeated.

By the end of that war in 1835, the British and Boers had taken a heavy toll on the Xhosas. They had killed thousands of the best fighters, seized innumerable cattle, burnt homes and crops, and generally disrupted Xhosa society.

But the Xhosas had still not been conclusively defeated—and the settlers knew it. The Xhosas' continued independent presence on the eastern frontier of the colony blocked further white expansion for a time and was one of the factors that impelled a section of the Boer settler population to break away from the colony in the late 1830s and skirt around the Xhosa territories in search of new areas that might be easier to conquer and settle.

The Boers were unaware, however, that just a few years before their move, the entire region north and east of the Xhosas had been transformed by a revolution in traditional African society.

At the end of the eighteenth century, new forms of social organization had arisen among the northern Nguni-speaking peoples as a result of growing population density and increasing wars, leading to a process of national consolidation. Several Nguni tribes developed a system of military regiments that allowed them to expand and gain dominance over neighboring tribes. Shaka, a member of a hitherto unimportant tribe called the Zulu, greatly accelerated this process by introducing a new weapon, the *assegai* (a short stabbing spear) and new, more effective battle tactics. His most radical innovation was the organization of a standing army that could quickly absorb recruits from defeated tribes. Basing himself on a dynamic, new social structure capable of rapid expansion, Shaka embarked on a campaign of nation building. In the brief period of a decade before his death in 1828, he overwhelmed his main rivals. The defeated peoples were not subjugated, but directly assimilated, losing their previous tribal allegiances and over time identifying themselves as part of a broader Zulu *umhlobo* (nation).

The meteoric rise of the Zulus sent social shockwaves throughout southern Africa. Wars, population dispersals, and mass migrations threw the whole region into turmoil. New peoples were forged in the heat of the disturbances. The Swazi and Ndebele evolved out of groups that split off from the main body of northern Nguni. In the mountains southwest of the Zulu territory, Moshweshwe molded together the Sotho people out of a disparate grouping of refugees from various tribes.

In some areas, the upheavals of this period facilitated the white advance. In others, the rise of powerful peoples like the Zulus and Sothos placed stubborn obstacles in its path.

One early grouping of Boer trekkers moved into what is now the Transvaal, where they immediately encountered one of the newly emergent peoples, the Ndebele. After two fierce battles in 1837, the Ndebele (who had only recently arrived in the area) decided to migrate further northward, most of them settling in what is now Zimbabwe.

Another band of Boers chose to take on a far more formidable people, the Zulus, who were now led by Shaka's successor, Dingane. Although the Boers made a pretense of coming in peace, their predatory aims were soon evident. In a preemptive strike, Dingane's troops fell on the Boers in 1838, killing 370 of them and destroying Port Natal (now Durban). But in December of the same year, a band of well-armed Boers, drawn up in a highly defensible *laager,* (wagon encampment), managed to beat back an attack by twelve thousand Zulus, killing about three thousand of them, in what is known as the Battle of Blood River, a battle that is celebrated every year by the white supremacists as a victory for white civilization. The Zulu defeat at Blood River soon led to Dingane's downfall and to the rise of Mpande, a chief who sought collaboration with the settlers. Although the Zulus were temporarily weakened, they had not been decisively defeated.

Meanwhile, the British-Boer onslaught against the Xhosas continued to face resistance as the various Xhosa tribes began to further unify in face of the white invaders. In the War of the Axe of 1846-47, and again during a massive Xhosa rebellion in 1850-52, broad intertribal alliances were formed. Some Khoikhoi, who had previously fallen under the influence of the colonialist missionaries, broke away and joined the anticolonial forces. The Coloured Cape Mounted Police mutinied and did likewise. Commenting on the growing Xhosa unity, Commander Andries Stockenstrom warned, "With their late acquired knowledge of their strength . . . their power must be broken. . . ."[3] Fearing that similar African alliances would spread to other peoples, the authorities rushed in reinforcements from Britain. In a massive, determined counterinsurgency drive, eleven British battalions spent half a year in suppressing the Xhosa uprising.

Except for a final brief war in 1877-78, Xhosa resistance to the colonial conquests had been broken. The devastations of the wars and the severe famine of 1857 had dealt irreparable blows to

3. Nosipho Majeke, *The Role of the Missionaries in Conquest,* p. 59.

Xhosa society and undermined what remained of i
dence.

Just north of the Xhosa region, across the Drakensber
tains, lay the territory of the Sotho people led by Moshw
His efforts to break down tribal divisions and to build a broader African alliance were a particular threat to the colonialists, who feared that he could provide the focus for a general uprising. For that reason, they set a high premium on defeating Moshweshwe. But their efforts to conquer the Sotho were repeatedly stymied by the Sothos' formidable military prowess; unlike most other African peoples, the Sotho had managed to obtain large numbers of guns (purchased by Sotho diamond miners) and had bred their own swift Basuto ponies, quickly becoming expert mounted fighters.

When the Sothos refused to accede to a whittling away of their lands by Boer settlers, the British governor of the Cape decreed that Moshweshwe "must be humbled."[4] But it was the British who were humbled. Three times during the 1850s Sotho fighters trounced British and Boer forces.

The inability of either the Cape administration or the Boer settlers to defeat Moshweshwe prompted London to step in directly, with a deft political maneuver. In 1868 it annexed Basutoland to the British crown. Weakened by the loss of considerable land and cattle and by the defeat of some of his allies, Moshweshwe was forced to agree to the move as the only alternative to eventual and complete military defeat.

Though Moshweshwe soon died and the military strength of the Sothos had been greatly sapped, they were still able to resist attempts to physically disarm them. This heroic resistance was an important factor blocking South Africa from incorporating Basutoland directly, as it did most other African territories. Basutoland survives today as the formally independent country of Lesotho.

With the British annexation of Basutoland, the Zulus were left as the most powerful African people in South Africa still independent of direct white rule. By the time Cetshwayo formally succeeded Mpande as head of the Zulus in 1872, the Zulu nation had recovered from its initial defeats and was stronger than ever, with about fifty thousand troops in thirty-five regiments. Many of them were now armed with guns. The example of continued Zulu independence kept alive the flame of resistance among other

4. Mnguni, *Three Hundred Years,* 2:109.

African peoples. The British could not countenance such a situation for long.

With an army of 16,800 troops, Lord Chelmsford began a major drive into Zululand in January 1879, expecting to defeat Cetshwayo's forces with a heavy first blow. But Chelmsford had underestimated the Zulus' military abilities, and his forces were outmaneuvered. At a place called Isandhlwana, six British infantry companies were overrun and virtually wiped out by the Zulus. All together, 895 whites and 850 Africans serving with the British forces were killed in the battle (the Zulus lost thousands of their own troops). It was one of the most stunning defeats ever suffered by the British in the long annals of their colonial wars.[5]

The Zulus won the first battle, but Zulu society could not long stand up to the overwhelming firepower and vast resources of an imperialist country like Britain. More than ten thousand reinforcements were quickly sent from Britain for the second round of the war. In late May Chelmsford's army again invaded Zululand. The British slaughtered thousands of Zulus and burned down every Zulu hut they came across. After the final Zulu defeat at Ulundi, the conquerors broke up the Zulu nation into thirteen petty chiefdoms. Zululand was finally annexed to Natal in 1897.

The Zulu defeat eliminated the last major obstacle to the completion of the colonial conquests. In rapid succession, the British and Boer forces overran the Pedi, Hlubi, Griqua, Rolong, Venda, and other peoples who had still retained a measure of independence.

Though all the indigenous African peoples of South Africa had been conquered by the beginning of the twentieth century and subjected to the colonial rule of British imperialism or the local white settlers, there was one final rebellion of an essentially tribal character.

In Natal, a section of the Zulus under Bambata rose up in 1906 against the imposition of stiff taxes by the white authorities.

5. Frederick Engels, who was himself quite knowledgeable in military affairs, commented just a few years after Isandhlwana: "The Zulu . . . did what no European army can do. Armed only with pikes and spears and without firearms, they advanced, under a hail of bullets from the breech loaders, right up to the bayonets of the English infantry—acknowledged as the best in the world for fighting in close formation—throwing them into disorder and even beating them back more than once; and this, despite the colossal disparity in arms. . . ." (Frederick Engels, *Origin of the Family, Private Property and the State* [New York: Pathfinder Press, 1972] p. 100-101.)

Bambata, a chief who had been deposed by the British, led his followers into the Nkandla Mountains, where he built up a rebel army of up to a thousand fighters. But his forces were cornered in June by the British and about five hundred of them were cut down by machinegun fire. Bambata himself was killed, and his head cut off—for "identification" purposes. Following an even bigger uprising by other Zulus in the Mapumulo division, hundreds were butchered there as well; Zulu crops and homes were burned. The governor himself referred to the crushing of the revolt as a "slaughter" and another official termed it a "massacre."[6] All together, some three thousand to four thousand Africans were killed, compared to only thirty whites.

The form of the Bambata rebellion—a tribally based armed uprising—placed its historical roots in the preceding era of resistance, in which Africans fought back basically as separate peoples, each trying to preserve its own independent position and way of life, with little actual coordination and unity among them. The crushing of the rebellion brought that era to a definitive close. Henceforth, the struggle of Blacks would take on new forms, on a different and broader social basis.

6. Shula Marks, *Reluctant Rebellion*, p. 239.

14

Class and Color

Disarmed and defeated in the colonial wars, stripped of their independence, deprived of their land, and compelled by legislation and economic necessity to labor for a white *baas*, millions of Africans were engulfed by the new colonial society.

Though many retained their tribal loyalties for years to come, the days of separate tribal resistance were over. The traditional African societies themselves had been shattered by the upheavals of the colonial conquest and an expanding capitalist economic system. Subjected to a common national oppression, Africans of varied tribal backgrounds gradually acquired a new sense of solidarity and of a common identity and purpose. And as a large section of the African population became urbanized through the forging of a strong Black working class, evolving class consciousness combined with a new national awareness to produce more modern forms of organization and struggle.

Blacks were now disarmed, but they were not powerless. They had two mighty weapons on their side: their vastly superior numbers and their social position as the producers of South Africa's wealth. As South African capitalism developed and Blacks became correspondingly more urbanized and proletarianized, they became increasingly aware of this strength and of how best to utilize it.

Blacks formed numerous organizations—political, cultural, trade union, neighborhood—to try to advance their struggles for class and national emancipation. Scarcely a decade went by without major battles being fought: the first mass Black demonstrations and strikes in the 1910s; the meteoric growth in African unionization in the 1920s; the attempts at forging broad African unity in the 1930s; the work stoppages, urban uprisings, and mass protest campaigns of the 1940s; the boycotts, general strikes, and massive civil disobedience actions of the 1950s; the widespread upsurge following the Sharpeville massacre in the early 1960s; the labor unrest, student rebellions, and township explosions of the 1970s. Throughout this rich history of struggle, the Black working class—numbering in the millions—took on an ever more central role. Even when workers were not in the leadership of the various political campaigns (which was often the case), their class interests nevertheless left a strong imprint on the demands raised and the forms of struggle undertaken.

The first Black political groups surfaced in the early 1880s, largely among the Xhosas of the Eastern Cape. They included the Native Electoral Association, Imbumba Yama Afrika (Union of Africa), and the Native Educational Association. The most prominent political figure was John Tengo Jabavu, the editor of *Imvo Zabantsundu* (African Opinion), the first African-run newspaper in the country. Jabavu's literary works, political activities, and organizing efforts on behalf of Africans marked a symbolic watershed in the African struggle. They were among the first attempts by Africans to press for their democratic rights from *within* the colonial-settler state, by means of organized political agitation.

Jabavu himself, however, directly represented the interests of only a small layer of Africans in the Cape, those relatively prosperous few who qualified for the restricted voting franchise. More seriously, he sidetracked any independent initiatives his followers might have taken by openly supporting a wing of the oppressor class, represented by the South African Party and the Afrikaner Bond. When Jabavu's white "friends" in parliament supported further restrictions on the African vote, he failed to put up any real opposition. He publicly declared that he was against "native preponderance."[1]

A different current of political thought among Africans was expressed through the formation of separate African churches, a trend known as Ethiopianism. Rather than accepting white cultural standards or seeking political and social integration into a white-dominated society, as Jabavu's followers did, leaders and members of these churches tended to stress African advancement through the efforts of Africans themselves. In its most political form (though Ethiopianism was not a political movement), this concept was crystallized in the anticolonialist slogan, "Africa for the Africans."

1. Edward Roux, *Time Longer Than a Rope,* p. 72.

The first significant Coloured formation arose in 1902: the African Political Organisation (APO)—later renamed the African People's Organisation, headed by Abdullah Abdurahman. Though it remained a largely Coloured group, the APO had an explicit position in favor of Black unity, as exemplified in Abdurahman's statement that "there will one day arise a solid mass of Black and Coloured humanity whose demands will be irrepressible."[2] Like Jabavu, however, Abdurahman avoided mass actions and sought instead to use the voting power of Coloureds and Africans to influence legislation by supporting certain white candidates, in his case members of the Progressive (later Unionist) Party. His efforts, like Jabavu's, were singularly unsuccessful.

The first mass political protests were launched by Indians, who were led by a young lawyer from India, Mohandas K. Gandhi, later to become a towering figure in the independence struggle in India. He had founded the Natal Indian Congress in 1894, shortly after his arrival in South Africa. Though he often took a militant stance on behalf of his Indian followers, he had no perspective of trying to link up their struggles with those of other oppressed Blacks, either African or Coloured.

In 1906, Gandhi led a campaign against the imposition of passes for Indians in the Transvaal. During it he developed his idealistic concept of *satyagraha* (soul force), which postulated "the conquest of the adversary by suffering in one's own person."[3] In line with this emphasis on personal sacrifice, he called on his followers to court arrest by defying the pass laws, an approach that tended to limit the resistance campaign to only the most dedicated, those who were willing to face certain imprisonment. These ideas of Gandhi's were to have a long life in South Africa, influencing some Black political leaders through to the early 1960s.

The disobedience campaign nevertheless attracted thousands of participants, who packed the Transvaal's jails and prisons. A second phase of the campaign began in 1908 with a spectacular burning of several thousand passes in Johannesburg. By 1913, however, the struggle had grown beyond Gandhi's direct control. Women joined the fight as a result of new marriage laws that recognized the legitimacy of Christian marriages only. In Natal,

2. A Lerumo, *Fifty Fighting Years,* p. 32.

3. Mohandas K. Gandhi, *Satyagraha in South Africa,* p. 179.

Indian workers for the first time became active in large numbers. They struck the Newcastle coal mines and some two thousand of them marched into the Transvaal in solidarity with Gandhi's *satyagraha* campaign. The strikes spread throughout Natal, affecting sugar plantations, railways, factories, and offices.[4] Among the strikers' demands was abolition of a £3 poll tax. In one incident, police attacked a group of Indian sugar workers, killing nine. Striking miners were forced back into the mines at gunpoint.

This militant working-class response achieved what Gandhi's "soul force" had been unable to. It forced the regime to make some major concessions. Indian marriages were recognized as legal, the Transvaal Indian pass law was repealed, and the Natal poll tax was abolished.

The example of the Indian strikes and defiance campaign did not pass unnoticed by other Blacks. Shortly after the beginning of the antipass actions, Africans throughout the country launched their first large-scale, coordinated political campaign, directed against the establishment of a "whites only" government over all of South Africa. Protest meetings, petition drives, and congresses were held in all four of the South African colonies to fight the racist provisions of the new constitution.

Although the campaign had no impact on the actual laws of the new Union of South Africa, it did represent a monumental development in the struggle for Black rights, providing a powerful impetus to unity among Africans by cutting across old tribal allegiances. At a national convention in Bloemfontein in March 1909, at which a broad range of African organizations were represented, Pixley ka Izaka Seme, a young lawyer, stressed the importance of such unity: "The demon of racialism, the aberrations of the Xosa-Fingo feud, and the animosity that exists between Zulus and Tongaas, between the Basutos and every other Native must be buried and forgotten. . . . We are one people."[5]

4. Gandhi had opposed the extension of the strikes beyond the initial one at Newcastle. He later wrote, "I had warned my co-workers against allowing any more labourers to go on strike. . . . But when the flood-gates are opened, there is no checking the universal deluge. The labourers everywhere struck work of their own accord. . . ." (Gandhi, *Satyagraha,* p. 478.)

5. Thomas Karis and Gwendolen M. Carter, eds., *From Protest to Challenge,* 1:72.

In January 1912, delegates from throughout southern Africa again gathered in Bloemfontein, this time to found the South African Native National Congress, which was renamed the African National Congress (ANC) in 1923. In his opening address, Seme told the delegates, "The white people of this country have formed what is known as the Union of South Africa—a union in which we have no voice in the making of laws and no part in their administration. We have called you therefore to this Conference so that we can together devise ways and means of forming our national union for the purpose of creating national unity and defending our rights and privileges."[6]

The establishment of the ANC as a countrywide organization was a historic step in the evolution of the national liberation struggle. For the first time, Africans of all backgrounds and regions of the country could join a central political organization that claimed to represent their national interests. It raised hopes among many Africans that their demands would now be articulated and acted upon.

But the promise shone brighter than the reality. In its early days in particular, the ANC was dominated by an essentially conservative leadership of lawyers, teachers, religious figures, small businessmen, and tribal chiefs, who were content to issue periodic verbal appeals, attend government-initiated "native conferences," and dispatch an occasional delegation to London or Cape Town. Nevertheless, the very existence of the ANC inspired Africans to initiate their own struggles, knowing that they could at least count on the ANC to extend political support.

In 1913, African women in the Orange Free State repeatedly took to the streets to protest new requirements that they buy monthly passes. Hundreds marched in Bloemfontein, Jagersfontein, and Winburg, dumping their passes at the feet of startled officials. Hundreds went to jail. Many of the women were supporters of the ANC, which petitioned Prime Minister Smuts on their behalf. These actions marked the first sizable protest by Black women in South Africa, as well as the first organized campaign by Africans against the passes.

The young African working class also began to flex its muscles. There had already been advance tremors of Black labor unrest in the gold mines in 1901-02 and the diamond mines in 1907, when African miners, organized almost exclusively on a tribal basis,

6. Peter Walshe, *The Rise of African Nationalism in South Africa*, p. 34.

embarked on a series of sporadic strikes and mass desertions from work.[7] But the first large and sustained African strike erupted in 1913. It began after white miners walked off their jobs in the gold mines in June of that year. At first the African workers stayed away under pressure from the white strikers, but soon began to hold meetings and discuss demands, refusing to go to work as a result of their own grievances. The strike grew, until thirteen thousand African miners had downed their tools. The authorities, who had treated the white workers cautiously, were alarmed at the African strike. They leaped into action to crush it. Demonstrations and meetings were broken up by police. Strike leaders were arrested. Finally, the army was sent in to force them back to work.

African industrial and political action died down for a while during World War I, though there were sporadic outbreaks in some mines. The ANC leaders, who mistakenly looked to British imperialism as a "progressive" force, used their political influence to try to halt the ferment in the name of aiding the British war effort (of which the South African military was a part). They took the logic of their policy to its tragic conclusion, agreeing to help the South African government recruit twenty-four thousand African laborers to assist the military campaign against the German forces in Namibia, a campaign that was to bring the Namibian population under direct South African colonial rule.[8]

Even before the end of the war, however, African workers took the lead in resuming protests. In early 1918, African workers on the Rand launched a boycott of trading stores in protest against rising prices and low wages. In May of that year, African sanitation workers in Johannesburg struck to demand higher pay. When they refused to return to work, 152 were arrested and sentenced to two months' hard labor.

Some ANC leaders had by this time been influenced by the labor militancy, and the Transvaal congress organized a campaign in defense of the sanitation workers. This gradually developed into a movement for a general wage increase of one

7. For details of this little-known chapter of Black labor history, see Peter Warwick, "Black Industrial Protest on the Witwatersrand, 1901-1902," and Sean Moroney, "Mine Worker Protest on the Witwatersrand, 1901-1912," in Eddie Webster, ed., *Essays in Southern African Labour History*, pp. 20-46.

8. Mary Benson, *The Struggle for a Birthright*, p. 34; Walshe, *Rise of African Nationalism*, pp. 53, 80.

shilling a day for all African workers. At a meeting of a thousand Africans in June 1918, a resolution was adopted calling for a general strike to back up the demand, although some ANC leaders were opposed to striking. Later in the month, a crowd of ten thousand Africans tore up a British flag in protest. Yet when Prime Minister Botha wrote to the ANC stating that he was willing to discuss their demands, the ANC leaders called off the threatened general strike. About fifteen thousand African workers at three mines struck anyway. Police and troops rushed in to break the strike. Several leaders of the ANC and the largely white International Socialist League were arrested for "incitement." An ANC deputation met with Botha, but all that eventually came of it was another government-sponsored "inquiry."

The issue of passes, a widespread grievance among Africans, again came to the fore. Fearing a renewal of the massive women's demonstrations of 1913, the Orange Free State government had chosen not to implement its pass laws and the provincial officials in the Transvaal had decided not to introduce them for women there. But they still applied to men. In March 1919, a massive protest campaign was initiated in the Transvaal, with ANC participation. Thousands of Africans demonstrated, rallied, and turned in their passes, particularly in Pretoria and on the Rand. Protesters in some areas clashed with police and white civilians, and a few unsuccessful attempts were made to bring African workers out on strike. The regime, aided by white vigilantes, cracked down hard, shooting several Africans and arresting more than seven hundred.

The recurrent protests among African workers in the Transvaal for wage increases prompted the employers to agree to pay hikes for many workers—but not for gold miners. The African miners responded in fury, prompting the largest African strike anywhere in South Africa up to that time. Beginning on February 17, 1920, about 71,000 African miners in twenty-one mines came out on strike. The president of the Chamber of Mines admitted that it "practically paralysed the industry."[9] The miners were well organized and disciplined. Referring to the strike, the chamber warned the regime "that the native is advancing more rapidly than we had anticipated, and that we should take measures accordingly."[10] As in other strikes, troops rushed in and shot into

9. Frederick A Johnstone, *Class, Race and Gold*, p. 180.
10. Ibid., p. 183.

the crowds of workers, killing eleven. The strike lasted for ten days before finally collapsing.

Out of these simmering labor struggles of the immediate postwar period emerged the most massive and powerful Black organization South Africa had yet seen—the Industrial and Commercial Workers' Union of Africa.

It grew out of union organizing drives in a number of cities. In Cape Town, the Industrial and Commercial Union (ICU) was established in January 1919 under the leadership of Clements Kadalie, who led two thousand African and Coloured dock workers out on strike later that year. Other unions were formed in Port Elizabeth, East London, Aliwal North, and Bloemfontein. Blacks in one area soon learned of developments in another, and a broader sense of class solidarity began to emerge. Selby Msimang, a young lawyer and a founder of the ANC, who had helped organize a union in Bloemfontein, contacted Kadalie; they agreed to try to bring the local bodies together into a national union.

Although Msimang was unsuccessful in winning the ANC's support for the project, a labor conference was held in Bloemfontein in July 1920. The delegates decided to inaugurate the Industrial and Commercial Workers' Union of Africa, which eventually came to be known by the initials of Kadalie's original Cape Town union, the ICU. It was projected as "one great union of skilled and unskilled workers of South Africa, south of the Zambezi."[11]

The ICU was soon catapulted into national prominence. The Cape Town union won a wage increase for the Black dock workers in August 1920, through the mere threat of a strike. Two months later, the Port Elizabeth workers struck for higher pay. When thousands of Blacks marched to the Port Elizabeth police station to protest the arrest of ICU leader Samuel Masabalala, police and white vigilantes opened fire, killing twenty. Some thirty thousand angry Blacks responded by flocking to a funeral demonstration in a massive display of solidarity and defiance.

By late 1920, when Kadalie was elected national secretary, the ICU was fast on its way to becoming an important factor in South African political life.

The period around World War I also witnessed considerable

11. Peter L. Wickins, *The Industrial and Commercial Workers' Union of Africa,* p. 61.

ferment among white workers, who carried out a series of militant strikes in the mines. But because of their narrow craft unionist outlook and their racist attitudes toward Blacks, they combined actions against the mineowners and other employers with attempts to exclude Blacks from the more skilled and semiskilled jobs. In general, they refrained from any common action with Black workers against the bosses.

There were white trade unionists and political activists, however, who were more radical. Some were attracted by communist ideas. Repelled by the prowar stance of the reformist South African Labour Party (SALP), a group broke away in 1915 and formed the International Socialist League (ISL), led by David Ivon Jones and William H. Andrews. Though still rooted in the white labor milieu, the ISL took a few steps in the direction of Black workers, calling for the abolition of the pass laws, contract labor system, and mining compounds. It urged "the lifting of the Native worker to the political and industrial status of the white."[12] In 1915, Jones wrote, "An internationalism which does not concede the fullest rights which the native working class is capable of claiming will be a sham."[13] The ISL protested against the Native Administration Bill of 1917, and its leaders shared platforms with ANC speakers.

The ISL at the same time displayed a sectarian attitude toward the national liberation struggle of Blacks, artificially counterposing to it an abstract conception of "pure" class struggle. In doing so, its leaders failed to recognize that the nationalism of an oppressed people could play a progressive, even revolutionary, role and that in South Africa the Black liberation struggle is the central axis of the class struggle itself. Their formalistic calls for "class unity" were greatly weakened by their failure to project the only effective basis on which Black and white working class solidarity could conceivably be built: unconditional and active support by white workers for the struggles of the most oppressed segment of the working class—Blacks.

Following the Russian revolution of 1917, the ISL and other South African socialist groups moved closer to revolutionary Marxism. Jones and another ISL leader published and distributed a leaflet in English, Zulu, and Sotho addressed, "To the

12. H. J. Simons and R. E. Simons, *Class and Colour in South Africa, 1850-1950*, p. 193.

13. Anthony J. Southall, "Marxist Theory in South Africa Until 1940," p. 23.

Workers of South Africa—Black and White," which hailed the Russian revolution.[14] A year later the ISL issued a May Day manifesto bearing portraits of the two main leaders of the revolution, Lenin and Trotsky.

As early as July 1920, the ISL applied for affiliation to the Communist International, the world revolutionary socialist body founded in 1919 and headquartered in Moscow. One year later, at a conference in Cape Town from July 30 to August 1, the ISL merged with a number of smaller groups to form the Communist Party of South Africa (CPSA), the South African section of the Communist International. It was the first serious attempt to build a revolutionary party in South Africa.

The CPSA manifesto declared that "the main duty of the party and of every member of it is to establish the widest and closest possible contact with workers of *all ranks and races* and to propagate the Communist gospel among them. . . ."[15] Like its predecessor, however, the CPSA still bore the legacy of its origins in the politically backward white labor movement. All the delegates at the founding congress were white and all the members of the executive were white. The manifesto, while openly calling for a socialist revolution, did not have a word to say about the national liberation struggle of Blacks.

The Communist Party's mistaken perception of the nature of the class struggle in South Africa was revealed in practice by its role during the massive revolt of white workers on the Rand in 1922. In response to a decision by the Chamber of Mines to cut costs by opening some semiskilled jobs to lower-paid Africans, the white miners called a strike in January to safeguard their craft positions. William H. Andrews and Ernie Shaw, both members of the CPSA, were prominent leaders of the strike, and many of the strike activities were organized out of the party's headquarters in the Trades Hall in Johannesburg.

Though the CPSA declared that the strike was "essentially . . . a fight against the rule of the capitalist class,"[16] the conflict had more than just a few racist overtones. In a travesty of proletarian internationalism, the strike leaders put forward the slogan, "Workers of the World, Fight and Unite for a White South

14. Lerumo, *Fifty Fighting Years,* pp. 39, 155.
15. Ibid., p. 119. Emphasis in original.
16. Ibid., p. 121.

Africa."[17] Armed strike commandos were formed. Their main purpose was to defend the strikers from the police and troops, but they also participated in physical attacks on Blacks. The killing of about thirty Blacks by white commandos prompted protests by the ANC, ICU, and APO, among others.

While deploring the murders of Blacks, the CPSA nevertheless tried to justify the racist demands of the strikers, claiming that the abolition of the job color bar in the mines would aid the mineowners.[18] The party failed to realize that *retention* of the color bar aided the capitalist class as a whole—and in the long run the mining companies themselves. It preserved racial job differentiation, which made it possible to continue the superexploitation of Black workers and heighten the racial frictions between Black and white workers, thereby weakening both in the face of the bosses. A revolutionary response to the mining companies' efforts to undercut the positions of white skilled workers would have been to fight to raise Black wages to the same levels.

The Smuts government, concerned not only about the spread of the white labor unrest, but also about the possibility that it could spur Black workers into action, declared martial law two months after the strike began. Some 1,500 strikers and their leaders were summarily arrested. This provoked an armed insurrection by the strike commandos. Police and troops retaliated with aircraft, artillery, machine guns, and tanks, killing up to 220 strikers. Four members of the strike commandos were later executed.

Following the strike, the Communist Party leaders compounded their error by giving political support to the SALP-Nationalist Party electoral bloc in the 1924 elections, claiming that the coalition was aimed at "the overthrow of the orthodox colonial imperialist government."[19] When the two parties came to power and formed the Pact government, they rammed through a series of segregationist and repressive legislation.

To its credit, the CPSA soon recognized some of its initial errors and adopted a more positive approach toward the Black struggle. At its December 1924 conference in Johannesburg, the party

17. Simons and Simons, *Class and Colour*, p. 285.

18. Ibid., p. 276.

19. Ibid., p. 313.

elected a new leadership, with Sidney Percival Bunting as chairman and Edward Roux as vice-chairman. Both stressed the importance of mobilizing Blacks. From that point onward, the party's Black recruitment gradually picked up, while some of its more conservative white leaders, such as Andrews and Shaw, drifted away.

The Black organization for revolutionists to try to work in during the 1920s was most obviously the Industrial and Commercial Workers' Union. Members of the CPSA joined the union and helped build it. Some union leaders were recruited to the party. By 1926, five Black party members held important leadership positions in the ICU: James La Guma, John Gomas, R. G. de Norman, E. J. Khaile, and Thomas Mbeki, all of whom were on the union's National Council. Following the expulsion of known Communist Party members from the ICU that same year, the CPSA turned its attention toward other Black unions and toward the ANC. Members helped organize Black unions in the laundry, baking, clothing, and furniture industries, most of which had their headquarters at the party's offices in Johannesburg. The Native Clothing Workers Union, led by CPSA member Gana Makabeni, received some backing from the white-led but predominantly Coloured Garment Workers Union of Solly Sachs. In 1928 these unions were drawn together into the Federation of Non-European Trade Unions, with a total membership of ten thousand. The CPSA also worked with the ANC and had especially close relations with such figures as Josiah Gumede, who was elected ANC president-general in 1927. The same year, CPSA leader E. J. Khaile was elected secretary-general of the ANC.

This shift in the CPSA's emphasis inevitably affected the party's composition. Though the top leadership remained largely white, a new layer of Black leaders began to emerge; Khaile, Makabeni, and T. W. Thibedi were elected to the Central Committee. Changes were even more striking in the party ranks. In a period of just one year, from 1927 to 1928, the CPSA's Black membership swelled from 200 to 1,600 (out of a total membership in 1928 of 1,750). At the January 1929 conference, two-thirds of the delegates were Black, representing at that point an estimated membership of 3,000.[20] For a party seeking to lead a revolution in

20. *International Press Correspondence* (Inprekorr), 8, no. 78 (November 8, 1928), p. 1452; Roux, *Time Longer Than Rope*, p. 217.

South Africa, its transformation into a largely Black organization was indispensable.

In a booklet published in 1928, Bunting explained the party's view toward the Black struggle:

> Real liberation means not just formal independence . . . but freedom of the S. African natives, as a race, and also freedom of the S.A. working class and peasantry. . . . The primary struggle of the S. African natives for liberation, as it must apparently be carried out in practice, is in substance the same as, or part of, the struggle of the exploited in all countries for the overthrow of their own bourgeoisie and of the entire bourgeoisie as an international class, and for the rule of the workers and peasants. In political form, it is a struggle for a S. African Workers' and Peasants' Republic, as contrasted with the present regime of white rule over black and capitalist rule over worker.[21]

Despite these promising moves, the CPSA's overall approach toward the national liberation struggle was still conservative. It tended to portray national oppression as somehow secondary to class exploitation. It called for the abolition of the pass laws, for an end to all racial discrimination, and for full equality. But the CPSA left out of its program the central democratic demand for Black majority rule, a demand that expresses the political aspirations of the struggle for national liberation and that is fully realizable only through a socialist revolution and the establishment of a workers' state.

As a result of its own experiences and with the advice of revolutionists in other countries, the CPSA might have been able to correct this failing on its own. It was already moving in that direction. But in 1928 the Communist International intervened to abruptly and bureaucratically alter the party's programmatic line. By then the International was no longer a revolutionary organization, but a foreign-policy vehicle to advance the narrow interests of the privileged bureaucratic caste that had usurped political power in the Soviet Union under Joseph Stalin. Its intervention in South Africa, while superficially improving some of the CPSA's positions, at the same time caused considerable political disorientation.

The Executive Committee of the Communist International

21. Sidney P. Bunting, *Imperialism and South Africa*, pp. 51-52.

(ECCI) passed a resolution ordering the CPSA to adopt "the slogan of an independent native South African republic as a stage towards a workers' and peasants' republic, with full equal rights for all races, black, coloured and white."[22] This formally corrected the CPSA's weakness on the all-important national question through the call for an "independent native republic." But the way it was packaged—and later interpreted in practice—simultaneously stripped the slogan of much of its revolutionary content by separating it from the socialist revolution itself. First there had to be a bourgeois-democratic revolution, the ECCI maintained, and then only later—at some distant and undefined future stage—could the working class come to power and initiate a socialist revolution.

Within the CPSA, the Communist International's intervention aroused some opposition, led by Bunting and Roux, both of whom spoke at the Sixth World Congress of the Communist International in Moscow in 1928. Rejecting the Stalinist theory of a revolution in "two stages" implicit in the ECCI resolution, Bunting accurately pointed out that "the class struggle is here practically coincident and simultaneous with the national struggle."[23] To bolster his contention that a socialist revolution was on the order of the day and not a bourgeois-democratic revolution, Bunting quoted the "Theses on the National and Colonial Question" of the Second Congress of the International in 1920, which stated that in the colonial world it was the foremost task of revolutionists to "organize the peasants and workers and lead them to the revolution and to the establishment of soviet republics."[24]

Roux also recoiled at the Stalinists' attempts to bureaucratically impose the slogan. Although he did not challenge the "two stage" theory in general, he did question its applicability to South

22. Lerumo, *Fifty Fighting Years,* p. 129.

23. *International Press Correspondence* (Inprekorr), 8, no. 78 (November 8, 1928), p. 1452.

24. *Theses and Statutes of the Third (Communist) International, Adopted by the Second Congress, July 17th-August 7th, 1920* (Moscow: Publishing Office of the Communist International, 1920), p. 74.

Africa.[25] He also offered an amendment that combined the call for a Black majority government with the seizure of power by the workers and peasants: "an independent workers' and peasants' S. African Republic, with equal rights for all toilers irrespective of colour, as a basis for a native majority government."[26] The ECCI rejected Roux's amendment.

At the same time, both Bunting and Roux reflected the CPSA's continued backwardness on the national question, by emphasizing that the call for a Black republic would arouse opposition from white workers. Bunting went so far as to declare that a Black republic could possibly lead to a "black race dictatorship."[27] In raising such objections, Bunting and Roux were bending to the racist attitudes of whites, an opportunism that—if persisted in—would have done far more damage to the party than the ECCI slogan.

What was wrong with the ECCI's slogan was not the call for a Black republic—that was the most progressive thing about it. Nor was the refusal of the ECCI to explicitly link the Black republic demand with the socialist revolution its central failing; given the fact that national liberation is the central axis *of* the class struggle in South Africa, the most crucial task for any organization that calls itself revolutionary is to begin mobilizing the oppressed. Even if the social character of the revolution is not correctly defined in theory, the nature of South African society and the class dynamic of the national liberation struggle will in practice lead in the direction of challenging capitalism itself. The

25. "The resolution of the E.C.C.I.," Roux stated at the congress, "suggests that the independent native republic will not be founded on the proletarian dictatorship. It is merely a stage towards a Workers' and Peasants' Republic. . . . The possibility of the *complete telescoping* of the bourgeois nationalist revolution and the development of the proletarian revolution in the *absence* of a native bourgeoisie is not admitted in the thesis of the C.I." ("Official Stenograms of the Speeches of the South African Delegates to the VI World Congress of the Communist International," July 28, 1928, 8761/6, pp. 1-2. Emphasis in original. Copy on microfilm in "South Africa: A Collection of Political Documents," Hoover Institution, Stanford, California.)

26. Letter by Roux to CPSA General Secretary Douglas Wolton, September 5, 1928. Copy on microfilm in Hoover Institution collection.

27. *International Press Correspondence* (Inprekorr), 8, no. 78 (November 8, 1928), p. 1452.

crucial mistake was insisting that a Black republic would be brought about through a bourgeois-democratic revolution. In this way the ECCI ensured that the CPSA would be unable to fight for a Black republic in an effective, revolutionary manner.

As the party's record showed after it adopted the slogan, the stress on the bourgeois-democratic nature of the struggle led the CPSA to de-emphasize the leading role of the Black working class, to look toward Black petty-bourgeois figures as the "natural" leaders of the struggle, and even to flirt with supposedly "democratic" sectors of the white ruling class. All this disoriented the party's ranks, and prevented it from developing in a healthy direction.

Throughout the period in which the CPSA was groping toward involvement in the national liberation struggle, it was the Industrial and Commercial Workers' Union that dominated Black politics. At a time when the ANC's influence remained limited and its actual membership was relatively small, the ICU adopted a perspective of organizing the masses of Black workers into a militant organization capable of standing up to the white bosses and their racist regime. Its members included laundry workers, farm laborers, municipal employees, domestic servants, and factory workers—those who felt the brunt of South Africa's severe class oppression.

The ICU did not limit itself to the economic concerns of Black workers, though that was a main emphasis. It also addressed itself to the major political questions affecting Black people in general: the pass laws, the color bar in employment, high taxation, police repression, landlessness, and many other grievances. It sought to combine aspects of the struggles of Black workers as a class and as an oppressed people. Despite the limitations of Kadalie's leadership, the ICU had a tremendous potential and was an inspiration to millions of Blacks.

By the time of the January 1923 conference of the ICU, the union had seventeen registered branches in various parts of the country. At the end of the following year, Kadalie began an organizing tour that resulted in the formation of important new branches in Durban and Johannesburg, while the ICU's membership rose to some thirty thousand, about one-third of them women. Members of the Communist Party helped in the formation of the Johannesburg branch; the ANC, on the other hand, proved somewhat hostile. The formation of the ICU branch in Bloemfontein helped pressure the Wage Board there to set a minimum wage for Blacks. The national ICU launched its own newspaper, the *Workers Herald.*

Although the leadership of the ICU did not in practice follow socialist policies, the union was nonetheless influenced by socialist ideas, most directly through its Communist members. This influence was especially evident in the ICU's 1925 constitution, whose preamble declared:

> Whereas the interest of the workers and those of the employers are opposed to each other, the former living by selling their labour, receiving for it only part of the wealth they produce; and the latter living by exploiting the labour of the workers; depriving the workers of a part of the product of their labour in the form of profit, no peace can be between the two classes, a struggle must always obtain about the division of the products of human labour, until the workers through their industrial organisations take from the capitalist class the means of production, to be owned and controlled by the workers for the benefit of all, instead of for the profit of a few.[28]

One of the key grievances that the ICU sought to initiate action on was the system of pass laws. An ICU resolution stated, for instance, "that Passes, no matter what shape or form, are nothing more or less than an institution of the present capitalist system of government to reduce the African workers to a state of abject servility so as to facilitate their utmost exploitation. . . ."[29] The ICU made a proposal in 1925 for a countrywide general strike against the passes, in collaboration with the ANC. But when the ANC proved reluctant to get involved, the general strike plan was dropped.

The ICU was harassed by the authorities, but its mass base dictated caution on their part. They generally avoided direct repression against the union and instead sought to blunt the ICU's effectiveness by diverting it toward class-collaborationist channels.

Kadalie fell under the influence of a group of white bourgeois liberals who urged him to adopt a "moderate" approach and to drive the Communists out of the ICU. At a December 1926 meeting of the National Council, a motion was narrowly passed calling for the expulsion of all Communist Party members, unless they resigned from the party. Among the CPSA members in the

28. Karis and Carter, *From Protest to Challenge,* 1:325.

29. Clements Kadalie, *My Life and the ICU,* p. 76.

union leadership, La Guma, Gomas, and Khaile refused and were expelled. The white-controlled press hailed the expulsions, while some ICU branches protested against them.

A few days after the expulsions, Kadalie assured the government and employers that the ICU now believed in "constitutional methods" and that "the strike weapon was obsolete."[30] Declaring himself "entirely opposed to revolutionary methods,"[31] Kadalie proceeded to dampen the ICU's militancy. While the ranks demanded action, the leadership temporized. This was glaringly evident during a series of spontaneous strikes in 1927 and 1928. About 4,500 coal miners struck in Natal, but were disowned by the ICU headquarters in Durban. Another 1,500 dockers in Durban walked off their jobs twice, with no help from the ICU. In Johannesburg, railway workers struck for higher wages, but were urged to go back by a senior ICU official. Though they rejected this "advice," the strike was quickly broken. The *Workers Herald,* the ICU paper, declared a week later that the "reasonable attitude of I.C.U. officials" during the Johannesburg strike "should prove to the Government that they are not dealing with a lot of hotheads. . . ."[32] In June 1928, some 30,000 African diamond miners in Lichtenburg struck against wage cuts; the ICU threw its weight behind a government-sponsored compromise offer. The ICU's general inaction weakened it politically, sapping the confidence of its members and tarnishing its credibility.

The ICU leadership's "reasonable attitude," however, did not win it the respectability among white trade union circles that it had hoped to achieve. In 1927 it applied for affiliation to the South African Trade Union Congress, but the white union bureaucrats, including former CPSA leader Andrews, recoiled at the prospect of tens of thousands of Blacks joining their federation. They rejected the application.

As an organization, the ICU had not yet passed its peak. It continued to stand as a beacon of hope to the laborers of the cities and the countryside. Tens of thousands still flocked to it. In

30. *International Press Correspondence* (Inprekorr), 7, no. 19 (March 11, 1927), p. 381.

31. Roux, *Time Longer Than Rope,* p. 168.

32. *International Press Correspondence* (Inprekorr), 7, no. 68 (December 1, 1927), p. 1538.

January 1927, the ICU claimed a membership of 57,760. By the end of the year, its claimed membership reached 100,000 and by early 1928 "very nigh to 200,000."[33] At its height, the ICU had some 100 branches around the country, including in each of the eleven biggest cities. Much of this new influx came from rural areas or the smaller towns, however, where agricultural laborers rallied to the union in search of relief from their onerous working conditions.

Kadalie and his lieutenants were certainly successful in forging a mighty working class weapon. But they shrank from using it.

The political upswing that began during World War I started to recede by the late 1920s, largely under the combined impact of a series of harsh repressive measures by the regime and the failure of the various political and trade union leaderships to give it a clear and audacious direction.

This downturn found its sharpest expression in the rapid decline of the ICU. The leadership's inability to establish a stable base among industrial workers, its failure to define the union's immediate tasks, and especially its refusal to use the ICU as a militant weapon of struggle against the white employing class all weakened the organization and left it more vulnerable to factional conflicts. By 1928, the year of the ICU's greatest membership, these conflicts burst into the open with the breakaway of the Natal section, the largest in the country. From that point on, generalized disintegration set in, and was accelerated by the interference of the white liberals. Within a few years, there were at least eight groups calling themselves the ICU.

The breakup gave the regime the opportunity it was waiting for. With less worry about having to face an organized response, it unleashed the police against strikers, arrested union leaders, and generally did its best to try to stamp out the fragmented remnants of the ICU. A general strike led by Kadalie in East London was crushed.

Kadalie tried to revive the ICU on a national basis during the early 1930s, but failed. The first mass Black workers' organization in South Africa had ceased to exist as anything more than a shadow of its former self.

With the dissipation of the ICU, some of its leaders and members gravitated toward the African National Congress, the only Black organization remaining on a national scale. This

33. Wickins, *Industrial and Commercial Workers' Union,* pp. 116, 202.

briefly injected some life into the ANC's mainly dormant body. More ANC leaders began to speak of mass action, including its president, Gumede.

The regime took careful note of these developments and adopted a policy of selective repression against the more radical elements in the ANC. In one case, after local ANC leaders held an illegal May Day demonstration in the Western Cape in 1930, the police invaded the African township in Worcester and gunned down five Africans. Having watched the disintegration of the ICU with great satisfaction, the authorities were hardly inclined to allow the ANC to try to fill the vacuum.

Nor were the more conservative leaders of the ANC itself interested in taking up the role vacated by the ICU. In the Western Cape, a radical wing of the ANC led by Bransby Ndobe and Elliot Tonjeni was forced out of the organization. Gumede, too, was soon ousted from the national leadership. With the challenge from the activists squelched for the moment, the ANC leadership reverted to its favored policy of *hambe khale* (go slow). It was once again a period of deputations, appeals, and collaboration with the white bourgeois liberals.

The Communist Party, too, went into sharp decline, asphyxiated by Moscow's tightening hold. At a time when Stalin's Communist International was going through an ultraleft and sectarian swing, the CPSA was forced to adopt a hostile attitude toward the existing Black organizations, including the ICU and ANC. Moscow ordered the dissolution of the League of African Rights, a Black united-front organization initiated by Bunting that was beginning to attract a following. The party embarked on an adventurist and politically isolated pass-burning campaign in 1930 that exposed its members to attack; a party leader in Durban, Johannes Nkosi, was killed during the campaign.

On top of all this, a series of devastating purges initiated by Moscow nearly destroyed the CPSA. Bunting was removed from the leadership and later expelled. Throughout the early 1930s many others were booted out as well, including many of its most prominent Black leaders. The party was reduced to a shell. From a largely Black membership of 3,000 in 1929, it had plunged by 1933 to 150 members, most of them white.[34]

34. Roux, *Time Longer Than Rope,* p. 269.

15

Exploring New Roads

The 1930s were a decade of rapid Black urbanization. The influx into the main cities of tens of thousands of Blacks swelled the ranks of the working class and filled the townships to overflowing. Blacks had only to look around to realize the strength of their numbers and the social power they held as the mainstay of the South African economy. This bolstered their self-confidence. It lessened the impact of political setbacks and gave the mass movement greater resilience.

Thus the collapse of the ICU, the degeneration of the Communist Party, and the dormancy of the ANC did not lead to a prolonged period of political demoralization or passivity. Rather, it prompted political activists to question old methods and seek new ways to move forward. While the 1920s were dominated by just a few groups, the 1930s and 1940s witnessed a proliferation. Alternative political strategies were hotly debated and put to the test of practice, against a background of sharpening working class militancy.

One of the earliest (and shortest lived) attempts to strike out along a new path was the formation in 1930 of the Independent ANC, based in the Western Cape and led by Bransby Ndobe and Elliot Tonjeni, who had been driven out of the ANC for their radical views. The Independent ANC favored the building of a "militant African liberation movement which will not bow the knee to British and Boer Imperialism." Unlike the ANC, which sought to avoid mass action and did not go much beyond an emphasis on the need of Blacks to achieve equality of opportunity, its militant offshoot called for the establishment of a Black republic through mass demonstrations and a "general stoppage of work."[1] If the Independent ANC had had a chance to consolidate itself, its slogan for a Black republic and its orientation toward the masses of Blacks could have transformed it into an important political force. But the regime was not about to give it a chance. Both Ndobe and Tonjeni, its guiding figures, were banished from the area, and the group soon collapsed.

The demise of the Communist Party as a revolutionary force also prompted the emergence of new groups. The most important current within the workers' movement to develop in opposition to the Stalinist policies of the CPSA were the supporters of Leon Trotsky, who was leading a fight internationally against the degeneration of the Russian revolution and the bureaucratization of the Communist International. Under the difficult conditions of a downturn in the world class struggle at that time, the Trotskyists attempted to keep alive the traditions of revolutionary socialism. Although they did not grow into a sizeable force in South Africa, they were to have a political impact out of proportion to their numbers, particularly in the 1930s and 1940s.

Some Trotskyists had been expelled from the Communist Party during the purges. Others developed outside of it. A small grouping arose in Johannesburg, but the bulk were centered around Cape Town, where they established the Lenin Club in 1932. Many were white, but there were also a number of Coloured members, some of whom were in the leadership of the Coloured Unemployment League, which had thirty thousand members in the year the Lenin Club was formed. The public forums of the Lenin Club drew large audiences.[2]

A May Day manifesto issued by the club in 1934 criticized the policies of the Third (Communist) International and of the CPSA. It called not only for the formation of a new communist party in South Africa, but also for a new, a fourth International. "We shall start," it declared, "richer from the experience of the past, to build a new Revolutionary International, a new Revolutionary Workers' Party, a party which will be true to the best traditions of Marx and Lenin and their achievement in the October [Russian]

1. Peter Walshe, *The Rise of African Nationalism in South Africa,* p. 183.

2. Anthony J. Southall, "Marxist Theory in South Africa Until 1940," p. 34; Hendrik W. van der Merwe and C. J. Groenewald (eds.), *Occupational and Social Change Among Coloured People in South Africa,* p. 192; Edward Roux, *Time Longer Than Rope,* p. 312.

Revolution, a party which will . . . win the confidence of the workers and oppressed masses of South Africa. . . ."[3]

The Lenin Club, however, was already stricken by disputes, and split into two public factions in 1934. One established the Workers Party of South Africa (WPSA), also known as the Spartacist Club. It published a mimeographed magazine, the *Spark,* for several years. The other was briefly known as the Communist League, but then renamed itself the Fourth International Organisation of South Africa (FIOSA). It linked up with a Trotskyist grouping in Johannesburg and published *Workers Voice* off and on during the 1930s and 1940s.

Among other political differences, the WPSA emphasized the centrality of the agrarian revolution and the role of the African peasantry, while the FIOSA stressed the leading role of the urban working class and placed the agrarian revolution within the context of the broader struggle for national liberation. Both favored the abolition of all repressive and racist legislation and the attainment by Blacks of their national liberation. But they were nevertheless quite hostile to the Communist Party's call for a Black republic, not only because it was couched in terms of a bourgeois republic, but *also* because of its national content. In this, their position was no better than that defended by Bunting and Roux in 1928. A central document of the WPSA rejected the call for a Black republic with the fallacious argument that "instead of uniting the workers it again splits them on racial grounds."[4] The FIOSA (when it was still called the Communist League) agreed with this rejection, adding that the slogan was "chauvinistic in its implication."[5]

Both groups sent copies of their main political theses to Trotsky, but only the WPSA's apparently reached him. In April 1935 Trotsky wrote a reply to the WPSA, taking up a few critical points, especially on the national question. Trotsky wrote:

> When the theses say that the slogan of a "black republic" is *equally* harmful for the revolutionary cause as is the slogan of a "South Africa for

3. Lenin Club, "Workers of South Africa, Awake!" manifesto issued in Cape Town, May 1, 1934. (Copy in author's files.)

4. Workers Party of South Africa, "Draft Thesis. The Native Question," [1934?]. (Copy in author's files.)

5. *Workers Voice* (Cape Town), February 1936.

the whites," then we cannot agree with the form of the statement. Whereas in the latter there is the case of supporting complete oppression, in the former there is the case of taking the first steps toward liberation.

We must accept decisively and without any reservations the complete and unconditional right of the blacks to independence. Only on the basis of a mutual struggle against the domination of the white exploiters can the solidarity of black and white toilers be cultivated and strengthened.[6]

Trotsky also noted that under the conditions of a victorious revolution,

the South African republic will emerge first of all as a "black" republic; this does not exclude, of course, either full equality for the whites or brotherly relations between the two races—depending mainly on the conduct of the whites. But it is entirely obvious that the predominant majority of the population, liberated from slavish dependence, will put a certain imprint on the state.

Insofar as a victorious revolution will radically change the relation not only between the classes but also between the races and will assure to the blacks that place in the state that corresponds to their numbers, thus far will the *social* revolution in South Africa also have a *national* character.[7]

In the light of Trotsky's suggestions, the South African Trotskyists subsequently laid greater stress on the national character of the South African revolution, although a strong sectarian streak continued to run through their political approach toward most of the existing Black organizations. This weakness—especially glaring in a country like South Africa—was to be a prime factor limiting the Trotskyists' growth and overall political effectiveness.

The introduction in 1934 of Prime Minister Hertzog's segregationist bills—which included the threatened abolition of the African vote in the Cape and the establishment of a quisling Natives' Representative Council (NRC)—provoked a sharp resurgence of African political activity.

Responding to a call issued by a wide range of Black organizations, more than four hundred delegates representing various groups throughout the country gathered for an All African Convention in Bloemfontein in December 1935 to discuss ways to oppose the bills. It was the broadest Black gathering in South

6. Leon Trotsky, "On the South African Theses," p. 250.

7. Ibid., p. 249.

African history up to that time and marked an impressive display of African unity in face of the regime's new attacks. It drew some of the most prominent Black leaders, including D. D. T. Jabavu, A. W. G. Champion, Selby Msimang, J. B. Marks, Clements Kadalie, and others, who represented groups ranging from local community organizations to such bodies as the ANC, ICU, Communist Party, and the Trotskyist groups.

Recognizing the potential of this broad national gathering of the oppressed, the Trotskyists pressed for the All African Convention's establishment as an ongoing body. Goolam Gool, a prominent Coloured activist and a leader of the FIOSA, proposed from the floor that the AAC "lay the foundations of a national liberation movement to fight against all the repressive laws of South Africa."[8] The convention, however, decided on very little. It called for another meeting, passed a resolution rejecting the Hertzog bills, and instructed a delegation to inform Hertzog of the AAC's decision.

The initial expectations aroused by the All African Convention of a united opposition to Hertzog's policies were soon dashed. Shortly after the convention, some AAC representatives agreed to a "compromise" with Hertzog (acceptance of the bills if Africans could elect three white members of parliament). At the second convention of the AAC, held in June 1936, the door to capitulation was opened even wider. Although the AAC was formally established as a standing body, it also sanctioned Jabavu's proposal that the AAC "evolve an intermediary policy of using what can be used and fighting against all that we do not want,"[9] a formula that was elastic enough to allow AAC leaders to sit on the government's Natives' Representative Council under the claim that they could use it against the government. (Although opposition to this course was defeated, Gool, one of the more outspoken advocates of boycotting the NRC, was elected to the AAC's Executive Committee.)

Following the conference, the majority of members of the AAC Executive fell over each other in their scramble to win seats on the council. The ANC fielded a number of candidates and several of its leaders won positions. The ANC also supported the election

8. D. D. T. Jabavu, *The Findings of the All African Convention* (n.p., 1935), p. 34.

9. D. D. T. Jabavu (ed.), *Minutes of the All African Convention* (n.p.: Lovedale Press, 1936), p. 43.

of some white liberals to fill the posts of "African representatives" in parliament. The Communist Party encouraged this collaboration on the ANC's part, and itself ran candidates for the NRC, including Edwin Mofutsanyana. CPSA leader George Hardy attacked "Trotskyists and other opportunists" for proposing a boycott of the elections.[10]

The conservative stance of the AAC was further codified at its third conference in December 1937, where a clause in its new constitution recognized the NRC members as "the accepted mouthpiece" of the AAC. However, despite the mistaken policies of the AAC leadership on the question of the NRC, the organization continued to call for an end to segregation, for franchise rights and direct representation of Africans in parliament, for equal pay for equal work, for freedom to organize trade unions and to strike, for an end to restrictions on African land ownership, and for other rights.[11]

To an extent, the participation of the African National Congress in the NRC gave the ANC leaders greater visibility and kept the name of the ANC alive, but it did nothing to shake the organization out of its lethargy. Nor was its collaboration with the NRC likely to attract to it much of a mass following. James Calate, a leader of the ANC, revealed in 1939 that the congress had a membership of only four thousand.[12]

Although both the AAC and ANC failed to rally Blacks against the government attacks, other groups with a more activist approach began to spring up, especially among the Coloured community in the Western Cape. The African People's Organisation of Abdullah Abdurahman was no longer a significant force, but it was younger members of Abdurahman's own family who helped spur Coloureds back into political action. Most notable of them were Zainunnissa (Cissie) Gool, who was a member of the

10. H. J. Simons and R. E. Simons, *Class and Colour in South Africa, 1850-1950,* pp. 495-96. A resolution of the Political Bureau of the CPSA that same year called for a "united front" of the Communist Party, the South African Labour Party, and "the rank and file of the Nationalist Party." It also called for a racially differentiated minimum wage—10 shillings a day for white workers but only 5 shillings for Africans. (Southall, "Marxist Theory in South Africa," p. 67.)

11. Thomas Karis and Gwendolen M. Carter, *From Protest to Challenge,* 2:61, 64.

12. Ibid., 2:85.

Communist Party's Political Bureau, and her brother-in-law, Goolam Gool, the Trotskyist leader. Both were central leaders of the National Liberation League (NLL), founded in Cape Town in late 1935. While it was largely Coloured in membership, it was one of the first groups to emphasize the necessity of building unity among all Blacks—Coloureds, Africans, and Indians—in a struggle against their common oppressors. With this aim in view, the NLL called a national conference of trade unions, cultural bodies, and political organizations in Cape Town in March 1938. The delegates agreed to form a new Black organization, the Non-European United Front (NEUF), open to all Blacks.

The NEUF soon faced the test of action. The Cape government had authorized municipal councils to enforce segregationist measures in housing and in public places, the first time Coloureds were threatened with legal segregation in more than a century. The NEUF demanded the repeal of racial laws and organized a mass demonstration in Cape Town in March 1939. Cissie Gool told the crowd, "Our weapons will be the strike, the boycott and peaceful demonstrations."[13] The protesters marched on the parliament buildings, where they were met by a police attack. But the demonstration achieved its goal. The government withdrew its ordinance and dropped its proposals for further segregationist measures, for the moment at least.

Fresh from this victory, the NEUF held a conference in Cape Town two weeks later. It was largely dominated by members of the Communist Party, but the participants also included Charles van Gelderen, who represented the FIOSA, and Ben Kies of the WPSA and the Trotskyist-influenced New Era Fellowship.[14] This broad political representation soon narrowed, however, as Gool and other Trotskyists were either expelled or forced out of the NLL and NEUF, leaving leadership of those organizations almost entirely in the hands of the Communist Party members.

In the years immediately preceding World War II, there was also a ripple of unrest on the labor front. An economic boom in South Africa in the mid-to-late 1930s had resulted in a rapid expansion of secondary industry, and the number of African workers in manufacturing doubled within just a two-year period.

13. Simons and Simons, *Class and Colour,* p. 502.

14. Non-European United Front, *NEUF of SA: Minutes of Conference, April 8-9, 1939* (Cape Town).

This growth was accompanied by a series of strikes and union organizing campaigns.

The Federation of Non-European Trade Unions, originally formed under Communist influence, had fallen apart by the early 1930s. But the Native Clothing Workers Union, led by Gana Makabeni (who had been expelled from the CPSA during the purges), managed to survive and become the nucleus of a new group of African-led unions. In 1938 Makabeni became the chairman of the Non-European Trade Union Coordinating Committee.

One of the most effective union organizers in the Transvaal in the late 1930s was Max Gordon. A young white member of the Trotskyist WPSA, he had moved to Johannesburg from Cape Town with the specific aim of helping to organize Black unions. In May 1935 he became secretary of the almost defunct African Laundry Workers Union, soon leading it out on a successful strike for higher wages. Together with African unionists like Daniel Koza, Gordon helped unionize Black workers in more than twenty trades, including construction, iron and steel, restaurant, motor, commercial, department store, printing, and warehouse workers. A Joint Committee of African Trade Unions was formed, with Gordon as secretary. By 1939 it included eleven unions claiming twenty thousand members, some six-sevenths of all organized African workers in Johannesburg at the time. Gordon's trade union activities were abruptly interrupted in May 1940 when he was interned by the Smuts regime as a "safety measure"; the authorities accused him of communist activities and of organizing African unions in order to foster unrest. Koza and other Black unionists took over Gordon's responsibilities. (After his release from internment in 1941, Gordon briefly resumed his work in Port Elizabeth, before retiring from trade union activities entirely.)[15]

The outbreak of World War II provided another catalyst to the struggles of South Africa's oppressed peoples and classes. But it

15. Roux, *Time Longer Than Rope,* pp. 327-28; Simons and Simons, *Class and Colour,* p. 511; Mark Stein, "Max Gordon and African Trade Unionism on the Witwatersrand, 1935-1940," in Eddie Webster (ed.), *Essays in Southern African Labour History,* pp. 143-57; Baruch Hirson, "The Reorganization of African Trade Unions in Johannesburg, 1936-42," in *The Societies of Southern Africa in the 19th and 20th Centuries,* vol. 7, University of London Institute of Commonwealth Studies Collected Seminar Papers No. 21 (London, 1977), pp. 182-94; taped interview with Joyce Meissenheimer, 1977.

also exposed how removed the Communist Party had become from the basic interests of those it claimed to represent and how much it had been transformed into an obedient appendage of Moscow, following without question every twist and turn in the Kremlin's foreign policy.

In the first two years of the war, the period of the Stalin-Hitler pact, the CPSA held an "antiwar" position, that is, it opposed South Africa's participation in the war on the side of Britain. Playing to the nearly universal sentiment among Blacks that their real enemy was in South Africa itself, and that they had nothing to gain by supporting one imperialist power against another, the CPSA Central Committee declared in June 1939, "The fight against Fascism must start in our own country."[16] Yusuf M. Dadoo, a CPSA leader, was jailed for four months for an antiwar leaflet put out by the Transvaal Non-European United Front, which he headed.

Simultaneously, however, the Communists bent toward the National Party, which opposed South African involvement in the war because it sympathized with Hitler. An Afrikaans pamphlet by CPSA leader Franz Boshoff called on Afrikaners to oppose both British imperialism and Afrikaans capital, but conveniently avoided mentioning that the National Party was a capitalist party.[17] Representatives of the Communist and National parties held a number of joint meetings to condemn the war. At one, CPSA leader Harry Snitcher, referring to the Nationalist speaker, declared, "I think if we scratch under Mr. Van Zyl's Nationalist skin, we will find a genuine socialist."[18]

When Hitler attacked the Soviet Union in June 1941, the entire nature of the war suddenly changed—according to the Stalinists. Overnight, the imperialist governments of Britain and its allies became defenders of "democracy." The white supremacist Smuts

16. *Must We Fight?* (Cape Town: Communist Party of South Africa, 1939), p. 15.

17. Boshoff also tried to pin the sole responsibility for South Africa's colonial policies on the British, absolving the Afrikaners of their role in the oppression of Blacks. "It is an irrefutable fact that the natives and the Afrikaners are both colonized peoples." (Franz Boshoff, *Die Afrikaner en Britse imperialisme*, p. 12.)

18. *Workers Voice* (Cape Town), November 1944. H. Morkel, a CPSA writer, later delicately explained that "before June 1941, we found ourselves in the company of the Nationalists, who also opposed the war but for different reasons" (*Freedom/Vryheid*, April 1942).

regime, which was fighting in the war on their side, was portrayed in a new light. Yusuf Dadoo, now released from prison, urged Blacks to support unconditionally the regime's war policies.[19] A statement of the CPSA Central Committee affirmed that "the Communist Party is fully aware of the importance of strengthening the Government in its war effort."[20] The party dropped its overtures toward the National Party and instead joined hands with various "liberal" bourgeois forces, including elements of the ruling United Party. In 1942 the CPSA launched a "Defend South Africa" campaign.

Following the logic of its position, the party muted its criticisms of the regime, and party activists tried to dampen the various struggles that they were involved in. A pamphlet addressed to workers stated, "Today, above all things . . . workers must try all ways of settling disputes with the bosses before calling strikes. For strikes hold up the supply of weapons, of arms, of uniforms, to our armies fighting for freedom."[21]

The Trotskyists, on the other hand, maintained that the Soviet Union's involvement in the war—while it did necessitate calling for military defense of the Soviet Union—did not alter the class character of the war between the Allied imperialist powers and Japan and Germany. It was still an interimperialist conflict for a redivision of the world's markets and colonies. They thus argued that working people should not support the Smuts government's war effort and should continue fighting for their rights at home.

The Communist Party had much greater political influence, however, and with at least tacit government approval was able to widely propagate its position on the war. It was largely successful in transforming the NEUF into a prowar body—but not without some resistance from the front's ranks. According to Edward Roux, "In 1942 at a local conference of the Non-European United Front at Port Elizabeth, the communists moved a motion urging a second front in Europe. A Coloured follower of the Trotskyist organisation opposed the motion from the body of the hall and secured its rejection by the meeting, which then affirmed its belief

19. Roux, *Time Longer Than Rope*, p. 310.

20. *Communists' Plan for Victory: Reports of the Central Committee of the Communist Party of South Africa to the National Conference held at Johannesburg, January 1943*, p. 10.

21. *More Money* (Johannesburg: Communist Party of South Africa, n.d.), p. 22.

that non-Europeans should not support an imperialist war."[22]

The African National Congress, while not as rabidly prowar as the CPSA, likewise softened its already mild criticisms of the Smuts regime.

The Black masses themselves saw little reason to forego their own fight against white supremacy and class rule simply to allow Smuts to carry on unhindered. Spontaneously, and in some cases by throwing up new leaderships, they participated in their tens of thousands in a series of massive strikes, demonstrations, and boycotts that swept from one corner of the country to the other and that involved all three sectors of the Black community—African, Coloured, and Indian.

Hit hard by wartime inflation, Black workers initiated a new wave of strikes beginning in 1941. Municipal workers, railway and dock laborers, milk distributors, and coal miners walked out on the Rand and in Natal. In one strike near Pretoria, sixteen African strikers were shot to death by white police and troops. Smuts clamped down with War Measure Act No. 145, which prohibited "all strikes by all Africans under all circumstances."[23]

The Communist Party, as part of its support to the regime's war drive, urged Africans to return to work. In criticizing a strike by Durban dockers in July 1942, it tried to justify its stance by pointing out that they had been involved in "vital work for the war effort."[24] Three months later, the Central Committee of the party urged African workers to avoid "any stoppage of work."[25]

Black workers ignored both Smuts and the CPSA, engaging in some sixty illegal strikes between 1942 and 1944. In some cases, all the strikers were arrested or fired.

Black unionization expanded rapidly, reaching a level comparable to that of the heyday of the ICU in the 1920s. Founded in 1942, the Council of Non-European Trade Unions (CNETU) developed into the major Black labor federation in the country, claiming 119 affiliated unions and 158,000 members by 1945, about 40 percent of all Africans employed in commerce and

22. Roux, *Time Longer Than Rope,* p. 313.

23. Mary Benson, *The Struggle for a Birthright,* p. 78.

24. David Hemson, "Dock Workers, Labour Circulation, and Class Struggles in Durban, 1940-59," *Journal of Southern African Studies* (Oxford) 4, no. 1 (October 1977), p. 98.

25. *Communists' Plan for Victory,* p. 47.

manufacturing. The fifty or so African unions on the Rand fell into four rough political categories: those under the leadership of Gana Makabeni, the chairman of the CNETU; those influenced by the Communist Party; those initiated by Max Gordon, and now under the leadership of Daniel Koza; and those influenced by the Workers International League, a Trotskyist group that emerged during the war through a split in the Johannesburg section of the FIOSA.[26]

One of the most important unions to arise during the war was the African Mine Workers Union (AMWU), headed by J. B. Marks of the CPSA. It was the first—and to this day only—union to win any significant backing from the largely migrant African workers in the crucial gold mines. By 1944, the AMWU had enlisted twenty-five thousand members.

Hundreds of miles away, in the Western Cape, the Coloured population again mobilized to counter new government threats against them: Smuts's proposal to set up a Coloured Affairs Department (CAD) and a Coloured Advisory Council (CAC), as a prelude to even greater segregation against Coloureds. They rallied around a newly formed group, the Anti-CAD, to oppose the establishment of the CAD and CAC and to "canalize all non-European sentiment and endeavour—economic, political and social—in one mighty stream that will expunge from the statute book all discriminatory legislation."[27]

The Anti-CAD had a very broad base. At its first national conference in May 1943, some two hundred delegates attended, representing 109 organizations, including trade unions, teachers' groups, student associations, and such political formations as the APO, AAC, Communist Party, NEUF, and FIOSA. The original initiative for the formation of this united-front body came from the New Era Fellowship, a Trotskyist-influenced discussion and education group; many of the top leaders of the Anti-CAD were Trotskyists, including Goolam Gool, I. B. Tabata, Ali Fataar, Ben Kies, and Hosea Jaffe. The Teachers League of South Africa, which in 1944 began to play an increasingly central role in the fight against the CAD and CAC, was also under Trotskyist leadership.

The Anti-CAD held innumerable rallies and meetings throughout the Western Cape, many of them drawing thousands of

26. Roux, *Time Longer Than Rope*, pp. 332-33.

27. Simons and Simons, *Class and Colour*, p. 541.

participants. It ran candidates for community-elected school boards, winning control of some high schools and transforming them into organizing centers. It won support from as far away as Port Elizabeth, where a meeting of twenty-five hundred African workers expressed solidarity with the struggle against the CAC. It launched a broad boycott of the CAC and put considerable social and political pressure on Coloured collaborators who sought positions on it.[28]

The Anti-CAD gave expression to a popular protest against segregation and, according to Farieda Khan, it "did more than any other single organization in the Cape, to politicize and shake out of its lethargy and comfort, that section of the population classified as Coloured."[29]

This upsurge in the Western Cape provided a promising basis for leaders of the Anti-CAD to try to solidify links with other Black organizations, in what was projected as an attempt to build unity among all sectors of the oppressed.

The All African Convention, by that time, had been transformed; the ANC's decision to pull out of it reduced its base, but it also left the AAC in the hands of a more militant leadership, which included I. B. Tabata (an African Trotskyist who also played a role in the Anti-CAD). Under this new influence, the AAC turned its back on its past policy of collaboration with the Natives' Representative Council and called for boycotting all government-sponsored bodies. It also pressed for broader Black unity, noting that "the striving for freedom of all the oppressed people in South Africa, the Africans, the Coloured, and the Indians, is identical in aim and methods."[30]

In a bid to concretize the latter goal, the AAC and Anti-CAD (along with a variety of unions, community bodies, and political groups) united in December 1943 to found the Non-European Unity Movement (NEUM). It issued a ten-point program that called for complete equality; a full franchise for all; free, compulsory, and uniform education for every child; freedom of speech, press, association, movement, and occupation; land reform; and other democratic demands.

To try to make the organization more representative, the

28. Farieda Khan, "The Origins of the Non-European Unity Movement," pp. 60-82; taped interview with Joyce Meissenheimer, 1977.

29. Khan, "Origins of the Non-European Unity Movement," p. 81.

30. I. B. Tabata, *The Awakening of a People*, p. 55.

leaders of the NEUM called on the ANC and the South African Indian Congress (SAIC) to join in the new movement on the basis of the ten-point program. But the political differences among the leaderships of the groups were too sharp. The ANC was still reluctant to boycott the Natives' Representative Council, and the SAIC was beginning to come under the political influence of the Communist Party. The NEUM leaders were also sectarian, refusing to seek collaboration with the ANC and SAIC around specific united-front actions, and in fact spurning such proposals when they were made.

The program for democratic rights put forward by the NEUM could have provided an important impetus to the overall fight for national liberation had it been more closely linked to the ongoing, day-to-day struggles of the masses of Blacks. But the leaders of the NEUM limited themselves to expounding the program in a propagandistic—and in later years virtually ritualistic—fashion. Failing to absorb the experience of the Anti-CAD struggle in the Western Cape, they advanced no coherent program of *action,* no set of concrete, immediate demands that could have been used to help mobilize the oppressed around specific issues. They in fact counterposed such limited struggles to the goal of attaining the full ten-point program. Tabata, for instance, denounced those who sought to focus on the issue of the pass laws, stating that to do so would "deflect the attention of the people from the fundamental cause of their disabilities and at the same time distort the nature of the campaign."[31] The NEUM thus failed to appreciate that battles around immediate demands, through which the masses gain political experience and confidence in their abilities, can provide a basis upon which broader struggles can then be built.

Connected with this ultimatistic conception of how to win democratic rights, the NEUM elevated the use of the boycott weapon (against the NRC, local advisory bodies, and other institutions) into a virtual principle, applicable at all times and under all circumstances, as the *main* form of struggle. It consequently tended to stand aside from many of the demonstrations, strikes, and other mass actions that were unfolding around it.

From its formation, the NEUM became the central focus of activity for most of the South African Trotskyists, who in the process dropped their efforts to maintain an independent organizational existence. The WPSA (with which Tabata was con-

31. Khan, "Origins of the Non-European Unity Movement," p. 125.

nected)[32] had already suspended its public activities a few years earlier. By the end of the 1940s the FIOSA had done likewise. Thus at the very point when the political influence of the Trotskyists was at its widest, they abandoned their efforts to build a revolutionary socialist party in South Africa.

Despite its political weaknesses, some of the NEUM's component organizations and some of its leaders did play an important role in leading mass struggles, most notably the Anti-CAD campaign and actions by the AAC in rural areas of the Transkei and other reserves in support of peasant struggles. In addition to this immediate impact, the Unity Movement helped popularize the concepts of noncollaboration with government bodies and of African, Coloured, and Indian unity in a common struggle against the oppressors.

The upsurge in the Western Cape was not an isolated event. In both 1943 and 1944, thousands of African residents in Johannesburg's Alexandra Township boycotted buses to protest against fare hikes (some members of the Trotskyist Workers International League played a leading role in the second boycott). Both times, the boycotters were successful in driving the bus fares back to their old rates.

The rapid influx of Africans into the main urban centers during the war, combined with the regime's refusal to build additional housing for them, produced a rash of squatters' actions, as homeless Africans built illegal shantytowns. The largest and most organized began in April 1944, when twenty thousand Africans near Johannesburg occupied municipal land. Spontaneous rebellions swept a number of African townships. In 1944, up to five thousand African teachers marched through central Johannesburg to demand higher pay.

Confronted with an obvious rise in mass combativity and pressure for action from its own supporters, the ANC leadership roused itself somewhat. In 1943, the ANC, for the first time, endorsed the demand for an unqualified universal franchise in "the extension to all adults, regardless of race, of the right to vote and to be elected to parliament. . . ."[33] The following year it organized a number of demonstrations, including one of twenty thousand in Johannesburg against the pass laws.

32. Author's taped interview with I. B. Tabata, April 18, 1978.

33. Karis and Carter, *From Protest to Challenge,* 2:217.

Similar pressures for action were developing within the Indian community as well, particularly in response to new moves against Indian rights. In October 1945, a conference attended by seven thousand Indians dumped the conservative, merchant-dominated leadership of the Natal Indian Congress (NIC) and elected new leaders. Twelve of them were members of the CPSA, and G. M. Naicker, a Communist, was elected president (a few years later he became president of the South African Indian Congress as a whole). Dadoo of the CPSA had already become head of the Transvaal Indian Congress earlier, so now the main leadership of the SAIC had been brought under strong Communist Party influence.

The new leadership was much more susceptible to the rank-and-file pressures for action. Recalling the campaigns initiated by Gandhi, the NIC in March 1946 launched a "passive resistance" campaign against the government's new segregationist measures. The campaign was accompanied by large meetings and rallies, as well as some *hartals*, a form of protest in which shopkeepers closed down their businesses. The main form of mass action involved token occupations of white-owned land, resulting in nearly two thousand arrests. However, although no concessions had been won, the NIC called off the campaign just before the 1948 elections so as not to embarrass the reelection bid of Smuts, the very architect of Indian segregation. Despite this conciliatory approach of the leadership, the NIC's new policy of action won it considerable support; it quickly grew from a few hundred members to thirty-five thousand.[34]

On the labor front, the end of the war brought even greater ferment among Black workers, resulting in the biggest African strike the country had yet seen. The Communist leadership of the African Mine Workers Union had urged patience for several years and had turned down earlier rank-and-file demands for strike action. But it could no longer keep the miners in check. In August 1946, some one thousand union delegates met and approved a motion from the floor calling for a strike to press for a minimum wage and other demands.

On the first day of the walkout, August 12, fifty thousand miners refused to work. The strike quickly gained support and drew the participation of more than seventy-three thousand miners all together, affecting about twenty of the forty-five mines on the Rand. Leaflets were distributed declaring "Ikona mali—

34. Ibid., 2:114; Freda Troup, *South Africa*, p. 284.

ikona sebenza" (no money, no work). Truckloads of police were rushed to the East and West Rand. They surrounded the miners' compounds, attacked the strikers with clubs and firearms, and forced many miners back to work at bayonet point. Numerous clashes broke out, with a number of casualties, and in one incident police moved in to prevent four thousand miners from marching on Johannesburg itself.

The leaders of the strike were quickly rounded up, as was the Communist Party leadership, while the death toll among the strikers rose to thirteen. The crackdown was so severe that even those Africans sitting on the regime's Natives' Representative Council decided to protest—by adjourning the council. By August 16 the strike was over.

The union never recovered from the defeat, and the workers received only a small raise three years later. But the sheer size of the strike and its ability to paralyze the key mines again showed the country the power that African workers could wield once they decided to act. This had a profound effect on the future course of organized Black political opposition, helping to push it away from an emphasis on patient and dignified pleas for reforms and more in the direction of mass action, a proletarian form of struggle.

Above, mass rally during Defiance Campaign, 1952. Below left, Sydney P. Bunting. Below right, Clements Kadalie.

Above, police attack women demonstrators at Cato Manor, Durban, 1959. Below left, John B. Marks. Below right, Lilian Ngoyi.

Above left, Yusuf Dadoo. Above right, Albert Lutuli. Below, 30,000 protesters march into Cape Town, March 30, 1960.

Sharpeville, 1960. Above, protesters flee from police firing guns (inset). Below, aftermath of massacre.

Above, funeral for victims of Sharpeville massacre. Below left, Nelson Mandela. Below right, Robert Sobukwe.

Above, strikers in Durban, 1973. Below, outside courtroom at trial of National Youth Organisation members, Johannesburg, March, 1976.

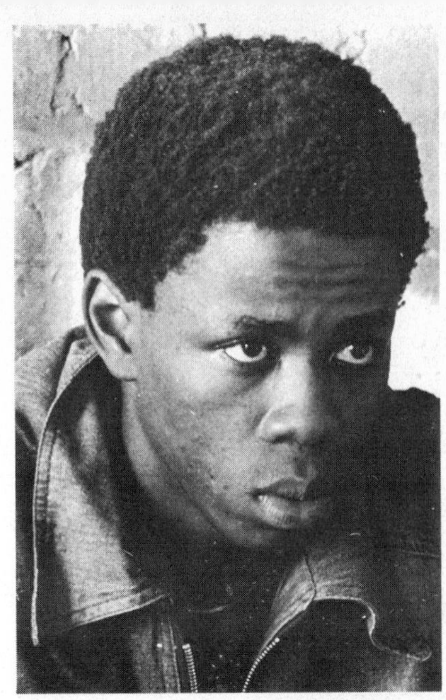

Above left, Tsietsi Mashinini. Above right, Khotso Seatlholo.
Below, Soweto demonstration, August 4, 1976.

Above, funeral procession for Steve Biko (right) in Kingwilliamstown.

16

The Awakening of African Nationalism

The political turbulence of the 1940s demonstrated that significant layers of the Black population were ready to move into action. They had mobilized repeatedly, in sufficient numbers, to reveal the potential that existed for the construction of a militant and broadly based movement for national liberation. The ranks were there. But sadly, they still lacked a determined political leadership.

The African National Congress, which claimed to be the paramount African organization, had played no more than a peripheral role. Its traditional leaders remained wedded to a policy of negotiation and compromise, an approach reflected in the willingness, even eagerness, of prominent ANC figures to sit on the regime's Natives' Representative Council. The congress's perspective at the time was not to organize the masses of Blacks and lead them in struggle against the racist regime, but to plead with the authorities for "reasonable" concessions and reforms.

Nevertheless, the ANC retained a real following. It could not remain immune from the spirit of militancy among its members and supporters. The wartime upsurge thus breathed new life into the organization.

As early as 1943, a group of young ANC activists who were buoyed by the struggles breaking out around them initiated the ANC Youth League. Its two hundred members, many of whom were students, included such future luminaries of the ANC as Nelson Mandela, Oliver Tambo, and Walter Sisulu.

The driving force behind the Youth League, however, was Anton Muziwakhe Lembede, who vocalized the aspirations of many of the younger militants and (together with A. P. Mda) formulated a newer, more radical, current of African nationalist thought.

Anticipating a later emphasis of the Black Consciousness movement, Lembede argued that one of the greatest handicaps toward an effective mobilization of the African masses was their psychological oppression resulting from the system of white supremacy, which produced among Africans a "loss of self-confidence, inferiority complex, a feeling of frustration. . . ." He stressed the need to propagate a new spirit of African nationalism as a way to raise their consciousness and mobilize them for action, declaring that "the dynamic human energy that will be released by African nationalism will be more powerful and devastating in its effects than . . . atomic energy."[1] Lembede repeatedly underlined the importance of forging solidarity among all the African language groups in South Africa (although he failed to extend this concept of Black unity to include the other oppressed peoples—the Indians and Coloureds). Unlike the older ANC leaders, Lembede and his comrades insisted that South Africa belonged to the indigenous African population by *right,* and therefore should be wrested out of the hands of the white minority. Also, unlike the older ANCers, the Youth League members recoiled from the policy of collaboration with government institutions.

Cautiously at first, but later more vociferously, the Youth League challenged the ANC leadership's conservative approach. Lembede publicly pressed for boycotting the Natives' Representative Council and branded those African leaders he considered collaborators with the regime as "traitors and quislings."[2] Gradually, the Youth League won increasing support for its positions from the ANC ranks, putting considerable heat on the leadership. In 1946, Lembede and Mda were named to the ANC's National Executive as representatives of the Youth League. The same year, under Youth League prodding, the ANC formally voted to boycott the Natives' Representative Council.

The young activists faced resistance to their militant course, both from the old-guard leaders, represented by ANC President A. B. Xuma, and from the Communist Party. Xuma obstructed the decision to boycott the NRC, and in 1947, J. B. Marks, a Communist and member of the ANC National Executive, moved

1. Gail Gerhart, *Black Power in South Africa,* pp. 58, 62.
2. Ibid., p. 81.

a resolution to allow the election of candidates to the council on a "boycott ticket." The leadership's acceptance of this permitted continued participation by members of the ANC and CPSA in the regime's fraudulent "representative" machinery. One white CPSA leader, Sam Kahn, won election in 1947 as a "Native representative." The CPSA also tried to moderate the league's militant nationalism, accusing its members of "racialism" and "chauvinism" and claiming that African domination would lead to "endless wars between black and white."[3] By doing so, the CPSA was not only bending to white racist attitudes, but was also ignoring the progressive role that the nationalism of an oppressed people can play in awakening them to political consciousness and action.

Some leaders of the Youth League responded to these attacks by the CPSA with red-baiting diatribes, and at one point even pressed for the expulsion of Communists from the ANC. But their reaction was more against the specific policies of the CPSA than against socialist ideas in general. Lembede occasionally made references to the need for "African socialism," which he described in idealistic and utopian terms.[4] A. P. Mda, on the other hand, was influenced more directly by Marxist ideas, stating that African nationalism as he understood it should aim for "full political control by workers, peasants and intellectuals," for "the liquidation of capitalism," and for the "equal distribution of wealth." He criticized both the Communist Party and the Trotskyist groups, however, for failing to appreciate the role of militant African nationalism as a catalyst for mass action. Accusing the South African Trotskyists of passivity, he nevertheless expressed admiration for Trotsky himself. "Leon Trotsky," he wrote, "was a man of action: he was a doer, a thinker, a theoretician and an orator."[5] Such views notwithstanding, Mda failed to see the interconnection between national and class oppression, insisting that while Africans suffered national oppression, "they do not suffer class oppression."[6]

3. Ibid., p. 76; Peter Walshe, *The Rise of African Nationalism in South Africa,* pp. 368-69.

4. Thomas Karis and Gwendolen M. Carter, *From Protest to Challenge,* 2:315, 318.

5. Gerhart, *Black Power,* pp. 130-31.

6. Karis and Carter, *From Protest to Challenge,* 2:320.

Despite the obstacles the Youth League faced within the ANC and despite Lembede's early death in 1947, the league continued to gain ground. By 1949 it won a decisive influence within the ANC leadership. More Youth Leaguers were elected to the National Executive, and J. S. Moroka, with Youth League backing, was chosen president to replace the more conservative Xuma.

Most significantly, the Youth League's Programme of Action, initially presented the year before, was adopted as official ANC policy, signaling a significant shift in the organization's political orientation. It went beyond the ANC's earlier timid calls for abolition of legal discrimination and recognition of equality of opportunity. It now demanded no less than "freedom from White domination and the attainment of political independence. This implies the rejection of the conception of segregation, apartheid, trusteeship, or White leadership which are all in one way or another motivated by the idea of White domination or domination of the White over the Blacks. Like all other people the African people claim the right of self-determination." This was to be achieved "under the banner of African Nationalism."[7] What governmental form "political independence" and "self-determination" should take was still left up in the air, however.

Equally important, the program recognized the burning need to begin mobilizing the masses of Africans in action. It called for an end to collaboration with the regime's segregationist institutions and pledged "to employ the following weapons: immediate and active boycott, strike, civil disobedience, non-co-operation and such other means as may bring about the accomplishment and realisation of our aspirations."[8] The days of exclusive reliance on deputations and "gentlemanly" pleas were over.

With the election of the National Party to power in 1948, and with its more rigorous implementation of white supremacy and segregation, the new leadership of the ANC was soon put to the test. Some ANC leaders who were members of the Natives' Representative Council, such as Z. K. Matthews and Moroka himself, continued to waffle, refusing to resign their seats until just before the council was abolished by the government in 1950. But others moved quickly into action.

Against the background of a series of urban uprisings in the African townships of the Rand and earlier strikes by African railway and dock workers in Durban, the ANC called a one-day

7. Ibid., 2:337, 339.

8. Ibid., 2:338.

general strike (formally termed a "work stoppage" since African strikes were illegal) on May 1, 1950. While the response to the strike call was uneven, substantial numbers of African workers heeded it in the Johannesburg area. Police intervention left eighteen Africans dead in clashes in Benoni, Orlando, Alexandra, Sophiatown, and Brakpan.

To protest this bloodbath, the ANC organized another general strike for June 26. It was called as a day of mourning for those who had given their lives in the freedom struggle and as a display of massive opposition to the newly adopted Group Areas Act, which intensified urban segregation for Coloureds and Indians, and the Suppression of Communism Act, which outlawed the Communist Party. The last measure in particular was seen as a mortal threat to the entire liberation struggle, since a successful attack against the party promised new assaults against other forces as well. Just before the act came into effect, the CPSA, more than three-quarters of whose two thousand members were Black, formally dissolved itself. The protest strike garnered significant support in some areas, most notably in Alexandra, Evaton, and the East Rand. Port Elizabeth was virtually paralyzed.

In 1951, the apartheid regime's drive to remove Coloured voters from the common franchise rolls met with stiff resistance. Demonstrations were held throughout the Cape. In April 1951 the Franchise Action Council, in which the ANC participated, called a protest strike that was widely supported by Coloureds in Port Elizabeth and the Cape Peninsula, as well as by Africans and Indians.

The ANC, in collaboration with the South African Indian Congress (SAIC) and the Franchise Action Council, embarked on a more sustained campaign in June 1952, known as the Defiance Campaign. It was called to protest six specific segregationist and repressive measures: the pass laws, the forcible reduction of livestock in African rural areas, the Suppression of Communism Act, the Group Areas Act, the imposition of the Bantu Authorities system in the reserves, and the threat against the limited Coloured voting rights.

On the pattern of the civil disobedience actions initiated by Gandhi several decades earlier, participants in the Defiance Campaign were to court arrest by breaking segregationist laws. This form of struggle tended to limit direct participation, since most Blacks were not ready to risk imprisonment as an expression of moral protest. With the conscious aim of further restricting the size of the campaign, the ANC leaders carefully screened prospective "defiers," keeping them down to several thousand disciplined volunteers over the course of the entire campaign. A later, mass phase was initially envisaged, including the use of strikes, but the ANC leaders never gave the go-ahead for it.

On June 26, the first day of the campaign, nearly 140 defiers were arrested for deliberately breaking one or more of the six target laws. In the weeks and months that followed the number of arrests rose, reaching a peak from August through October, when it climbed to 5,000. The regime quickly fashioned new repressive measures, providing for stiff penalties, including lashings, for anyone who broke a law by way of protest. This further reduced the number of volunteers willing to court arrest, and the campaign began to peter out.

The ANC leaders finally suspended the campaign before the 1953 legislative elections, so as not to detract from the election bid of the bourgeois opposition United Party, which some ANCers naively believed would adopt more favorable policies toward Blacks if elected. Yusuf Dadoo of the South African Indian Congress (and formerly of the CPSA) openly called on Coloured and Indian voters in the Cape to vote for the United Party.[9]

Despite the limitations of the protest actions and the reluctance of the ANC leadership to mobilize large numbers of Blacks, the Defiance Campaign was tremendously popular and established the ANC as the strongest Black political organization in the country. During the course of the campaign, the ANC's dues-paying membership skyrocketed from 7,000 to 100,000, the majority of them in the Eastern Cape.[10] For the first time in its history, the ANC had a real mass base.

Unfortunately, this rise in the ANC's base of support was accompanied by a decline in the organized Black labor movement, a decline that had begun with the defeat of the 1946 African miners strike. By 1950 the government was able to report that sixty-six African unions had recently ceased to function and that total African trade union membership had fallen to 38,000. Some of the leaders of the defunct unions shifted their energies toward the ANC, helping to introduce an element of working class influence into the ANC leadership. But the lack of a strong,

9. Ibid., 3:6.

10. Walshe, *Rise of African Nationalism,* pp. 402-3.

independent Black trade union movement was still a serious weakness of the national liberation struggle.

The ANC's turn toward a more active policy was like a red flag in the face of the apartheid bull. Whatever the subjective intentions of the ANC leadership and whatever unclarity still existed in its overall strategy, the white authorities feared that the organization, with its new mass following, could present a major challenge to the stability of the white supremacist order. The regime instinctively acted to hamper the ANC's activities through intimidation of its members and bannings of key leaders. Both Nelson Mandela, president of the Transvaal ANC, and Walter Sisulu, secretary general of the congress, were declared "statutory communists" under the Suppression of Communism Act and barred from attending gatherings or leaving Johannesburg. Sisulu was later ordered to resign from the ANC entirely. Chief Albert Luthuli, who was elected president-general of the ANC in December 1952, was five months later issued with similar, though less stringent restrictions. Police surveillance increased and many meetings were prohibited.

The banned ANC leaders tried to carry on from behind the scenes, while others persevered in face of the most extreme intimidation. But the repression had an impact. For more than two years after the Defiance Campaign, the ANC engaged in few significant mass activities, thus dissipating its base of support. By the end of 1953, the estimated paid-up membership had plunged to 28,900, less than a third of what it had been a year earlier.

Disillusionment in the ANC ranks spread further as a result of two dismally unsuccessful campaigns in 1955, both of which were poorly organized and executed.

The first was against government measures to forcibly evict Africans from Sophiatown, Martindale, and Newclare, all just west of Johannesburg, to a new African township (now part of Soweto), where Africans would have no land ownership rights at all. The ANC called on residents to resist the relocations, under the slogan "asi hambi" (we will not be moved). The form the resistance was to take was left unclear and the issue that the ANC focused on—the loss of land ownership rights—directly concerned only the minute layer of relatively prosperous Africans who could afford to buy land. This misdirection, combined with police intimidation, doomed the campaign to failure.

The second campaign was in opposition to the regime's new policy of Bantu Education, which sought to teach Africans, in the words of the ANC, "unquestioning acceptance of the *status quo*."[11] The ANC mapped plans for a complete and indefinite boycott of schools. It promised parents that it would set up an alternative network of schools, though it had absolutely no resources to do so. Many ANC leaders recognized that the population was unprepared for the campaign, and the National Executive Committee left the decision to go ahead with it to ANC supporters in local areas. As a consequence, the boycott was actually launched in only a few places. It quickly collapsed.

Without a clear political perspective, the ANC leadership reverted to a more cautious and conservative stance, muting the African nationalist course it had adopted with the Programme of Action. It believed that it was possible to win substantial white support by moderating its demands. While formally endorsing the concept of majority rule, ANC representatives frequently rejected the prospect of "Black domination."

In 1955, the ANC joined with several other groups to form the Congress Alliance. In the process it accepted as its new program the Freedom Charter, which had been put forward at a mass gathering, called the Congress of the People, held in Kliptown, near Johannesburg, in June of that year. The main groups that joined the ANC in organizing the conference and forming the alliance were the South African Indian Congress (SAIC), the South African Coloured People's Organisation (SACPO), and the Congress of Democrats (COD). The COD was a white organization formed in 1953 by members of the outlawed Communist Party, in alliance with some bourgeois liberals. The South African Congress of Trade Unions (SACTU), a nonracial labor federation that was also formed in 1955, likewise adhered to the alliance.

The Freedom Charter, which the ANC officially adopted in 1956, marked a partial pullback from the African nationalist positions put forward several years earlier. While the earlier Programme of Action had stressed the attainment of self-determination and political independence "under the banner of African nationalism," the Freedom Charter glossed over the nationalist side of the liberation struggle. It refrained from advocating outright Black majority rule, speaking instead of a "democratic state, based on the will of all the people" and emphasizing that "South Africa belongs to all who live in it,

11. Edward Feit, *African Opposition in South Africa,* p. 151.

black and white."[12] In a later letter to Prime Minister Strijdom, ANC President General Lutuli explicitly affirmed that it was not ANC policy to set up a "Native State."[13]

Although the Freedom Charter included a vague nationalization plank, Mandela took care to explain that "it is by no means a blueprint for a socialist state."[14]

The ANC's de-emphasizing of the national character of the struggle was accompanied by greater overtures to white "opposition" circles. This approach involved the erroneous conception that it was the National Party alone that was primarily responsible for segregation and other facets of national oppression, rather than the white ruling class as a whole. It also revealed considerable illusions in the "antiapartheid" stance of the bourgeois opposition forces, such as the United Party, which was actually invited to attend the Congress of the People (it chose not to). Lutuli even declared in a November 1957 interview that he favored a "United Party victory" in the impending elections, although he later adopted a formally "neutral" stance.[15]

The Communist Party, which had dissolved itself in 1950 under the threat of the Suppression of Communism Act, had reorganized underground about two years later as the South African Communist Party (SACP). Because of its hostility to militant African nationalism and its policy of seeking blocs with white "democratic" bourgeois forces, it bore a certain responsibility for this mutation in the ANC's policies. The party had a few key figures in the leadership of the ANC, and it politically dominated both the Congress of Democrats and the South African Indian Congress. The organizational structure of the Congress Alliance, moreover, tended to give a decision-making role to both the COD and SAIC (as well as the South African Coloured People's Organisation) that was far out of proportion to their real popular influence. While the ANC was far and away the largest of the groups, all four had a formally equal status in deciding the policies of the Congress Alliance.

The course adopted by the ANC leadership aroused dissension within the organization, especially among a sector of the younger and more militantly nationalist members. Some of them co-

12. Karis and Carter, *From Protest to Challenge,* 3:205.

13. Ibid., 3:399.

14. Nelson Mandela, *The Struggle Is My Life,* p. 55.

15. Karis and Carter, *From Protest to Challenge,* 3:282.

alesced into a tendency known as the Africanists. Its most prominent figures were A. P. Mda and Robert Mangaliso Sobukwe.

The Africanists directed their fire at the ANC's turn away from African nationalism and its openness to collaboration with white bourgeois liberals (who in the Africanists' opinion included members of the Communist Party). They attacked the phrase in the Freedom Charter that "South Africa belongs to all who live in it, black and white," charging that the ANC had thereby forfeited the African population's inalienable right to South Africa as a whole. They rejected the charter's call for equal status "for all national groups and races," proclaiming themselves "nonracialists" who recognized democratic rights only on an individual basis.[16] An editorial in the December 1955 *Africanist* accused the ANC leadership of frittering away the organization's potential "by a superfluous multiplicity of pacts with insignificant organizations." It castigated "collaborators who postpone our day of liberation by supporting dummy institutions" such as local advisory boards and administrative councils in the Bantustans. Hearkening back to the Programme of Action, it propounded "African nationalism as the sole ideological basis for the salvation of our people."[17] The Africanists likewise criticized the ANC's lack of any concrete plans for mobilizing the African masses in action.

The ANC, however, remained a real national liberation organization, with a significant following. The apartheid regime was still deathly afraid of it and of what it symbolized to millions of Blacks. Even the most moderately phrased demands for democratic rights cut to the very roots of the colonial-settler state. Nor did the white supremacists look kindly on the ANC's attempts to forge some form of unity with Indians and Coloureds.

In September 1955, just three months after the Congress of the People in Kliptown, Special Branch officers raided the homes and places of work of some four hundred persons and the offices of a number of organizations. They seized books, letters, documents, and other "incriminating" evidence. A little more than a year later, in December 1956, a total of 156 persons were arrested throughout the country and brought to Johannesburg to face charges in what came to be known as the Treason Trial. The

16. Ibid., 3:65.
17. Ibid., 3:209.

prosecution charged the defendants with membership in a "countrywide conspiracy" inspired by "international communism" to overthrow the state through force and violence. But it was the accused's political beliefs that were really in the dock. (The trial dragged on for several years, until March 1961, when the judges found the remaining defendants not guilty. By then, however, the ANC had already been banned.)

Despite the repression and the ANC hierarchy's inability to provide consistent leadership, the Black community remained far from quiescent. Throughout the second half of the 1950s, Blacks engaged in battle after battle, displaying a growing restiveness and combativity in both the cities and the countryside.

Women set a particularly militant example. They defiantly stood up in many different parts of South Africa to resist new government measures extending the despised passes to African women. In the first two years of the protests, 1955 and 1956, some forty thousand women demonstrated on thirty-eight occasions in thirty locations. The mobilizations peaked on August 9, 1956 (since celebrated as Women's Day in South Africa), when twenty thousand women converged on the Union Buildings in Pretoria. They deposited hundreds of thousands of signatures at the prime minister's office protesting the imposition of passes. Freedom songs filled the air of South Africa's capital, including a new one with the refrain, "Wathint' abafazi, way ithint' imbolodo uzo kufa" (You have touched the women, you have dislodged a boulder, you will be crushed).

The women's spirited actions continued into the following year, flowing over into some rural areas, such as Zeerust in the western Transvaal. On the first anniversary of the big protest in Pretoria, about eight thousand women demonstrated at various places throughout the country.

The women received some leadership from the Federation of South African Women, which was an adjunct of the Congress Alliance, and from the ANC's Women's League. Lilian Ngoyi, president of both organizations, assumed a prominent role in the demonstrations. Yet the women faced tremendous obstacles. Through repression and trickery, the regime eventually succeeded in foisting passes on them.

In June 1959, the anger of women, this time centering around economic issues and frequent police raids, erupted again. About two thousand women gathered to demonstrate in Cato Manor in Durban. They were charged on by the police, who brutally clubbed many. This attack provoked big protests, whose echoes spread out into the countryside of Natal. Hundreds of women were arrested and jailed.

Workers sporadically struck for higher wages or against victimization. Some of the strikes in the textile industry, most notably in Cape Town in 1956 and Durban in 1957, involved actions by African workers side by side with Coloured or Indian workers.

From 1955 to 1957, tens of thousands of Blacks in Evaton, Alexandra, and other townships in the Transvaal conducted a series of militant bus boycotts to protest fare hikes. They were successful in forcing the regime to lower the fares.

The bus boycotts gave rise to a popular demand for a £1 a day minimum wage. The ANC, in a new spurt of activity, called a general strike for June 1957 to protest against apartheid and to demand £1 a day. Despite a government crackdown before the strike, more than half of all Black workers in Johannesburg and about three-quarters of those in the industrial areas west of the city stayed away from work. There was also a notable response among dock workers in Port Elizabeth, and solidarity demonstrations were held in other towns. The following two years witnessed a series of smaller strikes, many of which were met with wholesale firings and prosecution of the strikers.

There were numerous other instances of urban strife during this period. Some twenty thousand Indians demonstrated in Durban in 1958 to condemn the Group Areas Act. Significant demonstrations were held against the extension of Bantu Education to the university level, with three thousand turning out in both Johannesburg and Cape Town. The ANC organized a popular boycott of potatoes to protest against forced prison labor on the farms. Demonstrations were staged in support of the defendants in the Treason Trial.

Provoked beyond endurance by years of police repression, poverty, poor housing, and a host of irritating regulations, African anger flared up at the slightest pretext; a series of spontaneous uprisings swept Black townships in Port Elizabeth, Johannesburg, Kimberley, East London, Cape Town, Krugersdorp, and Durban. In the worst unrest in Johannesburg, more than forty Africans were killed, many by the police. Thousands of Namibians demonstrated in 1959 in Katutura Township in Windhoek; eleven were cut down by police fire.

Popular rebellions flared up in the countryside too. The women's antipass protests in Zeerust had quickly evolved into acts of resistance against the newly imposed system of Bantu

Authorities, the tribal hierarchies set up by the regime.

In Sekhukhuneland, in the Transvaal, African peasants rallied in mass meetings to voice their rejection of the Bantu Authorities and Bantu Education. When their chief was deposed by the regime and replaced with a more subservient one, the peasants rose up.

In Tokazi (Zululand) and Pondoland (Transkei) popular opposition to government-imposed land rehabilitation schemes was so great that clashes broke out between the masses of peasants and the few supporters of the policy. The police rushed in and conducted mass arrests.

Many of those struggling against the regime and its policies looked to the ANC to provide a lead. In some cases it had responded, as in the women's antipass actions and the June 1957 general strike. But the ANC failed to provide any effective overall direction or even to set a consistent example through its own actions. Under the resulting strains, the factional conflicts within the organization sharpened.

Despite opposition from the central leadership of the ANC, the Africanist current gradually grew in strength and influence, with Robert Sobukwe emerging as one of its chief spokesmen. The current grew particularly strong in Orlando, part of present-day Soweto, where the ANC had its largest and most active branch.

The Africanists amplified their criticisms of the ANC leadership. An editorial in the December 1957 *Africanist* declared, "We have witnessed during 1957 a desire for unity and solidarity among the masses and a tendency towards crippling and contemptuous bureaucracy on the part of our leaders."[18] In an article in the same issue, Potlako K. Leballo, a leading Africanist, chided the ANC leaders for their "renunciation and denunciation of the Nationalistic" side of the struggle.[19]

The ANC leaders reacted to these criticisms in a bureaucratic manner. Africanist delegates were barred from conferences or were intimidated through strong-arm tactics. Leballo, who had been elected chairman of the ANC Youth League in Orlando, was expelled from the league. In May 1958, he and Josias Madzunya, a prominent leader in Alexandra, were ousted from the ANC itself.

This bitter factionalism finally boiled over at the November

18. Ibid., 3:498.
19. Ibid., 3:500.

1958 Transvaal provincial conference. A successful effort by ANC loyalists on the second day of the conference to bar Africanists from entering the session nearly ended in a physical confrontation. A major split ensued. In announcing their withdrawal from the organization, the Africanists declared, "We are launching out openly, on our own, as the custodians of the A.N.C. policy as it was formulated in 1912 and pursued up to the time of the Congress Alliances."[20]

During the months following this initial rupture, ANC factions and branches in Natal and the Cape also left the organization to rally around the Africanist banner. The Orlando branch went over to the Africanists in its entirety. So too did many members in Alexandra and Newclare. The Africanists struck especially firm roots in Langa, an African township near Cape Town inhabited largely by Xhosa migrant workers.

In April 1959, about three hundred delegates converged on Orlando for the first Africanist conference. They launched a new organization, the Pan Africanist Congress (PAC), electing Sobukwe president.

Unlike the ANC, which envisaged a vaguely defined sharing of governmental power between Blacks and whites, the PAC unambiguously emphasized the goal of African rule. In his opening address before the Orlando conference, Sobukwe proclaimed: "We aim, politically, at government of the Africans, by the Africans, for the Africans, with everybody who owes his only loyalty to Afrika and who is prepared to accept the democratic rule of an African majority being regarded as African. We guarantee no minority rights, because we think in terms of individuals, not groups."[21]

Sobukwe, like Lembede and Mda, viewed African nationalism as the only instrument capable of successfully mobilizing the Black masses for the overthrow of white domination. "African nationalism," he said in an interview, "is the only liberatory outlook that can bind together the African masses by providing them with a loyalty higher than that of the tribe and thus mould them into a militant disciplined fighting force."[22] It was from this standpoint that Sobukwe criticized the ANC's emphasis on

20. Ibid., 3:506.

21. Ibid., 3:516.

22. Ibid., 3:506.

multiracialism. The PAC maintained that the ANC's approach confused Blacks and dissipated their nationalist sentiments against the white oppressors. It was also from a nationalist stance that the PAC called for noncollaboration with government institutions or white political parties. "We believe that co-operation is possible *only between equals,*" Sobukwe explained. "There can be no co-operation between oppressor and oppressed, dominating and dominated. That is collaboration, *not* co-operation. And we cannot collaborate in our own oppression!"[23]

As exemplified by its name, the PAC was strongly influenced by the pan-Africanist sentiments that were sweeping the continent at the time. It called for the eventual establishment of a strong continent-wide government, a "United States of Africa." Its inaugural conference was decked out with slogans such as "Africa for Africans, Cape to Cairo, Morocco to Madagascar," "Imperialists Quit Africa," and "Izwe Lethu iAfrika" (Africa, our land). Greetings were received from Kwame Nkrumah of Ghana and Sékou Touré of Guinea, the leaders of two African countries that had just achieved their independence from British and French colonial rule. Those victories of the anticolonial upsurge in the rest of the world inspired the youthful PAC members with an optimism and confidence that they too could achieve political independence and African rule in the near future, by the same methods employed by their colleagues elsewhere.

The PAC was branded by its detractors, including the ANC and the white liberals, as a "racialist" organization. Sobukwe answered them, "We are not anti-white. . . . We do not hate the European because he is white! We hate him because he is an oppressor."[24]

The PAC was also accused of being anticommunist, especially by the ANC and the South African Communist Party. Some PAC statements lent credence to the charges, and a number of PAC leaders used strongly anticommunist language at times. The white-run press, as part of its red-baiting campaign against the ANC, picked up and amplified such PAC statements.

But the Africanists appear to have been responding largely to their experiences with the Stalinist SACP and its efforts to dampen the ANC's earlier militancy. Extremely contemptuous of the SACP, Sobukwe maintained that there never were any real

23. Ibid., 3:507. Emphasis in original.
24. Ibid., 3:508.

communists in South Africa, just "quacks."[25] Moreover, in his opening address to the PAC inaugural conference, Sobukwe noted the advantages of a planned economy, as in China, over one based on "private enterprise." He declared that the PAC stood for an "Africanist Socialist Democracy."[26] At the same time, however, the PAC denied that class conflict played any appreciable role in the liberation struggle, although some PAC leaders did note the social power of the Black working class.

By the time of the PAC's first full congress in Orlando in December 1959, the organization had grown to 153 branches and claimed a dues-paying membership of 31,000. It had a larger formal membership than the ANC at the time. As in the case of the ANC, however, the official membership figures did not give a true picture of the group's strength, since many of its supporters were reluctant to become full members for fear of police reprisals or because they could not afford the dues.

Two months before the PAC congress, Jacob D. Nyaose, the group's secretary for labor, managed to unite nine African unions, with a formal membership of 17,000, into a new African trade union association, the Federation of Free African Trade Unions of South Africa (FOFATUSA). Like other African unions, it was severly hampered by the regime's antilabor restrictions. It never gained much real influence or organized strength, and was much weaker that the rival SACTU, which was allied with the ANC and could boast a membership in 1960 of 52,600 in forty-five affiliated unions.

Although many young militants had been attracted to the PAC by its promise of imminent action, the leadership initially resisted the pressures of its more impatient followers to directly confront the white regime, perhaps sensing that a premature confrontation could prove costly to the young organization. But under the pressure of its followers, the PAC leadership had decided by the time of its December 19-20, 1959, conference to openly challenge white authority. It called for a broad campaign of civil disobedience against the unpopular pass laws. Africans were to leave their passes home and court arrest—methods similar to those employed by the ANC during the 1952 Defiance Campaign, but with one notable difference: While the 1952 action was consciously limited in scope and restricted to several thou-

25. Ibid., 3:509.

26. Ibid., 3:512, 516.

sand hand-picked defiers, the PAC, sensitive to the militancy and angry frustration of the Black population, stressed the *massive* character of its antipass campaign. When the details of the campaign were later mapped out, the PAC extended the proposed forms of struggle to include a general strike and raised the additional demand of a minimum wage of £35 per month.[27]

In projecting the antipass campaign, the PAC leadership maintained that it was part of a broader offensive that would lead to the overthrow of white supremacy itself. Somewhat optimistically, if not naïvely, it declared, "In 1960 we take our first step, in 1963 our last, towards freedom and independence."[28] Yet the PAC leaders did not explain what subsequent steps would be pursued following the antipass campaign, nor how the campaign related concretely to the liberation struggle as a whole. What course of action and what political program should the masses of Blacks follow once they were mobilized? The PAC leaders implied they had an overall plan, but there are no indications that they actually had one. In a spontaneist manner, they believed that all that was really necessary was to move the masses into action; the rest would naturally follow.

Aside from their lack of any real strategic orientation, the PAC leaders also made a tragic tactical error by insisting that the participants in the campaign voluntarily go to jail under the slogan, "no bail, no defence, no fine." Since Sobukwe, Leballo, and other top PACers intended to lead the campaign personally, to stand in the front ranks of the protesters, this policy was to facilitate a rapid beheading of the PAC at the precise moment when the mass movement needed its leaders the most.

Popular pressures for action were evident as well within the ranks of the ANC. A week before the PAC decided to call its antipass protests, the ANC held a conference in Durban attended by nearly four hundred delegates and more than five thousand observers. The participants demanded mass demonstrations, and one delegate, amidst thunderous applause, proclaimed, "Let us force our leaders into a tight corner!"[29] The result was an ANC call for commemoration of March 31, 1960 (the anniversary of an antipass demonstration in 1919), as antipass day, to be followed

27. Ibid., 3:556, 564-65.

28. Ibid., 3:556.

29. Mary Benson, *Struggle for a Birthright,* p. 219.

by protest actions. When Sobukwe later invited the ANC to join the PAC's own antipass actions, ANC leader Duma Nokwe replied that his organization would not support "sensational actions that might not succeed. . . ."[30]

As the year 1960 opened, social tensions were obviously sharpening. At Cato Manor, protests in January by African women against police raids sparked an uprising in which nine policemen were killed. Another revolt began in Pondoland against the government-installed tribal figureheads.

During the first months of 1960, the PAC leaders made preparations for their campaign. Sobukwe addressed enthusiastic audiences in some areas, receiving an especially favorable response in Cape Town. Leaflets signed by Sobukwe were distributed, announcing that the antipass actions would begin on March 21. "In every city, town and village," the leaflets declared, "the men must leave their passes at home," converge on police stations, and demand that they all be arrested. In addition, "So long as the Campaign is on, *nobody will go to work.*"[31] At a March 18 news conference in Johannesburg, Sobukwe officially set the date for the beginning of the campaign. He stressed that "the Pass Laws must go. We cannot remain foreigners in our own land." He urged the protesters to observe "a spirit of absolute non-violence." And he added, prophetically, "If the other side so desires, we will provide them with an opportunity to demonstrate to the world how brutal they can be. We are ready to die for our cause. . . ."[32]

30. Ibid., p. 222.

31. Karis and Carter, *From Protest to Challenge,* 3:564-65.

32. Ibid., 3:566-67.

17

Sharpeville

"We are fighting for the noblest cause on earth, the liberation of mankind. They are fighting to retrench an outworn, anachronistic vile system of oppression. *We* represent progress. They represent decadence. We represent the fresh fragrance of flowers in bloom; they represent the rancid smell of decaying vegetation. We have the whole continent on our side. We have history on our side. *We will win!*"[1]

It was with a sense of confidence and anticipation that Robert Sobukwe's words were read out on the eve of the PAC's antipass campaign to a series of preparatory meetings and rallies around the country. It was to be the young organization's first major effort at mass mobilization. And coming after several years of militant, but uncoordinated struggles, it promised to galvanize Black resistance again on a national scale.

On the morning of Monday, March 21, 1960, the demonstrators began to gather. Although participation was uneven (few turned out in Johannesburg, and no actions were organized in Durban, Port Elizabeth, or East London), tens of thousands of Blacks around the country responded to the PAC's call. The most massive turnouts were in Cape Town and in several towns south of Johannesburg.

Sobukwe, Leballo, and other members of the PAC Executive presented themselves with about 150 volunteers at the Orlando police station, where they were arrested. At Evaton, a crowd estimated at between ten thousand and twenty thousand gathered at the police station and demanded to be jailed. The police refused. Military aircraft dived low over the heads of the protesters to disperse them. At Vanderbijlpark, an industrial town

1. Thomas Karis and Gwendolen M. Carter, *From Protest to Challenge*, 3:570. Emphasis in original.

twelve miles from Evaton, a group of several thousand demonstrators stood their ground, refusing to disperse even after aircraft swooped over them and the police threw tear gas. The police then leveled their weapons and fired into the crowd, killing two Blacks. A baton charge finally scattered the demonstrators. In Cape Town, many Africans followed the strike call and stayed away from work. A large throng marched from Nyanga Township to a nearby police station, where fifteen hundred Africans presented themselves for arrest. The police declined to take them into custody and told them to go home. More than a thousand were arrested in Wynberg, just south of Cape Town.

In Sharpeville, an African township just outside Vereeniging, south of Johannesburg, a crowd of several thousand gathered early in the morning. The protesters formed a procession three-quarters of a mile long and marched to the municipal offices at the entrance to the township. Police threw tear gas and charged with batons to disperse the protesters. A little later, about ten thousand African men, women, and children surrounded the police station in the township. Nyskane Tsolo, one of the leaders of the protest, explained to a police lieutenant that they wanted to be arrested for not having their passes with them. The lieutenant replied that that was impossible for lack of jail space. Although the tensions rose somewhat, journalists described the crowd as "perfectly amiable."[2]

Shortly after 1:30 p.m., without any warning, several police began shooting. The others followed. A number of demonstrators started to laugh, apparently thinking that the police were firing blanks. But the laughter quickly turned into terror as protesters crumpled to the ground. Volley after volley of pistol and automatic weapons fire tore into the fleeing crowd. Scores of people fell under the hail of bullets. According to one eyewitness account, "One of the policemen was standing on top of a Saracen [armored car], and it looked as though he was firing his sten gun into the crowd. He was swinging it around in a wide arc from his hip as though he were panning a movie camera."[3] The shooting lasted for less than a minute, but when it stopped the area around the police station was cluttered with dozens of bodies. The wounded had fled into backyards and side streets. A few hours later a thunderstorm washed away most of the blood.

2. Mary Benson, *Struggle for a Birthright,* p. 222.
3. Edward Roux, *Time Longer Than Rope,* p. 407.

According to the official count, sixty-seven demonstrators died in Sharpeville that day. More than 180 were injured. The overwhelming majority had been shot in the back.

Across the country, in Langa, a crowd of ten thousand rallied several hours later, despite a police ban on all further meetings in the township. The police arrived in force and tried to break up the gathering. When some protesters resisted, the police shot into them, killing yet two more Blacks. This provoked an uprising in Langa that lasted for several hours and that marked the beginning of three weeks of upheaval and confrontation in the Cape Town area.

As news of the killings at Sharpeville, Langa, and Vanderbijlpark spread, so did the Black fury against the government. More demonstrations erupted in Cape Town and more workers walked off their jobs in that city and in the Vereeniging area. By the end of the week the strike was virtually total in Cape Town, crippling the city's docks and industries.

In a dramatic gesture of solidarity with the victims of the repression, Chief Albert Lutuli of the ANC publicly burned his pass. Many others followed his example. The ANC, with the support of the PAC, called a "stay at home" strike on March 28 as an expression of mourning. Several hundred thousand Black workers around the country observed the strike call. In Langa, an estimated fifty thousand Blacks gathered for the burial of those killed the week before. PAC speakers urged Blacks to continue striking until the passes were abolished, a £35-a-month minimum wage had been won, and the authorities had pledged not to victimize strikers.

The big outpourings after the Sharpeville massacre won the protesters a brief victory: The government ordered the temporary suspension of the pass laws.

The Verwoerd regime may have hoped that this ephemeral concession would dissipate the protests, but the anger of the Black population was now too great. The ferment continued to mount. For a week following the March 28 strike, the sixty thousand African workers in Cape Town continued to stay away from their jobs. On March 30 the regime declared a state of emergency and assumed broad powers to detain indefinitely anyone suspected of antigovernment activity. The entire Citizen Force was placed on alert. A series of police swoops and mass arrests began.

Partly in response to the crackdown, Cape Town was shaken the same day, March 30, by a huge demonstration. A procession of five thousand Africans led by Philip Kgosana of the PAC marched out of Langa and Nyanga toward the center of Cape Town to demand the release of the arrested leaders. They were joined by thousands of Black workers on the way, and by the time the crowd reached the Caledon Square police station it had swelled to about thirty thousand persons. The police and troops were extremely hesitant to attack such a large number of angry Blacks in the middle of "white" Cape Town. Instead, the police negotiated with Kgosana and offered to arrange a meeting between the leaders of the PAC and the justice minister if the crowd would disperse. Kgosana agreed and urged the protesters to go back to the townships, not realizing that he was at the same time dissipating his only real bargaining power. The meeting never took place and Kgosana was arrested later that day. Heavily armed police, troops, and naval personnel threw up tight cordons around Langa and Nyanga to prevent any repetition of the march.

From March 30 until April 2, a series of demonstrations and strikes swept other towns in the Western Cape. On April 1, rebellions erupted in Durban's Cato Manor slums and thousands of Africans marched in to downtown Durban, where they rallied in front of the main prison to demand the release of the political detainees. Police fired into the crowd, killing at least three. Outbreaks of unrest and pass burning also took place in Port Elizabeth, Bloemfontein, and other urban centers. All were met with swift police retaliation.

According to official sources, a total of eighty-three Blacks were killed between March 21 and April 9.

In an agitated speech before parliament, Minister of Justice François Erasmus declared of the demonstrators, "Their aim is to bring to its knees any White Government in South Africa which stands for White supremacy and for White leadership. . . . [They] do not want peace and order; what they want is not £1 a day for all the Bantu in South Africa; what they want is our country!"[4] Parliament quickly adopted the Unlawful Organisations Act, and on April 8 the regime invoked it to outlaw both the PAC and ANC as serious threats "to the safety of the public."[5]

By that time, overt resistance had already begun to recede in the cities. A joint call by the ANC and PAC for a week-long

4. Gail Gerhart, *Black Power in South Africa,* p. 247.
5. Benson, *Struggle for a Birthright,* p. 225.

general strike beginning April 19 met with almost no response.

The countrywide upheaval unleashed by the Sharpeville massacre had been unprecedented in its scope and militancy. It clearly revealed the growing social strength of the Black urban population, especially of the working class, which had demonstrated its ability to shut down much of the economy. The authorities were painfully aware that with better organization and a clearer political leadership, urban Blacks could soon threaten the very survival of white supremacy and the capitalist system on which it rests. They were determined that that should not happen.

To prevent a quick resurgence of the mass movement, police and troops descended on Black locations in cities throughout the country. They sealed off the townships, patrolled the streets, and conducted house-to-house searches, arresting thousands for such offenses as rioting, incitement, possession of dangerous weapons, vagrancy, violation of the pass laws, and so on. By May 6 the regime admitted that more than eighteen thousand Blacks had been arrested in these raids. In the same period, a total of seventeen hundred political activists were detained under the emergency regulations, including leaders of the ANC, PAC, SAIC, Congress of Democrats, and other organizations. Many were sentenced to prison terms, Sobukwe drawing a three-year jail sentence that was later extended by a special law to nine years.

While the authorities were successful for the moment in regaining control in the urban areas, African resistance broke out on a large scale in some rural districts.

The simmering unrest in Pondoland, in the Transkei, began to boil over in March 1960 when thousands of peasants held regular mass meetings to discuss their grievances against the imposition of government-paid tribal chiefs, unpopular taxes, and arbitrary land rehabilitation schemes. They came on foot and horseback to rally on ridges and mountain tops, in a movement that came to be known as Intaba (mountain) or Ikongo (congress). When the peasants discovered that their meetings were being reported to the authorities by tribal agents, they burned down the huts of the informers and drove them from the area.

On June 6, troops and police attacked a rally of African peasants. Although the peasants raised a white flag, eleven of them were shot to death. This only provoked greater resistance and prompted the peasants to take up arms. More than two dozen government collaborators, including two chiefs, were killed. By

September the rebellion had spilled over into Thembuland and threatened to affect other parts of the Transkei as well. Two months later the regime invoked Proclamation 400, imposing a state of emergency throughout the Transkei and abolishing all civil liberties. Thousands of suspects were detained and taken to Bizana for screening, where many were beaten and subjected to electric shock torture. According to official figures, 4,769 persons were detained in the Transkei that year. Thirty were sentenced to death and about twenty executed.

The dramatic events of 1960 had jarring repercussions on Pretoria's international position. The ferocity of the repression drew sharp protests from many quarters and scuttled the regime's initial attempts to establish diplomatic and trade ties with the emerging Black regimes. Fearing continued instability in South Africa, many foreign investors quickly dumped their South African shares; in 1960 alone, there was a net outflow of $194 million in private capital (it was to take several more years before foreign businessmen fully regained their confidence in Pretoria's ability to rule).

Meanwhile, within South Africa, the banned political groups were struggling to survive and to maintain some form of organized resistance under the new conditions of illegality and of increasing Black demoralization. Neither the ANC nor PAC had been prepared for the bannings, and many of their leaders were swept into police custody during the crackdown. A few top ANC leaders like Nelson Mandela and Walter Sisulu managed to evade the police for a while, but the PAC leaders were detained down to the third and fourth levels of the organization, causing considerable disruption. Despite these handicaps, the groups attempted to reorganize. By September, an ANC "care-taker" committee had formed a number of clandestine cells and began to issue leaflets and paint slogans in various parts of the country. The PAC also ordered its branches to disband and re-form into small cells of a few trusted members each.

For a fleeting moment, the repression forced the ANC and PAC to set aside their factional differences and attempt to unite their forces against the regime. In December 1960, a diverse group of Africans—including Govan Mbeki and W. Z. Conco of the ANC, Joe Molefi and Z. B. Molete of the PAC, Jordan Ngubane of the multiracial Liberal Party, and other, more conservative, Black figures—gathered in Orlando to discuss the new situation. They agreed on the "urgent need for African unity" and called for an "all-in conference representative of African people" to demand the holding of a "National Convention representing all the people of South Africa."[6] A thirteen-member continuation committee that included three ANCers and one PACer was set up to organize the proposed conference.

By the time it was actually held in Pietermaritzburg on March 25-26, 1961, the unity had broken down. The PAC objected to the participation of members of the Liberal Party and the white Congress of Democrats and to what it saw as ANC domination of the continuation committee. Its representative on the committee, Molete, withdrew just before the conference.

The conference itself, which drew fourteen hundred participants, was dominated by ANC speakers and slogans. Nelson Mandela made a dramatic appearance and addressed the audience, the regime having overlooked the expiration of his banning order a few days earlier. A resolution was adopted demanding that the Verwoerd regime call a democratically elected and nonracial national convention for the purpose of drawing up a new constitution. If the regime did not accede to the conference's demands by May 31, 1961, the day the Union of South Africa was to become a "republic" outside the British Commonwealth, the conference resolved to "stage country-wide demonstrations." The resolution also called on Indians, Coloureds, and "all democratic Europeans" to join with Africans in opposing Verwoerd's policies.[7] (The term "democratic Europeans" was apparently flexible enough to include the bourgeois opposition United Party, to which Mandela appealed for support to the convention call.)

Immediately after the Pietermaritzburg conference, a warrant was issued for the arrest of Mandela, who had already disappeared from public view. Both he and Sisulu traveled clandestinely around the country to organize a three-day strike that was planned to pressure the regime into calling the national convention. Since the PAC did not support the convention call, it refused to back the strike.

The regime was concerned not so much with the ANC's convention call—that could be easily enough ignored—but with the possibility that the strike itself could open the way to another massive upheaval against white supremacy like that of the year before. New repressive measures were adopted, and in the days

6. Karis and Carter, *From Protest to Challenge*, 3:626-27.
7. Ibid., 3:632.

before the scheduled start of the strike police conducted large-scale raids, arresting ten thousand Africans.

Verwoerd got an invaluable assist in his terror campaign from the United States Marines, who stopped off in South Africa on a "courtesy call" on the eve of the strike. They demonstrated flamethrowers and machine guns to the South African army and flew helicopters low over African townships. According to sociologist Pierre van den Berghe, ". . . almost all Africans interpreted the American visit as a show of force in favour of Verwoerd."[8]

Nevertheless, tens of thousands of Black workers, especially in Johannesburg and Port Elizabeth, stayed away from their jobs on May 29, the first day of the planned three-day strike. Mandela acknowledged, however, that the strike was "not the national success I had hoped for" and called it off on the second day.[9]

It was shortly after the partial failure of this strike effort that the ANC leadership began to veer away from strikes, demonstrations, boycotts, and other forms of mass mobilization toward acts of individual resistance, including sabotage and guerrilla-type operations.

In November 1961 Mandela and others participated in the formation of Umkhonto we Sizwe (Spear of the Nation), a paramilitary body formally separate from the ANC but composed largely of members of the ANC and the South African Communist Party. A month later, Umkhonto carried out its first sabotage actions, exploding bombs near electrical installations, pass offices, courts, and other government buildings and facilities in Durban, Port Elizabeth, Johannesburg, and elsewhere.

A leaflet by Umkhonto claiming credit for the bombings made it clear that Umkhonto's aim was to pressure the regime into making concessions, rather than to mobilize the Black population to take power itself. "We hope that we will bring the Government and its supporters to their senses before it is too late," the leaflet declared, "so that both Government and its policies can be changed before matters reach the desperate stage of civil war."[10]

Predictably, Umkhonto's bombing campaign had no impact on the government. Rather than marking a shift by ANC activists toward more "radical" forms of struggle, it actually denoted a turn away from the absolutely essential task of continuing—even

8. Pierre van den Berghe, *South Africa,* pp. 258-59.

9. Karis and Carter, *From Protest to Challenge,* 3:364.

10. Ibid., 3:716-17.

under conditions of severe repression—to organize the masses of Blacks to defend themselves and fight for their rights. Preparations for insurrection and armed self-defense would eventually have to be made, but to have any effect against a regime as deeply entrenched as that in Pretoria, they would have to be directly based on a strong mass movement that was politically prepared to lead the Black majority to power. The most effective weapon in South Africa is the organized social strength of the Black working class and its allies. The military exploits of a handful of combatants—or even several hundred fighters—cannot substitute for that, no matter how heroic or dedicated they may be.

While the leaders of the ANC placed their faith in a policy of sabotage against government property, followers of the PAC, in a parallel development, moved toward isolated attacks against whites. Spontaneously, with little overall coordination or direction and with only the most tenuous ties, if any at all, to the surviving fragments of the PAC leadership, young activists in the Western Cape and the Transkei came together to form loosely organized groups. They called themselves Poqo, a Xhosa word meaning "independent" or "standing alone," which had sometimes been used to refer to the PAC.

Beginning in November 1962, groups of Africans carried out a series of attacks against police stations and individual whites, killing several. Open-air meetings in the Cape Town area publicly discussed assassinating Chief Kaiser Matanzima of the Transkei. Such adventurist actions exposed many of the PAC's most committed activists to swift government retaliation.

While the remnants of the PAC leadership could not be held directly responsible for the actions of Poqo, neither could they be credited with trying to turn the energies of their youthful followers in a more fruitful direction. Potlako Leballo, who managed to flee South Africa and set up a temporary exile base in Basutoland, initially alternated between boastfully claiming that Poqo was part of the PAC and denying any connection. Then at a March 1963 news conference he maintained that the PAC and Poqo were one and the same, that Poqo had 155,000 members in South Africa, and that they were preparing to launch an imminent insurrection.[11] All that followed Leballo's news conference was a massive crackdown against suspected PAC supporters that virtually crippled the organization within the country.

11. Ibid., 3:671.

The failure of Leballo and other leaders to try to conserve the PAC's strength and reforge the mass movement was especially tragic given the indications of continued widespread support for the PAC among the African population. For instance, a survey on "African attitudes" published by the South African Institute of Race Relations in 1963 found that 57 percent of those asked expressed a preference for the PAC.[12]

The authorities used the specter of an alleged Poqo and Umkhonto "menace" to justify the most brutal methods of repression against followers of the PAC, ANC, and other groups. Newer, even more stringent laws were pushed through, including one known as the "Sobukwe clause," which permitted indefinite detention of political prisoners after their sentences had been served (Sobukwe was imprisoned on Robben Island until 1969 under this measure, after which he was banned and confined to Kimberley). The minister of justice acknowledged that by June 1963 no less than 3,246 Africans alleged to be members of Poqo had been arrested, 124 of whom were charged with murder.[13] The PAC has named seventy members who were executed between 1962 and 1967 and another eight who were tortured to death during the decade of the 1960s (more than a dozen others had been killed in clashes with the police).[14]

The ANC and its allied organizations did not escape this repression. Mandela was captured in August 1962 and nearly a year later, in July 1963, police raided a farm near the Johannesburg suburb of Rivonia, rounding up most of the prominent leaders of the ANC, Communist Party, and Umkhonto we Sizwe still at large, including Walter Sisulu, Govan Mbeki, and Ahmed Kathrada. They were charged with sabotage and brought to trial.

During the trial, Mandela presented the main speech on behalf of the defendants, concluding it with the words: "I have cherished the ideal of a democratic and free society in which all persons live together in harmony and with equal opportunities. It is an ideal which I hope to live for and to achieve. But if needs be, it is an ideal for which I am prepared to die."[15]

12. Richard Gibson, *African Liberation Movements,* p. 62.

13. Benson, *Struggle for a Birthright,* p. 244.

14. *P.A.C. in Perspective: Sobukwe, the Man Who Still Walks Tall* (London: Pan Africanist Congress of Azania, 1973), pp. 25-28.

15. Karis and Carter, *From Protest to Challenge,* 3:679.

The danger of death sentences was real, but was averted largely as a result of international protests. Nevertheless, all but one of the nine defendants—including Mandela—were found guilty and sentenced to spend the rest of their lives in jail.

Numerous other organizations and individuals fell victim as well. The South African Indian Congress lapsed into a comatose state with the banning of most of its leaders. The South African Congress of Trade Unions, associated with the Congress Alliance, was crippled by the banning, arrest, or execution of its leaders. The Federation of Free African Trade Unions of South Africa, allied with the PAC, dissolved itself in 1966 under the shadow of the regime's repressive and antilabor measures. The Communist Party-influenced Congress of Democrats was banned in 1962, and four years later Abram Fischer, a prominent lawyer and underground leader of the SACP, was captured and sentenced to life imprisonment. A number of publications, including the Unity Movement's newspaper the *Torch,* were forced to shut down. The predominantly white African Resistance Movement, a sabotage group, was crushed and one of its members executed. Neville Alexander and several other members or former members of the Unity Movement were arrested and sentenced to jail terms on Robben Island for conspiring to commit "sabotage," that is, for reading Marxist literature. In 1966, the Defence and Aid Fund, which had been set up to assist political prisoners and their families, was outlawed.

From January 1963 to December 1965, nearly two hundred political trials, involving more than two thousand accused, were held in courts throughout the country. Many others were simply detained without ever being charged or brought to trial. An average of two Africans were hanged every week.

This extensive crackdown caused barely a ripple in the daily lives of most whites, but it cast a tangible pall of terror over the Black population as a whole, an intimidating atmosphere that was to linger throughout much of the decade and inhibit all but the most veiled displays of antigovernment sentiment. No more than two thousand Africans a year dared to strike between 1962 and 1968.

Bereft of much of their direct influence on political life inside South Africa, the various national liberation groups—the ANC, PAC, and Unity Movement—set up offices abroad. As part of their efforts to secure financial assistance from African governments, political parties in Europe, the Organization of African Unity, and other sources, they all claimed to have continued mass support within South Africa. There was a degree of truth to their claims, as shown by the recurrent political trials in South Africa, especially of alleged ANC members. But in general the organizations were reduced to marking time. Their activities focused largely on building up and maintaining apparatuses and on arming and training guerrilla forces. In this, the ANC had an advantage over the other groups, since its ties with the SACP and bourgeois liberal forces opened all sorts of doors to financial and political support from foreign governments and parties, some of whom recognized the ANC as the only "authentic" liberation movement.

The South African Communist Party itself assumed more of an open role in exile than it had been able to inside South Africa. With its main leadership now based in London, it published the quarterly *African Communist,* lobbied on behalf of the ANC, and sent speakers to conferences and public meetings. Its basic political positions had not changed. In the SACP's new program, adopted in 1962, the socialist revolution in South Africa was still relegated to the nebulous future, while the immediate aim was defined as a "national democratic revolution" to establish an "independent state of National Democracy," in which "the interests of private business where these are not incompatible with the public interest" would be protected. Despite all the concrete lessons of the class struggle in South Africa and despite its own advocacy of guerrilla warfare, the SACP held out the possibility of a "non-violent," negotiated end to white supremacy and even of a "gradual and peaceful transition to socialism." Although it was opposed to white supremacy, the SACP continued to denounce what it called "narrow nationalism" and "Black chauvinism."[16]

In the late 1960s, both the ANC and PAC embarked on abortive guerrilla campaigns. The ANC sent some two hundred guerrillas into Zimbabwe in 1967 to fight with the Zimbabwe African People's Union against the Smith regime; nearly all were killed or captured. The following year, the PAC tried to infiltrate a number of guerrillas into South Africa, but they were discovered passing through Mozambique and some were killed by the Portuguese.

A Unity Movement faction led by I. B. Tabata also tried to

16. South African Communist Party, "The Road to South African Freedom," program adopted at the Fifth National Conference, 1962, pp. 42, 52, 54, 58.

establish its own armed units, but was never successful in training more than a handful of recruits.

The long-standing factional disputes among the groups were further amplified in exile by the strains and tensions of relative isolation and by bitter competition for foreign financial support. Charges and countercharges flew fast and heavy. "Unity" negotiations were initiated and broken off. The Sino-Soviet dispute became an additional obstacle to united-front action, as the ANC looked to Moscow for support, while the PAC hopefully cast its net in the direction of Peking. All the groups were rent to one degree or another by internal disputes, as contesting factions and individuals charged each other with being corrupt, counter-revolutionary, racist, or any of the numerous other "crimes" that have become standard fare among nationalist movements in exile. Differences were usually resolved through splits, if not by expulsions or "disappearances."

Meanwhile, the groups waited for an opportunity to reenter the main stage, to take up their old roles, and once again to have some direct impact on the course of the freedom struggle.

Political developments, however, wait for no one. Despite the prevalent police surveillance and the severe, far-reaching repression within South Africa, new Black leaders and organizations began to arise—as inevitably they would.

18

The Rise of Black Consciousness

The relative political quiescence of the 1960s was not to last very long, much to the dismay of the apartheid authorities. They had thought that by clamping the lid on virtually all Black dissent, by unleashing their police and hangmen, they could eliminate or sufficiently terrorize the most active leadership of the Black community. They had calculated that the stultifying atmosphere of Bantu Education, given enough time, would smother any independent thought among young Blacks and produce a new generation schooled in docility and subservience. They had gambled that the Bantustan charade, the policy of divide and rule, and constriction of the few remaining Black rights would push Black aspirations into carefully prescribed channels, breeding divisiveness and factionalism to such an extent as to facilitate prolonged white control.

The 1970s proved them wrong on all counts. With a rapidity that few would have predicted, new Black political organizations sprang up, new struggles were launched in the townships and factories, new militant ideas took root and spread.

Ironically, the reawakening of Black political activity was bolstered by the very same economic expansion that the white ruling class thrived on. The growth of the urbanized Black working class provided a solid foundation for the emergence of new forms of struggle and gave Blacks greater social power.

The initial steps toward Black political revival were not taken by workers themselves, however. During the late 1960s and early 1970s, the initiative lay primarily with the Black student movement. Black students had always been politically active, but with the banning of the major Black parties and the destruction of the most important Black unions, they soon found themselves in the forefront of the national liberation movement. Moreover, while most Black university students had previously been almost exclusively from better-off families, an increasing number were now from working class backgrounds, adding a new element to Black student radicalism.

Following the collapse of the main Black student organizations of the early 1960s (the African Students' Association and the African Students' Union of South Africa, linked to the ANC and PAC, respectively), some Black student activists tried to work through the National Union of South African Students (NUSAS), a white-dominated federation that had a "liberal" image and formally opposed segregation. But since the NUSAS leadership paid scant attention to the real problems of Blacks, discontent soon developed among the group's Black members. This surfaced for the first time during a 1967 NUSAS annual conference, during which the Black criticisms of the leadership were vocalized by a twenty-year-old student from the Black section of the University of Natal—Steve Biko.

By late 1968, discontent with NUSAS developed to such an extent that the Black students within it decided to break away. Biko and his colleagues joined with other Black student leaders in December of that year to form a new all-Black students' body, the South African Students' Organisation (SASO). It held its inaugural conference in July 1969 at the University of the North at Turfloop, where the delegates adopted a constitution and elected an executive, which included African, Coloured, and Indian members. Steve Biko, who had been chosen as the first president of SASO, then toured the various Black campuses to address students and garner support for the new organization.

At first, SASO maintained cordial, but cautious, relations with NUSAS. At SASO's 1970 conference, however, it withdrew its formal recognition of NUSAS as a body claiming to represent all students, declaring that "the emancipation of the black peoples in this country depends on the role the black people themselves are prepared to play. . . ."[1] SASO had embarked on the path of independent Black political activity.

In attempting to define its political identity in a more comprehensive manner, SASO elaborated its own particular current of nationalist thought and action, known as Black Consciousness. Many of the concepts SASO advanced were not really new and had been previously presented in one form or another by the

1. Ben A. Khoapa, ed., *Black Review 1972*, p. 20.

African National Congress Youth League, the Unity Movement, or the Pan Africanist Congress. Others had been influenced by the struggle for Black rights in the United States and by the ideas of Black American radicals like Malcolm X, Stokely Carmichael, and Eldridge Cleaver. Yet others were inspired by the colonial revolution and by the speeches and writings of such figures as Franz Fanon and Julius K. Nyerere. Elements of all these various strains of Black nationalist thinking were blended, developed, and shaped by SASO under the specific conditions of South Africa in the 1970s. SASO's aim was not to mimic, but to apply the useful lessons of other struggles.

Black Consciousness, as outlined in SASO's 1971 "Policy Manifesto," meant resistance to the dehumanizing and demoralizing influences of the apartheid system. It sought to foster a sense of self-respect and confidence among Blacks. "The basic tenet of Black Consciousness," the manifesto emphasized, "is that the Black man must reject all value systems that seek to make him a foreigner in the country of his birth and reduce his basic human dignity."[2] As part of this process, SASO dismissed use of the term "nonwhite" to describe Africans, Coloureds, and Indians collectively, since it characterized them negatively, in relation to whites. SASO preferred the more positive term *Black* to describe "those who are by law or tradition politically, economically and socially discriminated against as a group in the South African society. . . ."[3] In a similar vein, SASO condemned the entire system of Bantu Education, seeing it as a mechanism designed to stunt Black creativity and assertiveness and keep Blacks in a position of educational and social inferiority. SASO viewed the liberation of Blacks from their "psychological oppression" not as an end in itself, but as a prelude to their struggle for physical liberation.

A central aim of Black Consciousness, according to a 1970 SASO editorial statement, was "to define one's enemy more clearly and to broaden the base from which we are operating."[4] In other words, SASO sought to draw a sharp line between the oppressors and the oppressed.

This involved a campaign to unify all sectors of the Black

2. Ben Langa, ed., *SASO on the Attack*, p. 10.
3. Ibid.
4. *SASO Newsletter* (Durban), September 1970.

population—African, Coloured, and Indian—and to heighten their nationalist awareness. Blacks, SASO stressed, needed to recognize the "power they wield as a group, both economically and politically," and needed to "close their ranks . . . to oppose the definite racism that is meted out by the White society, to work out their direction clearly and bargain from a position of strength."[5]

The complementary effort "to define one's enemy more clearly" resulted in part from SASO's realization that it was futile to make overtures to white bourgeois opposition parties (as the ANC had done in the past), just because they criticized the ruling National Party. Biko explained in a 1972 article:

> The biggest mistake the black world ever made was to assume that whoever opposed apartheid was an ally. For a long time the black world has been looking only at the governing party and not so much at the whole power structure as the object of their rage. In a sense the very political vocabulary that the blacks have used has been inherited from the liberals. . . .
>
> For a long time, in fact, it became the occupation of the leadership to "calm the masses down," while they engaged in fruitless negotiation with the status quo.[6]

A later SASO publication put it more sharply: "Our parents had too much tea with the—liberals. Now they expect us to be tea lovers as well. Tea with the liberals is an imperialist enjoyment that we completely reject."[7]

Although there were always some individual exceptions, SASO members in general tended to lump all whites—racist, liberal, or radical—together as part of the oppressor camp. As a consequence, SASO stipulated that whites must be excluded "in all matters relating to the struggle towards realizing our aspirations. . . . SASO believes that a truly open society can only be achieved by blacks."[8]

Nevertheless, SASO did not spurn all contact with whites. Some SASO leaders acknowledged that a few whites—the small

5. Langa, *SASO on the Attack*, p. 10.
6. Steve Biko, *I Write What I Like*, pp. 63-64.
7. *SASO Newsletter* (Durban), March-April 1976.
8. Langa, *SASO on the Attack*, p. 10

handful who were sincerely committed to a victory of the Black liberation struggle—could play a supportive role. "The more radical whites," a SASO discussion paper observed, "have in fact rejoiced at the emergence of SASO and some of them have even come up with useful support in terms of valuable contacts etc., but radical whites are very rare creatures in this country."[9]

The white bourgeois liberals, however, did not rejoice at the emergence of SASO. Finding themselves barred from direct meddling in the Black student movement, they screamed that SASO was a "racist" organization, which used methods similar to those of the National Party. Ridiculous though they were, Biko replied to the charges, in the process defining the true nature of racism in South Africa, not in terms of the abstract moralism used by the liberals but in its proper social context. "Racism," he pointed out, "does not imply exclusion of one race by another—it always presupposes that the exclusion is for the purposes of subjugation."[10]

Another Black Consciousness leader later explained to me in Johannesburg that the racial exclusiveness of the movement was simply a "means to an end," the ultimate goal being a nonracial society.

Ironically, some government figures initially misread the motivation behind SASO's spurning of the white liberals and greeted SASO's split from NUSAS as a vindication of their segregationist policies. They soon realized their error.

Within the first few years after its birth, SASO began drifting in an increasingly radical direction. One sign was its changing attitude toward the Bantustan system, Urban Bantu Councils, and other similar government-established bodies. Initially SASO was noncommittal on whether Blacks should or should not participate in those bodies in an effort to work for change from "within the system." Some SASO leaders actively wooed figures like Gatsha Buthelezi of KwaZulu and David Thebehali of the Soweto UBC. But by the time of SASO's July 1972 conference, when outgoing SASO President Temba Sono presented a formal proposal to work through the Bantustans, feeling among the rest of SASO had hardened considerably against the Bantustans and

9. "Understanding SASO," in Hendrik W. van der Merwe et al., eds., *African Perspectives on South Africa*, p. 105.

10. Biko, *I Write What I Like*, pp. 97-98.

similar institutions. Sono was censured for his speech and expelled from the conference.[11]

As the student activists radicalized, they increasingly saw the need to reach out to other Blacks and popularize the concepts of Black Consciousness more broadly. They set out to radically influence the mass thinking and political outlook of much of the Black population, an endeavor made easier by the Black population's growing sense of its own social power.

On April 24, 1971, SASO participated with four educational, religious, and community groups in a conference in Bloemfontein to begin exploring new avenues for broader Black collaboration. This was followed four months later, on August 14, by a larger conference in Pietermaritzburg, which drew more than a hundred representatives from a wide variety of groups and was addressed by such speakers as Steve Biko, Drake Koka (a trade unionist), and Chief Gatsha Buthelezi. As the participation of Buthelezi indicated, conservative Black figures were seeking to dampen the radical thrust of SASO's initiative and steer the new organization into safe channels.

The differences between the moderates and the radicals came to a head at the next conference, held in Soweto, December 17-19, 1971. Some forty delegates discussed and debated the form and aims of the new national organization. The conservatives, rallied around M. T. Moerane of the Association for the Educational and Cultural Advancement of the African People of South Africa, argued for a purely culturally oriented African umbrella group. The SASO delegation, led by SASO Permanent Organizer Ranwedzi Nengwekhulu, pressed for an openly political Black organization. When it came to a vote, the SASO view won out. Moerane and his colleagues subsequently withdrew from any direct involvement in the organization.

The conference elected a ten-member Ad Hoc Committee, chaired by Drake Koka, to lay the organizational groundwork for the Black People's Convention. On January 24, 1972, the committee issued a press release announcing that the new group would strive "towards the formation of a Black People's political movement whose primary aim is to unite and solidify black people with a view to liberating and emancipating them from both psychological and physical oppression."[12]

11. Gail Gerhart, *Black Power in South Africa*, pp. 288-90.
12. Khoapa, *Black Review 1972*, pp. 9-10.

In early 1972, while the budding Black Consciousness movement was beginning to extend its reach outward, SASO itself experienced its baptism of action—the May-June student revolts.

The ferment actually began during the April 29 graduation ceremonies at the University of the North at Turfloop, one of the relatively new African universities, where SASO had a following. Onkgopotse Ramothibi Tiro, a former president of the Students' Representative Council at the university, delivered a scathing attack on the racist educational system during his address to the graduates. He urged them to become politically active. "We black graduates, by virtue of our age and academic standing, are being called upon to greater responsibilities in the liberation of our people," he declared.[13] Tiro was expelled by the university authorities a few days later. When the student body of 1,150 voted to boycott all lectures until Tiro was readmitted, they were all suspended and forced off the campus.

Solidarity actions quickly spread to other campuses around the country. Hundreds of students from the universities of Fort Hare, the Western Cape, Durban-Westville, and Zululand protested and boycotted classes. Those at other higher educational institutions also joined in. Mass assemblies of students took place in Durban, Johannesburg, and elsewhere. A parents' committee was formed in Johannesburg in support of the students.

Significantly, white students at a number of English-speaking campuses staged a series of protests in solidarity with the Black student actions and against apartheid education. Enraged by this violation of "white unity," police attacked and viciously beat white student demonstrators on the steps of St. George's Cathedral in Cape Town.

Following further Black student actions, the Vorster regime, on June 6, banned most political gatherings, marches, and protests at sixteen campuses around the country. The wave of student revolts receded.

The Black student upsurge won only a few minor concessions from the university authorities. But more important than any concrete success or failure was its impact on the political consciousness of young Blacks. For the first time in more than a decade they had openly demonstrated in large numbers against the regime's white-supremacist policies. The sense of Black solidarity generated by the actions and the mood of self-

13. Ibid., p. 175.

confidence they engendered could only encourage those who were seeking to rebuild a broad-based liberation movement.

SASO itself continued to grow and gain in influence. Despite opposition in some cases from university authorities, SASO branches had been set up at all the main Black campuses, and even at some of the smaller theological seminaries and teacher-training institutions. A branch to accommodate correspondence and other students was set up in Johannesburg under the direction of Nengwekhulu. By 1972, the *SASO Newsletter* was coming out regularly and had reached a circulation of four thousand.

Against this background, the moves toward the establishment of a national Black political organization reached fruition at a conference in Pietermaritzburg, July 8-10, 1972. More than a hundred Blacks from a variety of political backgrounds formally launched the Black People's Convention (BPC). Most of those in attendance were African, of course, but Coloureds also participated and the BPC drew a degree of Indian support; under the leadership of such activists as Saths Cooper and Strini Moodley, the largest and most active branch of the Natal Indian Congress joined the BPC almost in its entirety.

The conference adopted a constitution, the preamble of which stated, "It is necessary and essential for Blacks in South Africa to unite and consolidate themselves into a political movement if their needs, aspirations, ideals and goals are to be realised and actualised. . . ."[14] The BPC pledged to work outside of the government-created institutions like the Bantustans, the Coloured People's Representative Council, and the South African Indian Council; establish and promote Black businesses on a cooperative basis; and set up and coordinate Black trade unions.

The conference elected an interim executive (to hold office until the BPC's first full convention later that year) with Rev. Mashoabado Mayathula as president and Drake Koka as secretary-general. Following the conference, the BPC began to build branches in Johannesburg, Pretoria, Pietermaritzburg, Cape Town, and other areas.

Although Drake Koka, the BPC secretary-general, was himself a unionist, the direct links between the Black Consciousness groups and the Black labor movement were nevertheless quite limited. Leaders of the BPC and SASO recognized this as a

14. "BPC Constitution," in Sipho Buthelezi, ed., *The Black People's Convention (BPC)—South Africa*, p. 12.

problem and attempted to rectify it. In July 1972, SASO established the Black Workers' Project for the purpose of contacting existing Black unions to lay the basis for a national workers' conference. The project was headed by two field officers, Mthuli Shezi, the BPC vice-president and a leader of SASO, and Bokwe Mafuna, a former trade unionist who was now with the Black Community Programmes (a Black Consciousness group that concentrated on establishing community welfare projects and publicizing information of particular interest to Blacks). A month later, on August 27, the Black Allied Workers Union (BAWU) was founded near Johannesburg on the initiative of Koka's Sales and Allied Workers Association. It was projected as an "*umbrella trade union* that would cater for and embrace all workers in various job categories. . . ."[15]

Shortly before the BPC's first full convention in Hammanskraal, December 16-17, 1972, it suffered the loss of one of its leading figures in this labor outreach effort. Twenty-three-year-old Mthuli Shezi was pushed in front of a moving train in Germiston by a white railway employee, dying in the hospital on the last day of the BPC convention. The BPC resolved to continue Shezi's work and charged the new National Executive Committee with the task of encouraging closer collaboration among all Black workers' organizations. The BPC's new secretary-general, Sipho Buthelezi, emphasized the role of Black workers as "the vanguard of the struggle" and argued that it was imperative for the BPC to make it the "number one priority to mobilize the black working-class."[16]

Related to this explicit approach toward Black workers, the BPC also began to pay more attention to economic questions. In particular, it zeroed in on the role of imperialist investments in helping to prop up white supremacy. The BPC publicly resolved to "reject the involvement of foreign investors in this exploitative economic system" and to "call upon foreign investors to disengage themselves form this white-controlled exploitative system."[17] This issue was so important in the view of the BPC leaders that they were willing to openly defy the regime's Terrorism Act, which outlaws any such calls for investment or

15. Khoapa, *Black Review 1972*, p. 123.

16. Buthelezi, *Black People's Convention*, p. 7.

17. *U.S. Business in South Africa: Voices for Withdrawal*, Southern Africa Perspectives No. 1-78 (New York: Africa Fund, 1978), p. 3.

trade boycotts against South Africa. Following the conference, the BPC acted on the resolution by writing to more than thirty foreign companies specifically demanding that they pull out.

The Black Consciousness movement's first concrete steps toward trying to link up with the Black labor movement came at a time of rising combativity among Black workers in general.

In December 1971, more than thirteen thousand Ovambo migrant workers in the South African colony of Namibia began a strike against the contract labor system and "for human rights to work in peace and order like people all over the world."[18] The militancy of this strike gave a boost to the Namibian independence struggle—and inspired Black workers in South Africa, who discussed it in the townships, migrant labor hostels, and factories.

In early June 1972, hundreds of striking African bus drivers in the Johannesburg area refused to return to work despite the arrest of more than three hundred of them; their determination won them a 33 percent pay hike and laid the basis for a new Black union, the Transport and Allied Workers Union. In October, two thousand African dockworkers struck for higher pay in Durban and another two thousand African and Coloured dockers launched a month-long slowdown in Cape Town.

Just three weeks after the BPC convention in Hammanskraal, South Africa began to feel the first tremors of one of the biggest Black strike waves in its history.

Early on the morning of January 9, 1973, a group of workers at the Coronation Brick and Tile Company on the northern outskirts of Durban called their two thousand coworkers together for a rally at a nearby football stadium to mark the beginning of a strike for higher wages. The Coronation strike lasted a week, with the workers finally accepting a lower pay hike than they had demanded. The strike was widely reported in the local press, with banner headlines and photos of marching workers.

The Coronation workers' example quickly caught on. A series of minor strikes broke out among transport workers, tea packers, and ship painters. By January 25 the trickle began to swell into a massive and spontaneous outpouring of working class action, as hundreds of African men and women downed their tools at several textile mills in the Pinetown–New Germany industrial complex just east of Durban. By the following day, about six thousand African textile workers, and many Indian workers too,

18. Roger Murray et al., *Role of Foreign Firms in Namibia*, p. 164.

were out on strike. They rallied at the plant gates, chanting, "We are now a united nation" and "Usuthu," a traditional Zulu battle cry.[19]

Within days the strikes spread like a brushfire throughout the Durban area, with sparks landing in other parts of Natal as well. Workers in the sugar, rubber, chemical, bakery, metallurgical, construction, carpet, fruit, meat, and textile industries joined the great strike wave. By force of example, strikes swept up and down whole streets, with thousands of striking workers from one establishment marching en masse to another to pull more workers out, until about 150 firms in the Durban area alone had been hit. The strikers held numerous impromptu rallies, often in an atmosphere of joyous celebration, and sang traditional freedom songs, such as "Nkosi Sikelel' iAfrika" (God Bless Africa).

On February 5, thousands of Durban municipal workers jumped into the fray, many of them marching to the city hall waving sticks and clenched fists. Two days later, Hammarsdale, an industrial area twenty-five miles from Durban, was paralyzed by a virtual general strike of the town's Black work force.

The Black Consciousness movement did not have any direct influence on the striking workers, although the activities of the BPC, SASO, and other groups may have added to the generally defiant mood of the workers. During the strikes, Saths Cooper and four other BPC members were arrested for distributing pamphlets in English and Zulu urging solidarity among African, Coloured, and Indian workers.

The white employers and their government were more than alarmed at the massive display of Black working class strength. Police reinforcements were flown in from Pretoria, and police with riot equipment, guns, and dogs turned out in force. But aside from a few tear-gas attacks against marching workers and in some cases the arrest of strikers, the police exercised considerable restraint. Faced with tens of thousands of angry workers, and the possibility of similar outbursts in other parts of the country, the authorities were worried that a serious attack on the strikers might only aggravate the situation. They chose to wait the strike out.

The extremely low wages of Black workers, the very issue that impelled them to strike in the first place, eventually forced them to return to work. They simply could not afford to stay away from

19. Mafika Pascal Gwala, ed., *Black Review 1973*, p. 132.

their jobs for more than several days at a time. Nevertheless, most Black workers, including those who did not join the strikes, won modest wage increases, making the strike wave the most successful Black industrial action in South Africa's history. In addition, the regime amended its labor legislation, conceding a very limited right to strike to some African workers under certain conditions.

Although the big strike wave had begun to recede by mid-February, new strikes flared up in Natal and other parts of the country at a much higher rate than in previous years. On September 11, 1973, gold miners at the Western Deep Levels pit in Carletonville, near Johannesburg, struck to protest the big wage differential between white and Black miners. The "antiapartheid" Anglo American Corporation, which owned the mine, called in the police, who shot and killed eleven of the protesting miners.

Almost every one of the strikes of 1973 revolved around economic grievances, especially pay demands. Yet the political implications of the strike wave were considerable. Whatever the immediate aims of the strikers, the very logic of their independent mobilizations as workers *of an oppressed people* presented a fundamental challenge to the white supremacist system. This was reflected in the frequency with which the strikers sang traditional Black freedom songs. The high degree of solidarity exhibited between African and Indian workers also did much to reinforce the concept of Black unity. Even more importantly, the sheer size of the strike wave (involving sixty thousand workers in Natal alone) gave Black workers—and the Black population as a whole—a sense of their potential power that could only enhance their political militancy.

While underscoring the social weight of the Black working class, the strike wave at the same time revealed the relative disorganization of the Black labor movement as such, a disorganization that the regime constantly tries to foster through restrictions on Black trade union rights and the outright banning or imprisonment of the most effective labor organizers. As a result of the weakness of the existing Black unions, the strikes were largely spontaneous, with little identifiable leadership or coordinated direction. In only a handful of cases did Black unions attempt to negotiate on behalf of the strikers. The workers themselves generally refused to elect strike representatives, for fear that their rank-and-file leaders would later be victimized by management and the police. Yet rudimentary forms of organization existed and some leaders did arise in the heat of the upsurge, though they took care to remain anonymous.

To the regime's obvious concern, Black workers began to move toward greater organization in the wake of the strikes. Although they were still not legally recognized by the government (a secondary issue in any case), a number of Black unions were established, including the Metal and Allied Workers Union in Natal.

The Black Allied Workers Union itself grew from its modest beginnings in 1972, reaching eight thousand members within less than three years and establishing offices in Johannesburg and Durban. BAWU did not consider the lack of legal recognition of Black unions of immediate importance. "By virtue of our existence and strength," BAWU Secretary Cecil Fanekiso said, "employers would be forced to accord us *de facto* recognition."[20] BAWU also viewed the position of Black workers in a broader context, pointing out that "black Worker interests extend beyond the factory: they extend to the ghetto where black workers stay together in hostels under squalid conditions; to the crowded trains and buses—to the absence of amenities—to the stringent, irksome and humiliating application of influx control laws . . . to the lack of proper channels whereby people could equip themselves with basic skills."[21]

By mid-1974, some thirty thousand Black workers in Natal had been organized. But the goal originally outlined by the Black Workers' Project for a national conference of Black labor organizations failed to materialize.

The Black Consciousness movement itself nevertheless continued to spread its influence. By early 1973, SASO had grown to six thousand members, or nearly half of the entire Black university student population at that time (within two more years it was to increase to nine thousand members), making it the recognized voice of Black student opinion. The Black People's Convention, after a little more than a year since its inaugural conference, had by late 1973 established forty-one branches spread throughout the country.

Other Black Consciousness groups sprang up. The South

20. Thoko Mbanjwa, ed., *Black Review 1974/75*, p. 136.

21. Black Allied Workers Union, "Call to Organise & Form Black Trade Unions in S. Africa" (Johannesburg: n.d. [1973?]), p. 5. (Copy in author's files.)

African Student Movement (SASM), which was initially founded by high school students in Soweto, started to expand into other regions of the country and took on the character of a high school equivalent of SASO. In early June 1973, four youth organizations from different parts of South Africa partipated in a seminar in Kingwilliamstown sponsored by the Black Community Programmes (BPC) and SASO, at which they decided to unite and form the National Youth Organisation (NAYO). During the same month, the Black Consciousness movement extended its banner beyond South Africa's immediate borders; Black students from South Africa, Namibia, Zimbabwe, Botswana, Lesotho, and Swaziland came together in a conference in Lesotho, founding the Southern African Students' Movement (also known by the initials SASM), with O. R. Tiro as its first president.

The Black Community Programmes set up various community projects—such as health clinics, publishing ventures, cooperative building schemes, political prisoner relief funds, and leadership training programs. It aimed to broaden the appeal of the movement, open new avenues of communication with segments of the Black community, and, according to Nengwekhulu, instill "a sense of self-reliance and initiative in our people."[22]

Black religious figures were likewise open to the influence of Black Consciousness, partly through the medium of Black Theology, which was defined as a "theology of liberation."[23] A number sought to use the churches as platforms for propagating Black Consciousness ideas.

Some of the basic concepts of the Black Consciousness movement spread well beyond the actual membership of the BPC, SASO, and other groups and helped engender a greater sense of Black self-confidence. The movement itself, however, remained organizationally weak. Formal membership could only be counted in the thousands, while there were any number of groups that identified with the movement. Although there was some overlap of membership, there was no single authoritative body that could direct the political energies of the movement as a whole. The BPC, which most closely resembled a national

22. Ranwedzi Nengwekhulu, "The Meaning of Black Consciousness in the Struggle for Liberation in South Africa," United Nations Centre Against Apartheid, Notes and Documents No. 16/76, July 1976.

23. Nyameko Pityana, "What Is Black Consciousness?" in Basil Moore, ed., *The Challenge of Black Theology in South Africa* (Atlanta: John Knox Press, 1973), p. 59.

political organization, did not grow big enough to fill that role.

Connected with this organizational weakness was the lack of a coherent program of concrete demands that could be used to actively mobilize Blacks in struggle. The leaders, it appears, consciously held back from solidifying the movement's organizational base and hammering out a program of action.

This was partly in response to the likelihood of government repression. A decentralized movement, with leadership responsibilities spread around to a large number of activists, made it more difficult for the authorities to cripple it by simply detaining or banning a few recognized leaders. Similar considerations were involved in the hesitancy to spell out a precise political platform; it is dangerous in South Africa to openly state what one thinks.

However, the reluctance of the BPC and SASO leaders to take the initiative in organizing Blacks around political campaigns—or even to get more directly involved in the various struggles that were already going on—also flowed from their conception of how the fight for liberation would develop. In a schematic and idealist fashion, they thought that it was sufficient for the moment to simply popularize the ideas of Black Consciousness. Later, after the Black community had gained greater confidence—its "psychological liberation"—it could then fight for specific gains, for "physical liberation." They did not seem to think that these processes could be intertwined or realize that concrete struggles generally provide the best vehicles for advancing mass political consciousness. In practice, of course, layers of the Black population (university students, workers in Natal) were already mobilizing against specific aspects of their oppression. Some in the Black Consciousness movement saw the need to provide political direction to these struggles, but the general attitude was that the Black masses, in a more or less spontaneous manner, would find their own way. The weakness of this approach was to become evident during the 1976 uprisings.

To an extent, the Black Consciousness movement's unwillingness to rush into immediate battle with the regime was a healthy reaction to the PAC's mistakes during the Sharpeville crisis, when it prematurely, without any real strategy, marched into a confrontation for which neither the PAC nor the masses in general were prepared. To Biko, for one, Black Consciousness needed to avoid "precipitate and shot-gun methods which may be disastrous," and instead had to "channel the pent-up forces of the angry black masses to meaningful and directional opposition."[24] But the lack of a comprehensive and clear political strategy left the movement without an effective means for harnessing those energies—or later for checking the impatience of its more youthful followers.

One of the factors handicapping the movement's political development was its failure to establish a *strong* organized base in the Black working class, despite the growth of Black trade unionism at the time and despite its own stated objectives. Such a base would have done much to help politically orient the movement.

The young activists of the Black Consciousness movement nonetheless took heart from the rise in working class combativity, which helped reinforce their own militancy.

There were numerous expressions of this during 1973. The BPC held large rallies on Heroes' Day—March 21—to commemorate the anniversary of the Sharpeville massacre. Students at the University of Fort Hare conducted mass walkouts to protest harassment of SASO, while the student body at the University of the North voted overwhelmingly for automatic membership in SASO. In some parts of Durban, many Indian voters participated in organized boycotts of elections for local advisory committees, which were rejected as "meaningless bodies" with "no real power."[25] Coloured students at the University of the Western Cape mobilized in a series of large demonstrations to protest against the regime's educational policies and to demand community control of the university.

As the Black Consciousness movement's influence continued to spread, the security police began to seriously appreciate the inherent threat that it posed to apartheid stability. In March 1973, right after the Durban strike wave, eight top leaders of the movement were banned: Steve Biko, Nyameko Barney Pityana, Drake Koka, Saths Cooper, Ranwedzi Nengwekhulu, Strini Moodley, Jerry Modisane, and Bokwe Mafuna. Minister of Justice P. C. Pelser raised the ludicrous claim that the eight had advocated "arson, rape and bloody revolution," but refused to

24. Biko, *I Write What I Like*, p. 31.

25. Leonard Thompson and Jeffrey Butler, *Change in Contemporary South Africa*, pp. 269-70.

allow them an opportunity to defend themselves, declaring that they would not be charged and brought to trial since they would have used the courtroom as a political platform.[26] Throughout the rest of the year, scores of other Black activists met a similar fate, including Sipho Buthelezi, the BPC secretary-general. All together, more than a hundred militants were banned or placed under house arrest. Mosibudi Mangena, the BPC national organizer, was tried under the Terrorism Act and sentenced to five years on Robben Island.

One of the most chilling reminders of the white supremacists' brutal reaction to Black dissent came on February 1, 1974. On that day, O. R. Tiro, the president of the Southern African Students' Movement, was killed by a parcel bomb at his home in Gaborone, Botswana. The Bureau of State Security was widely believed to have been behind the murder.

White student and academic radicals, including some who supported the Black Consiousness movement, were also picked up and banned. Richard Turner, an avowed socialist, was banned in Durban, and several top leaders of NUSAS, including Glenn Moss, Charles Nupen, Karel Tip, and Cedric de Beer, were detained and tried for their ideas under the Supression of Communism Act (they were eventually acquitted).

The crackdown against the Black Consciousness movement eliminated almost the entire official leadership of the major groups. The blow was a heavy one, but it did not cripple the movement as such. New figures soon arose to fill the vacuum of formal leadership, while those who had been banned functioned as best they could from behind the scenes.

This resilience and continued determination of the movement's activists was further reinforced by the gains of the national liberation struggle elsewhere in Africa, especially in the Portuguese colonies. In an audacious expression of defiance against their own colonial oppressors, the BPC and SASO jointly called for rallies in Durban, Cape Town, Port Elizabeth, and Johannesburg for September 25, 1974, to express solidarity with the Mozambican freedom fighters, who were close to achieving their country's independence from Portugal. The Students' Representative Council at the University of the North planned a similar action there. The night before the demonstrations, Minister of Justice James Kruger banned all gatherings by the BPC and

26. *SASO Newsletter* (Durban), March-April 1973.

SASO for a one-month period. At least two of the actions nevertheless went ahead as planned.

At Turfloop, about twelve hundred students rallied and listened to speeches at the university hall. Police armed with rifles, pistols, clubs, and dogs arrived in riot vans and ordered the students to disperse. Although the students complied with the police order and headed back to their dormitories, the police unleashed their dogs anyway, inflicting some serious injuries.

In Durban, the rally at Curries Fountain began at 5:30 p.m., with more than two thousand Black protesters already in attendance. The crowd quickly grew. Within ten minutes of the start of the demonstration, according to a SASO pamphlet, "the number of people had increased to between 4000 and 5000. . . . The National Anthem, 'Nkosi Sikelela iAfrika,' was chanted, the Black power salute was given, and many people shouted slogans including 'Viva Frelimo.' "[27] About a half hour later the police attacked. Fleeing demonstrators were bitten by police dogs. Many were arrested on the spot and others were picked up at hospitals when they went for treatment of their injuries.

Beginning the same night, the security police began a countrywide raid against SASO, the BPC, the Black Allied Workers Union, and other organizations, arresting about forty top leaders, including several who had already been banned. Many lower-echelon leaders went underground and some left the country, but within weeks the groups had once more reorganized.

The ideas of the Black Consciousness movement were tenacious and continued to spread through the Black community. In December 1974, some three hundred delegates attended a Black Renaissance Convention in Hammanskraal, called by a committee of Black church figures. In terms of its size and breadth, it was one of the most representative Black conferences yet. The participants expressed their militant opposition to the institutions of "separate development" by expelling from the convention those who held positions in the Bantustan administrations or in the Coloured People's Representative Council.

In a significant development, reflective of the rising radicalization among Blacks, the convention raised a series of demands more specific than those put forward at most previous Black Consciousness gatherings. It called for "the release of all political prisoners, detainees and banned people." It appealed to "all the countries of the world to withdraw all cultural, educational,

27. Mbanjwa, *Black Review 1974/75*, p. 80.

economic, manpower and military support to the existing racist institutions." It demanded that the government "immediately recognise African unions" and declared that "there is a need for workers to organise themselves into trade unions free from government interference." It maintained that Blacks would strive for a society "free from all forms of oppression and exploitation," in which "all people participate fully in the government of the country through the medium of one man one vote." It affirmed, "Blacks demand their freedom now! They want their land; they want political and economic powers; and they want to be masters of their own destiny."[28]

During the same month, a bus boycott to protest fare hikes on the pattern of those in Alexandra in the 1940s and 1950s began in Mdantsane Township, which is located near East London but within the Ciskei reserve. After six weeks, the boycotters were successful in forcing the fares back to their original level.

The simmering disaffection among Coloureds toward the Coloured People's Representative Council reached new heights in early 1975 during elections to the CRC. A countrywide boycott campaign was launched in February by the Anti-CRC Committee. Thousands of "Don't Vote" pamphlets were distributed and large posters proclaiming "Don't Vote for Apartheid—Don't Vote for the C.R.C." were plastered up, especially in the Western Cape. In the March elections, less than half of the 550,000 registered Coloured voters went to the polls. Combined with the 144,000 eligible voters who failed even to register, this showed a marked increase in the number of Coloureds abstaining from any involvement with the CRC. Even those who cast ballots expressed opposition to the CRC by voting overwhelmingly for the Labour Party, which campaigned on a platform that promised to *close down* the CRC through a boycott by Labour Party representatives. (Once elected, however, the Labour Party leadership betrayed its followers by refusing to implement its declared boycott policy. Party leader Sonny Leon claimed that it was better to "stay put to destroy the C.R.C. from within." Nothing of the kind happened, and the CRC continued to function for several more years.)[29]

Industrial unrest among Black workers during 1974 and 1975

28. Black Renaissance Convention, "Declaration and Resolutions, 1974" in van der Merwe et al., *African Perspectives*, pp. 118-19.

29. Mbanjwa, *Black Review 1974/75*, pp. 61-69.

also remained at a high pitch. During 1974, some 189 strikes involving African workers erupted sporadically in various regions of the country, mostly for higher pay. The following year saw 119 African strikes. In addition, discontent among Black miners, which often did not take the form of explicit strike action, contributed to a series of "riots" (some over wage grievances) in which scores were killed.

In October 1975, another mass bus boycott began, this time near the steel town of Newcastle in northern Natal. For four weeks, up to forty thousand Black industrial workers walked from eight to fourteen miles to and from work each day between Newcastle and the townships of Madadeni and Osizweni, both located within KwaZulu.

The impact of such ongoing mass struggles and the glaring need to define more precisely the goals of the liberation struggle impelled the Black Consciousness movement to begin grappling more seriously with the question of political program. As this process advanced, the political heterogeneity of the movement became increasingly apparent.

In two conferences—one held in Kingwilliamstown in December 1975 and the other in Mafeking in May 1976—the majority of the BPC leadership formally outlined proposals for the kind of society it envisaged to replace the existing white supremacist state. A document adopted at the Kingwilliamstown conference stated that the government of a free Azania (which would be the new name of the country) would be based on democratic elections through a universal adult franchise—in other words, majority rule.[30] Although the document also briefly touched on economic and social policies, those were spelled out in greater detail at the Mafeking conference. According to the BPC's thirty-point economic program adopted at Mafeking, all land "should be owned by all the people, with the state being entrusted with its control"; "industries that are of vital importance to the economy of the nation such as major corporations and major finance institutions, should be owned by the state"; and the "state should play a leading role in the planning and development of commerce and industry."[31]

While the BPC did not yet try to set forth a strategy for

30. "Towards a Free Azania—Projection: Future State," in Buthelezi, *Black People's Convention*, p. 29.

31. "The BPC Economic Policy," in ibid., pp. 24-25.

reaching this goal, the presentation of a more specific program of social and economic measures—and the political discussions the program would engender—was an important step forward in defining the movement's objectives.

Partly to avoid the charge that it was communist—a label that could bring with it a quick banning order—the BPC wrapped its economic and social program in the cover of Black Communalism, a concept that hearkened back to the relative egalitarianism of precolonial African society. Security considerations aside, however, such a presentation of the BPC's aims also corresponded to the view that many Black Consciousness leaders had in that period of the nature of the liberation struggle. Implicitly, and at times explicitly, they denied that class interests were a factor, or even that distinct social classes existed within the Black community.

The elasticity of the Black Communalism concept allowed some sections of the movement to interpret it as being compatible with capitalism. According to a BAWU document, for instance, "The idea mooted here was not an intention to destroy the existing system and substitute it with the other, but to introduce and implement Black Communalism within the Capitalistic structure."[32] In immediate terms, this was reflected in the emphasis on trying to establish Black-run clinics, services, and cooperative small-scale businesses through the activities of the Black Community Programmes. More seriously, it led to neglecting the central importance of organizing Black workers *as a class,* through unions and other organizations, to enable them to lead all Blacks in the fight for national liberation.

There were members and leaders of the Black Consciousness movement, however, who differed with this approach. According to Sipho Buthelezi, a former BPC secretary-general, by the time of the Mafeking conference there already existed a "proletarian" tendency within the BPC that stressed the need to mobilize the working class.[33] Another activist of the BPC in the Johannesburg area told me in 1978 that a good number of members had been dissatisfied with the emphasis on Black Communalism. "South Africa is an industrialized country," he said. "We must move

32. Black Allied Workers Union, "On Black Communalism" (London: n.d.), p. 2. (Copy in author's files.)

33. Personal correspondence with the author from Sipho Buthelezi, August 5, 1979.

forward to socialism, not backward to tribal communalism."

To an extent, such views were also expressed publicly, particularly by SASO leaders. An anonymous "Black student leader" wrote in the *SASO Newsletter* in 1975:

> First, it is important for us to accept the fact that any meaningful change in this country's social, political and economic situation, shall be brought about by the proletariat—the people who really feel the pinch of white domination, exploitation and oppression. They possess the power to effect radical changes because they are at the base, and thus shoulder the whole weight of all social, economic and political pyramids of this country.[34]

Henry Isaacs, a former president of SASO, stated:

> But if the Black Consciousness Movement is going to pursue the struggle to its logical conclusion, then it has to prepare for revolutionary action by the oppressed against the oppressors. Proletarian forces of the people will have to be formed, trained and steeled for the seizure of power. . . . *Above all, it must help the people understand the class nature of the conflict between oppressor and oppressed.*[35]

The apartheid authorities were seriously concerned about the political discussions going on within the Black Consciousness movement, and especially the BPC's moves toward hammering out a more concrete program. They were determined to head off these developments before the movement gained even more strength. The result was the longest trial held under the Terrorism Act up to that time.

Nine leaders and members of the BPC and SASO, including Cooper, Moodley, and SASO President Muntu Myeza, were brought to trial on charges stemming from the political *ideas* they defended as advocates of Black Consciousness. They were accused of conspiring between 1968 and 1974 to "transform the State by unconstitutional revolutionary and/or violent means"; "denigrate Whites and represent them as inhuman oppressors of Blacks"; "make, produce, publish or distribute subversive and anti-White utterances, writings, poems, plays and/or dramas"; "organise and hold subversive and anti-White rallies and/or gatherings"; and "discourage, hamper, deter or prevent foreign

34. *SASO Newsletter* (Durban), May-June 1975.

35. Henry Isaacs, "The Emergence and Impact of the Black Consciousness Movement," *Ikwezi* (London), December 1976. Emphasis in original.

investments in the economy of the Republic."[36] All of this was considered "terrorism." The evidence against them included more than a hundred pages of poems, speeches, plays, and resolutions produced over the years by various Black Consciousness groups or members.

The Vorster regime clearly hoped that by putting the Black Consciousness movement in the dock and by removing its most articulate representatives from active leadership it would be able to stifle the further development of the national liberation struggle. But it was too late for that. Despite the relative organizational weakness of the movement, some of its ideas had already had a profound impact on Black political consciousness, helping to inspire a generation of young Blacks to stand up to the racist regime and demand their basic human rights. Moreover, the ideas of the Black Consciousness movement, while contributing to greater Black assertiveness and determination, were at the same time but a reflection of a more general Black radicalization.

That new militancy had only begun to make itself felt. It would soon break over the country with unprecedented force.

36. Mbanjwa, *Black Review 1974/75*, pp. 82-83.

19

1976 —Year of Rebellion

1976, as I see it, will be a decisive year. I think it will bring most of the answers to questions about which we are wondering now and speculating on.

—John Vorster

As 1976 opened, the regime still appeared to be in firm control. At least superficially, most of the overt challenges to white authority in the previous few years had been dispensed with through bannings, detentions, trials, and generalized terror tactics. The white rulers counted on maintaining their supremacy through the same methods that had worked so well over the decades: instilling fear in the Black population to such an extent as to make the entire system of domination workable.

But among Blacks themselves, profound changes had already taken place on a wide scale, changes that could only reduce the power of the bullet and the jail cell to keep them in line. Strengthened on the social level by their growing urbanization and proletarianization, awakened politically by the young advocates of Black Consciousness, encouraged by the big gains of the national liberation struggles in Mozambique and Angola, Blacks acquired a greater sense of self-confidence. Especially inspiring was the outcome of the Angolan war, which shattered the myth of white invincibility. Blacks had eagerly consumed whatever news of the war they could get, and discussed it in their classrooms and factories. The BPC, at its December 1975 conference in Kingwilliamstown—at the height of the Angolan war—openly sided with the MPLA against the South African army.

The pervasive fear that enveloped the Black townships had

begun to erode. A cornerstone of white control was weakening.

The increasingly defiant mood among Blacks was especially evident by March 1976. During that month, about twenty-five thousand Black commuters in the township of KwaThema, east of Johannesburg, launched a boycott of buses to protest against fare hikes. Black Consiousness supporters staged a protest in Johannesburg March 18 against a trial of seven members of the National Youth Organisation; the demonstration developed into a four-hour street scuffle with police when the demonstrators were joined by Black workers waiting for trains, swelling the crowd to about two thousand. Thousands of Blacks rallied in Soweto three days later, on the anniversary of the Sharpeville massacre. And a week after that several hundred Black workers seeking union recognition demonstrated outside the American-owned Heinemann electrical equipment factory in Germiston.

The ideas of the Black Consciousness movement reached an even broader audience in May, when Steve Biko testified for the defense in the ongoing trial of nine leaders of the SASO and BPC. Biko used the courtroom as a platform to explain the movement's advocacy of a universal adult franchise, an end to white supremacy, and "the creation of a nonracial society without any particular minority protection."[1] Every day after his testimony, Blacks pored over the newspaper reports of the trial. Biko quickly became the toast of Soweto.

Given the highly charged atmosphere, and the scores of Black grievances ranging from low pay and poor housing to the pass laws and political repression, virtually any issue could have set off a generalized upheaval. The one that finally did was the regime's decision to implement a policy of teaching half the courses in African secondary schools in the southern Transvaal through the medium of Afrikaans. This roused the ire of African students, parents, and teachers, both because of the practical difficulties of forcing students suddenly to learn through a language in which they were not fluent and because of the deep hatred among Blacks for the language used by the police, the courts, and the apartheid administration.

On May 17, students in Soweto began to take action. Some sixteen hundred pupils aged twelve to fourteen initiated a class boycott at Orlando West Junior Secondary school, declaring that they would not return until the Afrikaans language policy was withdrawn. Within days, more schools went out. Pickets were

1. Steve Biko, *Black Consciousness in South Africa,* p. 318.

set up. Responding to police provocations and arrests, students at Naledi High School stoned police and burned their car. Those at Morris Isaacson High School put up a placard at the main gate reading, "Notice—no S.B.s [Security Branch police] allowed. Enter at risk of your skin."[2]

On June 12, Tsietsi Mashinini, the president of the South African Student Movement chapter at Morris Isaacson, got together with student leaders from other schools and formed an ad hoc action committee. They decided to mobilize all high school and junior secondary school students in Soweto for a mass demonstration four days later.

On the morning of Wednesday, June 16, students from all over Soweto began to gather at Orlando West Junior Secondary. The crowd of twelve-to-twenty-year-old students had already reached more than ten thousand before 7:00 a.m. Some carried placards made out of old cardboard boxes and exercise-book covers reading, "Down With Afrikaans," "Afrikaans Is Oppressors' Language," "Blacks Are Not Dustbins," and "Viva Azania!" Toward the end of the morning rush hour they started a peaceful march toward Orlando Stadium, singing "Nkosi Sikelel' iAfrika," shouting "Amandla!" (power), and giving clenched-fist salutes. As they passed schools on the way, they called out other students to join them. According to observers, the atmosphere was jovial.

The march had barely begun, however, when ten vanloads of white and Black police arrived, armed with semiautomatic rifles, submachine guns, tear gas, and batons. They had megaphones, but made no attempt to talk to the students. Without warning, they fired tear-gas canisters into the crowd. Enraged protesters answered with stones and other objects.

Col. Johannes Kleingeld, the white officer in charge, drew his revolver, aimed at the students just in front of him, and fired. Thirteen-year-old Hector Petersen, who had his back to the policeman, crumpled to the ground, dead. Other police began firing, and more students fell. Kleingeld then opened up with a machine gun, he later explained, because "it has a more demoralizing effect than a pistol shot."[3]

The news of the shootings raced through the township. Youths responded to the murders by unleashing all their pent-up anger and frustration at the police and other symbols of white suprem-

2. *South Africa in Travail,* p. 6.

3. Denis Herbstein, *White Man We Want to Talk to You,* p. 13.

acy. Virtually oblivious to the danger, they stoned the police and engaged in running street battles. Scores of government buildings, administrative centers, post offices, beer halls, liquor stores, and other white-owned or run facilities were attacked, smashed up, and burned. Barricades were hastily built. Bakery vans were stopped, the bread distributed to bystanders, and the vans set alight. At Orlando High School, students painted on a wall, "Victory is certain—Orlando MPLA."

The police swarmed in with greater force, firing rifles and submachine guns into the crowds of young Blacks, often indiscriminately. Bodies dotted the streets.

By mid-afternoon, the ranks of the protesters had swelled to about thirty thousand, as unemployed youths joined the students. The regime's new paramilitary antiterrorism unit was brought into action for the first time. One unit of nearly sixty police led by Col. Theunis Swanepoel, who had previously acquired an international reputation for his torture methods as chief "interrogator" for the security police, fired at Blacks with high-velocity rifles. Dressed in camouflage uniforms, the police went out on sorties from the central station in Soweto, attacking large groups of youths to disperse them, shooting down any who stood their ground. The air was filled with smoke, cries of pain, and the constant "drrrr" sound of automatic weapons fire. French-supplied Alouette helicopters hovered overhead, dropping tear-gas canisters. When evening arrived, workers returning from their jobs in Johannesburg joined their children in the streets. By nightfall the township was ablaze. The authorities sealed Soweto completely off from the outside world, allowing only troop reinforcements in.

The official toll of that first day's police carnage was twenty-five persons dead, scores of others wounded. But given the persistent reports of secret burials and burning of bodies by the police, the real figure could have been much higher.

Rather than "pacifying" the township, as intended, the massacres of June 16 only heightened the fury of Soweto's Blacks and buttressed their determination to strike out at white authority in any way they could. Rebellions continued to flare up throughout Soweto, as Blacks, most of them very young, attacked those white-owned shops and administrative buildings that had somehow escaped the previous day's anger. Trucks were overturned and cars set on fire. Thousands of Black workers stayed away from their jobs. At various points the protesters and residents erected barricades and established "no-go" zones. In Dube, a more prosperous section of Soweto, a branch of the British-owned Barclays Bank was burned.

The police adopted a new tactic on the second day of the uprising, shooting down Blacks at random to instill a general atmosphere of terror. Anyone who raised a clenched fist or shouted "amandla" became a prime target. Bodies of children riddled with bullet holes lay scattered about.

The unrest spread almost as quickly as the news did. Alexandra, on the other side of Johannesburg from Soweto, was one of the first townships to join in solidarity with the Soweto students. Protesters built a huge roadblock in the center of Alexandra, covered with the slogan, "Why kill kids for Afrikaans?"

The day after the initial Soweto massacre, some four hundred white students from the University of the Witwatersrand began a solidarity march through Johannesburg. As they reached the downtown area, the protesters were joined by Black workers and white bystanders. Linking arms, they shouted, "Power to Soweto!" They were soon attacked by 150 club-swinging police and white thugs.

At the University of Zululand, students burned down the administration building. Several hundred African and Indian students in Durban marched in solidarity with Soweto. Police charged two thousand students at the University of the North who were holding a prayer meeting for those killed by the police. Rebellions erupted in Tokosa, Daveytown, Natalspruit, Katlehong, Vosloorus, Thembisa, Kagiso, Seshego, and elsewhere.

In a statement broadcast June 18, Prime Minister Vorster took a hard stance. "This Government will not be intimidated," he affirmed, "instructions have been given to maintain law and order at all costs."[4] While scores of teenagers were already being gunned down in the streets, Assistant Police Commissioner Brig. J. F. Visser warned the same day, "From now on we will use tougher methods."[5] The army, navy, and other military units were put on alert and James Kruger, the minister of justice, police, and prisons, outlawed all public gatherings until the end of the month. Given a free hand by their superiors, the police went on a rampage, unleashing a wave of killings unprecedented since the early part of the century. By June 19 the official death toll had risen to 109. But Chief Gatsha Buthelezi, hardly a

4. *New York Times,* June 19, 1976.

5. *Washington Post,* June 19, 1976.

radical, claimed after visiting the main hospital in Soweto that the real figure was closer to seven hundred.[6]

The bloodbath notwithstanding, new protests began in the Pretoria area June 21. In Atteridgeville, schools were spray-painted with the slogans "Don't pray, fight" and "Support Soweto." Crowds of students moved from one school to another, recruiting more and more protesters. The most serious unrest took place in Mabopane, a township of more than a hundred thousand Blacks located sixteen miles north of Pretoria and within the BophuthaTswana reserve. According to the police, the demonstrations began after 170 employees at the local waterworks went out on strike for higher pay.[7] Although Chief Minister Lucas Mangope of BophuthaTswana appealed to all of the Bantustan's "citizens" to refrain from protesting, Tswana students at Ga-Rankuwa ignored him.

The uprisings in the urban centers also spilled over into three other Bantustans: Lebowa, Venda, and QwaQwa. By the time the first wave of upheavals began to subside on June 23, it had already swept through more than twenty townships.

Despite their spontaneous character, the uprisings carried a clear message to the apartheid authorities: A new militancy and determined antigovernment sentiment had spread to an extremely large number of young Blacks. Both Kruger and Willem Cruywagen, a deputy minister in the Department of Bantu Administration and Development, later maintained that "only" about 20 percent of Soweto's population had participated in the protests—that is, more than a quarter of a million persons in one township alone.[8]

Fired by the ideas of the Black Consciousness movement, these young militants had learned to throw off the yoke of fear. They were no longer afraid to stand up before the armed might of the apartheid state, although in their impatience they did so recklessly. They had initially been impelled into action around a specific grievance, but were driven onward by the whole system of national and class oppression that blighted their lives and those of their parents. They instinctively understood that their struggle was not just for a few reforms, but for a complete change

6. Herbstein, *White Man*, p. 27.
7. *Times* (London), June 22, 1976.
8. John Kane-Berman, *Soweto*, p. 6.

in society. Their frequently shouted slogan of "amandla" raised the supreme political question of the day—who will rule, who will hold power? In this, the youth of Soweto and other Black townships articulated the more generalized aspirations of the Black population as a whole.

The authorities understood that. More than anything else, they feared that the students' lead would be followed by the more powerful Black social sectors, especially the working class, and that the mobilizations would soon give rise to a more organized and politically conscious leadership that could direct the upsurge in a more focused manner against the very structure of white supremacy.

Lacking a concrete strategy for mobilizing Blacks in political action, the main Black Consciousness groups had been overtaken by events. But the informal links between the student rebels and some of the Black Consciousness leaders raised a clear possibility that greater coordination and direction of the revolt would develop over time.

Trying to head off such a prospect, the Vorster regime pursued a course of combining a few concessions with massive repression. On July 6 it officially backtracked on the language issue, allowing school principals a choice of whether to use English or Afrikaans as a medium of instruction. In subsequent weeks, other small concessions were made, such as the easing of restrictions on Black home occupancy.

Overt repression, however, was the main axis of Pretoria's response, as it has been during every major crisis in South African history. "We are determined to stamp this out—and very fast," Kruger annouced.[9] Black schools and universities were closed. All public gatherings were banned. The regime admitted that 1,298 persons had been arrested by June 25. Kruger for the first time invoked the preventive detention provisions of the newly adopted Internal Security Act on July 16, putting them into effect in the Transvaal for one year. This was accompanied by another, more selective, wave of detentions, as police fanned out into the townships and began seizing scores of well-known Black figures, especially leaders of the BPC, SASO, and SASM. Dozens of children, some as young as eight years, were caught up in the security net. Gen. Gert Prinsloo, the commissioner of police, quipped that "the children are probably better looked after in a police cell than they would be in a place of safety. It is not

9. *Washington Post*, June 21, 1976.

unusual to keep juveniles in cells for long periods before trials."[10]

How well Black political prisoners were treated was underscored by the death in detention on August 5 of Mapetla Mohapi, a leading figure in the Black Consciousness movement, who was alleged to have hanged himself in his cell. (Mohapi's "suicide" note was later revealed to have been a forgery, and an inquest magistrate refused to accept the security police's version of his death.) In the subsequent weeks and months, Mohapi's killing was followed by many others.

While Vorster's lieutenants were busy trying to clamp the lid down, the prime minister received a valuable political boost from Washington. American Secretary of State Henry Kissinger agreed to meet directly with Vorster in West Germany June 23-24, a move that the South African rulers greeted as a major breakthrough after years of relative diplomatic isolation. The meeting allowed Vorster to show South Africa's Black population that he had powerful friends.

Vorster's crackdown made only a temporary impression. Black youths launched a new series of demonstrations and rebellions from July 17. On that day, students at the University of Fort Hare held a mass meeting to discuss a day of prayer for Soweto; the meeting spilled over into a few days of protests. On July 20 unrest erupted both west and east of Johannesburg, as thousands of students again went out onto the streets in Lynnville, Mhluzi, and Khutsong.

In Soweto itself, Black students began to organize themselves in preparation for further demonstrations. On August 2, each school sent two representatives to a meeting at which the Soweto Students Representative Council (SSRC) was established, with Tsietsi Mashinini as its first president. Adults in Soweto also formed a new umbrella group, the Black Parents' Association, which embraced a variety of prominent Black figures ranging from leaders of the Black Consciousness movement to members of the YMCA, YWCA, and Housewives' League. It was the more militant SSRC, however, that emerged for the moment as the spearhead of the struggle in Soweto. It also provided an example to young activists around the country and inspired the formation of similar councils in Katlehong, Randfontein, Mamelodi,

10. *South Africa in Travail,* p. 14.

Atteridgeville/Saulsville, Sibasa, Seshego, Port Elizabeth, the Vaal Triangle townships, and elsewhere.[11]

The SSRC's first step was to call a demonstration for August 4 to demand the release of the hundreds of Black activists who had been detained since the initial wave of protests in June. For the first time since the upheavals began, the students appealed directly to Black workers to stay away from their jobs.

Soon after daylight on August 4, students began to gather at Orlando Stadium. Giving clenched-fist salutes and carrying placards reading "Release all detainees!" they started a march from Soweto to Johannesburg, with the intention of rallying outside John Vorster Square, the main police headquarters. Their numbers quickly grew to twenty thousand. As the crowd reached the police barricades that had been erected on the outskirts of Soweto, the protesters were again attacked. They regrouped twice in an effort to continue their march, but were unable to break through the police lines. When the tear gas and gunfire subsided, three Black youths lay dead. The students were more successful in urging Black workers to stay at home. According to news reports, up to 60 percent of the Black labor force in many Johannesburg businesses failed to show up for work.

The following day, the Soweto students attempted a repeat performance. They rallied at Morris Isaacson High School and embarked on another march toward John Vorster Square. This time about five thousand students and adults participated. They were again prevented from completing the march by police barricades and gunfire. Earlier in the day, the students had set up their own well-organized roadblocks and pickets to dissuade workers from going into Johannesburg, with some success.

The August 4-5 demonstrations in Soweto signalled the beginning of another big wave of protests, one that was to spread through the entire country, affecting some eighty Black townships by the middle of the month.

One of the most significant new developments in the upsurge was its extention to Cape Town, the second-largest city in the country. On August 2, about a thousand Coloured students at the University of the Western Cape began a class boycott. A little more than a week later, on August 11, African high school

11. Kane-Berman, *Soweto,* p. 148.

students in Langa, Nyanga, and Guguletu began demonstrating. In Guguletu an angry crowd converged on the police station to demand the release of about thirty marchers who had been arrested earlier in the day. Surrounded by a large number of militant and determined protesters, the police gave in and released all those who had been detained. As night fell, the youths were joined by migrant workers returning to their hostels.

The next day, hundreds of students and workers marched to the Langa police station to demand the release of arrested students. The African townships were completely cordoned off, as police reinforcements were flown in from the Rand aboard American-supplied Hercules transport planes. By the evening of August 12, nearly thirty Blacks had been officially reported as killed, but residents of the townships revealed that police took away some bodies for secret burial.

Significantly, the unrest began to gather more steam among the Coloured population of Cape Town, in a clear setback to the regime's efforts to fuel divisions between Coloureds and Africans. Students from at least ten Coloured high schools rallied, boycotted classes, and expressed solidarity with their compatriots in the African townships. Students from the University of the Western Cape clashed with police on campus.

These protests, plus the growing resentment among Coloureds in general toward the regime's racist policies, prompted seventeen religious ministers of the Coloured Nederduitse Gereformeerde Sendingkerk to issue a statement August 16 rejecting "in the strongest possible terms the sinful structure of apartheid." In a direct slap in the face to Pretoria's attempt to buy off Coloureds with a few minor concessions, the ministers declared that "we refuse to accept privileges that are not given to the rest of the black community and we refuse to be used any longer by the divide and rule politics of the white government."[12]

Several hundred white students at the University of Cape Town held a solidarity action, some of them attempting to march to the Black townships to join the demonstrators there. The march was dispersed by police and seventy-six white students were detained.

Rebellions, meanwhile, continued to blaze away in other cities. Soweto itself was in a virtually constant state of turmoil. Indian students in Durban boycotted classes, and youths in the Transkei and BophuthaTswana staged sit-ins and demonstrations. Port

12. *Cape Times,* August 17, 1976; *Christian Science Monitor,* August 18, 1976.

Elizabeth was rocked by renewed unrest, as thousands of Black students and workers took part in a series of militant actions in the townships of New Brighton, KwaZekele, and Zwide. They attacked police stations, burned down government buildings, and attempted to march on the white areas of the city.

Despite an escalating repression in which scores of prominent Black Consciousness and community leaders were detained by the security police, the militant young activists in Soweto made preparations for a second general strike. The call for a three-day *azikhwelwa* (we will not ride) was initially relayed to Black workers through their children. It was then formally announced through thousands of leaflets, posters, and pamphlets put out by the SSRC, one of which demanded the "scrapping of Bantu education, the release of prisoners detained during the demos, and the overthrow of oppression."[13] According to SSRC leader Mashinini, "We had realised we had gone as far as we could, and it was now important that we strike at the industrial structure of South Africa."[14]

Even before it got light on August 23, students had set up pickets at the train stations. But they proved largely unnecessary. Although large contingents of police swarmed into the township to "protect" workers from student "intimidators," the overwhelming majority of Soweto's workers supported the strike call. No taxis were operating and the trains into Johannesburg ran virtually empty. The City of Gold, dependent as it is on the Black labor force of the surrounding townships, was brought to a standstill. Between 150,000 and 200,000 Black workers were estimated to have taken part on the first day of the strike.

Unable to intimidate the Black population through police terror, the authorities tried to weaken resistance by pitting Black against Black. During the strike's second day, which was as successful as the first, the police instigated a large group of migrant workers—who had been poorly informed about the aims of the strike—to attack Soweto residents, particularly students. The regime and the white-controlled press tried to make it appear as a spontaneous "backlash" by angry Soweto workers against student "hooligans." But there was considerable evidence pointing to police direction. Nat Serache, a Johannesburg reporter, hid in a coal box near one of the migrant hostels and overheard a

13. *Financial Times* (London), August 24, 1976.

14. *Black South Africa Explodes,* p. 22.

policeman telling the migrants, "We didn't order you to destroy West Rand property. You were asked to fight people only. . . ."[15] Other reporters overheard similar instructions, and one photographed a policeman talking to the strike-breakers just before they went on one of their rampages. Armed with sticks and long knives, the large groups charged through the streets, broke into homes, and beat or stabbed to death youths and older residents. In some cases they were openly accompanied by police in armored cars.

But the strike held firm. Large pickets were out on August 25, the third day. And although the police had been able to turn several hundred migrants against their fellow workers, there was no reported increase in the overall number of migrant workers who showed up at their jobs.

While the *azikhwelwa* was not able to force any concessions from the regime, it did reveal the social and political power of the Black working class, and reinforced the Black community's growing sense of its own strength. The students in particular were becoming increasingly conscious that they alone could not change society, that it was Black workers who had the power to do so. One leaflet issued just after the August 23-25 strike declared:

> The students believe that South Africa is what it is, and has been built by the blood, sweat and broken bodies of the oppressed and exploited Black workers, it is a well known fact that the Blacks carry the economy of this country on their shoulders. All the sky-scrapers, super highways, etc., are built out of our undistributed wages.
>
> It is because of these facts that the students realise that in any liberatory struggle, the power for change lies with the workers.[16]

About the time of the strike, Tsietsi Mashinini, the president of the SSRC, was forced to flee the country to escape a police dragnet that had been put out for him, including a R500 bounty placed on his head. Khotso Seatlholo, an eighteen-year-old student from Naledi High School, was chosen the new president.

The Johannesburg strike did not spread to Cape Town, but the port city was far from quiet. On August 23, about five hundred Africans in Guguletu again demonstrated. Langa high school students issued a declaration stating, "We want our fellow

15. *Rand Daily Mail* (Johannesburg), August 26, 1976.

16. No Sizwe, *One Azania, One Nation,* p. 193.

students who have been detained to be released, and other detainees regardless of colour. Equal job, equal pay. Free education."[17] On the same day, Coloured high school students in Bonteheuwel, outside Cape Town, held solidarity demonstrations. Over the next few days the entire township erupted, as Coloured youths and adults attacked police and government buildings. Police described Bonteheuwel as a "slagveld" (battlefield).[18]

One leaflet, issued anonymously in Cape Town, raised a series of popular demands: "We want free and equal education for all. . . . Give the workers equal wages and work according to merit. Stop influx control."[19] A pamphlet by Coloured students of the University of the Western Cape addressed itself to a different question. In a strong appeal for Black unity, it proclaimed, "We maintain that Black people all over the country suffer in the same manner and feel the pains of oppression in a common way. It is not only true but necessary, that the only effective way in bringing about a new society is for *Black people to stand together.*"[20]

That goal was already becoming a reality. On September 1, while large crowds clashed with the police in the Coloured township of Athlone, some two thousand African students took their protests into the heart of Cape Town itself, snarling rush-hour traffic and startling white onlookers with their peaceful but audacious march around the downtown area. During the following two days, hundreds of Coloured youths also marched into Cape Town, mingling with African protesters and even some sympathetic whites. The authorities were stunned. The failure of their divide-and-rule strategy was staring them in the face. Their immediate reflex was to crack down hard.

In protest after protest, the police covered the streets with tear gas and waded into the seething crowds with swinging batons. But the protesters continually reassembled and were joined by office and factory workers. The assault by the riot police climaxed

17. *Black South Africa Explodes,* p. 20.

18. *Cape Times,* August 26, 1976.

19. "A Call to All," hand stenciled leaflet issued in Cape Town, 1976. (Copy in author's files.)

20. "Soweto—UWC?" leaflet by students of the University of the Western Cape, Belville, n.d. Emphasis in original. (Copy in author's files.)

with a sweep down Adderley Street, the city center's main thoroughfare, as they blasted into a large racially mixed crowd with birdshot. The police assaulted anyone within reach, threw them into police vans, and dragged them off for further beatings in jail. The repression in downtown Cape Town was matched by similar attacks in the Coloured and African townships, claiming an unknown number of dead and wounded. Luke Mazwembe, a detained African trade unionist, died in police custody in Cape Town that day.

With Cape Town at the hub, the rest of the Cape Province also rose up. Stellenbosch, Parow, Cradock, Hout Bay, Somerset West, Paarl, George, Beauford West, Oudtshoorn, Wellington, Knysna, Mossel Bay, all were engulfed by the uprisings. Large crowds of youths stoned cars, burned shops, and screamed out their hatred of white supremacy. They were met by withering barrages of gunfire from the police and groups of armed white vigilantes. The number of Black bodies counted in just two hospitals in the Cape Peninsula on September 8 reached a total of seventy-three. The police in the Cape had earned their popular nickname—the "terroriste."

The two main flashpoints of the upsurge, Johannesburg and Cape Town, were now beginning to fall into step. The SSRC distributed leaflets in Soweto calling for yet another three-day general strike September 13-15. Drake Koka, the banned leader of the Black Allied Workers Union, helped by arranging for the printing of forty thousand strike leaflets and smuggling them into Soweto.[21] In English, Zulu, and Sotho, the SSRC leaflets condemned the police killings, the deaths in detention of political prisoners, and the "cutting down of our parents' wages" for observing the August strikes.[22]

For the first time, similar leaflets were passed out in Cape Town, calling for a general strike in that city September 15-16. The plea for Black unity was explicit, with denunciations of the Coloured People's Representative Council, the South African Indian Council, and the Bantustans. "All Black people suffer alike," one declared, going on to point out, "If you strike you will hit the system where it hurts."[23]

21. Herbstein, *White Man,* p. 190.

22. "Azikhwelwa!" leaflet issued by the SSRC, September 1976. (Copy in author's files.)

23. *Black South Africa Explodes,* p. 39.

On September 13, an estimated half-million Black workers in the Johannesburg area stayed away from their jobs. Almost nothing moved. Not only did Soweto respond to the strike call, but so too did the townships of Alexandra and Krugersdorp. Some industries reported only a 2 percent attendance by their Black workers. The Johannesburg Chamber of Commerce estimated that between 75 and 80 percent of the city's Black workers stayed home.

The strike organizers scored a notable victory by winning the support of many of the migrant workers who had opposed the previous strike. Some one thousand Soweto residents, students, and migrant workers had met the day before to smooth over the frictions and to discuss the reasons for the strike. The students emphasized to the migrants that as workers they too were victims of oppression.

Confronted with a solid Black front, the regime could do little to break the strike, except to continue its direct terror tactics. Alexandra was completely sealed off, and police conducted house-to-house raids, carting off and jailing about eight hundred Blacks. As pickets were set up the next morning, police opened fire on them, killing a number of protesters. But the strike remained firm.

Wednesday, September 15, was the day that the Cape Town workers joined in. The docks, construction sites, textile factories, bakeries, shops, and other businesses ground to a near standstill, as about a quarter of a million Coloured and African workers—some three-quarters of the entire work force—heeded the strike call.

Combined with the half-million strikers in Johannesburg, this made it the biggest strike South Africa had ever known. Johannesburg and Cape Town, the two largest cities in the country, were crippled by an explicitly political workers' action that the authorities were virtually powerless to do anything about.

On Thursday the Johannesburg strike had ended, but the Cape Town strike picked up even more support than the day before. In the evening, protesters took to the streets, setting up barricades in the Coloured areas of Athlone, Manenberg, Grassy Park, Bishop Lavis, and Kewtown. Police vented their frustrations by shooting dead twelve demonstrators (according to official figures) and wounding more than fifty.

A series of one-day strikes subsequently swept through many of the smaller towns in the Cape and on September 20-21 thousands of Black workers in Thembisa, east of Johannesburg, followed a strike call that had been announced in anonymous leaflets.

That month's issue of *Umanyano,* a Xhosa- and Afrikaans-language newspaper aimed at Black workers in Cape Town, drew attention to some of the basic political lessons of the general strike. "It is the workers who keep the factories, stores, mines, and farms running," it said. "The workers are strong, because they are so vital to the entire country. . . . They have greater strength than the students." Noting that Black workers view "exploitation in the factory and apartheid as the same thing," *Umanyano* pointed out that in participating in the strike, "workers had struck in protest against both the government and the bosses."[24]

Virtually ignoring the massive rebellions against white rule, Kissinger, the American secretary of state, arrived in Pretoria on September 17. His visit was widely interpreted in the Black townships as a form of diplomatic backing for the Vorster regime at a time of crisis. As the Christian Institute of Southern Africa pointed out on the eve of the visit, "A foreign statesman visiting the South African Government bestows a respectability and approval upon the apartheid regime, unless he specifically rejects it."[25] Vorster made little effort to conceal his glee over the visit.

Just before Kissinger's arrival, however, Black students from at least eight high schools in Soweto held demonstrations to condemn him. They put up hundreds of placards denouncing Kissinger as a "murderer." Others protested American support for the South African regime, or simply declared, "Kissinger, go home." One huge sign tacked up on a church yard wall read, "Kissinger, get out of Azania—don't bring your disguised American oppression into Azania."[26] At Sekano Ntoane High School, students rallied on the school grounds, singing freedom songs and waving placards. The police drove up, blasted open the gate, and charged into the grounds firing shotguns. Similar attacks were launched at other high schools, claiming the lives of at least six students. The anti-Kissinger signs were removed.

Less than a week later, on September 23, Black students for the first time managed to take their opposition into the heart of Johannesburg itself, consciously following the example of the

24. *Umanyano* (Cape Town), September 1976.
25. *New York Times,* September 17, 1976.
26. *Cape Times,* September 18, 1976.

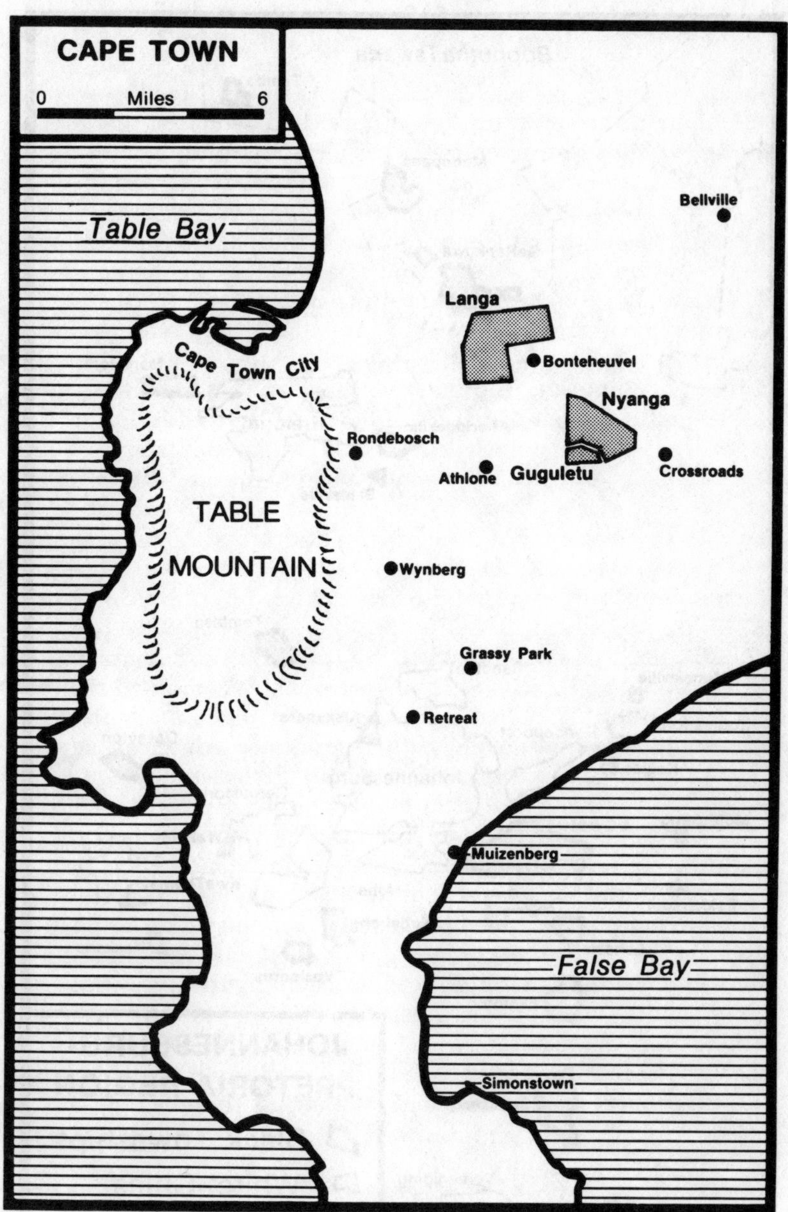

CAPE TOWN
0
Miles
6
Table Bay
Cape Town City
TABLE
MOUNTAIN
Langa
Bonteheuvel
Nyanga
Bellville
Rondebosch
Athlone
Guguletu
Crossroads
Wynberg
Grassy Park
Retreat
Muizenberg
False Bay
Simonstown

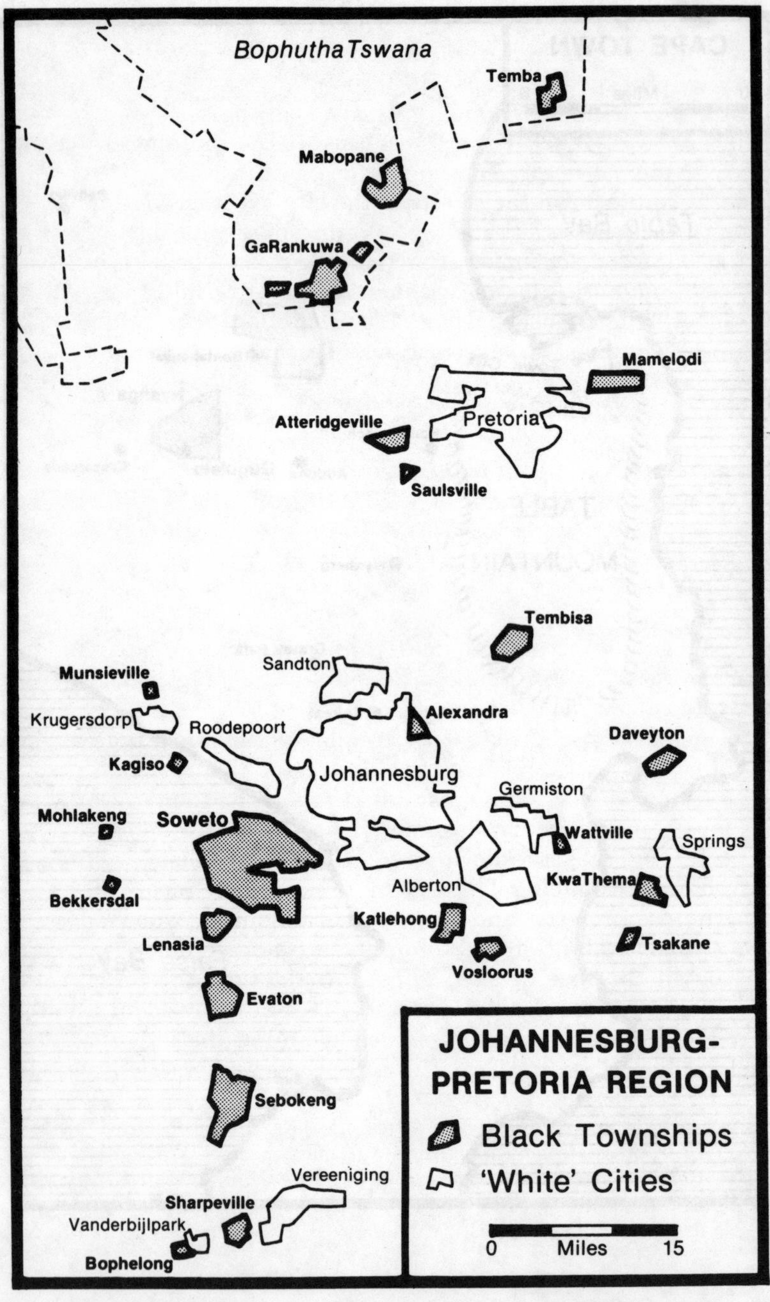

BophuthaTswana
Temba
Mabopane
GaRankuwa
Mamelodi
Atteridgeville
Pretoria
Saulsville
Tembisa
Munsieville
Sandton
Krugersdorp
Alexandra
Roodepoort
Daveyton
Kagiso
Johannesburg
Germiston
Mohlakeng
Soweto
Wattville
Springs
Bekkersdal
Alberton
KwaThema
Katlehong
Lenasia
Tsakane
Vosloorus
Evaton
JOHANNESBURG-
PRETORIA REGION
Sebokeng
Black Townships
'White' Cities
Vereeniging
Sharpeville
Vanderbijlpark
0
Miles
15
Bophelong

demonstrations in downtown Cape Town earlier that month. Some fifteen hundred students managed to slip past police security checks and reach the center of Johannesburg. They unfurled a banner reading, "Release our people." Chants of "Black power! Black power!" echoed off the buildings. Within minutes the police arrived and charged with batons, leading to a running battle down the streets of the city. At least four hundred young Blacks were arrested in Johannesburg that day.

Following the September 23 action, the overt rebellions against the white minority regime went into a relative lull for a while, having already touched some 160 Black locations around the country. The masses paused to size up the situation and catch their breath.

Taking advantage of this lull, the police escalated detentions and other reprisals. According to a report by the South African Institute of Race Relations, nearly 4,200 persons were arrested and charged between June 16 and October 31. Hundreds of them, mostly youths, were sentenced to whippings. In addition, Kruger announced in October, 697 persons were under detention for "security reasons."[27] They included almost every prominent leader of the Black Consciousness movement, among them Steve Biko, Nyameko Pityana, Mongezi Stofile, Silumko Sokupa, Thomas Manthatha, Hlaku Kenneth Rachidi, Aubrey Mokoena, Thadisizwe Mazibuko, and others.

The police dragnet was rather broad, sweeping up a wide range of other figures, from Winnie Mandela of the Black Parents' Association to Rev. Mangaliso Mkatswa of the Roman Catholic Bishops Conference. Two groups of people who were especially hard hit by the crackdown were Black journalists, who had played an invaluable role in trying to accurately report the antigovernment protests, and Black trade unionists, who had continued their valiant efforts to organize Black unions.

Even in the face of such fierce intimidation, the SSRC continued to defy the regime. On October 29, SSRC President Khotso Seatlholo issued a press release condemning the imposition of "independence" on the Transkei three days earlier. He affirmed:

> We shall rise up and destroy a political ideology that is designed to keep us in a perpetual state of oppression and subserviency. We shall oppose the economic system that is keeping us in [a] non-ending state of poverty. We shall not stand a social system of discrimination that has become an insult to our human dignity. We shall reject the whole system of Bantu

27. *Star Weekly* (Johannesburg), November 13, 1976.

Education whose aim is to reduce us, mentally and physically, into "hewers of wood and drawers of water" for the White racist Masters. Our whole "being" rebels against the whole South African system of existence, the system of Apartheid that is killing us psychologically and physically.[28]

Seatlholo also issued a call for another national stay-at-home strike, to be held November 1-5, to demand the resignation of the regime, the release of political detainees, and an end to the killings.[29] Several leaflets were distributed by the SSRC to publicize the strike call.

Except for the closing down of many shops and stores in Soweto itself, the strike failed to materialize, an indication of the relative downturn of the mass upheaval, a tougher stance by employers (who threatened to dismiss strikers), and the extent and ferocity of the police repression.

Mass police raids were launched against townships in the Johannesburg area, especially Soweto, throughout late October and early November. Their objective was to crush the SSRC and intimidate activists in general. Soweto, Alexandra, and other locations were sealed off and subjected to house-to-house searches, the police seeking to track down student leaders on their wanted list.

As the jails filled up with even more political prisoners, the number of deaths in detention rose sharply. From the June protests through the end of the year, at least a dozen jailed activists were alleged to have committed suicide, fallen down stairs, or died of "natural" causes. Many more suffered injuries, some of them permanent, at the hands of Vorster's interrogators.

The killings of hundreds of protesters, the jailings of thousands more, and the regime's systematic campaign of terror forced many student activists to flee the country for their lives. Up to eight hundred refugees had fled to neighboring Botswana by the end of the year, and more than a hundred others went to Swaziland. Thousands more were later forced to follow them.

During this severe crackdown, the embers of the youth revolt continued to sputter here and there. In October and November, students in Soweto and in the African townships around Cape Town carried out campaigns to shut down *shebeens* and other

28. "Students Representative Council," press release by Khotso S. Seatlholo, October 29, 1976. (Copy in author's files.)

29. Ibid.

establishments that sold liquor to Africans (widespread alcoholism among Black workers was recognized as an impediment to the struggle). Some thirty thousand African students in Cape Town observed a boycott of classes for several months, while a similar boycott of matriculation examinations in Soweto and Katlehong was carried out with full participation.

In December, the SSRC called on all Blacks to refrain from Christmas celebrations as an expression of mourning for those killed by the police. The call was widely followed. Students in Cape Town issued a similar call, but there the police again applied their tactic of instigating misinformed migrant workers to attack students and residents, leading to some thirty deaths in several days of clashes.

By the end of the year, police repression throughout the country had succeeded in putting an end to most of the massive, spontaneous outbursts, but it did not destroy the SSRC or the other groups opposed to minority rule. Rather than receding, the confrontation between the apartheid authorities and the Black masses took on new forms. In the words of the SSRC leaflet announcing the Christmas boycott in Soweto, "There is no peace, there shall be none until we are all free."[30]

30. "Soweto Students Representative Council," leaflet issued December 1976. (Copy in author's files.)

20

South Africa After Soweto

Like a violent electrical storm that cleanses the morning air, the social crisis brought on by the Soweto upheavals left the political atmosphere crisp and clear. Any illusions that the basic conflict between white supremacy and Black aspirations was somehow reconcilable had been washed away. Increasingly, majority rule appeared to Blacks to be the only alternative that could offer an end to the centuries of oppression, impoverishment, and racist violence.

Though the upheavals of 1976 had a profound radicalizing effect in the Black townships, mass resistance remained at an ebb throughout the first months of 1977. The Black population needed time to recover from the repression, time to absorb the political lessons of the previous year.

Benefitting from the experience of Soweto, sectors of the Black leadership had already come to an important realization: Uncoordinated and unfocused assaults against the white supremacist system, even massive ones, were unlikely to achieve very much. What was needed above all was greater organization and political leadership. Efforts to move in that direction were not long in coming.

The senior Black Consciousness groups, though decimated by detentions, strove to keep on functioning. But the repression against the Black People's Convention and the South African Students' Organisation—combined with their lack of a well-organized base and concrete political perspective—nevertheless prevented them from playing the kind of leading role that was needed to weld the disparate strands of resistance together into a mighty opposition movement.

As a result, much of the political responsibility fell onto the shoulders of the Soweto Students Representative Council. Throughout much of 1977, the SSRC remained the most powerful political organization in Soweto, commanding wide respect and authority. According to Khotso Seatlholo, "Most of the people, if they want to do something that has to do with politics, consult with the SSRC members. . . . In that way, the SSRC has become the 'government.'"[1]

Frequent detentions and police sweeps made it more difficult for the SSRC to operate, but the organization was quite resilient. The SSRCers found ways to circumvent Pretoria's informer network. If a leader was arrested or forced into exile, a new one was quickly chosen to fill the vacancy. Seatlholo, who took over after Mashinini left the country, operated underground for several months, moving secretly from house to house, before going into exile himself in January 1977. Sechaba Daniel Montsitsi, the chairman of the Sekano Ntoane High School branch of the SASM, immediately assumed the SSRC presidency.

Despite the youth and relative inexperience of its leading militants, the SSRC consciously tried to broaden its following beyond students. It addressed itself to some of the basic concerns of Blacks in general.

In April 1977, the West Rand Administration Board, which ran Soweto, announced that rents on all homes in the township would be raised by 40 to 80 percent. Soweto reacted in anger. In response to an SSRC call, thousands poured into the streets, carrying placards ranging from "We will not pay" to "Away with capitalism."[2] The regime quickly backtracked and temporarily shelved the rent increase.

Fresh from this victory, the SSRC moved on to its next target, the collaborationist Urban Bantu Council. It had already issued a call during the rent protests for the dissolution of the UBC, declaring that its members "have consistently been used by the authorities to oppress their own people."[3] In subsequent weeks, UBC members came under even more heat, both from the students and from the Black community as a whole (the UBC

1. Author's taped interview with Khotso Seatlholo, New York, February 24, 1977. Excerpts in *Intercontinental Press* (New York), March 14, 1977.

2. *Washington Post,* April 28, 1977.

3. *Star Weekly* (Johannesburg), April 30, 1977.

was never very popular; only 14 percent of the township's qualified voters turned out for council elections in 1974). Under popular pressure, most of the councillors had resigned by early June.

The collapse of the Soweto UBC was one of the most graphic illustrations of the SSRC's power and prestige. But the student activists did not stop there. They called on the residents of Soweto to choose their own democratically elected representative body. Montsitsi explained that the SSRC itself "cannot suggest the alternative," but made it clear that the SSRC favored the setting up of a council free of all government ties.[4]

While this challenge to Pretoria's day-to-day authority over Soweto was emerging, the first anniversary of the June 16, 1976, student protests drew near, bringing with it a new round of mass actions. The SSRC announced plans to commemorate the occasion June 13-19, calling on the township's million-and-a-half inhabitants to demonstrate, rally, and strike.

In a vain attempt to nip the planned anniversary demonstrations in the bud, the police swept through Soweto June 10-11, arresting almost the entire top leadership of the SSRC, including Montsitsi.[5] But the SSRC barely missed a step. It quickly chose a new leadership and reaffirmed its commemoration plans.

Significantly, the Black People's Convention, in a move toward greater direct involvement in political action, openly threw its own authority behind the SSRC call; in a June 13 statement BPC President Hlaku Kenneth Rachidi urged Blacks to take part in the commemorative actions.

Tens of thousands of Black workers observed the SSRC strike call on June 16 and 17, despite a police show of force and warnings by employers that those who did not report for work would not be paid. According to company estimates, at least half of the Johannesburg industrial work force stayed home; Black leaders claimed an even greater response.

Most Black schools in South Africa were shut down on the anniversary date, and protest meetings and demonstrations were held in many areas. In Soweto itself, thousands demonstrated or

4. *Southern Africa* (New York), August 1977.

5. Montsitsi and ten other SSRCers were later brought to trial for their role in the 1976 and 1977 protests. Montsitsi received an eight-year prison sentence in May 1979, of which four years were suspended.

attended church services to pay tribute to the martyrs of 1976. In Mamelodi, east of Pretoria, the police broke up a demonstration of ten thousand. In Uitenhage, in the Eastern Cape, the Black townships of Kabah and Kwanobuhle exploded in big mobilizations. Over a period of several days many schools and government offices were put to the torch. Protesters clashed with police units. Ten Blacks had been shot dead by the police by June 19.

On June 23, between four hundred and five hundred Soweto youths slipped into Johannesburg and rallied outside the police headquarters at John Vorster Square (the police had managed to turn back a thousand others who tried to march to the city along the main highway from Soweto). The demonstrators shouted slogans, sang Black freedom songs, and gave clenched-fist salutes, which were returned by Black workers watching from the sidewalks. Their placards demanded the release of the detained SSRC leaders and proclaimed, "Bantu Education is for the education of slavery!"[6] The police plowed into the demonstration with clubs and detained more than 140 of the Black youths.

Meanwhile in Soweto, tens of thousands demonstrated in various parts of the township. One march, in the Phefeni district, stretched for more than half a mile in rows of twenty persons across. Riot police, backed up by reinforcements flown in from Pretoria, attacked crowds in at least seven areas, shooting to death several more protesters. A few days later, some five thousand mourners in Soweto turned out for the funeral of a seventeen-year-old student who had been beaten to death by the police on the eve of June 16.

This new upsurge impelled the Black-run *Weekend World* to adopt a more militant editorial stance than before: "We say to the Government and the whites in general, your choice is simple. Either abandon all your privileges now and submit yourselves to majority rule in a nonracial society, or face certain destruction in the future."[7]

Especially significant was the political evolution of some of the younger leaders of the Black Consciousness movement, who began to focus more explicitly on the role of capitalism in the oppression and exploitation of Blacks. Diliza Mji, then the SASO president, declared in a speech published that month, "Apartheid

6. John Kane-Berman, *Soweto,* p. 4.

7. *Weekend World* (Johannesburg), June 19, 1977.

as an exploitative system is part of the bigger whole, capitalism. . . . If Black Consciousness must survive as a viable philosophy and continue to articulate the aspirations of the masses of the people, it must start interpreting our situation from an economic class point of view. . . . we have to align ourselves with the majority of the working people and be with them."[8]

On the crest of this rising militancy, the SSRC's earlier call on the Black community to set up its own representative body began to bear fruit. In late June, ten prominent Soweto leaders formed the Soweto Local Authority Interim Committee—known as the Committee of Ten—as a preliminary step toward a popularly based community council. Dr. Nthato Motlana, a former secretary of the ANC Youth League and a founder of the Black Parents' Association, chaired the committee. His colleagues included Lekgau Mathabathe, the principal of the volatile Morris Isaacson High School; Leonard Mosala, a former Urban Bantu Council member; Veli Kraai of the Soweto Traders' Association; and four current or past officers of the Black People's Convention—Thandisizwe Mazibuko, Sedupe Ramsy Ramakgopa, Mashoabado Mayathula, and Thomas Manthata. The committee had the SSRC's blessing. Speaking at the committee's inaugural meeting, the new SSRC president, Trofomo Sono, urged the members to form a council "that will not be indoctrinated into the government way of controlling the black man in the country."[9]

On July 26, the Committee of Ten, challenging the government's right to wield authority over the township, issued a "blueprint" for the establishment of a democratically elected council. Though couched in diplomatic terminology, the plan unequivocally rejected any contact with "imposed appointees of the central government," thus opposing Pretoria's schemes to install a new Community Council subject to government supervision and veto. Instead, it called for free elections to a council that would have final authority over all of Soweto's internal affairs, including legislation, taxation, education, and the police. It also held out the promise of full home and land ownership rights to Soweto's residents, against Pretoria's efforts to limit Black residency rights in the townships. "The time has come for us to

8. *SASO Bulletin* (Durban), June 1977.

9. *Times* (London), July 26, 1977.

manage our own affairs," Motlana proclaimed.[10]

From their public statements, some of the more moderate committee members appeared to view the proposed council as an alternative to sustained mass mobilization and organization. But their limited aims did not lessen the plan's objectively radical thrust. The very concept of a *democratically* elected Black council, one that reflected the true political leadership of the Black community of Soweto, could have a profound impact in a country where the most fundamental democratic rights are denied. The regime realized, moreover, that if Blacks actively mobilized around such a demand, they would not only raise the question of political control over one township, but also of who would rule the country as a whole. The fact that most of the blueprint's supporters openly favored Black majority rule indicated that they too viewed its realization as simply a first step toward their ultimate goal.

As if to confirm the government's fears, the Committee of Ten announced plans for a mass rally in Soweto to mobilize popular support for its demands. The rally was promptly banned. Another was called and it too was outlawed. The regime had no intention of allowing the committee to actively demonstrate its popularity.

Although the Committee of Ten continued to exist and to wield a degree of political influence in Soweto, its members made little real effort to circumvent the administrative obstacles thrown up by the regime. They did not try to mobilize their followers or build up an organized base of support. That very much limited the committee's effectiveness.

Almost simultaneously with the Committee of Ten's formation, students and other political activists stepped up opposition to two of the more detested aspects of apartheid, the Bantustans and the racist education system.

On July 16, ten major Black organizations held an all-day seminar in Hammanskraal to discuss how to organize opposition to Pretoria's Bantustan policy. The seminar was called by the BPC, which was starting to take greater initiative in organizing activities in its own name. The ten groups unanimously agreed to "mobilize all black people in Azania to demonstrate in no uncertain terms their rejection of Bantustan independence."[11]

The potential of such a campaign was already being demon-

10. *Star Weekly* (Johannesburg), July 30, 1977.

11. *Christian Science Monitor*, July 26, 1977.

actice. At the very time of the conference, Black aheng, ninety miles away, were protesting against s Mangope's agreement that BophuthaTswana become pendent" in December 1978.

Black students also initiated a new offensive against Bantu Education. On July 25, some twenty thousand students in Pretoria's Black townships of Atteridgeville and Saulsville walked out of their classes. The boycott then spread to Soweto and Alexandra in late July and early August. SSRC President Sono called for the complete scrapping of Afrikaans as a medium of instruction, for an end to government control of the schools, and for education that was relevant to the needs and aspirations of Blacks.[12] Sono, who was in hiding from the police, was forced to flee into exile shortly thereafter.

On September 14, while the school boycotts were continuing to gain momentum, the morning newspaper headlines stunned the country. Steve Biko, one of the people most identified with the birth of the Black Consciousness movement, whose ideas had helped inspire an entire generation of young Blacks, was dead. He had died alone, in a police cell, two days earlier, following his arrest August 18 at a roadblock near Kingwilliamstown.

If Biko had not been widely seen as a symbol of Black Consciousness, his death might have received the same perfunctory treatment in the press as the preceding forty-five deaths in security police detention since 1963. The circumstances of his death, hidden behind impenetrable jail walls, beclouded by brusque bureaucratic explanations, might have remained a mystery. But the thirty-year-old Black leader had been too well known, both in South Africa and abroad. For those who were responsible for his death, a cover-up was required.

Underscoring the importance of the case, James Kruger himself gave a relatively extended "explanation" on the day after Biko's death. He implied that Biko had died as a result of a hunger strike. The next day, before a congress of the National Party, Kruger quipped that Biko's death "leaves me cold," and added amid snickering and laughter from the audience that prisoners in South Africa had "the 'democratic right' to starve themselves to death. It is a democratic land."[13]

In the face of widespread disbelief, the hunger-strike claim fell

12. *Star Weekly* (Johannesburg), August 20, 1977.
13. *Rand Daily Mail* (Johannesburg), September 16, 1977.

to pieces. Details of the official autopsy report soon leaked out, revealing that Biko had died of "extensive brain injury" caused by several blows to his head and that his body was covered with bruises and abrasions. The public furor over Biko's killing, both at home and abroad, forced the regime to order an inquest. Although it brought to light further evidence of how Biko was mistreated by the police, the chief magistrate ruled that no one was responsible for Biko's death.[14]

To the many Blacks who had looked up to Biko, who had taken inspiration from his example and his ideas, no inquest or other court proceeding was needed to convince them of how he had died. The reality of life under apartheid made that fairly obvious. The murder only gave them a new source of anger and led to yet more outpourings of mass defiance across the country.

Within hours of the announcement of Biko's death, some four hundred Blacks and whites gathered for an impromptu memorial service in Johannesburg. The BPC, of which Biko was honorary president, condemned Pretoria as "a violent police state."[15] The entire student body of fifteen hundred at the University of Fort Hare, which Biko once attended, turned out September 15 to commemorate him. Protest meetings and memorial services, many of them called by the BPC, spread to campuses in every major city in the country. Hundreds gathered at the University of the Witwatersrand in Johannesburg and at the University of the Western Cape. Thousands attended a series of memorials in Soweto. A Black churchman told an angry audience at one of them, "Steve Biko has not died in vain. For among us there will rise 100 Steve Bikos."[16]

At another Soweto service, police shot and killed a fifteen-year-old youth. At several they assaulted and whipped mourners with *sjamboks*. In an attempt to cut down attendance at Biko's funeral in Kingwilliamstown, bus transportation from Soweto was halted; when a crowd of a thousand protested they were fired on and several hundred were dragged off to jail.

The September 25 funeral for Biko was an appropriate tribute to the fallen fighter. Despite roadblocks around Kingwilliams-

14. For details of Biko's death and the inquest proceedings, see Hilda Bernstein, *No. 46—Steve Biko* (London: International Defence and Aid Fund, 1978).

15. *Washington Post*, September 15, 1977.

16. *Washington Post*, September 19, 1977.

town and police action in other cities, nearly twenty thousand Blacks turned out for a massive and militant farewell. The mourners marched for more than a mile from Biko's home in the township of Ginsburg to a local sports field, following Biko's coffin on the back of an ox-drawn wagon, a traditional Xhosa display of respect usually reserved for chiefs. A banner bearing the BPC slogan "One Azania, one nation" was carried near the front of the entourage.

For three and a half hours, speaker after speaker paid tribute to Biko's life and work, mixing their remarks with sharp condemnations of the system that had killed him. BPC President Rachidi told the mourners, "We vow to carry the yoke he helped us to shoulder. Steve ranks as one of the dedicated liberators of the oppressed people."[17] As Biko's coffin was lowered into the grave, thousands of clenched-fists shot into the air amid shouts of "Amandla!"

The rage over Biko's death did not die down after the funeral. It simply merged with other grievances, spurring a new surge of antigovernment upheavals. In Mdantsane, in Queenstown, in Grahamstown, in Whittlesea, in Soweto youths demonstrated and clashed with police. In Port Elizabeth, students shut down their schools in response to a call by the Students Representative Council there. In Dimbaza, in the Ciskei reserve, hundreds demonstrated on several occassions and put government offices to the torch. In Durban, Indian university students demonstrated against chief Gatsha Buthelezi, denouncing him as a government "puppet." In GaRankuwa, in BophuthaTswana, youths burned down a branch of Barclays Bank and attacked the African Bank Building and the offices of the National African Federated Chambers of Commerce.

The school boycott that had begun in July gathered momentum. All forty-two of Soweto's secondary schools were shut down as 27,000 students walked out; a majority of the teachers resigned their posts in solidarity. By early October, more than 190,000 students were refusing to attend classes around the country, some 50,000 of them in the Ciskei and nearly 115,000 in the Venda reserve. The unrest in Venda, which is near the northern border with Zimbabwe, was also marked by a demonstration in solidarity with the Zimbabwean struggle for Black majority rule. The boycotts spread to Port Elizabeth and East London. In mid-October sporadic outbursts swept the Port Elizabeth townships,

17. *Star Weekly* (Johannesburg), October 1, 1977.

during which the police shot and killed at least six Black youths. New protests erupted in the KwaZulu, QwaQwa, and Bophutha-Tswana Bantustans.

To the authorities, the situation threatened again to get out of control, the atmosphere becoming dangerously reminiscent of 1976. Events moved quickly toward a showdown.

The government, after a month of deliberation, finally decided to strike a sudden blow, in the hope of turning back the new groundswell of opposition. In predawn raids on October 19, police seized about fifty prominent political activists, community figures, teachers, journalists, and students. A few hours later, Kruger decreed the banning of eighteen organizations and a number of individuals under the terms of the Internal Security Act, marking the most dramatic crackdown on Black political organizations since 1960.

The outlawed groups included virtually every major component of the Black Consciousness movement: the BPC, SASO, SASM, SSRC, Black Community Programmes, Black Women's Federation, Black Parents' Association, National Youth Organisation, and Union of Black Journalists.[18] Also banned were the *World* and *Weekend World,* which had large, predominantly Black readerships. Those swept up in the police dragnet included Motlana and the nine other Committee of Ten members; Percy Qoboza, editor of the *World* and *Weekend World;* and Hlaku Rachidi, Aubrey Mokoena, Jairus Kgokong, Sadeque Variava, Mongezi Stofile, and other Black Consciousness leaders.

As his justification for the bannings and detentions, Kruger claimed that the opponents of the regime were just "a small group of anarchists" who had attempted to manipulate Black grievances so as to "create a revolutionary climate" and bring about a "confrontation between black and white." He warned that "should it become necessary, new measures will be considered."[19]

Coming only a little more than a month after the killing of Biko, the banning of the Black Consciousness groups provoked a sharp international outcry against Pretoria.

18. The other groups were the Medupe Writers' Association, Zimele Trust Fund, Association for the Educational and Cultural Advancement of African People, Border Youth Organisation, Natal Youth Organisation, Transvaal Youth Organisation, Western Cape Youth Organisation, Eastern Cape Youth Organisation, and the Christian Institute of Southern Africa.

19. *New York Times*, October 20, 1977.

Reflecting the sentiments of people throughout Africa, the Organization of African Unity, representing forty-nine African states, demanded that the United Nations impose international economic and military sanctions against the apartheid regime. Pretoria's Western allies, particularly the American, British, and French governments, were put on the spot when the demand was raised within the UN Security Council. To protect their own substantial economic interests in South Africa and to soften the direct impact of the protests against Pretoria, the three powers on October 31 vetoed resolutions before the Security Council calling for a ban on foreign investments and credits to the white minority regime, a halt to arms sales and other military collaboration, and a move toward UN punitive measures. Four days later, however, they reluctantly agreed to a largely symbolic arms embargo.

This latter move was greeted with little enthusiasm in Soweto. One Black worker told an American reporter, "Carter should have done more than this. An arms embargo is cosmetic. South Africa is already producing 90 per cent of its own arms." A community leader declared, "The trade and commercial enterprises are the topmost priority. They should have been first priority—cut off completely—because, as they say, we blacks have got nothing to lose."[20]

Despite the apparent determination among many young Blacks not to be cowed into submission by the regime's crackdown, the banning of the most representative Black groups was a severe blow. The ties that had been built up between the political leaders and their followers were disrupted, the traditional organizations were no longer able to function as they had, and open political activity became much riskier. All this made it harder for activists to mobilize mass support without immediately facing the prospect of banning, detention, or worse.

By outlawing the major Black Consciousness groups, the regime hoped to create a vacuum of political leadership in the Black community, thereby providing greater opportunities for Bantustan officials and other collaborationist figures to try to dominate political life in the townships.

The most concerted effort to take advantage of the bannings came from Chief Gatsha Buthelezi of KwaZulu. Despite his participation in the Bantustan system, Buthelezi had carefully sought to nurture an "antiapartheid" image for himself. He

20. *Washington Post*, October 29, 1977.

frequently criticized Pretoria's racist policies, including the imposition of "independence" on the Bantustans, and often struck a radical pose by giving clenched-fist salutes and shouting "amandla." He has, however, publicly rejected the popular Black demand for a universal adult franchise and has accused those who are involved in guerrilla actions against the regime of engaging in "barbarism."[21]

In 1975, Buthelezi set up the Inkatha YeNkululeko YeSizwe (National Cultural Liberation Movement), which claimed to favor the liberation of South Africa from racist rule. Its main function, however, was to provide Buthelezi with an organizational base, primarily in KwaZulu itself, but elsewhere as well. Although Inkatha tried to present itself as an "all-African" formation, it remained 90 percent Zulu. According to its constitution, all members of the Central Committee had to be Zulus and only a Zulu could be president of Inkatha.[22]

Despite Buthelezi's strident rhetoric (which annoyed some government officials), the authorities made little attempt to silence him. In their eyes, he was basically a tribal politician who could perhaps win some support for the Bantustan system and who could be presented abroad as a "true leader" of the Black population. According to a report in one South African newspaper:

> To an extent, elements within the Government—possibly the Security Police for a start—believe Chief Buthelezi is in fact an asset.
>
> They argue that at the time of the Soweto riots, Natal, where he exercises his greatest influence, was relatively quiet.
>
> At the same time his growing influence is regarded as an asset of sorts simply because it provokes such intense rivalry with the black consciousness movements.[23]

Following the October 1977 bannings, Buthelezi moved quickly to try to extend his influence beyond KwaZulu, into the townships. His Inkatha organization was expanded considerably, and by late 1978 was claiming two hundred thousand dues-paying members. Some had been recruited on the basis of Inkatha's

21. *Star Weekly* (Johannesburg), September 1, 1979.

22. Allan Boesak, "Amandla! Eendrag maak mag!—of so iets . . ." [Amandla! Unity means strength!—or something like that . . .], *Deurbraak* (Cape Town), April 1978.

23. *Rand Daily Mail* (Johannesburg), July 12, 1978.

"militant" claims, others through pressure (in Durban, township residents without Inkatha membership cards encountered greater difficulties and delays in getting housing allocations than those who had cards). Buthelezi staged several rallies in Soweto itself, drawing audiences of around ten thousand. The conservative National African Federated Chambers of Commerce, a Black businessmen's organization, declared its backing for Inkatha.

In early 1978, Inkatha held a series of meetings with the Indian Reform Party and the Coloured Labor Party, two other groups that collaborated with the regime through their participation in the South African Indian Council and the Coloured People's Representative Council. The three organizations established the South African Black Alliance (SABA), later joined by the Dikwankwatla Party of the QwaQwa Bantustan.

The efforts of Inkatha and SABA to garner support in urban areas met with only limited success, primarily from the older and more conservative sectors of the population. Those who had been most radicalized by the upheavals in the townships, especially the youth, reacted to Inkatha and SABA with open hostility.

The banning of the major Black Consciousness groups also had the effect of throwing greater press attention on the older liberation organizations, the ANC and PAC. Despite the fact that both groups still retained a certain political following and respect among Blacks within South Africa, neither had played any appreciable role in the mass urban uprisings of 1976 and 1977, aside from the issuing of a few leaflets and the participation of some of their supporters in the student protests. The bulk of their active members were still based outside South Africa, while those functioning underground within the country were engaged largely in guerrilla warfare and sabotage actions, not directly in the ongoing mass struggles. As a consequence, they were somewhat removed from the real tempo of political life in the townships and had been caught off guard by the reemergence of mass mobilization and open political organization, a possibility they had previously ruled out.

Nevertheless, the ANC and PAC did recruit new members, many of them young exiled activists who had participated in the upsurge. They even won over some Black student leaders, the PAC recruiting former SASO leader Henry Isaacs and SSRC President Trofomo Sono, for example, and the ANC picking up SASM Secretary-General Tebello Motapanyane and others. Many of the new recruits were given military instruction. South African police and military officials acknowledged that hundreds of

Black youths—especially those now adhering to the ANC—were being trained for guerrilla warfare and were beginning to filter back into South Africa. The number of reported armed clashes, including several attacks on police stations in Soweto, started to rise sharply.

Supporters of the Black Consciousness movement, confronted with the fact that many of them had been forced into exile by Pretoria's repression, also moved toward the establishment of an external wing. As early as February 1977, the BPC set up a secretariat of external affairs, headed by Ranwedzi Nengwekhulu and based in Botswana. In 1979, Black Consciousness supporters in Britain, the United States, and Botswana and other African countries held a series of conferences to reorganize themselves and better coordinate their activities. Exiled members of the BPC, SASO, SASM, BCP, Black Allied Workers Union, and National Youth Organisation began to function under the umbrella of the Black Consciousness Movement of South Africa.

In April 1979, the SSRC dissolved itself to make way for a broader Black Consciousness youth movement. The former SSRC leaders, together with young supporters of other Black Consciousness groups, met in Botswana that month to form the South African Youth Revolutionary Council (SAYRCO). Most of those who participated were exiles, but some delegates from South Africa managed to attend as well. Reflecting the growing influence of revolutionary socialist ideas among the young militants of the Black Consciousness movement, a SAYRCO statement pointed out that "revolutions if successful are led by workers," although in South Africa there was not yet a "vanguard party to tap this revolutionary situation." It maintained that the South African revolution would combine both a class struggle and a national liberation struggle. Khotso Seatlholo, the former SSRC leader, was elected as SAYRCO's first president.[24]

Although Black Consciousness supporters had always been open toward collaboration with the ANC and PAC, and viewed them as legitimate national liberation organizations that still had a role to play in the freedom struggle, the ANC failed to reciprocate. It even reacted with ill-disguised hostility toward the movement, consistently refusing to participate in joint activities with the Black Consciousness movement (or the PAC), and claiming in a sectarian fashion that the ANC was the only

24. *SAYRCO Special Edition on the 1st National Congress Held in April 1979* (n.p., n.d.), p. 4. (Copy in author's files.)

"legitimate" liberation movement. The South African Communist Party, based in London, adopted a similar stance.

Explaining the differences in orientation among the various currents, Nengwekhulu, of the Black Consciousness movement, stated that while the ANC and PAC concentrated on launching armed actions from abroad, the Black Consciousness movement spent "about 90% of our resources building up a strong internal resistance movement." He stressed, "No struggle has ever been won from outside, it's won from within. . . ."[25]

While those in the Black Consciousness movement who were living abroad sought to retain their links with the internal movement, the activists inside followed a perspective of trying to organize and function as best they could, through public organizations and activities where possible, but also clandestinely to evade the reach of the security police.

For a brief period following the October 1977 bannings, class boycotts by high school students expanded even further, at their peak involving up to three hundred thousand Black students around the country. But by early 1978 the boycotts had died down, marking the beginning of another ebb in the mass resistance.

Although 1978 and 1979 did not witness any generalized mass upsurges of the same impact and scope as those of the previous two years, things were far from quiescent. A strong current of militancy continued to survive in the townships. New struggles developed, largely on a local scale, and new organizations were formed.

Demonstrations and strikes, sometimes involving thousands of participants, sporadically flared up in Soweto, in the townships around Port Elizabeth, in the Transkei and KwaZulu, and elsewhere. Following the death in February 1978 of Robert Sobukwe, the banned leader of the Pan Africanist Congress, an estimated five thousand Blacks turned out in Graaff-Reinet for his funeral; while some of the participants were former PAC supporters, many were young adherents of the Black Consciousness movement.

In Soweto, during the elections in February and April 1978 to the newly imposed Soweto Community Council, about 94 percent of the eligible voters displayed their opposition or lack of interest by staying away from the polls. Turnouts were higher in some of

25. *SANA Bulletin* (London), August 1979.

the other townships where councils were set up, but hundreds of thousands of Blacks boycotted those elections as well.

Anniversaries of important political events were popular occasions. In June 1978, up to twenty thousand Blacks in Soweto rallied and some 40 percent of the township's labor force struck work to commemorate the second anniversary of the 1976 rebellions. Similar memorials were held in Cape Town, Kagiso, Mhluzi, Mamelodi, Kimberley, Mabopane, Queenstown, and elsewhere. The first anniversary of the 1977 bannings was also marked by rallies throughout the country that October.

Overt displays of white solidarity with the Black struggle were still few and far between, but there were some indications of growing white disenchantment with the government's policies, particularly with its stepped-up military mobilization of the white population.[26] Pretoria's response to white dissent was not that different from that toward Black opposition. During 1978, several prominent white critics of the regime were shot at or had their cars bombed by shadowy right-wing terrorist groups. In January of that year, Richard Turner, a banned lecturer and self-professed socialist, was assassinated at his home in Durban.

The continued political ferment in the Black townships laid the basis for the emergence of new Black organizations, which at least partially filled the vacuum that had been created by the October 1977 bannings. In fact, the authorities themselves expected as much. Kruger stated that when he outlawed the Black Consciousness groups, "I knew these organisations would not fade away. They are always there, busy reorganising and moving forward."[27]

Within weeks of the bannings, the Soweto Action Committee (SAC) was established, under the chairmanship of Ishmael Mkhabela, a former associate of Steve Biko's. A leader of the SAC explained that after the October bannings, "We had to reorganize." The group presented itself as an umbrella Black political

26. As many as three thousand young white men leave South Africa each year to avoid military induction. Between 1975 and 1979, some two thousand whites within the country were convicted of refusing to serve in the military. A small, but increasing, number of white soldiers have been deserting as well. In December 1978, a group of South African military resisters and deserters living in exile in Britain formed the Committee on South African War Resistance to publicize cases of draft resistance and desertion and to help others leave South Africa.

27. *Rand Daily Mail* (Johannesburg), August 17, 1978.

organization aiming to represent the interests of Soweto's inhabitants. It maintained a visible presence through occasional rallies and commemorative actions and defied the provisions of the Terrorism Act by openly advocating a complete international economic, political, and cultural boycott of South Africa.[28]

Another group formed shortly after the crackdown was the Soweto Students League (SSL). To an extent, it attempted to fill the vacuum created by the banning of the SSRC and organized continued resistance to Bantu Education.

In late April 1978, yet another new group, the Azanian People's Organisation (Azapo), was set up after sixty Black delegates from around the country held a conference in Roodepoort, near Johannesburg. Mkhabela, the chairman of the SAC, was also chosen as the Azapo chairman. Azapo openly declared its adherence to the ideas of the Black Consciousness movement. Adopting the slogan "one people, one Azania," it called for the establishment of a single parliament for everyone, within a unitary state. It demanded a common educational system to replace the current segregated one, and announced that it would direct its efforts toward Black workers.

These promising beginnings were soon stifled by new police action, as most of the central leaders of the SSL and Azapo were rounded up and either detained or placed under banning orders. The SSL never recovered, and Azapo was driven into a state of relative inactivity that lasted for many months.

The Committee of Ten, although it had escaped being outlawed, had nevertheless ceased to function for a while due to the detention of the bulk of its members. But after most of them were freed in late 1978, the committee was revived. It received a significant boost in March 1979, when the SAC announced that it was dissolving as a separate organization in order to give its full support to the Committee of Ten. The following month it held its first public rally in many months, drawing a crowd of two thousand supporters, who enthusiastically greeted the committee's revival. In September, the committee—in a change from its earlier orientation—took its first steps toward seeking to organize the mass of Soweto's residents. At a public rally, Dr. Motlana helped launch the Soweto Civic Association, which was projected as a mass organization that planned to recruit a hundred thousand members in Soweto and encourage the formation of similar groups in other townships. The political tone at the rally

28. *Vrij Nederland* (Amsterdam), April 1, 1978.

was militant, and Motlana reaffirmed that Blacks would settle for nothing less than majority rule.[29]

The second half of 1979 witnessed a revival of the Black Consciousness movement, as new groups sprang up and some of the older ones exhibited greater vitality.

In early June, a new national Black student body was formed to represent pre-university students, the first since the banning of the SASM more than a year and a half earlier. Some sixty delegates from around the country gathered at Roodepoort to establish the Congress of South African Students (COSAS). Eph Mogale, who was elected president, condemned the government's education policy and called on students to continue to "struggle for a better education."[30]

Two important Black Consciousness conferences took place in September, serving notice that the movement was still very much alive—and that its ideas were maturing.

At the beginning of the month, about 250 Blacks, many of them former members of the BPC and SASO, attended a three-day conference near Johannesburg of the Writers Association of South Africa (WASA). The organization, which had emerged after the banning of the Union of Black Journalists in October 1977, went beyond the early ideas of the Black Consciousness movement, laying greater stress on the class role of Black workers. The association maintained that "if black consciousness is indeed the necessary base on which workers become conscious of themselves as a class, it is our duty to conscientize black people along these principles." WASA pledged to cooperate closely with other Black organizations and to build solidarity with the struggles of Black workers.[31]

On September 29-30, the Azanian People's Organisation held a national congress near Roodepoort, marking its first significant activity in nearly a year and a half. Azapo reorganized itself, chose a new leadership, and adopted a constitution. Like WASA, it too stressed the key role of Black workers in the struggle, one of its aims being to "conscientise, politicise and mobilise black workers through the philosophy of black consciousness to strive

29. *Star Weekly* (Johannesburg), September 29, 1979.

30. *Rand Daily Mail* (Johannesburg), June 4, 1979.

31. *Southern Africa* (New York), October 1979.

for their legitimate rights."[32] After the conference, Azapo called mass rallies around the country, the first one in Soweto drawing a crowd of a thousand supporters.

On October 19, the second anniversary of the 1977 crackdown on the Black Consciousness movement, Azapo, WASA, and other Black groups held commemorative actions, in Soweto, Pietermaritzburg, East London, and Cape Town.

The following month, on November 23, Black university students once again sought to organize themselves on a national scale, to try to fill the gap left by the banning of SASO. Delegates from almost all the Black campuses around the country gathered at a conference in Pietermaritzburg to found the Azanian Students Organisation (Azaso). One of Azaso's declared aims was to "promote the role of the black student as a vanguard in the struggle for liberation."[33]

As it has in the past, this revival of Black political militancy and organization was accompanied by a resurgence of the Black labor movement, an important factor in the greater emphasis placed on the role of Black workers by the major political groups.

In April 1979, a new Black trade union federation was formed, the first since the destruction of SACTU and FOFATUSA in the 1960s. At a conference in Hammanskraal, representatives of twelve unions established the Federation of South African Trade Unions (FOSATU), which claimed a membership of forty-five thousand. Although it represented only some of the unregistered Black unions, FOSATU's formation was nevertheless a significant step forward and showed that Black workers were striving toward greater organization.

New Black strikes broke out. Textile workers in New Germany, railway employees in Johannesburg and Durban, furniture workers in BophuthaTswana, gold miners in Germiston and Carletonville, stevedores in Cape Town, and numerous others walked off their jobs in support of pay demands—and in some cases to press for union recognition. Reflecting Black workers' growing social leverage, some of the struggles were successful. Black construction workers at a Dutch-owned firm in the Cape, who were supported by the ten-thousand-member Western Province General Workers Union, won their demands for higher pay, retroactive for two years. After an eight-month consumer

32. *Post* (Transvaal), October 1, 1979.

33. *Post* (Transvaal), November 27, 1979.

boycott, Fattis and Monis, a Cape Town pasta, bread, and flour manufacturer, agreed to rehire fifty workers who had been dismissed for their union activities.

Confronted with new labor laws that threatened to bring the independent Black unions under strict government control, a number of them prepared to resist the regime's plans. The Western Province General Workers Union rejected registering for official recognition under the new labor law, stating that it was designed to impose "rigid control and supervision" over the affairs of Black unions.[34] The Black Allied Workers Union likewise rejected registration.

To strengthen their position in face of the government's antilabor drive—and to counter the attempts of some companies to set up subservient unions of their own choosing—a number of the independent Black unions initiated organizing campaigns in many plants and factories.

During the last months of 1979 and into early 1980, the Black industrial working class of Port Elizabeth provided Blacks around the country with a stirring example of combined industrial and political action. Their struggle showed that the regime's goal of rigidly controlling and "depoliticizing" the Black labor movement was little more than wishful fantasy.

In October, about seven hundred Black workers at Ford Motor Company's Struandale factory struck in protest against the forced resignation of a young political activist in the plant, Thozamile Botha, who was head of the Port Elizabeth Black Civic Organisation (PEBCO), a Black Consciousness group that had been set up in the area a month before. The workers won Botha's reinstatement within a few days, but the next month walked off their jobs three more times around pay demands and other grievances. Following the example of the Ford workers, more than a thousand other Blacks laid down their tools at a nearby paper plant and at General Tire and Rubber, a partially owned subsidiary of the giant American tire firm.

In carrying out their struggles, the Ford workers bypassed the conservative leadership of the United Automobile, Rubber, and Allied Workers' Union (a local Black union affiliated to FOSATU). They instead formed a strike committee and worked closely with PEBCO. According to Botha, "The union doesn't

34. *Post* (Transvaal), September 27, 1979.

35. *Southern Africa* (New York), February 1980.

want to involve itself in politics. I don't agree with that. The position of blacks in factories is political. So the problem is also a political one. . . ."[35] As a result of PEBCO's stance on behalf of the strikers, many workers at Ford and General Tire and Rubber began displaying PEBCO insignia.

As the labor disputes developed, PEBCO also began to organize a campaign on behalf of the six thousand residents of Walmer, a Black township in Port Elizabeth that was scheduled for demolition. PEBCO grew in strength and its public rallies regularly drew crowds of between ten thousand and fifteen thousand persons. At one rally in Walmer, Botha, speaking symbolically on behalf of Black workers in general, declared, "The country rests in my hands and in my numbers. If I don't go to work tomorrow the country is in trouble." In an especially defiant act, Botha also proclaimed his solidarity with Nelson Mandela and other imprisoned and exiled figures, telling his audience that they were the real leaders of the struggle.[36]

Later that month, Ford, which had tried to portray itself as one of the more "enlightened" American firms operating in South Africa, responded by firing all the striking Black workers at Struandale. General Tire and Rubber followed suit. But the working-class solidarity in Port Elizabeth was now so great that the management was unable to break the strike or recruit enough scab labor. The Azanian People's Organisation began organizing a national campaign on behalf of the strikers and collected financial support for them. Combined with expressions of international solidarity with the Ford workers, this resistance eventually forced the company to back down. In January 1980 it agreed to rehire all the workers, with full benefits and seniority.

Fearful that the Black victory at Ford could spur more militant labor struggles, the regime soon cracked down, detaining Botha and other top PEBCO leaders. Street demonstrations and calls for a general strike followed.

As the white supremacists saw it, however, serious political damage had already been done. The workers in Port Elizabeth had shown Blacks throughout the country that by combining working-class action with political organization it was possible to take on the ruling class and win. As the decade of the 1980s opened, that was an important lesson for the future of the Black freedom struggle.

36. *Evening Post* (Port Elizabeth), November 16, 1979.

21

Toward Azania

When we talk about freedom, we mean freedom from poverty and its associated evils, freedom to enjoy basic rights of food, shelter and clothing, education which teaches creativity not destruction, and access to the world of culture in which all those who have the gift can participate.

—SASO Bulletin

The Black population of South Africa has a three hundred year history of fighting for liberation. Today the forces exist that can lead that fight to victory.

The Black working class of South Africa is stronger than ever before, in its numbers, its position in the economy, and its political experience. Through the strikes and political mobilizations of the 1970s, Black workers have become increasingly aware of their social power. They have shown their ability to bring South Africa's economy to a halt. They have learned the importance of mass political action.

This growing strength of the Black working class and the political ferment of other layers of the Black population, such as the students, has had a profoundly radicalizing impact on the thinking of Blacks in general.

The defeat of Portuguese colonialism, the victory of Angolan and Cuban troops over the invading South African army, and the massive advances of the Zimbabwean liberation struggle also have left a big imprint on the consciousness of Blacks, as did the revolutions in Iran and Nicaragua. All have added considerably to the combativity and self-confidence of Blacks. For example, when the Zimbabwean election results were announced in early March 1980, revealing a sweeping victory for Robert Mugabe's

Zimbabwe African National Union, Soweto resounded with car horns and shouts of "Viva Mugabe!" and "Amandla ngwethu!" (Power to the people).

During the struggles of the past decade, every aspect of white supremacy has come under attack, from the pass laws and the migrant labor system to the Bantustans and racist education. The South African masses have shown that they will not stop fighting until Black majority rule and full democratic rights have been won.

The freedom struggle has also shown itself to be a struggle over who will control the tremendous economic wealth and resources of South Africa—the small circle of white bankers, industrialists, farmers, and foreign investors or the Black masses themselves. In one battle after another—for higher wages and union rights, against rent and transportation fare hikes, against land rehabilitation schemes and forced resettlement programs—Blacks have fought to take back some of that wealth, wealth originally created through their own labor.

The fight for Black majority rule has been totally intertwined with this struggle to end the poverty and exploitation of the Black population. By its very nature, majority rule points in the direction of a socialist transformation of society. Because of the inevitable resistance of the white ruling class, a Black majority government that strives to wipe out the accumulated legacy of centuries of white supremacy cannot hope to achieve its aims without at the same time storming the strongholds of white capitalist economic power.

The obvious links between the struggle for Black majority rule and the fight for control over the allocation of South Africa's wealth has led a growing number of militants to look toward socialist solutions to the problems that confront Blacks. They have come to recognize more clearly the close interrelationship between capitalist exploitation and national oppression, and the need to wage a combined struggle against them.

Sipho Buthelezi, a former secretary-general of the BPC, has maintained that "while the struggle is one for national liberation it also has to be raised at the level of the class struggle. We don't think that we should first simply achieve national independence and then after that struggle for socialism. We believe that we shall have the combination of the two stages into one."[1]

1. Interview obtained by John Blair in Britain, early 1979. Published in *Intercontinental Press / Inprecor*, May 14, 1979.

Other activists have pointed in a similar direction. "Our struggle against apartheid is a struggle against capitalism," one former militant of the BPC told me in Johannesburg. "We do not want to just take over the government and leave everything else as we find it. We want to run the economy, in the interests of the masses, to their benefit, not to profit some capitalist, white or Black."

By the late 1970s, a number of activists who had come out of the Black Consciousness movement were already describing themselves as Marxist-Leninists[2] or adherents of scientific socialism. Some of the student militants in Soweto preferred the term communist, according to one former leader of the BPC. If the BPC or SASO were not banned and were allowed to hold open conferences, another affirmed, their resolutions would be "definitely more to the left."

Despite the difficulties of obtaining socialist literature in South Africa, a certain amount circulates clandestinely. Among the Black Consciousness exiles abroad, where literature is more readily available and where there are fewer restraints on the expression of political ideas, this movement toward the left has been especially apparent.

The radicalization within the Black leadership is reflective of the growing popularity of socialist ideas among wider strata of the urban population itself, a development that has not escaped the notice of the white rulers of South Africa. An editorial in one of the major South African daily newspapers raised an alarm about the "steady drift towards communism/marxism/socialism on the part of South Africa's urban blacks. . . . This trend has been confirmed by three major surveys which show that the majority of urban blacks prefer to call themselves communists, marxists or socialists rather than capitalists."[3] While it would be unlikely that very many Blacks would consider themselves capitalists to begin with, it was nevertheless significant that so

2. In the past, the term "Marxist-Leninist" was frequently used as a self-descriptive label by those who considered themselves followers of Mao Zedong and the Stalinist leadership in Peking. But today the term has a broader usage. Because of Peking's foreign policy stance in Africa (open support for the reactionary Mobutu regime in Zaïre, opposition to Cuban aid to the African revolution), there are very few militants in South Africa who would now look to Peking for political inspiration.

3. *Star* (Johannesburg), May 4, 1979.

many would openly identify with socialism in a country where to do so can mean imprisonment or worse.

This growing identification with socialism reflects an understanding on the part of many Blacks about what they are fighting for. Education to meet the needs of the Black majority, decent housing and medical care, and an adequate living standard will never be granted under the apartheid system. To win them will require Black workers taking control over both the government and the economy and using them to advance the interests of the vast majority of the population.

The revolution in Cuba holds out an example of what can be done. As the workers and peasants of that Caribbean country were able to do once they had freed themselves from local and foreign capital, the masses of South Africa could use the resources of their country to fulfill their own immediate and pressing needs, to build housing and schools, clinics and hospitals, to eradicate unemployment and poverty. And all this not on the scale of a small island with a tiny industrial plant, but on the basis of the wealthiest, most industrialized country in Africa.

Because of the absence in South Africa of any strong working class political parties, much of the emerging prosocialist sentiment is still vague and diffuse, to a great extent divorced from any thought-out strategy of how to achieve a socialist society.

Some of the young militants, however, are already grappling with that problem. Especially significant has been the growing appreciation of the potential power of the Black working class and its political and social role as the spearhead of the revolution.

A group of exiled South African revolutionists, based in Botswana, stated in an interview: "It is the Black working class that carries the burden of history. It is on the shoulders of this class that the wheels of industry lie. This is the class that is the mainstay of the socialist revolution in South Africa. The mobilization of this class is a necessity and it would be a dream to think of bringing down the South African racist regime without the greatest role being played by this class." They added that while white workers were not yet conscious of their class position, and while it was necessary for revolutionists to concentrate on organizing and mobilizing Blacks, some white workers could be won over as class allies of Blacks.[4]

4. Interview obtained by author in Gaborone, Botswana, December 1978. Published in *Intercontinental Press / Inprecor*, February 5, 1979.

Many of those who understand the crucial role of workers as a class have already taken their thinking one step further by recognizing the need for workers to have their own political leadership, their own organization, through which they could defend and advance their class interests. Specifically, they favored the construction of a working-class party, based on a revolutionary program, which could lead and mobilize the oppressed and exploited.

The group in Botswana has stressed that such a party "should be based among the struggling masses, give direction to the day-to-day struggles against capitalism, coordinate the upsurge by the masses, and give them direction."[5]

Similarly, Sipho Buthelezi has stated:

> For Marxist-Leninists the most important thing is the formation of an independent working-class organization. . . . acting as the vanguard force in the struggle for national liberation. We appreciate that there should be a united front of all the "patriotic" forces in the country, but we recognize that we need to ensure, if we're to establish a socialist country, that the Black working class is the leading force. . . . We think this has to be built step by step through involvement in the day-to-day activity of the Black working class. At this stage it would be quite wrong for a small group of us, without any serious base inside the class, to proclaim ourselves the leadership. It is only after serious work with the class in its struggles that we shall see the emergence of a genuine proletarian party.[6]

Without such a party, a former BPC activist in Johannesburg has pointed out, future mass upsurges would "be like Soweto again, just hitting out blindly, not hitting the enemy where it really hurts. Soweto was good, it taught us many things, but it could have been better, more powerful. Now, we see we must organize ourselves into a strong force, a more disciplined force."

The armed strength of the apartheid state and the pervasiveness of its apparatus of political control dictate a highly organized response. A workers' party, in order to effectively challenge the apartheid regime, would require a political program based on the needs of all sectors of the oppressed, including Africans, Coloureds and Indians; urbanized workers as well as migrants; township residents and those in the Bantustans; women; the unemployed; squatters. As a number of South African revolution-

5. Ibid.

6. *Intercontinental Press / Inprecor* (New York), May 14, 1979.

ists have explained, a workers' party would have to participate in the struggles of the masses for day-to-day changes, and link them up with the broader struggle to transform all of South African society.

The South African ruling class will not give up power peacefully. As its brutal response to the Soweto uprisings showed, it will not hesitate to shed the blood of thousands upon thousands of Blacks to uphold its oppressive and profitable system of white capitalist supremacy. Arms will thus be of crucial importance in the struggle against apartheid, both for the defense of the mass movement and for the ultimate *disarming* of the white rulers. But arms alone cannot defeat the powerful colonial-settler state. It can only be defeated through the organization and mobilization of the masses of workers and peasants, which will provide the best political conditions for the final overthrow of the apartheid regime.

The mobilization of the Black majority is, of course, the central task if South African society is to be transformed. But it will also be vital for revolutionists to try to divide the white population along class lines, to undermine the regime's base of support. Despite the bombastic pronouncements of some National Party leaders, far from all whites will be willing to die for apartheid. And, although the vast majority are not yet conscious of it, the maintenance of white supremacy is not in their real interests: it divides white workers from Black weakening all of them in face of the employers and thus holding down the living standards of working people in general; it leads to increasing repression against political dissent from any direction; it degrades and dehumanizes whites, stifling their cultural and social development; it deprives them of real and lasting security. Unlike the white capitalists, white workers in South Africa do not have a vested class interest in the maintenance of the apartheid regime. They do not profit from the exploitation of Blacks.

While continuing to build a powerful struggle for Black majority rule and while not giving in one inch to white racist attitudes, it will be possible for revolutionists to convince at least a layer of whites that it is better to throw in their lot with the future than to perish with the past. As the struggle of Black workers gains in organized strength and presents a clear alternative to the present apartheid system, it will win the respect of more white workers, especially those in industry, and serve as a pole of attraction to all the exploited. Some whites may simply be neutralized. But others can be won over to active support for the struggle. Despite their limited scale, the white student protests in support of the Soweto rebellions, the solidarity shown by some white unionists with the wage demands of Black workers, and the small but growing number of white draft resisters and army deserters already reveal cracks in the white monolith.

The apartheid regime relies not only on the support of the white population to remain in power. Its police and troops would be helpless without the arms, the planes, the fuel, the funds, and the technology Pretoria has obtained from its allies abroad. Because of the international character of capitalism, and especially the South African ruling class's close ties with its allies in North America, Europe, and Japan, revolutionists in South Africa will find it imperative to maintain and reinforce ties of political solidarity with workers in other countries, to fight their common enemies.

Effectively organized international campaigns can do much to help expose and undermine the apartheid regime's avenues of foreign backing: trade union actions to block shipment of vital cargo to South Africa; demonstrations, rallies, and other forms of mass pressure to demand that foreign governments and companies stop aiding the white supremacist system. It is the duty of labor activists and antiapartheid fighters in other countries to help expose the true nature of the apartheid regime and its so-called reforms and extend solidarity to the struggle for majority rule. Direct material aid—such as that provided by Cuba to freedom fighters throughout southern Africa—can also play a vital role.

The liberation of South Africa from national oppression and capitalism will be a momentous event for all of Africa. South Africa would cease to be an imperialist power. The days of South African economic domination and military intervention would be replaced by an era of genuine fraternity. South Africa's abundant wealth could be made available to help other African peoples develop their own countries.

A revolution in South Africa would also be a devastating blow to world capitalism. With the loss of South Africa's superprofits and an end to control over its natural wealth (especially gold), imperialism would be weakened economically. And an end to South Africa's role as a regional gendarme would be a major political blow to imperialism's grip on the African continent.

Even more crucially, the South African revolution will provide a stirring inspiration to workers and other oppressed people in Africa and around the globe.

The struggle of South African Blacks is part of the struggle of people everywhere for a democratic and just society, for a socialist future. Their victory will be a victory for humanity. Their triumph will belong to the world.

List of Abbreviations

AAC	All African Convention
AMWU	African Mine Workers Union
APO	African Political Organisation; *also,* African People's Organisation
ANC	African National Congress
Azapo	Azanian People's Organisation
Azaso	Azanian Students Organisation
BAWU	Black Allied Workers Union
BCP	Black Community Programmes
BOSS	Bureau of State Security
BPC	Black People's Convention
CAC	Coloured Advisory Council
CAD	Coloured Affairs Department
CNETU	Council of Non-European Trade Unions
COD	Congress of Democrats
COSAS	Congress of South African Students
CPSA	Communist Party of South Africa
CRC	Coloured People's Representative Council
FIOSA	Fourth International Organisation of South Africa
FNLA	Angolan National Liberation Front
FOFATUSA	Federation of Free African Trade Unions of South Africa
FOSATU	Federation of South African Trade Unions
Frelimo	Mozambique Liberation Front
ICU	Industrial and Commercial Workers' Union
ISL	International Socialist League
MPLA	People's Movement for the Liberation of Angola
NAYO	National Youth Organisation
NEUF	Non-European United Front
NEUM	Non-European Unity Movement
NIC	Natal Indian Congress

NLL	National Liberation League
NRC	Natives' Representative Council
NUSAS	National Union of South African Students
PAC	Pan Africanist Congress
PEBCO	Port Elizabeth Black Civic Organisation
SABA	South African Black Alliance
SAC	Soweto Action Committee
SACP	South African Communist Party
SACPO	South African Coloured People's Organisation
SACTU	South African Congress of Trade Unions
SAIC	South African Indian Congress
SAIC	South African Indian Council
SALP	South African Labour Party
SASM	South African Student Movement
SASM	Southern African Students' Movement
SASO	South African Students' Organisation
SAYRCO	South African Youth Revolutionary Council
SSL	Soweto Students League
SSRC	Soweto Students Representative Council
SWAPO	South West Africa People's Organisation
TUCSA	Trade Union Council of South Africa
UBC	Urban Bantu Council
UNITA	National Union for the Total Independence of Angola
WASA	Writers Association of South Africa
WPSA	Workers Party of South Africa
ZANU	Zimbabwe African National Union
ZAPU	Zimbabwe African People's Union

Bibliography

Adam, Heribert. *Modernizing Racial Domination: The Dynamics of South African Politics*. Berkeley and Los Angeles: University of California Press, 1971.

——, and Giliomee, Hermann. *Ethnic Power Mobilized: Can South Africa Change?* New Haven: Yale University Press, 1979.

——, ed. *South Africa: Sociological Perspectives*. London: Oxford University Press, 1971.

Adler, Taffy, ed. *Perspectives on South Africa: A Collection of Working Papers*. African Studies Institute Communication No. 4. Johannesburg: University of the Witwatersrand, 1977.

Ainslie, Rosalynde. *Masters and Serfs: Farm Labour in South Africa*. London: International Defence and Aid Fund, 1973.

Albrecht, Gisela. *Soweto, oder der Aufstand der Vorstädte*. Hamburg: Rororo, 1977.

Amnesty International Report on Torture. London: Amnesty International, 1973.

Barber, James. *South Africa's Foreign Policy, 1945-1970*. London: Oxford University Press, 1973.

Beinart, Williams. "Peasant Production, Underdevelopment and Stratification: Pondoland c. 1880-1930." In *Africa Seminar: Collected Papers*, Vol. 1. Cape Town: Centre for African Studies, 1978.

Benians, E. A.; Butler, J. R. M.; Mansergh, P. N. S.; and Walker, E. A., eds. *The Cambridge History of the British Empire*. Vol. 8, *South Africa, Rhodesia and the High Commission Territories*. Cambridge: At the University Press, 1963.

Benson, Mary. *South Africa: The Struggle for a Birthright*. Rev. ed. Harmondsworth: Penguin Books, 1966.

Bernstein, Hilda. *For Their Triumphs and for Their Tears: Women in Apartheid South Africa*. London International Defence and Aid Fund, 1975.

——. *South Africa: The Terrorism of Torture*. London: International Defence and Aid Fund, 1972.

Biesheuvel, S. *The Black-White Wage Gap: What Can Be Done About It?*

Johannesburg: South African Institute of Race Relations, 1972.

Biko, Steve. *Black Consciousness in South Africa*, edited by Millard Arnold. New York: Vintage Books, 1979.

——. *I Write What I Like*, edited by Aelred Stubbs. London: Bowerdean Press, 1978.

Black South Africa Explodes. London: Counter Information Services, 1977.

Blueprint for Blackout. Johannesburg: Education League, 1948.

Boshoff, Franz. *Die Afrikaner en Britse Imperialisme* [The Afrikaner and British Imperialism]. Johannesburg: Die Ware Republikein, 1940.

BOSS: The First Five Years. London: International Defence and Aid Fund, 1975.

Brookes, Edgar H., ed. *Apartheid: A Documentary Study of Modern South Africa*. London: Routledge & Kegan Paul, 1968.

Brückner, Reinhard. *Südafrikas Schwarze Zukunft*. Frankfurt: Verlag Otto Lembeck, 1977.

Brute Force: Treatment of Prisoners in South Africa's Gaols. London: African National Congress, n.d.

Bryce, James. *Impressions of South Africa*. 3rd rev. ed. London: MacMillan and Co., 1899.

Bundy, Colin. "The Emergence and Decline of a South African Peasantry." *African Affairs* (London), no. 71 (October 1972).

Bunting, Brian. *The Rise of the South African Reich*. Rev. ed. Baltimore: Penguin Books, 1969.

Bunting, Sidney Percival. *Imperialism and South Africa*. Johannesburg: Communist Party of South Africa, 1928.

Burrows, Raymond. *Indian Life and Labour in Natal*. Johannesburg: South African Institute of Race Relations, 1952.

Business as Usual: International Banking in South Africa. London: Counter Information Services, n.d.

Buthelezi, Sipho, ed. *The Black People's Convention (BPC)—South Africa: Historical Background and Basic Documents*. New York: Black Liberation Press, n.d.

Butler, Jeffrey; Rotberg, Robert I.; and Adams, John. *The Black Homelands of South Africa: The Political and Economic Development of Bophuthatswana and KwaZulu*. Berkeley: University of California Press, 1977.

Carter, Gwendolen M. *The Politics of Inequality: South Africa Since 1948*. Rev. ed. New York: Praeger Publishers, 1959.

——; Karis, Thomas; and Stultz, Newell M. *South Africa's Transkei: The Politics of Domestic Colonialism*. Evanston, Ill.: Northwestern University Press, 1967.

Cockram, Gail-Maryse. *Vorster's Foreign Policy*. Pretoria and Cape Town: Academica, 1970.

Cook, Allen. *South Africa: The Imprisoned Society*. London: International Defence and Aid Fund, 1974.

Cronjé, Geoffrey. *Regverdige Rasse-apartheid* [Righteous racial apartheid]. Stellenbosch: Die Christen-Studenteverenigingmaatskappy van Suid Africa, 1947.

Davenport, T. R. H., and Hunt, K. S., eds. *The Right to the Land.* Cape Town: David Philip, 1974.

Davidson, Basil; Slovo, Joe; and Wilkinson, Anthony R. *Southern Africa: The New Politics of Revolution.* Harmondsworth: Penguin Books, 1976.

Davis, David. *African Workers and Apartheid.* London: International Defence and Aid Fund, 1978.

De Kiewiet, C. W. *British Colonial Policy and the South African Republics, 1848-1872.* London: Longmans, Green and Co., 1929.

——. *A History of South Africa: Social and Economic.* London: Oxford University Press, 1957.

——. *The Imperial Factor in South Africa.* London: Cambridge University Press, 1937.

De Klerk, W. A. *The Puritans in Africa: A Story of Afrikanerdom.* Harmondsworth: Penguin Books, 1976.

Denoon, Donald. *Southern Africa Since 1800.* New York: Praeger Publishers, 1973.

Desmond, Cosmas. *The Discarded People: An Account of African Resettlement in South Africa.* Harmondsworth: Penguin Books, 1971.

Detention and Detente in Southern Africa. Braamfontein: Christian Institute of Southern Africa, 1976.

The Durban Strikes 1973: "Human Beings With Souls." Durban: Institute for Industrial Education, in association with Ravan Press, 1976.

Du Toit, Bettie. *Ukubamba Amadolo: Workers' Struggles in the South African Textile Industry.* London: Onyx Press, 1978.

Edelstein, Melville L. *What Do Young Africans Think?* Johannesburg: South African Institute of Race Relations, 1972.

Ellis, George; Hendrie, Delia; Kooy, Alide; and Maree, Johann. *The Squatter Problem in the Western Cape: Some Causes and Remedies.* Johannesburg: South African Institute of Race Relations, 1977.

Feit, Edward. *African Opposition in South Africa: The Failure of Passive Resistance.* Stanford, Calif.: Hoover Institution on War, Revolution and Peace, 1967.

Ferguson-Davie, C. J. *The Early History of Indians in Natal.* Johannesburg: South African Institute of Race Relations, 1977.

First, Ruth. *South West Africa.* Baltimore: Penguin Books, 1963

——; Steele, Jonathan; and Gurney, Christabel. *The South African Connection: Western Investment in Apartheid.* Harmondsworth: Penguin Books, 1973.

Franklin, N. N. *Economics in South Africa.* 2nd rev. ed. Cape Town: Oxford University Press, 1954.

Gandhi, Mohandas K. *Satyagraha in South Africa.* Triplicane, Madras: S. Ganesan Publisher, 1928.

Gerhart, Gail M. *Black Power in South Africa: The Evolution of an Ideology.* Berkeley: University of California Press, 1978.

Gibson, Richard. *African Liberation Movements: Contemporary Struggles Against White Minority Rule.* London: Oxford University Press, 1972.

Gordon, Loraine, et al. *Survey of Race Relations in South Africa.* Johannesburg: South African Institute of Race Relations, 1977-78,

published annually.
Greyling, E. *Christelike en Nasionale Onderwys* [Christian-national education]. 2 vols. Bloemfontein: Nasionale Pers, 1941.
Gwala, Mafika Pascal, ed. *Black Review 1973*. Durban: Black Community Programmes, 1974.
Halpern, Jack. *South Africa's Hostages: Basutoland, Bechuanaland and Swaziland*. Harmondsworth: Penguin Books, 1965.
Harsch, Ernest. "South Africa: The Plight of the Urban Squatter." *Africa Report* (New York), May-June 1979.
——, and Thomas, Tony. *Angola: The Hidden History of Washington's War*. New York: Pathfinder Press, 1976.
Hartshorne, K. B. *Native Education in the Union of South Africa*. Johannesburg: South African Institute of Race Relations, 1953.
Harvey, Charles, et al. *The Policy Debate*. Study Project on External Investment in South Africa and Namibia (S.W. Africa). London: Africa Publications Trust, 1975.
Hepple, Alex. *South Africa: A Political and Economic History*. New York: Praeger Publishers, 1966.
——. *South Africa: Workers Under Apartheid*. 2nd ed. London: International Defence and Aid Fund, 1971.
——. *Verwoerd*. Harmondsworth: Penguin Books, 1967.
Herbstein, Denis. *White Man, We Want to Talk to You*. Hardmondsworth: Penguin Books, 1978.
Hirson, Baruch. *Year of Fire, Year of Ash: The Soweto Revolt—Roots of a Revolution?* London: Zed Press, 1979.
Hobson, J. A. *Imperialism: A Study*. 3rd rev. ed. London: George Allen & Unwin, 1938.
Hocking, Anthony. *Oppenheimer and Son*. New York: McGraw-Hill, 1973.
Horrell, Muriel. *The African Homelands of South Africa*. Johannesburg: South African Institute of Race Relations, 1973.
——. *Bantu Education to 1968*. Johannesburg: South African Institute of Race Relations, 1968.
——. *Laws Affecting Race Relations in South Africa, 1948-1976*. Johannesburg: South African Institute of Race Relations, 1978.
——, et al. *Survey of Race Relations in South Africa*. Johannesburg: South African Institute of Race Relations, 1971-76, published annually.
Houghton, D. Hobart. *The South African Economy*. 3rd ed. Cape Town: Oxford University Press, 1973.
——, and Dagut, Jenifer, eds. *Source Material on the South African Economy: 1860-1970*. 3 vols. Cape Town: Oxford University Press, 1972-73.
Hugo, Pierre, and Kotzé, Hendrik. *Suid-Afrika: Oorlewing in Politieke Perspektief* [South Africa: Survival in political perspective]. Johannesburg: Jonathan Ball, 1978.
Innes, Duncan, and O'Meara, Dan. "Class Formation and Ideology: The Transkei Region." *Review of African Political Economy* (London), no. 7 (1976).
Johnstone, Frederick A. *Class, Race and Gold: A Study of Class Relations and Racial Discrimination in South Africa*. London: Routledge &

Kegan Paul, 1976.

Kadalie, Clements. *My Life and the ICU: The Autobiography of a Black Trade Unionist in South Africa.* New York: Humanities Press, 1970.

Kane-Berman, John. *Soweto: Black Revolt, White Reaction.* Johannesburg: Ravan Press, 1978.

Karis, Thomas, and Carter, Gwendolen M., eds. *From Protest to Challenge: A Documentary History of African Politics in South Africa, 1882-1964.* 4 vols. Stanford, Calif.: Hoover Institution Press, 1972-77.

Khan, Farieda. "The Origins of the Non-European Unity Movement." Research essay in history, University of Cape Town, 1976.

Khoapa, Ben A., ed. *Black Review 1972.* Durban: Black Community Programmes, 1973.

The Kissinger Study of Southern Africa. London: Spokesman Books, 1975.

Kitazawa, Yoko. *From Tokyo to Johannesburg.* New York and Geneva: National Council of Churches and World Council of Churches, 1975.

Kuper, Leo. *Passive Resistance in South Africa.* New Haven, Conn.: Yale University Press, 1957.

La Guma, Alex, ed. *Apartheid: A Collection of Writings on South African Racism by South Africans.* New York: International Publishers, 1971.

Langa, Ben, ed. *SASO on the Attack: An Introduction to the South African Students' Organisation.* Durban: South African Students' Organisation, 1973.

Lee, Franz J. T. *Südafrika: Am Vorabend der Revolution.* 2nd rev. ed. Frankfurt: ISP-Verlag, 1976.

Lefort, René. *L'Afrique du Sud: Histoire d'une Crise.* Paris: Maspero, 1977.

Legassick, Martin. "Legislation, Ideology and Economy in Post-1948 South Africa." *Journal of Southern African Studies* (London) 1, no. 1 (October 1974).

——. "South Africa: Capital Accumulation and Violence." *Economy and Society* (London) 3, no. 3 (August 1974).

——. "South Africa: Forced Labor, Industrialization, and Racial Differentiation." In *The Political Economy of Africa*, edited by Richard Harris. Cambridge, Mass.: Schenkman Publishing Company, 1975.

Legum, Colin, et al., eds. *Africa Contemporary Record: Annual Surveys and Documents.* London and New York: Africa Research Limited and Africana Publishing Company, 1968-77, published annually.

Lenta, Giuseppe. *Development or Stagnation? Agriculture in KwaZulu.* Occasional Paper No. 7, Department of Economics. Durban: University of Natal, 1978.

Lerumo, A. *Fifty Fighting Years: The South African Communist Party, 1921-1971.* London: Inkululeko Publications, 1971.

Lever, Henry, ed. *Readings in South African Society.* Johannesburg: Jonathan Ball Publishers, 1978.

——. *South African Society.* Johannesburg: Jonathan Ball Publishers, 1978.

Lutuli, Albert. *Let My People Go.* New York: McGraw-Hill, 1962.

McHenry, Donald. *United States Firms in South Africa.* Bloomington, Ind.: African Studies Program, Indiana University, 1975.

MacMillan, W. M. *Bantu, Boer, and Briton: The Making of the South African Native Problem*. Rev. and enlarged ed. London: Oxford University Press, 1963.

Magubane, Bernard Makhosezwe. *The Political Economy of Race and Class in South Africa*. New York: Monthly Review Press, 1979.

Majeke, Nosipho. *The Role of the Missionaries in Conquest*. Cape Town: Society of Young Africa, 1952.

Mandela, Nelson. *The Struggle Is My Life*. London: International Defence and Aid Fund, 1978.

Marks, Shula. *Reluctant Rebellion: The 1906-1908 Disturbances in Natal*. Oxford: Clarendon Press, 1970.

Marlowe, John. *Cecil Rhodes: The Anatomy of Empire*. New York: Mason & Lipscomb Publishers, 1972.

Marquard, Leo. *The Peoples and Policies of South Africa*. 4th ed. London: Oxford University Press, 1969.

——. *A Short History of South Africa*. New York: Praeger Publishers, 1968.

Martin, Anthony. *Minding Their Own Business: Zambia's Struggle Against Western Control*. Harmondsworth: Penguin Books, 1972.

Mayer, Philip, and Mayer, Iona. *Townsmen and Tribesmen: Conservatism and the Process of Urbanization in a South African City*. 2nd ed. Cape Town: Oxford University Press, 1974.

Mbanjwa, Thoko, ed. *Black Review 1974/75*. Durban: Black Community Programmes, 1975.

Mbeki, Govan. *South Africa: The Peasants' Revolt*. Harmondsworth: Penguin Books, 1964.

Metrowich, F. R., ed. *Towards Dialogue and Détente*. Sandton: Valiant Publishers, 1975.

Mhlongo, Sam. "Zur Klassenanalyse Südafrikas." *Kritik der Politischen Okonomie* (Berlin), no. 11/12 (November 1976).

Mnguni [pseudonym]. *Three Hundred Years: A History of South Africa*. 3 vols. Cape Town: New Era Fellowship, 1952.

Molteno, Robert. *Africa and South Africa*. London: Africa Bureau, 1971.

Morris, Donald R. *The Washing of the Spears: The Rise and Fall of the Zulu Nation*. New York: Simon and Schuster, 1965.

Munger, Edwin S. *Afrikaner and African Nationalism: South African Parallels and Parameters*. London: Oxford University Press, 1967.

Murray, Roger; Morris, Jo; Dugard, John; and Rubin, Neville. *The Role of Foreign Firms in Namibia*. Study Project on External Investment in South Africa and Namibia (S.W. Africa). London: Africa Publications Trust, 1974.

Myers, Desaix, III. *Labor Practices of U.S. Corporations in South Africa*. New York: Praeger Publishers, 1977.

Neame, L. E. *The History of Apartheid*. London: Pall Mall Press, 1962.

Nolutshungu, Sam C. *South Africa in Africa: A Study in Ideology and Foreign Policy*. New York: Africana Publishing Company, 1975.

O'Meara, Dan. "The 1946 African Mine Workers' Strike and the Political Economy of South Africa." In *Contemporary Southern African Studies: Research Papers*, edited by Peter Kallaway and Taffy Adler. Vol. 2.

Johannesburg: University of the Witwatersrand, 1978.

Omer-Cooper, J. D. *The Zulu Aftermath: A Nineteenth-Century Revolution in Bantu Africa.* Evanston, Ill.: Northwestern University Press, 1969.

Pachai, Bridglal. *The South African Indian Question, 1860-1971.* Cape Town: C. Struik, 1971.

Pakenham, Thomas. *The Boer War.* New York: Random House, 1979.

Peterson, Robert W., ed. *South Africa & Apartheid.* New York: Facts on File, 1975.

Pienaar, S., and Sampson, Anthony. *South Africa: Two Views on Separate Development.* London: Oxford University Press, 1960.

Plaatje, Sol T. *Native Life in South Africa, Before and Since the European War and the Boer Rebellion.* 3rd ed. Kimberley: Tsala ea Batho; New York: Crisis, n.d.

Political Imprisonment in South Africa. London: Amnesty International Publications, 1978.

Potgieter, J. F. *The Poverty Datum Line in the Major Urban Centres of the Republic.* Research Report no. 12, Institute for Planning Research. Port Elizabeth: University of Port Elizabeth, 1973.

Potholm, Christian P., and Dale, Richard, eds. *Southern Africa in Perspective: Essays in Regional Politics.* New York: The Free Press, 1972.

Prison Conditions in South Africa. London: Amnesty International, 1965.

Rädel, F. E. *Progress or Exploitation?* Cape Town: Maskew Miller, 1978.

Randall, Peter, ed. *Power, Privilege and Poverty: Report of the Economics Commission of the Study Project on Christianity in Apartheid Society.* Spro-Cas Publication No. 7. Johannesburg: Spro-Cas, 1972.

Reid, J. V. O. *Malnutrition.* Johannesburg: South African Institute of Race Relations, 1971.

Republic of South Africa. *Report of the Commission of Inquiry into Labour Legislation.* Part 1. RP 47/1979. (Wiehahn Commission report.)

Rhoodie, N. J. *Apartheid en Partnership: 'n Rasse-Sosiologiese Ontleding van Afsonderlike Volksontwikkeling en Vennootskap, met Besondere Verwysing na die Motiewe vir hierdie Beleidsisteme* [Apartheid and partnership: a racial and social analysis of separate development and partnership, with particular reference to the motives for this administrative system]. Pretoria and Cape Town: H. & R. Academica, 1966.

——, and Venter, H. J. *Die Apartheidsgedate: 'n Sosio-Historiese Uiteensetting van sy Onstaan en Ontwikkeling* [The apartheid idea: a sociohistorical explanation of its origin and development]. Pretoria: Universiteit van Pretoria, 1960.

Roux, Edward. *Time Longer Than Rope: A History of the Black Man's Struggle for Freedom in South Africa.* 2nd ed. Madison: University of Wisconsin Press, 1964.

Rogers, Barbara. *Divide & Rule: South Africa's Bantustans.* London: International Defence and Aid Fund, 1976.

——. *White Wealth and Black Poverty: American Investments in Southern Africa.* Westport, Conn., and London: Greenwood Press, 1976.

Sachs, Albie. *Justice in South Africa.* Berkeley and Los Angeles: Univer-

sity of California Press, 1973.
Sachs, E. S. *The Anatomy of Apartheid.* London: Collet's, 1965.
St. Jorre, John de. *A House Divided: South Africa's Uncertain Future.* New York: Carnegie Endowment for International Peace, 1977.
Sandbrook, Richard, and Cohen, Robin, eds. *The Development of an African Working Class: Studies in Class Formation and Action.* Toronto and Buffalo: University of Toronto Press, 1975.
Schlemmer, Lawrence, and Stopforth, Peter. *A Study of Malnutrition in the Nqutu District of KwaZulu.* Fact Paper No. 2, Institute for Social Research. Durban: University of Natal, 1975.
——, and Webster, Eddie, eds. *Change, Reform and Economic Growth in South Africa.* Johannesburg: Ravan Press, 1978.
Scholtz, G. D. *Het die Afrikaanse Volk 'n Toekoms?* [Do the Afrikaner people have a future?]. Johannesburg: Voortrekkers, 1954.
——. *Die Ontwikkeling van die Politieke Denke van die Afrikaner* [The development of the political thought of the Afrikaner]. Vol. 2, 1806-1854. Johannesburg: Voortrekkerpers, 1970.
Seidman, Ann, and Seidman, Neva. *South Africa and U.S. Multinational Corporations.* Westport, Conn.: Lawrence Hill & Co., 1978.
Sikakane, Joyce. *A Window on Soweto.* London: International Defence and Aid Fund, 1977.
Simkins, Charles, and Clarke, Duncan. *Structural Unemployment in Southern Africa.* Development Studies Series No. 1. Pietermaritzburg: University of Natal Press, 1978.
Simons, H. J. *African Women: Their Legal Status in South Africa.* Evanston, Ill.: Northwestern University Press, 1968.
——, and Simons, R. E. *Class and Colour in South Africa, 1850-1950.* Harmondsworth: Penguin Books, 1969.
Sizwe, No. *One Azania, One Nation: The National Question in South Africa.* London: Zed Press, 1979.
Smit, P., and Booysen, J. J. *Urbanisation in the Homelands—A New Dimension in the Urbanisation Process of the Black Population of South Africa?* IPSO Monograph Series No. 3. Pretoria: University of Pretoria, 1977.
South Africa: An Appraisal. Johannesburg: Nedbank Group Economic Unit, 1977.
South Africa—A "Police State"? Braamfontein: Christian Institute of Southern Africa, 1976.
South Africa in Travail: The Disturbances of 1976/77. Johannesburg: South African Institute of Race Relations, 1978.
South Africa 1975: Official Yearbook of the Republic of South Africa. Johannesburg: Department of Information, 1975.
South Africa 1978: Official Yearbook of the Republic of South Africa. Johannesburg: Bureau of National and International Communication, 1978.
Southall, Anthony J. "Marxist Theory in South Africa Until 1940." Master's thesis, University of York, 1978.
Sprack, John. *Rhodesia: South Africa's Sixth Province.* London: International Defence and Aid Fund, 1974.

Stevens, Richard P., and Elmessiri, Abdelwahab. *Israel and South Africa: The Progression of a Relationship.* Rev. ed. New Brunswick, N.J.: North American, 1977.

Stockwell, John. *In Search of Enemies: A CIA Story.* New York: W. W. Norton & Company, 1978.

Suckling, John; Weiss, Ruth; and Innes, Duncan. *The Economic Factor.* Study Project on External Investment in South Africa and Namibia (S.W. Africa). London: Africa Publications Trust, 1975.

Tabata, Isaac B. *The Awakening of a People.* London: Spokesman Books, 1974.

——. *Education for Barbarism in South Africa: Bantu (Apartheid) Education.* London: Pall Mall Press, 1960.

——. *Imperialist Conspiracy in South Africa.* Lusaka: Prometheus Publishing Company, 1974.

Thomas, Tony. *The Freedom Struggle in South Africa.* New York: Pathfinder Press, 1976.

Thomas, Wolfgang H., ed. *Labour Perspectives on South Africa.* Cape Town: David Philip, 1974.

——, et al. *The Conditions of the Black Worker.* Study Project on External Investment in South Africa and Namibia (S.W. Africa). London: Africa Publications Trust, 1975.

Thompson, Leonard. *Survival in Two Worlds: Moshoeshoe of Lesotho, 1786-1870.* Oxford: At the Clarendon Press, 1975.

——, and Butler, Jeffrey, eds. *Change in Contemporary South Africa.* Berkeley and Los Angeles: University of California Press, 1975.

Torture in South Africa? Cape Town: Christian Institute of Southern Africa, 1977.

Trotsky, Leon. "On the South African Theses." In *Writings of Leon Trotsky, 1934-35.* 2nd ed. New York: Pathfinder Press, 1974.

Troup, Freda. *Forbidden Pastures: Education Under Apartheid.* London: International Defence and Aid Fund, 1976.

——. *South Africa: An Historical Introduction.* Harmondsworth: Penguin Books, 1975.

Turner, Richard. *The Eye of the Needle: Toward Participatory Democracy in South Africa.* Maryknoll, N.Y.: Orbis Books, 1978.

Union of South Africa. *Summary of the Report of the Commission for the Socio-Economic Development of the Bantu Areas Within the Union of South Africa.* UG 61/1955. (Tomlinson Commission report.)

United Nations Educational, Scientific, and Cultural Organization. *Apartheid: Its Effects on Education, Science, Culture and Information.* SHC. SS. 67/D.30/A. Paris, 1967.

U.S. Military Involvement in Southern Africa, edited by Western Massachusetts Association of Concerned African Scholars. Boston: South End Press, 1978.

Van den Berghe, Pierre. *South Africa: A Study in Conflict.* Berkeley and Los Angeles: University of California Press, 1970.

Van der Horst, Sheila T. *Native Labour in South Africa.* London: Oxford University Press, 1942.

Van der Merwe, Hendrik W.; Charton, Nancy C. J.; Kotzé, D. A.; and

Magnusson, Åke, eds. *African Perspectives on South Africa: A Collection of Speeches, Articles and Documents.* Cape Town: David Philip, 1978.

——, and Groenewald, C. J., eds. *Occupational and Social Change Among Coloured People in South Africa.* Cape Town: Juto & Company, 1976.

——, and Welsh, David, ed. *Student Perspectives on South Africa.* Cape Town: David Philip, 1972.
on South Africa. Cape Town: David Philip, 1972.

Vorster, B. J. *South Africa's Outward Policy.* Cape Town and Johannesburg: Suid-Afrikaanse Akademie vir Wetenskap en Kuns, 1970.

Walker, Eric A. *A History of Southern Africa.* 3rd ed. London and Harlow: Longmans Green and Co., 1957.

Walshe, Peter. *The Rise of African Nationalism in South Africa: The African National Congress, 1912-1952.* Berkeley and Los Angeles: University of California Press, 1971.

Webster, Eddie, ed. *Essays in Southern African Labour History.* Ravan Labour Studies No. 1. Johannesburg: Ravan Press, 1978.

Wickins, Peter L. *The Industrial and Commercial Workers' Union of Africa.* Cape Town: Oxford University Press, 1978.

Wilson, Francis. *Labour in the South African Gold Mines, 1911-1969.* Cambridge: At the University Press, 1972.

——. *Migrant Labour in South Africa.* Johannesburg: South African Council of Churches and Spro-cas, 1972.

——, and Perrot, Dominique, eds. *Outlook on a Century: South Africa 1870-1970.* Lovedale: Lovedale Press; Braamfontein: Spro-cas, 1973.

Wilson, Monica, and Thompson, Leonard, eds. *The Oxford History of South Africa.* 2 vols. London: Oxford University Press, 1969, 1975.

Wolpe, Harold. "Capitalism and Cheap Labour-Power in South Africa: From Segregation to Apartheid." *Economy and Society* (London) 1, no. 4 (November 1972).

Woods, Donald. *Biko.* New York and London: Paddington Press, 1978.

Newspapers and Periodicals

Africa (London)
Africa Research Bulletin (London)
African Affairs (London)
African Communist (London)
Argus (Cape Town)
Cape Times (Cape Town)
Christian Science Monitor (Boston)
Economist (London)
Facts and Reports (Amsterdam)
Financial Mail (Johannesburg)
Focus on Political Repression in Southern Africa (London)
Intercontinental Press / Inprecor (New York)
Le Monde (Paris)
Los Angeles Times
New African (London)
New York Times

Post (Transvaal)
Rand Daily Mail (Johannesburg)
Review of African Political Economy (London)
SASO Newsletter (Durban)
Sechaba (London)
Socialist Action / Lekgotla la Diketso (Johannesburg)
South African Labour Bulletin (Durban)
Southern Africa (New York)
Spark (Cape Town)
Standard Bank Review (Johannesburg)
Star (Johannesburg)
Times (London)
Washington Post
Work in Progress (Johannesburg)
Workers Voice (Cape Town)

Index